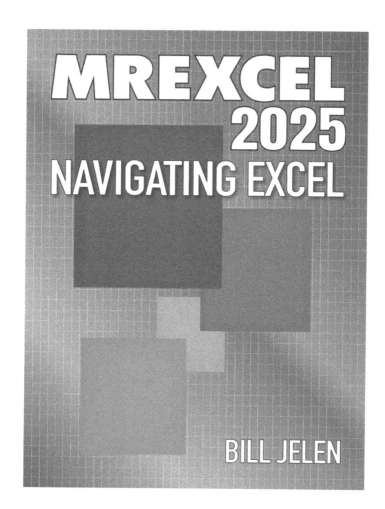

MREXCEL
2025
NAVIGATING EXCEL

BILL JELEN

Holy Macro! Books
PO Box 541731, Merritt Island FL 32954

MrExcel 2025 — Navigating Excel

© 2025 by Tickling Keys, Inc.

First Publication: July 1, 2025

Authors: Bill Jelen

Copy Editor: Kitty Wilson

Tech Editors: Roger Govier in 2020, Bob Umlas in 2021, 2022, and 2024

Formula Guru: Richard Simpson.

Indexer: Nellie Jay

Compositor: Jill Cabot

Cover Design: Kim Sekas

Illustrations: Cartoon Bob D'Amico, George Berlin, Walter Moore, Chad Thomas

Published by: Holy Macro! Books, PO Box 541731, Merritt Island FL 32954

Distributed by Independent Publishers Group, Chicago, IL

ISBN 978-1-61547-088-4 (print) 978-1-61547-175-1 (digital)

Library of Congress Control Number: 2025942270

Version 20250701

Table of Contents

Dedication

To Mary Ellen Jelen, again. Behind every Excel tip is someone who kept me from Ctrl+Alt+Freaking Out.

Thanks to

Suat Ozgur. Kim Sekas. Stacie Fuss. The Excel team. The Excel MVPs. The Morning Crew.

About the Author

Bill Jelen is the host of MrExcel.com and the author of 70 books about Microsoft Excel including *Excel Gurus Gone Wild and Excel Inside Out* for Microsoft Press. He has made over 80 guest appearances on TV's *The Lab with Leo / Call for Help with Leo Laporte* and was voted guest of the year on the *Computer America* radio show. He wrote the Excel column for *Strategic Finance* magazine. He has produced over 2,600 episodes of his daily video podcast Learn Excel from MrExcel. Social Media:

- YouTube: https://www.youtube.com/@MrXL
- X: https://x.com/MrExcel
- LinkedIn: https://www.linkedin.com/in/billjelen/
- Facebook: https://www.facebook.com/MrExcelSpeaker
- Instagram: https://www.instagram.com/mrexcelbill/
- Threads: https://www.threads.net/@mrexcelbill
- Pinterest: https://www.pinterest.com/mrexcel/

About the Illustrators

Cartoonist **Bob D'Amico** creates custom cartoons for business and more. See www.cartoonbob.com for more about his work.

George Berlin is all about delight and wonder! He puts a smile on the world's faces with illustration, animation, and interactive projection art. See more at www.georgeberlin.com.

Walter Moore is famous for his ape cartoons. If you need an illustration of the monkey business at your work, search Bing for Walter Moore Apes.

Chad Thomas is an illustrator who showcases his artwork on his website, www.whiterabbitart.com. His colorful and detailed artwork ranges from pet and people portraits to illustrations for children's books.

Foreword

After 17 years on the road, my live Power Excel seminars have been replaced by webinars. Check the MrExcel.com homepage for upcoming events. This book was built for those seminars and webinars. It is updated every couple of years with new features and techniques.

The book you are reading was the book that I used in those seminars. I would update the book for a new edition of Excel, print 5000 copies and hit the road. This 2025 update is current through July 1, 2025. See "What's new as of this 2025 edition:" on page 325

Much of the new content in this edition is about Copilot and Artificial Intelligence. This feature is constantly evolving. There are so many new features and they are arriving many times a year.

You will see a number of shortlinks in this book in the format mrx.cl/short. The idea is that it will be easier for you to type mrx.cl than a long URL.

Sample File Downloads

The files used in this book are available for download from mrx.cl/2025bookfiles.

Edge Index

The numbers in the color blocks on the right side of the numbered pages form an edge index in the printed book. The numbers roughly correspond to: 0 is front matter, 1 is favorite techniques, 2 is charting and visualization, 3 is data analysis, 4 is formulas, 5 is tools, and 6 is the index and back matter.

#1 Double-Click the Fill Handle to Copy a Formula

You have thousands of rows of data. You've added a new formula in the top row of your data set, some-thing like =PROPER(A2&" "&B2), or =TEXTJOIN(" ",A2:B2) as shown here. You need to copy the formula down to all of the rows of your data set.

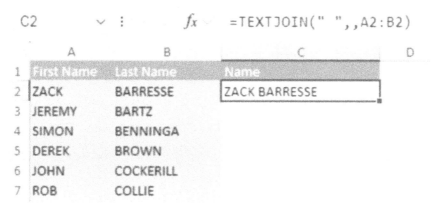

Many people will grab the Fill Handle and start to drag down. But as you drag down, Excel starts going faster and faster. There is a 200-microsecond pause at the last row of data. 200 microseconds is long enough for you to notice the pause but not long enough for you to react and let go of the mouse button. Before you know it, you've dragged the Fill Handle way too far.

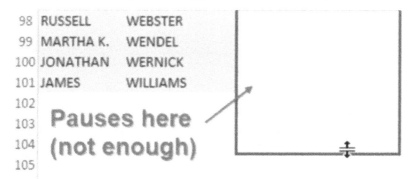

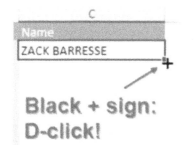

The solution is to double-click the Fill Handle! Go to exactly the same spot where you start to drag the Fill Handle. The mouse pointer changes to a black plus sign. Double-click. Excel looks at the surrounding data, finds the last row with data today, and copies the formula down to the last row of the data set.

In my live Power Excel seminars, this trick always elicits a gasp from half the people in the room. It is my number-one time-saving trick.

Alternatives to Double-Clicking the Fill Handle

This trick is an awesome trick if all you've done to this point is drag the Fill Handle to the bottom of the data set. But there are even faster ways to solve this problem:

- Use Tables. If you select one cell in A1:B112 and press Ctrl+T, Excel formats the range as a table. Once you have a table, simply enter the formula in C2. When you press Enter, it is copied to the bottom.

- Use a complex but effective keyboard shortcut. This shortcut requires the adjacent column to have no empty cells. While it seems complicated to explain, the people who tell me about this shortcut can do the entire thing in the blink of an eye.

Here are the steps:

1. From your newly entered formula in C2, press the Left Arrow key to move to cell B2.

2. Press Ctrl+Down Arrow to move to the last row with data—in this case, B112.

3. Press the Right Arrow key to return to the bottom of the mostly empty column C.

4. From cell C112, press Ctrl+Shift+Up Arrow. This selects all of the blank cells next to your data, plus the formula in C2.

5. Press Ctrl+D to fill the formula in C2 to all of the blanks in the selection. Ctrl+D is fill **D**own.

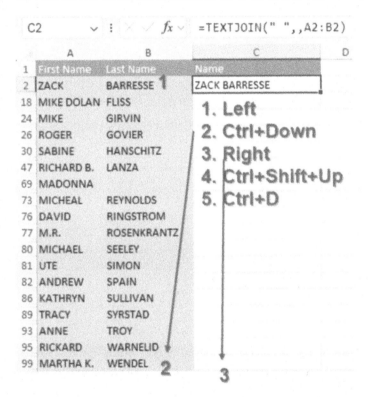

Note: Ctrl+R fills right, which might be useful in other situations.

As an alternative, you can get the same results by pressing Ctrl+C before step 1 and replacing step 5 with pressing Ctrl+V.

Be careful when you are joining text with a date or with currency. Even though your cells are formatted to show a currency symbol and two decimal places, the formula can't see the number formatting. You can explicitly add formatting using the TEXT function.

```
="Please remot "&TEXT(E18,"$#,##0.00")&" by "&TEXT(E12,"M/D/YYYY")
```

Thanks to the following people who suggested this tip: D. Carmichael, Shelley Fishel, Dawn Gilbert, @Knutsford_admi, Francis Logan, Michael Ortenberg, Jon Paterson, Mike Sullivan and Greg Lambert Lane suggested Ctrl+D. Bill Hazlett, author of *Excel for the Math Classroom,* pointed out Ctrl+R.

#2 Break Apart Data

You have just seen how to join data, but people often ask about the opposite problem: how to parse data that is all in a single column. Say you wanted to sort the data in the figure below by zip code:

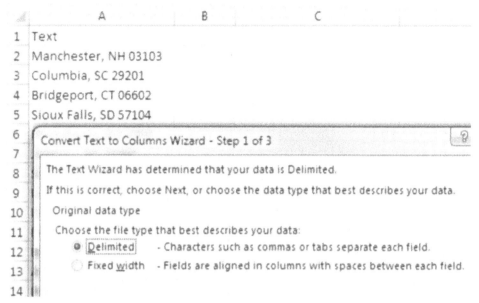

Tip: After March 2022, you could easily isolate the Zip code with =TEXTAFTER(A2," ",-1). See "#126 Text Before or After a Specific Delimiter" on page 241.

Select the data in A2:A99 and choose Data, Text to Columns. Because some city names, such as Sioux Falls, are two words, you cannot break the data at each occurrence of a space. Instead, you need to use a comma to get the city in column A and the state and zip code in column B, so choose Delimited in step 1 of the wizard and click Next.

In step 2 of the wizard, deselect Tab and select Comma. The preview at the bottom of the dialog shows what your data will look like. Click Next.

> **Aha**: For the rest of the day after you use Text to Columns, Excel will remember the choices you've chosen in step 2 of the Convert Text to Columns Wizard. If you copy data from Notepad and paste to Excel, it will be split at the comma. This is often maddening because most days, the data is not parsed at the comma, but for the rest of today, it will be. To fix it, close and re-open Excel.

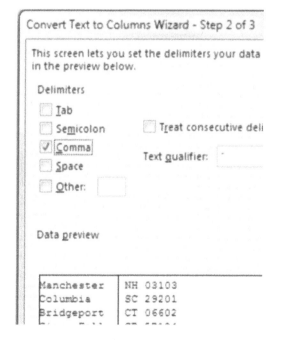

Step 3 of the wizard asks you to declare each column as General, Text, or Date. It is fine to leave the columns set as General.

After you've split the state and zip code to column B, select B2:B99 and again choose Data, Text to Columns. This time, since each state is two characters, you can use Fixed Width in step 1 of the wizard. To preserve leading zeros in the zip code, select the second column and choose Text as the data type in step 3 of the wizard.

New in 2023: Go to File, Options, Data. Turn off Remove Leading Digits and Convert to a Number.

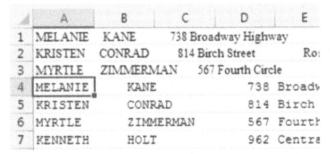

Tip: A lot of data will work well with Fixed Width, even it doesn't look like it lines up. In the next figure, the first three rows are in Calibri font and don't appear to be lined up. But if you change the font to Courier New, as in rows 4:7, you can see that the columns are perfectly lined up.

	A	B	C	D	E
1	MELANIE	KANE	738 Broadway Highway		
2	KRISTEN	CONRAD	814 Birch Street		Ro:
3	MYRTLE	ZIMMERMAN	567 Fourth Circle		
4	MELANIE	KANE		738 Broadw	
5	KRISTEN	CONRAD		814 Birch	
6	MYRTLE	ZIMMERMAN		567 Fourth	
7	KENNETH	HOLT		962 Centra	

Sometimes, you will find a data set where someone used Alt+Enter to put data on a new line within a cell. You can break out each line to a new column by typing Ctrl+j in the Other box in step 2 of the wizard, as shown below. Why Ctrl+j? Back in the 1980's IBM declared Ctrl+j to be a linefeed. Ctrl+j also can be typed in the Find & Replace dialog box.

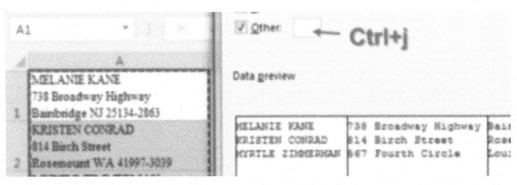

CONVERT TEXT NUMBERS TO NUMBERS QUICKLY

There are three special situations that Text to Columns handles easily:

- Dates in YYYYMMDD format can be changed to real dates. In step 3 of the wizard, click the column heading in the dialog, choose Date, then choose YMD from the dropdown.

- If you have negative numbers where the minus sign shows up after the number, go to step 3 of the wizard, click the Advanced Button, and choose **Trailing Minus for Negative Numbers**.

- Data copied from a Table of Contents will often have dot leaders that extend from the text to the page number as shown below. In step 2 of the wizard, choose Other, type a period, and then select the checkbox for Treat Consecutive Delimiters as One.

	A	B	C	D	E
1	Choose				Step 2
2	Date >	Step 3			Consecutive
3	YMD	Advanced >			Delimiters
4	in Step 3	Trailing Minus			as one
5	20201216	831.25-			A.......1
6	20201017	505.18			Bee....2
7	20190620	516.07-			C........2
8	20200302	674.98-			Dee......3

#3 Convert Text Numbers to Numbers Quickly

It sometimes happen that you end up with a long column of numbers stored as text and you need to convert those to real numbers.

During 2020, the logic behind Convert to Number was rewritten. In the past, using this feature could take minutes, as Excel would recalculate the worksheet after each cell was converted to a number. Today, however, it is super-fast. Simply select the range of cells where the first cell is a number stored as text. An on-grid drop-down will appear to the left of the top text number. Open the drop-down menu and choose Convert to Number.

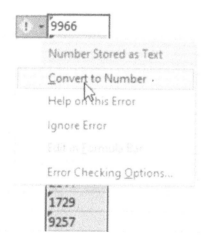

Note that this option only appears if you have File, Options, Formula set to these:

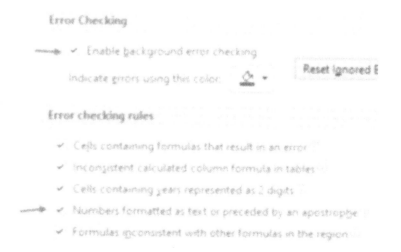

Before Convert to Number was rewritten, my favorite method of converting Text Numbers would be to select the column of text numbers and press Alt+D E F. This would run the column through the defaults of Text to Columns.

#4 Highlight the Active Cell with Focus Cell

Ever lose track of the active cell in a sea of data? As worksheets get larger, it can be tough to see where your cursor is—especially when you're just arrowing around. Good news: Excel now includes a feature called Focus Cell, which visually highlights the active cell with a crosshair overlay.

Go to the View, click Focus Cell, Choose a highlight color—green, red, blue, whatever helps it stand out.

As you move around the grid, a crosshair follows the active cell—one line for the row, one for the column. It's simple and effective.

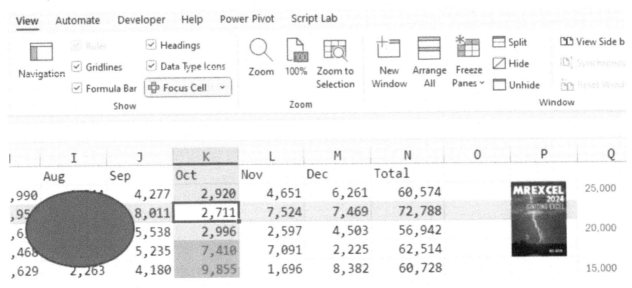

Smart Layering with Existing Formatting

The Focus Cell highlight doesn't replace any formatting. For example:

- If your cell is already shaded blue and you select it, the crosshair shows as a blend of green on top of the blue.
- When you move away, the original formatting returns.
- It plays nicely with charts and shapes on the drawing layer—Focus Cell appears under those.
- But it does appear over images inserted using Place in Cell (so it's not part of the drawing layer itself).

Behavior with Ranges and Merged Cells

If you select a range (like A2:C6), only the active cell (the one where you started) gets the crosshair. Merged cells? Yep, those highlight the full merged area—not just the top-left cell.

Combine with Find

This one's great. Press Ctrl + F to open Find and Replace, search for a word (say, "Apple"), and click Find All. Then as you click through each result, the Focus Cell crosshair clearly shows where you've landed in the sheet. This behavior is controlled by the Show Auto Highlight setting under Focus Cell.

> Tip: Before this feature, highlighting the active cell required VBA hacks or conditional formatting tricks that often broke your styling. With Focus Cell, it's built-in and just works—no code, no fuss.

#5 Filter by Selection

The filter dropdowns have been in Excel for decades, but there are two faster ways to filter. Most people select a cell in the data, choose Data, Filter, open the dropdown menu on a column heading, uncheck Select All, and scroll through a long list of values, trying to find the desired item.

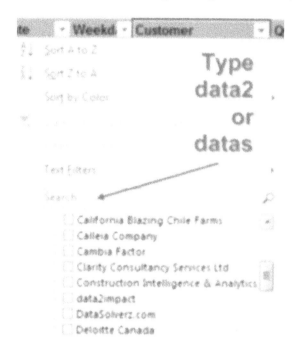

One faster way is to click in the Search box and type enough characters to uniquely identify your selection. Once the only visible items are (Select All Search Results), Add Current Selection to Filter, and the one desired customer, press Enter.

But the fastest way to Filter came from Microsoft Access. Microsoft Access invented a concept called Filter by Selection. It is simple: find a cell that contains the value you want and click Filter by Selection. The filter dropdowns are turned on, and the data is filtered to the selected value. Nothing could be simpler.

Starting in Excel 2007, you can right-click the desired value in the worksheet grid, choose Filter, and then choose By Selected Cells Value.

Guess what? The Filter by Selection trick is also built into Excel, but it is hidden and mislabeled.

Here is how you can add this feature to your Quick Access Toolbar: Right-click anywhere on the Ribbon and choose Customize Quick Access Toolbar.

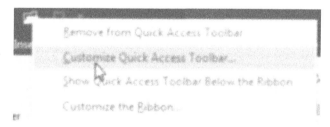

There are two large listboxes in the dialog. Above the left listbox, open the dropdown and change from Popular Commands to Commands Not In The Ribbon.

In the left listbox, scroll to the command AutoFilter and choose it.

In the center of the dialog, click the Add>> button. The AutoFilter icon moves to the right listbox, as shown below. Click OK to close the dialog.

That's right: The icon that does Filter by Selection is mislabeled AutoFilter.

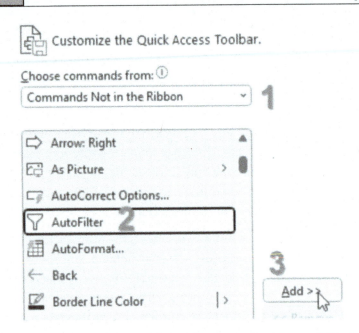

Here is how to use the command: Say that you want to see all West region sales of widgets. First, choose any cell in column B that contains West. Click the AutoFilter icon in the Quick Access Toolbar.

Excel turns on the filter dropdowns and automatically chooses only West from column B.

Next, choose any cell in column E that contains Widget. Click the AutoFilter icon again.

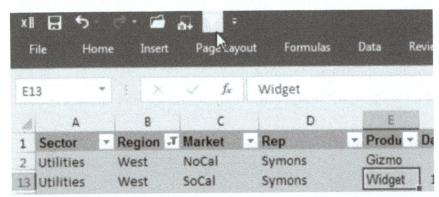

You could continue this process. For example, you could choose a Utilities cell in the Sector column and click AutoFilter.

Caution: It would be great if you could multi-select cells before clicking the AutoFilter icon, but that doesn't work. To see both widgets and gadgets, use Filter by Selection for widgets, then add gadgets from the Filter dropdown. Also. Filter by Selection does not work if you are in a Ctrl+T table. Instead, right click the cell, Filter, To Selected Cells Value.

Bonus Tip: Filter by Selection for Numbers Over/Under

What if you wanted to see all revenue greater than $20,000? Go to the blank row immediately below your revenue column and type >19999. Select that cell and click the AutoFilter icon.

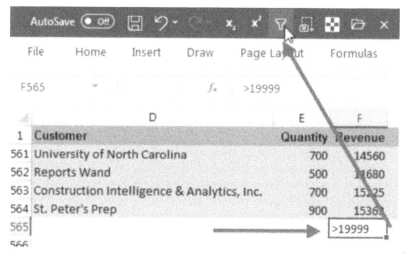

Excel will show only the rows of $20,000 or above.

	D	E	F
1	Customer ▾	Quant ▾	Reven ⊤
2	Vertex42	1000	22810
7	Excelerator BI	1000	21730
9	Berghaus Corporation	900	21438

Bonus Tip: Remove Filter Items Using Search Box

What if you wanted to hide all items that contain certain text? Use the Filter Search box to find all matches. Unselect the box for Select All Search Results. This turns off all of the items that contain "C" in this case.

Then, choose Add Current Selection to Filter.

Apparently, since everything in the Current Selection is unchecked, you are adding the unchecked state to the current filter.

It is a cool (but unintuitive) trick.

Fold the corner of this page down, because it is a difficult trick to remember.

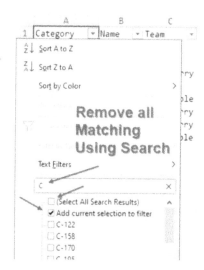

#6 Total the Visible Rows

After you've applied a filter, say that you want to see the total of the visible cells.

Select the blank cell below each of your numeric columns. Click AutoSum or type Alt+=.

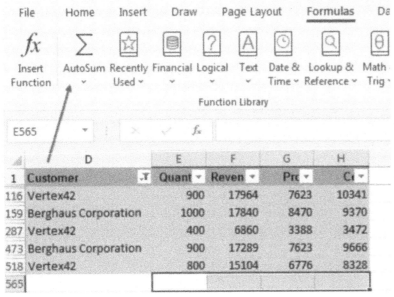

Instead of inserting SUM formulas, Excel inserts =SUBTOTAL(9,…) formulas. The formula below shows the total of only the visible cells.

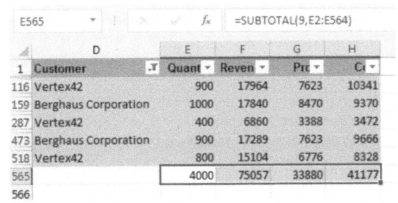

Insert a few blank rows above your data. Cut the formulas from below the data and paste to row 1 with the label Total Visible.

	E	F	G	H	I	J	K	L	M
I1				fx	=SUBTOTAL(9,I4:I566)				
1				Total Visible:	10200	196791	86394	110397	
2									
3	Produ ↪	Date ▾	Weekd ▾	Customer ▾	Quant ▾	Reven ▾	Prc ▾	C ▾	
20	Widget	1/24/2018	Wed	Excel Strategies, LLC	600	12606	5082	7524	
30	Widget	2/7/2018	Wed	All Systems Go Consult	1000	19890	8470	11420	
52	Widget	3/7/2018	Wed	Spain Enterprise	500	10155	4235	5920	

Now, as you change the filters, even if the data fills up more than one full screen, you will see the totals at the top of your worksheet.

Thanks to Sam Radakovitz on the Excel team for Filter by Selection – not for suggesting Filter by Selection, but for formalizing Filter by Selection! Thanks to Taylor & Chris in Albuquerque for the Over/under technique.

#7 The Fill Handle Does Know 1, 2, 3...

Why does the Excel Fill Handle pretend it does not know how to count 1, 2, 3? The Fill Handle is great for filling months, weekdays, quarters, and dates. Why doesn't it know that 2 comes after 1?

In case you've never used the Fill Handle, try this: Type a month name in a cell. Select that cell. There is a square dot in the lower right corner of the cell. This dot is called the Fill Handle. Hover over the Fill Handle. The mouse cursor changes from a white cross to a black plus. Click the handle and drag right or drag down. The tooltip increments to show the last month in the range.

> **Note**: If it is not working, select File, Options, Advanced. The third checkbox, **Enable Fill Handle and Cell Drag and Drop**, toggles the Fill Handle.

When you let go of the mouse button, the months will fill in. An icon appears, giving you additional options.

The Fill Handle works great with months or weekdays.

January	JAN	Monday	mon
February	FEB	Tuesday	tue
March	MAR	Wednesday	wed
April	APR	Thursday	thu
May	MAY	Friday	fri
June		Saturday	sat

The Fill Handle also works with quarters in many formats. There is even a secret custom list that will sort JFM, AMJ, JAS, OND into sequence (JFM is Jan, Feb, Mar and so on.)

To do both quarters and years, you have to type a number, then Q, then any punctuation (period, space, apostrophe, dash) before the year.

Q1	Qtr 1	1st Quarter	1Q-2032
Q2	Qtr 2	2nd Quarter	2Q-2032
Q3	Qtr 3	3rd Quarter	3Q-2032
Q4	Qtr 4	4th Quarter	4Q-2032
Q1	Qtr 1	1st Quarter	1Q-2033
Q2		2nd Quarter	2Q-2033

When you type 1 and grab the Fill Handle, Excel gives you 1, 1, 1, … Many people say to enter the 1 and the 2, select them both, then drag the Fill Handle. Here is a faster way.

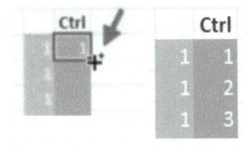

The secret trick is to hold down Ctrl while dragging. Hold down Ctrl and hover over the fill handle. Instead of the normal icon of a plus sign, you will see a plus sign with a superscript plug sign. When you see the $+^+$, click and drag. Excel fills in 1, 2, 3, ….

> **Note**: Andrew Spain of Spain Enterprise in Huntsville, Alabama taught me a cool variation on this trick. If you start dragging without Ctrl, you can press Ctrl during the drag. A + icon appears at the bottom of the drag rectangle to indicate that you are going to fill instead of copy. If you need a great Excel Consultant, find Andrew at spainenterprise.com

How were we supposed to figure out that Ctrl makes the Fill Handle count instead of copy? I have no idea. I picked up the tip from row 6 at the IMA Meonske seminar in Kent, Ohio. It turns out that Ctrl seems to make the Fill Handle behave in the opposite way: If you Ctrl+drag a date, Excel copies instead of fills.

I've heard another trick: Type 1 in A1. Select A1 and the blank B1. Drag. Excel fills instead of copies.

Right-Click the Fill Handle for More Options

If you right-click and drag the Fill Handle, a menu appears with more options, like Weekdays, Months, and Years. This menu is great for dates.

Normal	Ctrl	Weekday	Months	Years
1/31/2032	1/31/2032	1/31/2032	1/31/2032	1/31/2032
2/1/2032	1/31/2032	2/2/2032	2/29/2032	1/31/2033
2/2/2032	1/31/2032	2/3/2032	3/31/2032	1/31/2034
2/3/2032	1/31/2032	2/4/2032	4/30/2032	1/31/2035

What if your payroll happens on the 15th and on the last day of the month? Put in both dates. Select them both. Right-click and drag the Fill Handle. When you finish dragging, choose Fill Months.

Teach the Fill Handle a New List

The Fill Handle is a really handy tool. What if you could use it on all sorts of lists? You can teach Excel a new list, provided that you have anywhere from 2 to 255 items. Here is the easy way:

1. Type the list in a column in Excel.

2. Select the list.

3. Select File, Options, Advanced. Scroll almost to the bottom and click Edit Custom Lists.

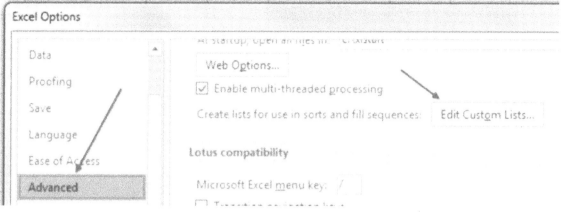

In the Custom Lists dialog, click Import.

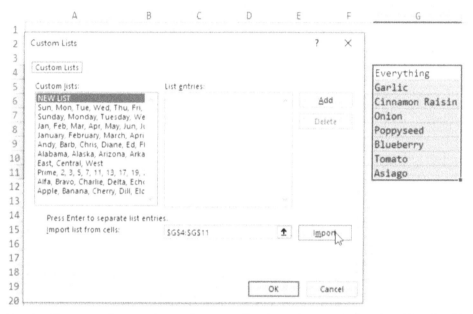

Excel will now understand your list as well as it understands Sunday, Monday, Tuesday. Type any item from the list It does not have to be the first item.

3	Bagels
4	ASIAGO
5	

Grab the Fill Handle and drag. Excel fills from your list.

3	Bagels
4	ASIAGO
5	EVERYTHING
6	GARLIC
7	CINNAMON RAISIN
8	ONION
9	POPPYSEED
10	
11	

I use this trick for lists that should be in Excel, such as a list of the U.S. states and a list of the letters of the alphabet.

Bonus Tip: Fill Jan, Feb, ..., Dec, Total

A person in one of my seminars wanted to have Jan fill into 13 values: Jan, Feb, Mar, Apr, May, Jun, Jul, Aug, Sep, Oct, Nov, Dec, Total.

While you can edit any custom list that you create, you cannot edit the first four lists in the Custom Lists dialog.

However, if you use the preceding tip to add a new custom list with the 13 values, that list wins. If two custom lists have the value Jan, the lowest one in the dialog box is the one that is used.

If you fiscal year ends March 31, you could set up a list with Apr, May, Jun, ..., Jan, Feb, Mar, Total.

Bonus Tip: Fill 1 to 100,000 in a Flash

What if you have so many items that you can't drag the Fill Handle? Follow these steps:

1. Type the number 1 in a cell.

2. Select that cell.

3. On the Home tab, toward the right, in the Editing group, open the Fill dropdown and choose Series.

4. Select Columns.

5. Enter a Stop Value of 100000.

6. Click OK.

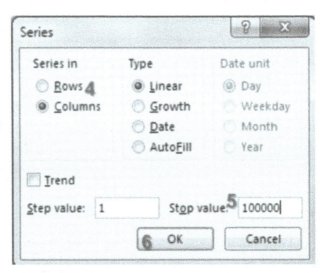

What if you have to fill 100,000 cells of bagel flavors?

1. Type the first bagel flavor in A1.

2. Select A1.

3. Type A100000 in the Name box and press Shift+Enter to select from the current cell to A100000.

4. Home, Fill, Series… and click AutoFill in the Type box. Click OK to fill from the custom list.

Thanks to the person in row 6 at the Meonske Conference in Kent, Ohio, for suggesting this feature.

#8 Fast Worksheet Copy

Yes, you can right-click any sheet tab and choose Move or Copy to make a copy of a worksheet. But that is the very slow way to copy a worksheet. The fast way: Hold down the Ctrl key and drag the worksheet tab to the right.

The downside of this trick is that the new sheet is called January (2) instead of February – but that is the case with the Move or Copy method as well. In either case, double-click the sheet name and type a new name.

January   January (2)

Ctrl+drag February to the right to create a sheet for March. Rename February (2) to March.

Select January. Shift+select March to select all worksheets. Hold down Ctrl and drag January to the right to create three more worksheets. Rename the three new sheets.

Select January. Shift+select June. Ctrl+drag January to the right, and you've added the final six worksheets for the year. Rename those sheets.

Using this technique, you can quickly come up with 12 copies of the original worksheet quickly.

Illustration: Walter Moore

Bonus Tip: Put the Worksheet Name in a Cell

If you want each report to have the name of the worksheet as a title, use either of these

```
=TEXTAFTER(CELL("filename",A1),"]")
```

CELL() returns [File Name]SheetName. Text after the] is the sheet name.

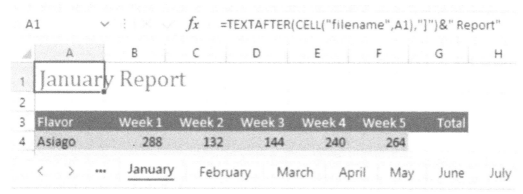

If you plan on using this formula frequently, set up a book.xltx as described in "#9 Use Default Settings for All Future Workbooks" on page 19. In book.xltx, go to Formulas, Define Name. Use a name such as SheetName with a formula of `=TEXTAFTER(CELL("filename",book.xltx!$A$1),"]")`. Then, in any new workbook `=SheetName&" Report"` will work.

Bonus Tip: Add a Total Row and a Total Column with One AutoSum

Say that you want to add a total row and a total column to a data set. Select all the numbers plus one extra row and one extra column. Click the AutoSum icon or press Alt+=.

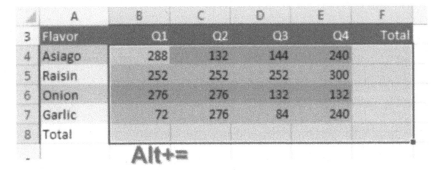

Excel adds SUM functions to the total row and the total column as shown in the figure below.

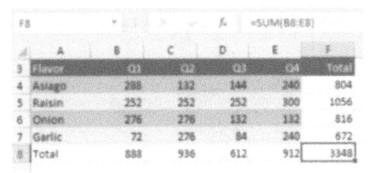

Bonus Tip: Power Up the Status Bar Statistics

When you select two or more numeric cells, the total appears in the status bar in the lower right of the Excel window. When you see a total, right-click and choose Average, Count, Numerical Count, Minimum, Maximum, and Sum. You can now see the largest, smallest, and average just by selecting a range of cells.

Aha!: Left-click any number in the status bar to copy that number to the clipboard.

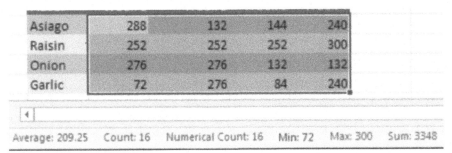

Caution: Here is a fun fact: The numbers in the status bar are shown in the number format of the active cell. This is generally very useful and allows the status bar to show the Min and Max date as a date for example. But in one very confusing trick, someone had applied a crazy number format to hide the negative sign from a number to the top cell in a range. If you selected the range from the top, you had one number as the Sum in the status bar. If you selected from bottom to top, you had a different number in the status bar. It through a lot of really smart Excel people for a loop. For details, see Episode 2566 at the MrExcel YouTube channel.

Bonus Tip: Change All Sheets with Group Mode

Any time your manager asks you for something, he or she comes
back 15 minutes later and asks for an odd twist that wasn't specified the first time. Now that you can create worksheet copies
really quickly, there is more of a chance that you will have to make
changes to all 12 sheets instead of just 1 sheet when your manager
comes back with a new request.

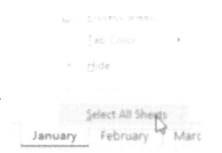

I will show you an amazingly powerful but incredibly dangerous
tool called Group mode.

Say that you have 12 worksheets that are mostly identical. You need to add totals to all 12 worksheets. To
enter Group mode, right-click on any worksheet tab and choose Select All Sheets.

The name of the workbook in the title bar now indicates that you are in Group mode.

Anything you do to the January worksheet will now happen to all the sheets in the workbook.

Why is this dangerous? If you get distracted and forget that you are in Group mode, you might start entering January data and overwriting data on the 11 other worksheets!

When you are done adding totals, don't forget to right-click a sheet tab and choose Ungroup Sheets.

Bonus Tip: Create a SUM That Spears Through All Worksheets

So far, you have a workbook with 12 worksheets, 1 for each month. All of the worksheets have the
same number of rows and columns. You want a summary worksheet in order to total January through
December.

To create it, use the formula =SUM(January:December!B4).

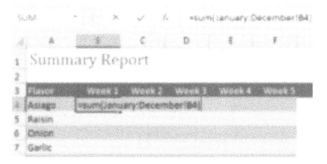

Copy the formula to all cells and you will have a summary of the other 12 worksheets.

	A	B	C	D	E	F	G
	B4				f_x	=SUM(January:December!B4)	
1	Summary Report						
2							
3	Flavor	Week 1	Week 2	Week 3	Week 4	Week 5	Total
4	Asiago	2400	2040	2004	2388	2688	11520
5	Raisin	2220	2244	2076	2160	1968	10668

Caution: I make sure to never put spaces in my worksheet names. If you do use spaces or punctuation, the formula would have to include apostrophes, like this: =SUM('Jan 2025:Mar 2025'!B4).

Tip: If you use 3D spearing formulas frequently, insert two new sheets, one called First and one called Last. Drag the sheet names so they create a sandwich with the desired sheets in the middle. Then, the formula is always =SUM(First:Last!B4).

Here is an easy way to build a 3D spearing formula without having to type the reference: On the summary sheet in cell B4, type =SUM(. Using the mouse, click on the January worksheet tab. Using the mouse, Shift+click on the December worksheet tab. Using the mouse, click on cell B4 on the December worksheet. Type the closing parenthesis and press Enter.

Bonus Tip: Use INDIRECT for a Different Summary Report

Say that you want to build the following report, with months going down column A. In each row, you want to pull the grand total data from each sheet. Each sheet has the same number of rows, so the total is always in row 12.

The first formula would be =January!B12. You could easily copy this formula to columns C:F, but there is not an easy way to copy the formula down to rows 5:15.

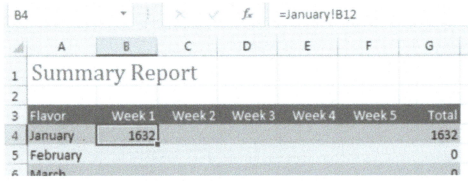

The INDIRECT function evaluates text that looks like a cell reference. INDIRECT returns the value at the address stored in the text. In the next figure, a combination of the ADDRESS and COLUMN functions returns a series of text values that tell Excel where to get the total.

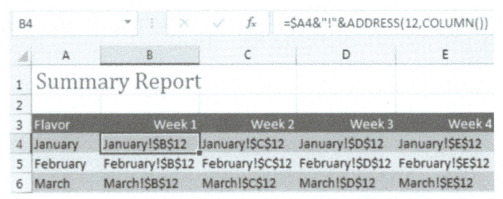

Wrap the previous formula in =INDIRECT() to have Excel pull the totals from each worksheet.

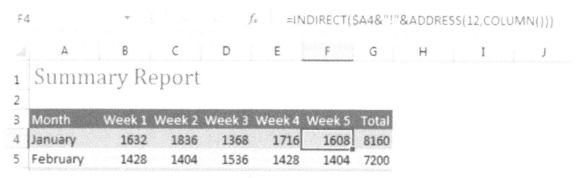

Caution: INDIRECT will not work for pulling data from other workbooks. Search the Internet for Harlan Grove PULL for a VBA method of doing this.

Thanks to Othneil Denis for the 3D formula tip, Olga Kryuchkova for the Group mode tip, and Al Momrik for status bar.

#9 Use Default Settings for All Future Workbooks

1

Do you have favorite worksheet settings in Excel? I do. There are things I do to every new workbook I create.

In a few minutes, you can teach Excel your favorite settings. Then, every time you create a new workbook with Ctrl+N or insert a new worksheet, the worksheet will inherit all of your favorite settings.

The key step is to save the workbook as a template into a specific folder with two specific names.

Start with a blank workbook with a single worksheet.

Apply all your favorite settings. There are dozens of possibilities. Here are a few that I use:

On the Page Layout tab, change the Scale to Fit so the Width is 1 page. Leave Height set to Automatic and Width set to 1 Page.

Create a custom header or footer. Use the dialog launcher in the bottom right of the Page Setup group. Go to the Header/Footer tab. Choose Custom Footer. Type whatever is your company standard in the footer.

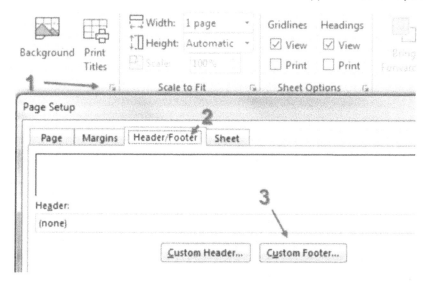

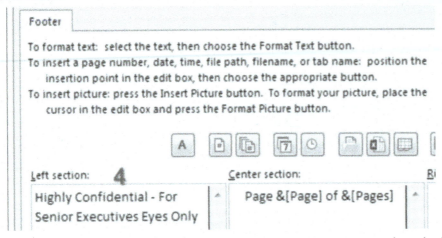

Create custom margins. I like narrow margins – even more narrow than the built-in Narrow margin settings. I've been using 0.25-inch margins since the 1990s, and they're automatically set for me because I've added that to my template.

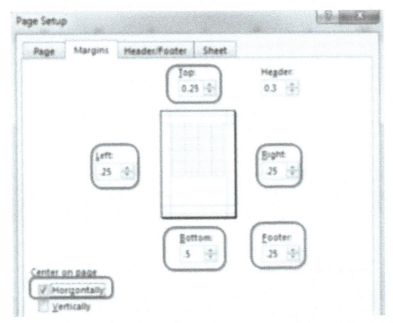

Choose a theme. I like the colors from Slipstream, but I prefer the Effects from Office 2007–2010.

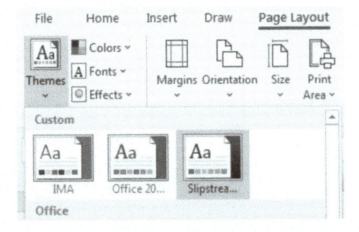

When you set a pivot table default theme, it only applies to the current workbook. Excel never saves your preference. Create a tiny two-cell data set. Create a pivot table. Change the default formatting. Delete the pivot table and the data set. The template will remember the setting.

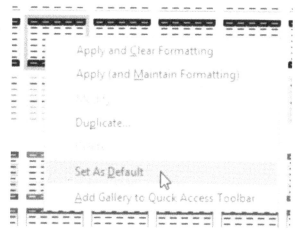

Would you use cell styles more often if they weren't so ugly? Do you hate that input cells are orange? Go to Cell Styles, right-click Input, and choose Modify as shown below. Click the Format button and choose a different input color.

If you develop some favorite functions stored as LAMBDA functions in the Name Manager, you can store those functions in your Book.XLTX workbook. Read more in "#122 Store Complex Formula Logic in LAMBDA function" on page 223.

I've just shown you some of my favorite settings. I'm sure you have your own favorites. Maybe you always set up a name to define the tax rate. Add it to your template, and you will never have to set it up again. Turn off gridlines. Do whatever you always do.

Once you've finished customizing your workbook, you need to figure out which file type you use most often. For people who never use macros, this is often XLSX. But I always use macros, so my default file type is XLSM. Maybe you want workbooks to open faster, and you use XLSB. There is a template format related to each of these file types, and you can just change the extension as needed. So, for me, I save the workbook as XLTM. You might save it as XLTX or XLTB.

As soon as you choose one of these file types, the Save As dialog box moves to a templates folder. You need to save the workbook in a different folder.

C:\Users\Bill\AppData\Roaming\Microsoft\Excel\XLSTART

In the folder bar, type %AppData% and press Enter to get to the AppData\Roaming\ folder on your computer. From there, navigate to Microsoft\Excel\XLSTART.

Save the workbook with the reserved name Book plus the appropriate extension. Use Save As again and save the workbook in the same folder but use Sheet plus the same extension as the name.

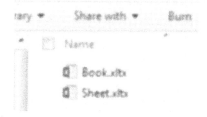

Of course, you only have to set this up once. After you do it, any time you use Ctrl+N to create a new workbook, the new workbook will inherit all of the settings from your template named Book.

Why did you have to also save templates named both Book and Sheet? Any time you insert a new worksheet into an existing workbook, Excel uses the Sheet template.

My Rant About New and New...

I've been using Book.xltm for 30 years. In all versions of Excel from Excel 95 up through Excel 2003, the Excel Standard toolbar had an icon called "New". Click that icon, and Excel loaded the Book template. Everything was great.

The File menu offered a New... option, but hardly anyone used it because it was half as many clicks to simply click the New icon on the Standard toolbar. New respects your custom settings in the Book template. New... does not.

If you've set up custom Book and Sheet templates, do not click the Blank Workbook template. Simply dismiss this opening screen by using the Esc key, and your custom Book template loads.

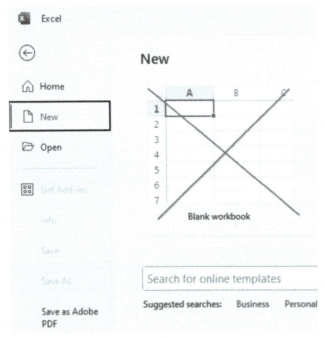

If you get tired of pressing Esc, go to File, Options, General and deselect the checkbox Show the Start Screen When This Application Starts.

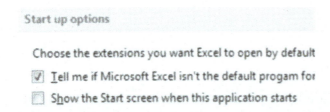

Bonus Tip: Replace the Comma Style in Book.xltx

The Excel team offers Currency, Percent, and Comma icons in the center of the Home tab of the Ribbon. The tooltip says the Comma Style formats with a thousands separator. I despise this icon.

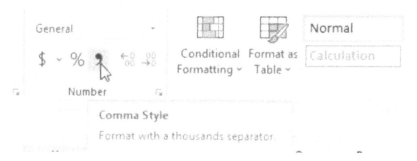

Why do I despise this icon? Because it turns on Accounting style. Sure, that gives you a thousands separator, but it also adds several things that I hate:

K	L
6,543.21	(4,321.00)
6,543.00	-

- It turns on two decimal places.

- It uses a right indent of 1 character to move the last digit away from the right edge of the cell.

- It uses parentheses for negative numbers.

- It displays zero with a single dash about four spaces away from the right edge of the cell.

There is no way to replace the Comma icon with my own icon or even to change what style it applies. So, I find that I have to click the Dialog Launcher icon at the bottom right of the Number group:

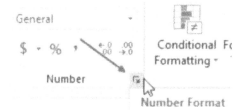

Tip: The Dialog Launcher icon is a diagonal arrow pointing down and to the right. It is found in many groups in the Ribbon and usually offers far more choices than are available in the Ribbon.

Then choose Number from the Category list, choose the checkbox for Use 1000 Separator, and click twice on the down arrow to change 2 decimal places to 0 decimal places. Click OK to close the Format Cells dialog. It takes six clicks to create a simple number format with a comma as the thousands separator. That is why I despise the Comma icon: People who can live with right indents, parentheses, and zeros displayed as dashes can apply that style in one click, but people who just want a comma have to go through six clicks.

The great news: There is a solution. The bad news: Microsoft makes it hard to use the solution. The good news: If you add the solution to the Book.xltx file, the solution will become mostly permanent for all files that you create. Here is what you do:

1. While you are creating Book.xltx, as discussed in "#9 Use Default Settings for All Future Workbooks", type 1234 in a cell. Format the cell using the six clicks discussed above (or your favorite format). Keep that cell selected.

2. Open the Cell Styles gallery. Near the bottom, choose New Cell Style....

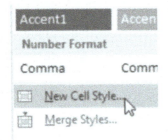

3. In the Style box that appears, type a descriptive name for your style, such as CommaGood.

4. If you only want to apply the Number format, unselect the checkboxes for Alignment, Font, Border, Fill, and Protection.

5. Click OK to create the new style.

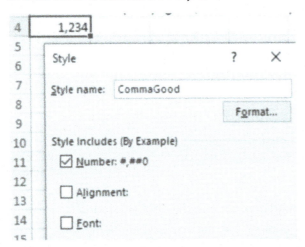

New styles appear at the top of the Cell Styles gallery, and you now have one-click access to the CommaGood style.

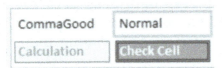

Caution: Any cell style added using this method applies only to the current workbook, making this tip almost useless.

Tip: If you add the CommaGood style to your Book.xltx file, the CommaGood style will be available on all future workbooks that you create with Ctrl+N.

Thanks to Jo Ann Babin for an idea similar to this one.

Bonus Tip: The Consolas Font Makes it Easy to Tell Zero from the Letter O

Way back in 2009, font designer Erik Spiekermann designed the Axel font specifically for use with Excel. You can still buy the font today, often for US $30 per computer. However, if your whole goal is to get a slashed zero, then the Consolas font is built in to Windows computers and is free to use.

Every half decade, Microsoft changes the default font in Excel. Today, we have Aptos that has taken over for Calibri which took over for Arial. How about adopting Consolas as the default font in your spreadsheets? You can either change the font in book.xltx or use File, Options, General, and Use This As The Default Font.

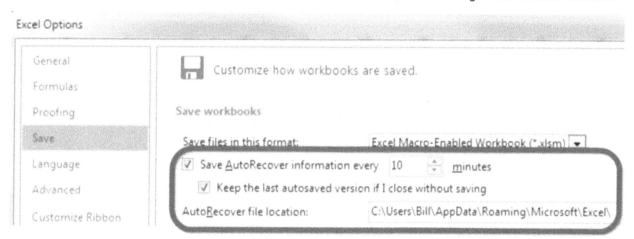

#10 Recover Unsaved Workbooks

The Auto Recover feature is a lifesaver. It debuted in 2010. It seems to be missing in 2024 builds of M365..

Say you have a bunch of files open in Excel and issue the Alt+F, X command to exit Excel.

There is no need to save this file, so you click Don't Save. Next file? Don't Save. Next file? Don't Save.

   Aha!: Hold Shift while clicking Don't Save to perform Don't Save All.

Now you are in a rhythm, clicking Don't Save in perfect synchronization with Excel presenting the message. Then, as you click Don't Save the last time, you realize that *this* workbook had a lot of unsaved changes. And you really needed to save it. You should have clicked Save.

You look at your watch. It will take two hours to re-create all of those changes. Your happy hour plans are sunk. But wait! Excel has your back. If the workbook was open for at least 10 minutes and created an AutoRecover version, Excel kept a copy for you.

Follow these steps to get it back:

1. Open Excel.

2. Go to File, Info, Manage Workbook, Recover Unsaved Workbooks.

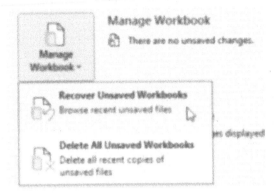

3. Excel shows you all the unsaved workbooks that it has saved for you recently.

4. Click a workbook and choose Open. If it is the wrong one, go back to File, Open and scroll to the bottom of the list.

5. When you find the right file, click the Save As button to save the workbook. Unsaved workbooks are saved for four days before they are automatically deleted.

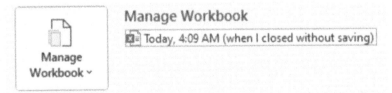

Use AutoRecover Versions to Recover Files Previously Saved

Recover Unsaved Workbooks applies only to files that have never been saved. If your file has been saved, you can use AutoRecover versions to get the file back. If you close a previously saved workbook without saving recent changes, one single AutoRecover version is kept until your next editing session. To access it, reopen the workbook. Use File, Info, Manage Workbook to open the last AutoRecover version.

Manage Workbook

Today, 4:09 AM (when I closed without saving)

You can also use Windows Explorer to search for the last AutoRecover version. The Excel Options dialog box specifies an AutoRecover File Location. If your file was named Budget2028Data, look for a folder within the AutoRecover File folder that starts with Budget.

While you are editing a workbook, you can access up to the last five AutoRecover versions of a previously saved workbook. You can open them from the Versions section of the Info category. You may make changes to a workbook and want to reference what you previously had. AutoRecover versions open in another window so you can reference, copy/paste, save the workbook as a separate file, etc.

Note: An AutoRecover version is created according to the AutoRecover interval AND only if there are changes. So if you leave a workbook open for two hours without making any changes, the last AutoSave version will contain the last revision.

Caution: Both the Save AutoRecover Information option and Keep The Last AutoRecovered Version option must be selected in File, Options, Save for this to work.

Tip: Create a folder called C:\AutoRecover\ and specify it as the AutoRecover File Location. It is much easier than trawling through the Users folder that is the default location.

Note: Under the Manage Version options on the Info tab you can select Delete All Unsaved Workbooks. This is an important option to know about if you work on public computers. Note that this option appears only if you're working on a file that has not been saved previously. The easiest way to access it is to create a new workbook.

Thanks to Beth Melton and Paul Seaman and for clarifying the differences between AutoRecover and Recover Unsaved Files.

#11 Search While Using File Open

When you choose File, Open, Excel will show you a list of recently opened workbooks. The size of this list is controlled by File, Options, Advanced, Display. The maximum numbers of recent workbooks or folders is 50. If you choose Quickly Access This Number Of Recent Workbooks, then a few workbooks will show in the left pane of the File menu, even in File, Home.

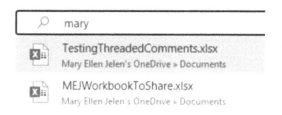

During 2020, a new Search box was added to the top of the File Open view. This Search box extends further back than the recent 50 workbooks. Type a word and Excel will present you with a list of workbooks previously opened with that word in the title. You can also search by collaborator.

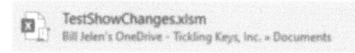

This search box uses a superset of Recommended Files, Most Recently Used, and Shared With Me. If you search for "cost accounting", Excel will return files that contain both cost and accounting in any order.

Bonus Tip: Pin an Item to the Top of the Recent Files

If you hover over any workbook in the File Open screen, a thumbtack appears. Click the icon to pin that item to the top of the recent files list.

What if you want to remove a sensitive item from the Recent files? Right-click it for options.

#12 Show Changes From Last One Year

The Show Changes feature debuted in June 2021. For any workbook that is stored in OneDrive or SharePoint Online, Excel is tracking every change to the workbook. Changes are saved for 365 days. The increase from 60 days to one year happened in May 2025 for Excel Online. It has not rolled out to Windows as of June 2025.

Let's say that you have a workbook which had been stored on your local hard drive. Do a File, Save As and save it in OneDrive and then continue editing in Windows. At that point, every change made to a worksheet will be logged. In the figure below, you type a new value in B5. The formulas in many other cells recalculate. But this is simply logged as a change to B5.

	A	B	C	D	E	F	G
1	Show Changes in Excel				Only "typing 1112 in B5"		
2	Type a value here...				is logged as a change.		
3	Name	Qty	Revenue	Cost	GP	GP%	Commission
4	Barb	5555	37095	9610.15	27484.8	74%	933.37
5	Chris	1112	6616.4	1923.76	4692.64	71%	171.41
6	Gary	1010	6009.5	1747.3	4262.2	71%	156.24
7	Ed	333	1971.36	576.09	1395.27	71%	55.28
8	Flo	2222	11132.2	3844.06	7288.16	65%	284.31
9	Diane	1000	4950	1730	3220	65%	129.75
10	Andy	999	3946.05	1728.27	2217.78	56%	104.65
11			...all of these cells change				
12	Total	12231	71720.5	21159.6	50560.9	70%	155672.679

If someone edits a formula, that will be logged as a change and is viewable in Review, Show Changes.

1. On the Review tab in Excel, choose Show Changes. A Changes panel appears on the right side with all changes made to the workbook.

2. A quick way to filter to only the changes for a cell or range is to select the cell, right-click, and choose Show Changes.

If you need to clear the Changes pane, use File, Info, Reset Changes Pane.

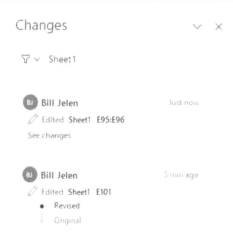

Bonus Tip: Roll Back to a Previous Version of the Workbook

The Show Changes log has dramatically improved the Version History available in Excel. When you go to File, Info, Version History, a panel is displayed with past versions that you can roll back to. Click a version in the Version History panel and you can cycle through each cell that was edited.

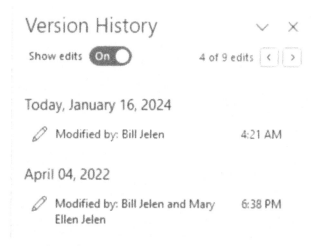

Note that when you are viewing a past version, it is in read-only mode. You can use File, Save As to save the old version with a new name. Or, if you prefer, you can use the Restore button that appears in the Info bar above the Formula Bar. This will replace the current version with the restored version.

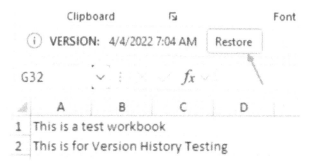

Tip: Microsoft isn't really saving many versions of the same workbook. They are saving the current workbook and the log of past changes. When you click Save a Copy, they are creating a new version of the workbook by reversing the changes saved in the Save Changes log.

#13 Add Interactive Checkboxes in Excel

Excel now has native checkboxes, and they're awesome. You will find the Checkbox on the left side of the Insert tab. Select the range where you want checkboxes. 2. Click Insert, Checkbox.

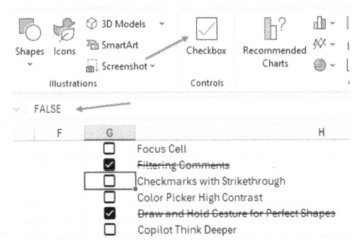

Each cell gets a clickable checkbox. You can toggle them with the space bar.

If you check the formula bar, you'll see the cell value is just TRUE or FALSE. And if you want to remove the checkbox, go to Home, Clear, Clear Formats, and you're back to plain old Boolean values.

Calculating the Checkbox with a Formula

Let's say column E is the quota, column F is sales, and column G calculates whether we met the goal: =F2 >= E2. You can format the G column with checkboxes, so each one automatically shows TRUE or FALSE as a checkbox.

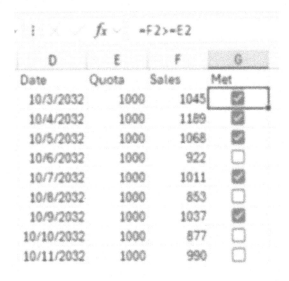

Using Conditional Formatting with Checkboxes

1. Select all checkboxes.

2. Change the font to red.

3. Home, Conditional Formatting, New Rule, Format Only Cells That Contain, Cell Value = TRUE.

4. Choose a green font for TRUE checkboxes.

Use Strikethrough in the cell to the right of the Checkboxes

1. Say you have checkboxes in A2:A9 and words in B2:B9.

2. Select B2:B9

3. Home Conditional Formatting, New Rule, Use a Formula

4. The formula is =A2. This might seem surprising. I initially thought the formula would be =A2=TRUE. But since A2 will either contain FALSE or TRUE, simply using =A2 works.

> Caution: If you send this workbook to someone who doesn't have the checkbox feature yet, their checkboxes will revert to True, False. No harm done, but no checkboxes either.

#14 Simultaneously Edit a Workbook in Microsoft 365

For decades, some people have been wanting a better way to have multiple people in the same workbook at the same time. The old Shared Workbook functionality was awkward. People resorted to "only one person having write access at a time", which led to someone opening the file and then forgetting to close it before going for a two-hour lunch and tying up the file that whole time.

After Google's spreadsheet product began offering the ability for multiple people to edit the same worksheet, the Excel team spent many years developing a feature that they call co-authoring. The feature was released to Microsoft 365 customers in the summer of 2017.

The feature works great if everyone you are sharing with are on the same tenant. For example, if everyone is using a signin ending @YourCo.onmicrosoft.com, then you are on the same tenant.

To start, choose one person to be the owner of the workbook. This person should already have a One Drive For Business or SharePoint Online folder set up. The owner of the document should use File, Save As and choose to save the document in either One Drive or SharePoint Online.

The owner of the workbook clicks the Share icon in the top right corner of Excel.

The Share panel asks you to invite people by e-mail address. The people you share with will receive an Outlook e-mail with a link to the file. They can also see the workbook in File, Open, Shared With Me.

If you are not in the same tenant, look at the bottom of the panel, you can generate a sharing link.

Generate a sharing link where anyone with the link can edit the workbook.

Copy the link and send it to others on your team.

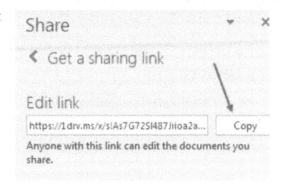

The next step is the annoying part. When they follow the link from Outlook, the workbook will open in Excel Online. At the top right, choose Editing, Open in Desktop.

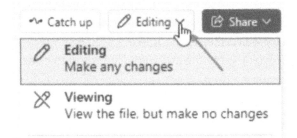

> **Tip**: I actually avoid opening the workbook from Outlook. Instead, I go to File, Home. In the middle of the screen is a tab for Shared With Me. I find the file there and open it in Excel for Windows.

While you and others are working in a document, your active cell will be outlined in green. The active cells for others will be other colors. If you want to know who is editing a cell, hover over that cell.

	A	B	C	D	E	F
1	Product	1Q 2020	2Q 2020	3Q 2020	4Q 2020	1Q 2021
2	Apple	1,446	1,540	1,244	3,137	3,296
3	Banana	1,923	1,851	2,311	1,830	2,399
4	Cherry	2,982	2,066	1,330	2,163	1,351
5	Date	1,838	2,547	2,390	1,371	1,622
6	Elderberry	2,549	2,557	2,798	2,591	2,992
7	Fig	1,308	2,854	2,280	2,108	3,318

Some people complain that when a dozen people are all moving around the same spreadsheet, having so many cell indicators moving around is annoying. Microsoft has heard this complaint and is trying to figure out the best way to mute or at least tone down Presence.

Co-authoring will work fine provided everyone avoids editing the same cell at the same time. When someone (probably your manager), dives in to edit a cell that you are already editing, then a confusing set of rules decides whose edit wins. Rather than dealing with these rules, be happy that co-authoring mostly works and have everyone agree not to edit the same cell at the same time.

Co-authoring is a whole new experience. There are good things and bad things that you need to get used to when you are co-authoring.

Bonus Tip: Avoiding the Veto

A "veto" is when Excel reports that your changes could not be synchronized. Microsoft is working hard to minimize these. They've already reduced them by 90%. But they still happen. One of my training clients learned that occassionally clicking Save will minimize the chance of a veto. Microsoft confirms this.

Bonus Tip: AutoSave is Necessary, But Turn it Off When Not Co-Authoring

The reason that co-authoring is possible is because of AutoSave. Every time that you make a spreadsheet change, that change will be saved to OneDrive so that others can (almost) instantly see what you just typed. AutoSave is necessary if you want ten accountants editing a budget worksheet at the same time.

But let's talk about workbooks that will never be used with co-authoring. These are the run-of-the-mill workbooks that I use 99.9% of the time. I do not want AutoSave to be active for those workbooks. I want to open Excel, know that I can do some "what-if" changes and then close the workbook without saving. If AutoSave is on, those changes are automatically saved. It is terrible.

Or - you likely recognize the scenario: You have a report for January. You need a report for February. You open the January report, change the headings, and then do File, Save As to save for February. This work-flow has been fine for decades. But if you allow AutoSave to be on, you will be destroying the January report as soon as you edit A1 and type February over January.

You have four choices. 1. Change your workflow to do the Save a Copy before you make any edits. 2. Always save to a local drive and AutoSave will not automatically be enabled. 3. Toggle AutoSave off for each workbook. Click the "On" icon shown here to turn AutoSave off for the current workbook.

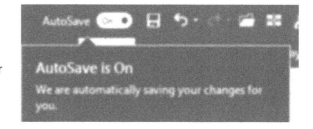

The best choice is 4. Go to File, Options, Save, and unselect the choice for AutoSave OneDrive and SharePoint Online Files By Default.

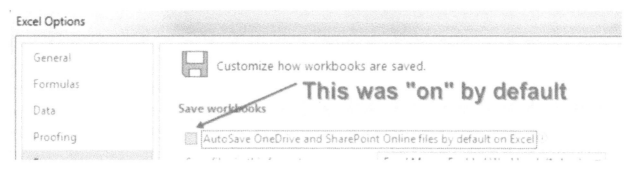

Bonus Tip: Undo an AutoSave

What if you have to undo an AutoSave? Your manager said to merge two regions and then 20 minutes later calls the merger off. AutoSave has been saving after every change in your workbook.

Click the drop-down menu next to the title bar. Click on Version History.

Excel will offer to let you open a previous version of the file. They don't save a version after every change. I (Bill Jelen) made 50 changes to this workbook in the last 20 minutes. The Version History is offering me three versions from those twenty minutes. Note that although all of the changes were made by Bill Jelen, AutoSave is crediting the changes to Mary Ellen Jelen. I have yet to find anyone at Microsoft who can ex-plain this apparent bug.

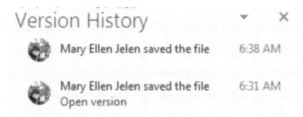

#15 Save Filter & Sorting in Sheet View

Do you share a workbook with co-workers? Does you co-worker want to Filter or Sort the workbook differently than you do? Eight years ago, I was ready to strangle my co-worker Scott when he kept filtering our project list to show only his projects.

Amazingly, the Excel team has provided a new solution called "Sheet View". It debuted for Microsoft 365 in March 2020.

Caution: Sheet View only works if you store your workbook in OneDrive or SharePoint online. It is fine for everyone to access the workbook on the PC, but it has to be saved in the cloud.

Caution: There is a pretty bad bug in Sheet View if you have a team of people working in Desktop Excel. Everything is fine when the first person creates a Sheet View. But when the second person creates a Sheet View, the default view changes for everyone. Microsoft's solution to this bug: If your team is all using Windows versions of Excel and people want to use Sheet View, then everyone needs to create a Sheet View and use it.

Tip: I will extend their advice and suggest that someone creates a Sheet View called Show All and have that view be unfiltered.

Below is a small workbook that Andy and Betty share. The Ribbon is showing the new Sheet View settings that are found on the View tab.

Tip: Before you create a view for Andy or Betty, create an unfiltered view called All or Everyone or Default.

	Project	Manager	Value
1	Project	Manager	Value
2	A001	Andy	$21,020
3	A002	Betty	22690
4	A003	Andy	$39,470
5	A004	Andy	$21,760
6	A005	Betty	$28,250
7	A006	Andy	$45,850
8	A007	Betty	44770
9	A008	Andy	$77,920
10	A009	Betty	29790
11	A010	Andy	$67,340
12			
13	Total Visible		$398,860

To create a new Sheet View, click New.

The new view is initially called Temporary View. Apply any formatting or sorting. In the image below, Andy has filtered to his records and sorted the projects high-to-low.

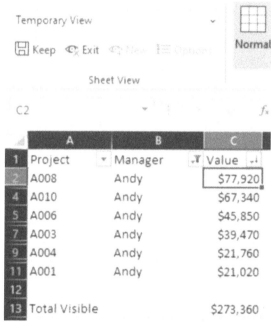

If you want to be able to return to this view in the future, you can either click the Keep icon or simply type a new name such as Andy Descending.

Notice that the Row and Column labels are now black. This is to alert you that you are seeing a Sheet View.

When Betty opens the workbook, she can filter to Betty and sort ascending. She might name her view as BettyAscending.

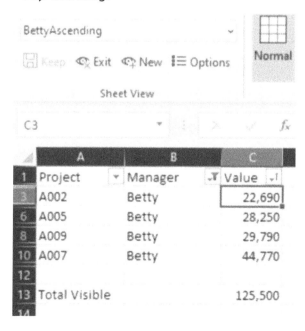

This next part is absolutely wild. Say that Andy edits cell C2 in his view and changes the value to $100,000.

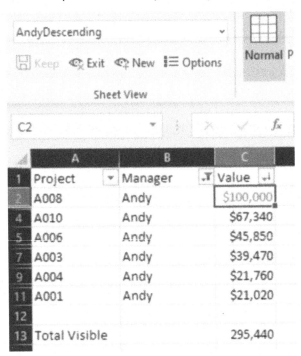

When anyone goes back to the Default view of the workbook, the original sort order is retained. But - the new value for Andy's project A008 is still $100,000!

I've asked the Excel team how they manage to do this behind the scenes, and I still don't know how they manage to keep it all tied together. But it works.

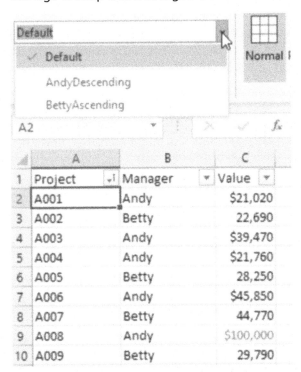

Tip: You might be happy having two different views of the workbook for your own use. But this feature is really designed for when you are collaborating with the whole department. See "#14 Simultaneously Edit a Workbook in Microsoft 365" on page 31.

#16 Threaded Comments Allow Conversations

Threaded comments debuted in 2018. When you insert a comment, Excel stores the comment, the author, the date, and time. You can @Mention a co-worker and optionally assign the comment to them. When a co-worker sees your comment, they can click Reply and add a new comment to the same cell. Each set of comments lists the author, date, and time. Use the ... menu to mark a comment as resolved. If you @Mention someone, they will be notified by Outlook. In the Show Comments pane, you can now filter comments by person or status.

These new threaded comments are indicated by a five-sided purple shape instead of the red triangle used for the old style comments (now known as Notes).

Bonus Tip: Old Style Comments Are Available as Notes

While the new threaded comments are cool, there are some great tricks that the old legacy comments offered that are lost with the threaded comments. Luckily, if you have a situation requiring one of the special tricks, the old comments are still available as Notes.

Here are some of my favorite Note techniques:

- Individual notes could be set to always show. This is useful for creating helpful instructions for a spreadsheet. Select a cell containing a red-triangle indicator and select Review, Notes, Show/Hide Note.

- Notes can be resized and located in a specific position. Right-click a cell with a note and choose Edit Note. Use the resize handle to change the size or drag an edge to move the comment.

- You can change the shape of a note. To start, Right-click the Ribbon and choose Customize Quick Access Toolbar. In the dialog box, change the top-left drop-down menu to All Commands. Find the Change Shape icon in the left list and click the Add>> button to add it to the Quick Access Toolbar. Right-click the cell containing the note and choose Show Note. Ctrl+Click on the edge of the note to select the note without entering text edit mode. Use the Change Shape icon in the Quick Access toolbar to choose a new shape. Note that you will often have to resize the note after choosing a shape. You also might try the Center and Align Middle icons to center the text in the shape. After changing the shape, you can return to Hide Note to make the note only visible when you hover over the red triangle indicator.

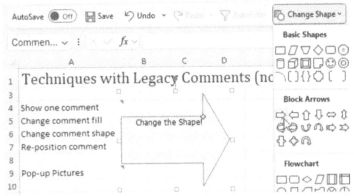

- You can change the color of a note. This one is tricky because there are two versions of the Format Comment dialog box. While in edit mode, click the border of the comment and then press Ctrl+1 to open the Format Comment dialog box. You should see nine tabs in the dialog. If you only see the Font tab, close the dialog and try clicking the comment border again or Ctrl+Click the comment to leave text edit mode. When you have the dialog with all 9 tabs, use the Colors and Lines tab, Fill Color to change the color of a comment. Use Fill Effects… to add a gradient or a picture.

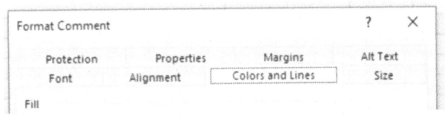

- To create pop-up pictures: edit a note and backspace to remove your name from the note. With a completely blank note, Ctrl+Click the edge and press Ctrl+1. Use Colors and Lines, Fill Color, Fill Effects, Picture and choose a picture from your computer. Hide the note and the picture will pop up when you hover over the triangle.

The following screenshot shows examples of notes with colors, shapes, and a pop-up picture.

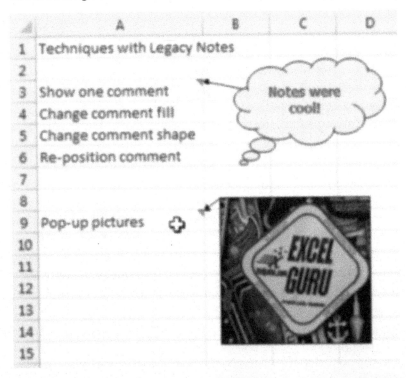

Bonus Tip: Add a Tooltip to a Cell with Validation

You can use the Data Validation dialog to set up a tooltip for a cell. The tooltip is only visible when the cell is the active cell.

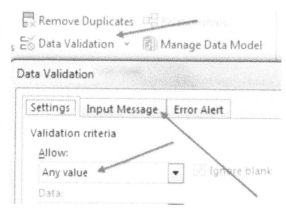

Data Validation is found towards the right side of the Data tab in the Ribbon. I end up using Alt+D L because I always have a difficult time finding the Validation icon. Normally, most people use the Settings tab in Data Validation to control what can be entered in a cell. You will skip the Settings tab and go to the Input Message tab.

On the Input Message tab, type a title and a message. Click OK.

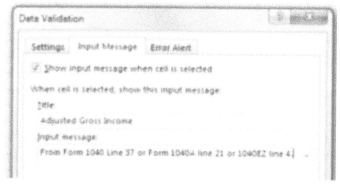

The result: a tooltip that will appear any time the cell is active:

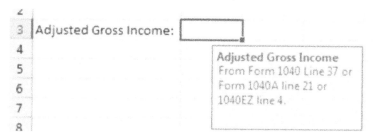

Bonus Tip: Data Validation Partial Matching Added in 2022

For many years, people were frustrated that a data validation drop-down list did not use partial matching. Starting in March 2022, Microsoft 365 customers will be able to use partial matching for their Data Validation lists. In this figure, the valid list for cell C2 is shown in E2:E9. Type "Ap" and Excel shortens the list to include entries where any word in the entry starts with "Ap". This means you get Apple, Fuji Apple, Crab Apple. But they don't see Pineapple as a match. Also note that the list is presented with Apple Butter higher in the list than Fuji Apple because Apple Butter starts with "Ap".

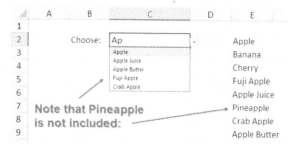

#17 Create Perfect One-Click Charts

One-click charts are easy: Select the data and press Alt+F1.

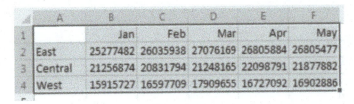

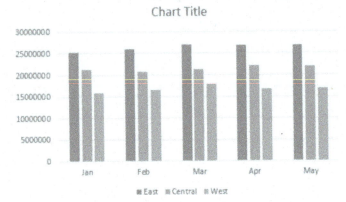

What if you would rather create bar charts instead of the default clustered column chart? To make your life easier, you can change the default chart type. Store your favorite chart settings in a template and then teach Excel to produce your favorite chart in response to Alt+F1.

Say that you want to clean up the chart above. All of those zeros on the left axis take up a lot of space without adding value. Double-click those numbers and change Display Units from None to Millions.

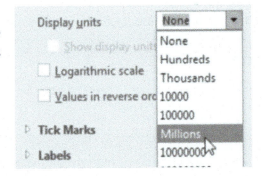

To move the legend to the top, click the + sign next to the chart, choose the arrow to the right of Legend, and choose Top.

Change the color scheme to something that works with your company colors.

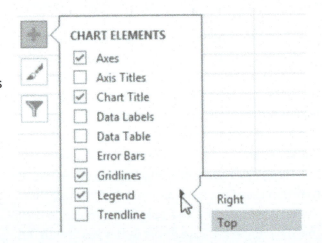

Right-click the chart and choose Save As Template. Then, give the template a name. (I called mine ClusteredColumn.)

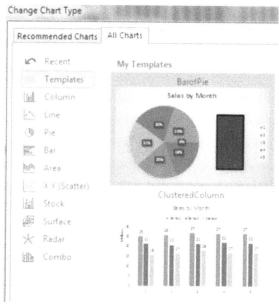

Select a chart. In the Design tab of the Ribbon, choose Change Chart Type. Click on the Templates folder to see the template that you just created.

Right-click your template and choose Set As Default Chart.

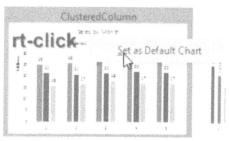

The next time you need to create a chart, select the data and press Alt+F1. All your favorite settings appear in the chart.

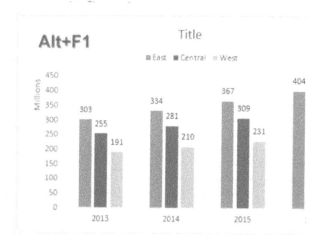

Thanks to Areef Ali, Olga Kryuchkova, and Wendy Sprakes for suggesting this feature.

#18 Paste New Data on a Chart

You might be responsible for updating charts every month, week, or day. For example, in my last job, a collection of charts were updated during the month-end close process. The charts would track progress throughout the year.

There is an easy way to add new data to an existing chart. Here, the chart shows data for January through May, and there is new data for June that is not on the chart.

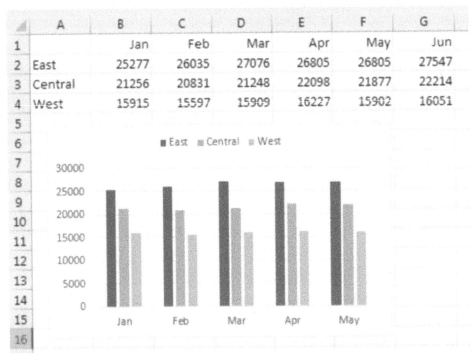

Rather than re-create the chart, you can paste new data on it. Select the new data in the worksheet, including the heading. Press Ctrl+C to copy.

Click on the chart and press Ctrl+V to paste the data on the chart. As shown below, the new data is added to the existing chart.

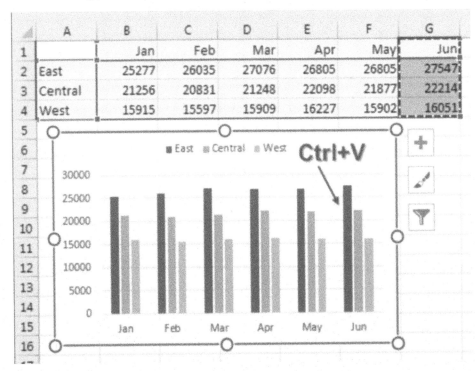

As you keep adding months to the right side, what if you want to remove data from the left side? Is there any way to Ctrl+X that data off the chart?

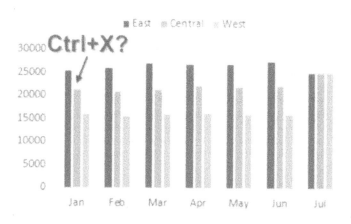

No, but there is another way. Select the chart. Outlines appear around the charted data in the worksheet. A blue box surrounds the data points for the charts, and in each corner of the blue box is a square dot as shown below. The square dot is a resizing handle.

Click on the lower-left resizing handle and drag to the right.

	Jan	Feb	Mar
	25277	26035	27076
	21256	20831	21248
	15915	15597	15909

■ East ■ Central ■ West

The data is removed from the left side of the chart.

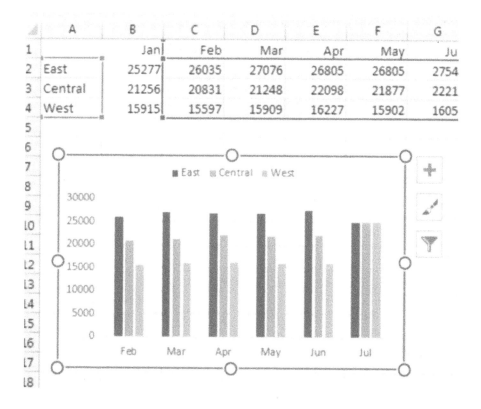

You can use resizing handles to resize or drag the blue box to change the data that appears on the chart. Of course, you could have dragged the bottom-right resizing handle to add June to the chart in the first place, but it is good to know this copy-and-paste trick in case the chart and data are on different sheets in the workbook.

> **Tip**: If you want to remove East from the chart, you can click on any East column in the chart and press Delete on your keyboard to remove that series. To temporarily hide a series, you can hide the row or column where the underlying data is stored. In Excel 2013 or newer, you can use the Filter funnel icon located to the right of the chart to hide any series or category from the chart.

#19 Create Interactive Charts

It is easy to create interactive charts without using VBA. By default, if you hide rows in Excel, those rows will be hidden in the chart. The technique is to build a chart with every possible customer and then use a slicer or a filter to hide all except one of the customers.

Say that you have the following list of customers. Make the data into a table by using Ctrl+T.

Company	Q1	Q2	Q3	Q4
Cambia Factor	814	838	897	1032
data2impact	860	877	886	877
Excel4apps	886	842	775	775
excelisfun	632	683	744	789
F-Keys Ltd	283	258	243	228
SpringBoard	259	220	211	222
Surten Excel	493	488	503	513
Vertex42	827	769	669	636
WSLCB	409	450	513	564
Yesenita	835	827	827	819

Select the table and insert a chart. In most cases, Excel will create the wrong chart, with customers along the X-axis.

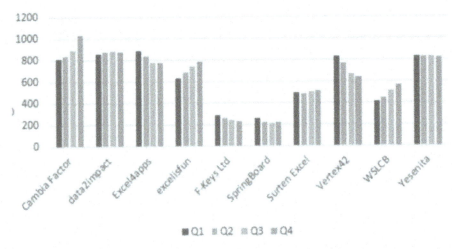

Click the Switch Row/Column icon in the Chart Tools Design tab of the Ribbon.

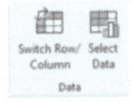

CREATE INTERACTIVE CHARTS

Select one cell in the table. In Excel 2013 or newer, go to the Insert tab of the Ribbon and choose Slicer. In Excel 2010 or earlier, you have to use the Company dropdown in A17 to choose a single company.

By default, every slicer starts as a single column in the middle of the screen. Plan on dragging the slicer to a new location and size. While the slicer is selected, you can use the Columns spin button near the right side of the Slicer Tools Options tab of the Ribbon to change the number of columns in the slicer.

In the following figure, choose one customer from the slicer and the chart updates to show just that one customer.

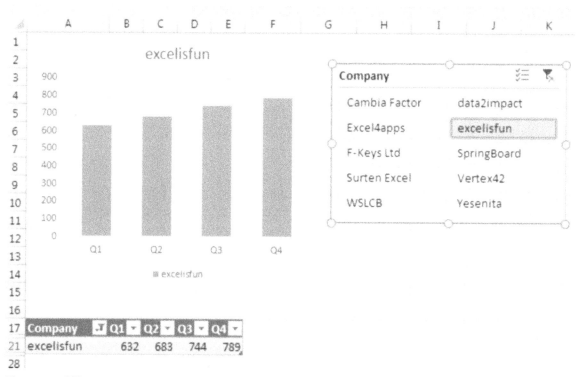

Choose a different customer, and the chart updates for that customer.

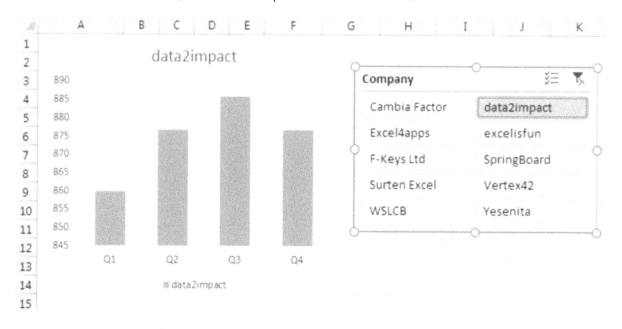

#20 Show Two Different Orders of Magnitude on a Chart

It is nearly impossible to read a chart where one series is dramatically larger than other series. In the following chart, the series for Year to Date Sales is 10 times larger than most of the monthly sales. The blue columns are shortened, and it will be difficult to see subtle changes in monthly sales.

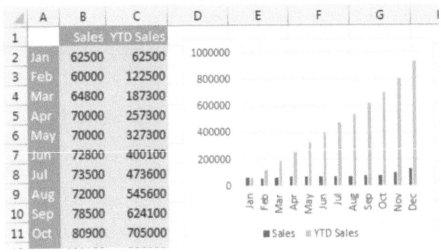

Combo charts are easy using the Combo Chart interface. Choose the chart above and select Change Chart Type. Choose Combo from the category list on the left. You then have the choices shown below. Move the larger number (YTD Sales) to a new scale on the right axis by choosing Secondary Axis. Change the chart style for one series to Line from Clustered Column.

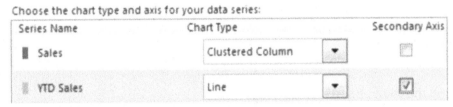

The result: Columns for the monthly revenue are taller, so you will be able to make out subtle changes like a decrease from July to August.

To get the additional formatting to the chart above, select the numbers on the left axis. Use the Font Color dropdown on the Home tab to choose a blue to match the blue columns. Select the green line. Select Format, Shape Outline to change to a darker green. Select the numbers on the right axis and change the font color to the same green. Double-click each axis and change Display Units to Thousands. Double-click a blue column and drag the Gap Width setting to be narrower. Double-click the legend and choose to show the legend at the top.

#21 Create Waterfall Charts

For 12 years, I worked at a company doing data analysis. One of my regular tasks was to analyze the profit on sales proposals before they went out the door. I did this with a waterfall chart. For me, the waterfall chart never would have to dip below the zero axis. I used a few tricks to make the columns float and drew the connector lines in by hand, using a ruler and a black pen.

Excel 2016 introduced a built-in Waterfall chart type. Select your range of data and create the chart. In the chart below, three columns are marked as total: Net Price, Gross Profit, and Net Profit. Excel won't automatically know which columns should be totals. Click any column to select all columns in the chart. Then single-click one total column. Right-click and select as Total. Repeat for the other columns that should touch the X-axis.

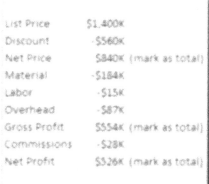

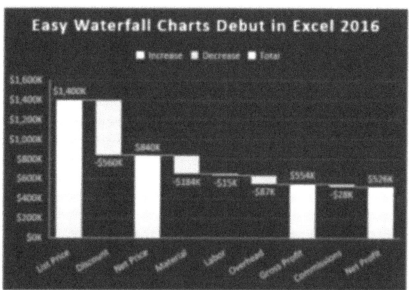

The waterfall charts even work for cash flow charts that might go below zero.

Open	$145K (mark as total)
Jan	$26K
Feb	-$68K
Mar	$20K
Apr	-$85K
May	-$76K
Jun	$59K
Jul	-$35K
Aug	$65K
Sep	$43K
Oct	-$37K
Nov	$79K
Dec	$99K
Close	$234K (mark as total)

Tip: To change the color for Increase/Decrease or Total: Click on the legend and then click on one item in the legend. Press Ctrl+1 to open the Format panel for that series and choose a new Fill Color.

#22 Create Filled Map Charts

Early in 2017, Map Charts appeared on the Insert tab in Microsoft 365. A Map chart shades closed regions on a map such as countries, states, counties, even zip code boundaries.

When you format a series in a Map, you can choose if it should show all 50 states or only the regions with data. Choose what makes the most sense for your data. In the chart on the left, the series color is a two-color gradient. You can choose three-color gradients or a category map, as shown on the right.

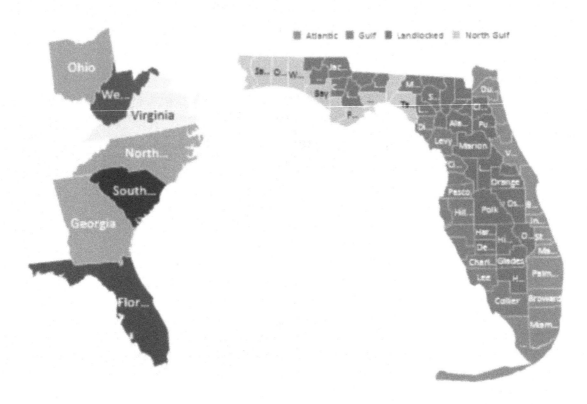

#23 Create a Bell Curve

A bell curve is based on a mean and standard deviation. In stats, 68% of values fall within 1 standard deviation, 95% within 2, and 99.73% within 3.

To plot a curve from 100 to 200 with a peak at 150: Use 150 as the mean. Since most of the results will fall within 3 standard deviations of the mean, you would use a standard deviation of 50/3 or 16.667.

1. Type 150 in cell B1. Type =50/3 in cell B2. Type headings of Point, X, Y in cells A4:C4.

2. Fill the numbers 1 to 61 in A5:A65. This is enough points to create a smooth curve.

B2		×	✓	fx	=50/3	
	A	B	C	D	E	
1	Mean	150				
2	Standard Deviation	16.66667	=50/3			
3						
4	Point	X	Y			
5		1				
6		2				
7		3				

3. Go to the midpoint of the data, point 31 in B35. Type a formula there of =B1 to have the mean there.

4. The formula for B36 is =B35+($B$2/10). Copy that formula from row 36 down to row 65.

5. The formula for B34 is =B34-($B$2/10). Copy that formula up to row 5. Note that the notes in columns C:E of this figure do not get entered in your workbook - they are here to add meaning to the figure.

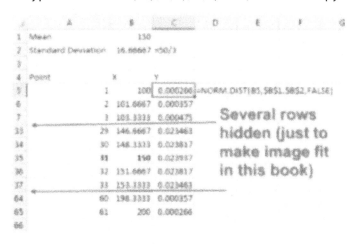

	A	B	C	D	E
1	Mean	150			
2	Standard Deviation	16.66667	=50/3		
3					
4	Point	X	Y		
32		28			
33		29			
34		30	148.3333	=B35-($B$2/10)	Copy up
35		31	150	=B1	
36		32	151.6667	=B35+($B$2/10)	Copy Down
37		33			
38		34			
39		35			

The magic function is called NORM.DIST which stands for Normal Distribution. When statisticians talk about a bell curve, they are talking about a normal distribution. To continue the current example, you want a bell curve from 100 to 200. The numbers 100 to 200 go along the X-axis (the horizontal axis) of the chart. For each point, you need to calculate the height of the curve along the y-axis. NORM.DIST will do this for you. There are four required arguments: =NORM.DIST(This x point, Mean, Standard Deviation, False). The last False says that you want a bell curve and not a S-curve. (The S-Curve shows accumulated probability instead of point probability.)

6. Type =NORM.DIST(B5,$B$1,$B$2,False) in C5 and copy down to row 65.

	A	B	C	D	E	F	G
1	Mean	150					
2	Standard Deviation	16.66667	=50/3				
3							
4	Point	X	Y				
5		1	100	0.000200	=NORM.DIST(B5,$B$1,$B$2,FALSE)		
6		2	101.6667	0.000357			
7		3	103.3333	0.000475	Several rows		
33		29	146.6667	0.023463	hidden (just to		
34		30	148.3333	0.023817	make image fit		
35		31	150	0.023937	in this book)		
36		32	151.6667	0.023817			
37		33	153.3333	0.023463			
64		60	198.3333	0.000357			
65		61	200	0.000200			
66							

7. Select B4:C65. On the Insert tab, open the XY-Scatter drop-down menu and choose the thumbnail with a smooth line. Alternatively, choose Recommened Charts and the first option for a bell curve.

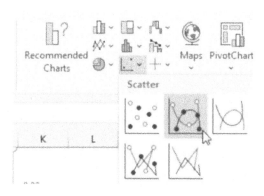

The result: a bell curve, as shown here.

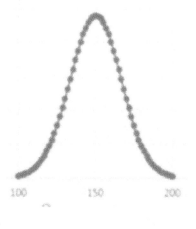

#24 Plotting Employees on a Bell Curve

Rather than creating a generic bell curve, how about plotting a list of employees or customers on a bell curve? Start with a list of people and scores. Use the AVERAGE and STDEV.P functions to find the mean and standard deviation.

	A	B	C	D	E	F	G
1	Name	Score					
2	Andy	62		Mean	78.231	=AVERAGE(B2:B14)	
3	Barb	64		St Dev	14.418	=STDEV.P(B2:B14)	
4	Chris	83					
5	Diane	68					
6	Ed	98					
7	Flo	85					
8	Gary	98					
9	Hank	49					
10	Ike	90					
11	Jared	81					
12	Kelly	93					
13	Lou	71					
14	Mike	75					
15							

Once you know the mean and standard deviation, add a Y column with the formula shown below.

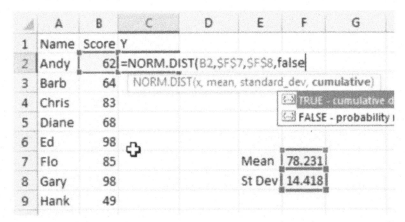

After adding the Y column, sort the data by Score ascending.

	A	B	C
1	Name	Score	Y
2	Hank	49	0.003544
3	Andy	62	0.014683
4	Barb	64	0.017
5	Diane	68	0.021512

Select Score & Y columns and add a Scatter with Smooth Lines as shown in the previous technique. Labelling the chart with names is tricky. Use the + icon to the right of the chart to add data labels. From the Data Labels flyout, choose More Options. In the panel shown below, click the icon with a column chart and then choose Value from Cells and specify the names in column A.

Tip: You will often have two labels in the chart that appear on top of each other. You can rearrange single labels so they appear with a small leader line as shown for Gary and Ed at the right side of the chart. Click on any label and all chart labels are selected. Next, click on either of the labels that appear together. After the second click, you are in "single label selection mode". You can drag that label so it is not on top of the other label.

The result:

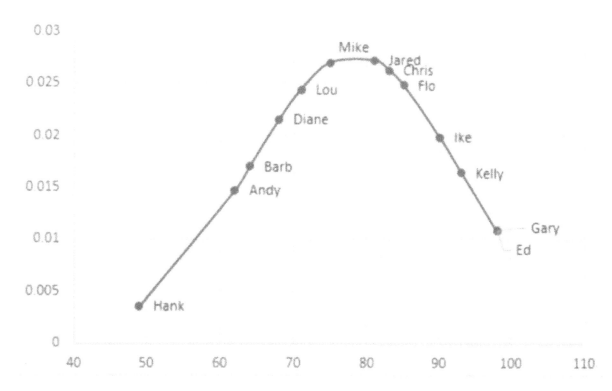

#25 Add Meaning to Reports Using Data Visualizations

Three easy visualization tools were added to the Conditional Formatting dropdown in Excel 2007: Color Scales, Data Bars, and Icon Sets.

Consider this report, which has way too many decimal places to be useful.

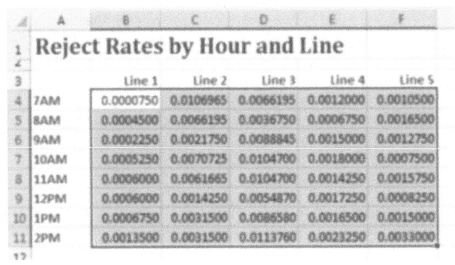

Select the numbers in the report and choose Home, Conditional Formatting, Color Scales. Then click on the second icon, which has red at the top and green at the bottom.

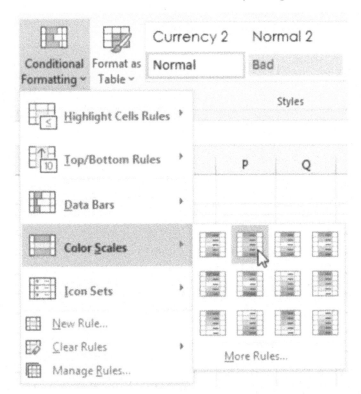

With just four clicks, you can now spot trends in the data. Line 2 started out the day with high reject rates but improved. Line 3 was bad the whole day. Line 1 was the best, but even those reject rates began to rise toward the end of the shift.

	Line 1	Line 2	Line 3	Line 4	Line 5
7AM	0.0000750	0.0106965	0.0066195	0.0012000	0.0010500
8AM	0.0004500	0.0066195	0.0036750	0.0006750	0.0016500
9AM	0.0002250	0.0021750	0.0088845	0.0015000	0.0012750
10AM	0.0005250	0.0070725	0.0104700	0.0018000	0.0007500
11AM	0.0006000	0.0061665	0.0104700	0.0014250	0.0015750
12PM	0.0006000	0.0014250	0.0054870	0.0017250	0.0008250
1PM	0.0006750	0.0031500	0.0086580	0.0016500	0.0015000
2PM	0.0013500	0.0031500	0.0113760	0.0023250	0.0033000

The next tool, Data Bar, is like a tiny bar chart that fills a cell. In the following figure, select all of the Revenue cells except for the grand total.

Choose Conditional Formatting, Data Bar, Green. Each number now gets a swath of color, as shown below. Large numbers get more color, and small numbers get hardly any color.

	A	B		B
1	Customer	Revenue		Revenue
2	Amazing Yardstick Partners	22810		22810
3	Inventive Opener Corporation	2257		2257
4	Magnificent Tackle Inc.	11240		11240
5	Leading Yogurt Company	9204		9204
6	Excellent Doorbell Company	18552		18552
7	Paramount Doghouse Inc.	9152		9152
8	Flexible Instrument Partners	8456		8456
9	Honest Chopstick Company	21730		21730
10	Wonderful Faucet Corporation	13806		13806
11	Special Doghouse Inc.	16416		16416
12	Ideal Vise Corporation	21015		21015
13	Guaranteed Bicycle Company	21465		21465
14	Astonishing Thermostat Corpora	21438		21438
15	Trustworthy Yogurt Inc.	9144		9144
16	Bright Toothpick Inc.	6267		6267
17	Remarkable Banister Supply	1740		1740
18	Safe Shoe Company	2401		2401
19	Vibrant Vise Company	9345		9345
20	Forceful Furnace Company	11628		11628
21	Guarded Zipper Corporation	5961		5961
22		244027		244027

Caution: Be careful not to include the grand total before selecting Data Bars. In the following example, you can see that the Grand Total gets all of the color, and the other cells get hardly any color.

2401
9345
11628
5961
244027

With the third tool, Icon Sets, you can choose from sets that have three, four, or five different icons.

Most people keep their numbers aligned with the right edge of the cell. Icons always appear on the left edge of the cell. To move the number closer to the icon, use the Increase Indent icon, shown below.

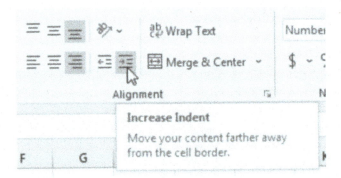

All three of these data visualization tools work by looking at the largest and smallest numbers in the range. Excel breaks that range into three equal-sized parts if you are using an icon set with three icons. That works fine in the example below.

	Q1	Q2	Q3	Q4
Andy	☆ 88	☆ 87	★ 94	☆ 85
Bob	☆ 87	☆ 94	☆ 89	☆ 94
Charlie	☆ 93	☆ 99	☆ 100	☆ 91
Dale	☆ 83	☆ 82	☆ 89	☆ 85
Eddy	☆ 80	☆ 83	☆ 82	☆ 91

But in the following figure, Eddy scored horribly in Q1, getting a 30. Because Eddy did poorly, everyone else is awarded a gold star. That doesn't seem fair because their scores did not improve.

	Q1	Q2	Q3	Q4
Andy	☆ 88	☆ 87	☆ 94	☆ 85
Bob	☆ 87	☆ 94	☆ 89	☆ 94
Charlie	☆ 93	☆ 99	☆ 100	☆ 91
Dale	☆ 83	☆ 82	☆ 89	☆ 85
Eddy	→ ☆ 30	☆ 83	☆ 82	☆ 91

You can take control of where the range for an icon begins and ends. Go to Home, Conditional Formatting, Manage Rules and choose Edit Rule. In the following figure, the Type dropdown offers Percent, Percentile, Formula, and Number. To set the gold star so it requires 90 or above, use the settings shown below. Note that the two other icons have been replaced with No Cell Icon.

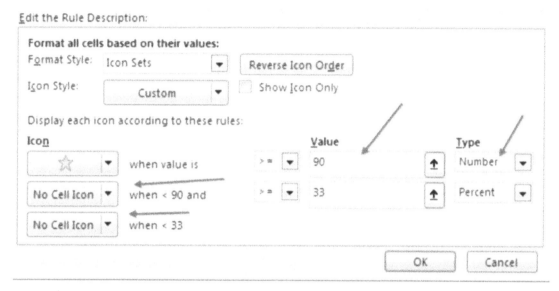

#26 Use People to Add Interest to Your Worksheet

Microsoft 365 subscribers now have access to 925 People in Excel. In a study conducted by YouTube, 90% of the most-watched videos have an emotive human face prominently on the title card. Photos of people attract attention because humans are naturally drawn to faces. Try adding a person to your next report to get someone to look at the report.

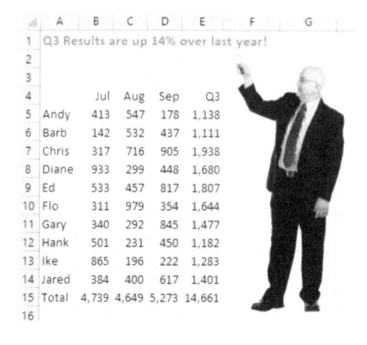

◢	A	B	C	D	E	F	G
1	Q3 Results are up 14% over last year!						
2							
3							
4		Jul	Aug	Sep	Q3		
5	Andy	413	547	178	1,138		
6	Barb	142	532	437	1,111		
7	Chris	317	716	905	1,938		
8	Diane	933	299	448	1,680		
9	Ed	533	457	817	1,807		
10	Flo	311	979	354	1,644		
11	Gary	340	292	845	1,477		
12	Hank	501	231	450	1,182		
13	Ike	865	196	222	1,283		
14	Jared	384	400	617	1,401		
15	Total	4,739	4,649	5,273	14,661		
16							

To insert a person, go to Insert, Icons. Across the top of the dialog, you can choose from Images, Icons, People, Stickers, Illustrations, and Cartoon People. Click on People.

There are 925 poses of 41 people. Each person has from 15 to 30 multiple poses, exhibiting different emotions. There are people holding their thumb up, or down. Seven of the people offer a series with 1, 2, 3, 4, or 5 fingers extended up.

To find all poses of one person, you might have to know their name to search. Small tiles identify 32 of the 41 people (chosen at random). If you want someone without a name tile, you can type their name in the search box.

The names of people in the photo below are: (Row 1) Addison, Alexander, Alfredo, Angela, Anthony, Babs, Basia, Carrie, Chantel, Charles, Christania, Deepika, Dennis, Elena, Fu, Herlinda, Jian, Jonathan, Kairy, Karun, and Kesha. Row 2: Kevin, Klein, Lance, Mara, Marci, Melanie, Melissa, Nicole, Noah, Pavan, Rachel, Randy, Shao, Sherri, Shreya, Soham, Stanley, Tanvi, Tiyna, and Ursula.

While you can search for people by name, you can also search by emotion or action. You can find people who are happy, excited, frustrated, pointing, or holding a sign. They're also grouped by angle. Searching for "Profile" will find people facing to the side, for example, while searching for "Back" will find people facing away from you.

Below, a series of photos of Karun could be used to illustrate five sequential steps.

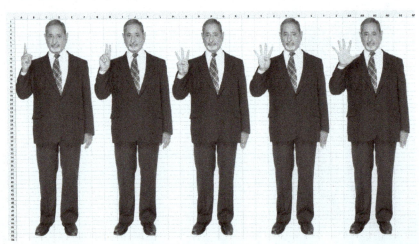

Bonus Tip: Add Text to the Sign Held by a Person

There are also poses where the person is holding a blank sign. You can add text to the sign, like in this image of Angela on the left or the tableau created from Cartoon People:

Here are the steps for adding text to a sign and making it look natural:

1. Use Insert, Icons, People, and search for "Sign."

2. Select a person and click Insert.

3. Resize the person as needed to fit the situation.

4. Click any cell outside of the picture to unselect the picture.

5. Use Insert, Shapes, Textbox. Draw a text box that aligns closely with the sign.

6. The color of the sign and the color of the white text box in Excel don't match exactly. With the text box selected, go to Shape Format, Shape Fill, & choose No Fill. This will make the background of the text box transparent and match the color of the sign. On the same tab, choose Shape Outline, No Outline.

7. Type your text to appear on the sign. On the Home tab, use Increase Font, Center, Middle Align, Font Color, and Font to make the text on the sign stand out.

> **Note:** I keep picturing the photo shoot where these people were put through the paces of being photographed with up to 30 different emotions. It had to be a tiring day. At the point where they asked people to hold a large blank sign, I doubt that anyone bothered to have a carpenter's level handy to make sure the sign was completely level. In most cases, the sign is tilted by a few degrees.

8. Align the top of the text box with the top of the sign. Make sure the text box is selected. Go to the Shape Format tab in the ribbon and look for the Arrange group toward the right side. The last drop-down in that group is called Rotate. Open the drop-down menu and choose More Rotation Options. This opens the Format Shape task pane. The Rotation spin button allows you to rotate in 1-degree increments. Rotate using the spin button until the text box lines up with the sign.

Bonus Tip: Make an Image Semi-Transparent

Semi-transparent images became easier in Microsoft 365 starting in the fall of 2019. If you use Insert, Image, the image always covers the data in the cells. Starting in 2019, you can use the Transparency drop-down on the Picture Format tab of the Ribbon to change the picture transparency.

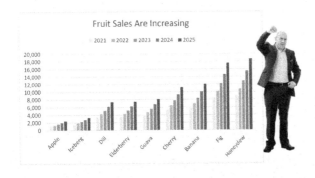

Tip: Picture Transparency is better than the old Page Layout, Background. When you choose a background image, it displays behind the numbers, but it will not print. With Picture transparency, you can control the size and shape of the image.

Caution: In the screenshot above, you will see the Remove Background tool. There is also a Set Transparent Color option under the Color drop-down menu. Both tools are finicky. The Set Transparent Color might work for a sign being held by a Person, but it won't work for a sky with many shades of blue. The Remove Background tool asks you to mark areas to keep and areas to remove. It seems that when you click a new area, the logic recalculates the old areas. As you remove a new section, the old sections come back. To painlessly remove backgrounds, try PhotoShop or Topaz Mask AI.

#27 Save Any Object as an Image

Starting in 2020 for Microsoft 365, you can right-click any object in Excel and choose Save As Picture. If you want to save a Chart plus a Person, you can select them both and then choose Group from the Format Picture tab of the Ribbon.

Tip: What if you want to save a picture of values in cells? You could use Paste Linked Picture, or simply use the Office Snipping Tool with Win+Shift+S.

	2021	2022	2023	2024	2025
Apple	1,143	1,372	1,646	1,975	2,370

#28 Display Online Pictures In a Cell Using a Formula

The IMAGE function debuted in August 2022. It is only for online images that are available through a URL.

The simplest case is =IMAGE(url). The first time you use it, Excel will show the #BLOCKED error and you will have to enable external content.

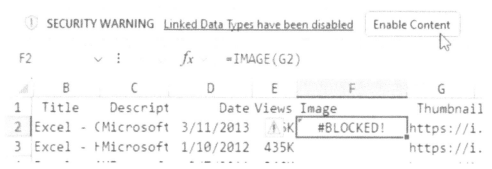

After you enable the external content, press F2 and Enter on the Image formula to have it re-render. Initially, the image will be resized to fit the cell.

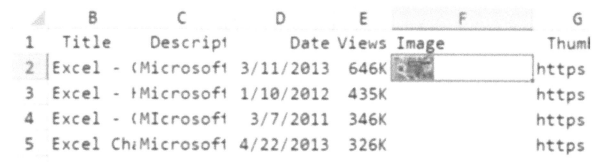

At this point, you could double-click the fill handle from cell F2 and the formula will copy down and you will have an image for each row in the data. Initially, the images are all very small. You can choose any cell and press Ctrl+Shift+F5 to see a larger preview of the image.

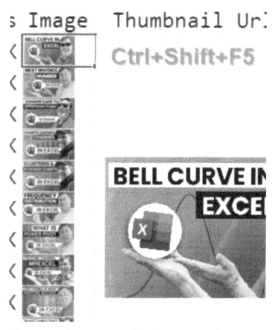

The complete syntax for the IMAGE function is =image(source,[alt_text],[sizing],[height],[width]). You will unlock some cool features if you include Alt Text. In my case, I have the video title in column A and that would make perfect Alt Text. Change the formula to =IMAGE(G2,A2).

The Alt Text that you specify in the formula will travel with the photo. You can bring the photos to other places by using formulas such as INDEX or XLOOKUP. In the following image, a formula brings the images to a dashboard. I've added a heading and turned on the filter drop-downs. When I attempt to filter by this column, the alt text appears in the filter drop-down. I can search for all photos about pivots.

The result will be just the images that have "pivot" in the alt-text.

You can also sort the data by the image and Excel will use the Alt Text for the sort order.

DISPLAY ONLINE PICTURES IN A CELL USING A FORMULA

The other arguments in the IMAGE function control the image size. First, understand that the image will never be larger than the cell. If you want a larger image, you need to increase the row height and column width (good) or merge a bunch of cells (evil).

In my opinion, the most useful image size setting is 0 to Fit Cell. The image will appear as large as possible, with either the row height or column width being the constraint. The rest of the cell is white space. This keeps the aspect ratio of the image correct.

If you change the size to 1 for Fill Cell, then the picture will be stretched or pinched to fill the entire cell. A setting of 2 keeps the image at the original size, but only shows you a portion of the image. A setting of 3 allows you to specify height, width, or both. Specify either height or width to keep the aspect ratio correct. If you specify both height and width, then the picture will stretch.

In this example, a slicer allows you to choose which image shows in a single large cell.

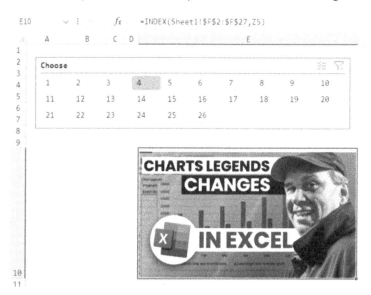

Below, the WRAPROWS brings all of the images into a dashboard.

Caution: The moment that you use the IMAGE function for a particular image, the current version of the image is cached in the workbook. If the image later changes on the website, your version in the workbook will stay the same. The only way to get Excel to refresh that image is to use Move or Copy Worksheet to move the sheet to another workbook. I don't like it either, but I don't suppose it would have been good to have Excel bringing the images in on every recalc. People smarter than me thought about this and came up with the current implementation.

As soon as the IMAGE function came out, many of the beta testers pleaded with Microsoft that we will really needed a way to embed images that were stored locally instead of online. It took ten months and the result was not what any of us expected. Read on.

#29 Place Pictures In Cell From Local Computer

For the last 30 years, you could use Insert, Picture in Excel. The image was added to a special drawing layer that floated above the grid. In June of 2023, that legacy experience became known as Place Over Cells. The new experience is to Place In Cell.

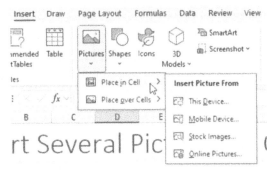

Here is a great use for Place In Cell. Arrange several photos in a folder on your computer. Insert a new picture worksheet in your computer. From a blank cell B4, use Insert, Picture, Place In Cell, This Device. If you specify several images, they will be arranged in a column.

This step is important. Right-click the first image and choose View Alt Text. An Alt Text pane will appear on the right side of the screen. Type some Alt Text for the image. With the Alt Text panel still showing, click the next image and type Alt Text for that image. Repeat for each image.

By Adding Alt Text to the image, you are making the images sortable and filterable. The Alt Text appears in the formula bar when you select the cell containing the image. And the Alt Text is available if you add the image to a pivot table.

Note: Typing Alt Text for hundreds of images might be a daunting task. You could use a macro like this one to add the text to the right of the image to the image:

```
Sub AddAltTextBulk()
    For Each cell In Range("B2:B6")
        cell.UpdatePictureInCellAlternativeText _
            AlternativeText:=cell.Offset(0, 1).Value
    Next cell
End Sub
```

Here is an example of using XLOOKUP to return an image:

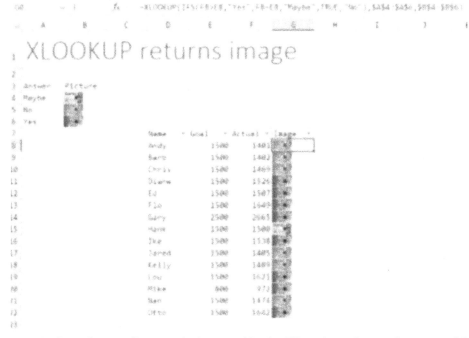

Here is the column of images being used in the Filter drop-down of a pivot table. Note that the image appears in the Filter area, but not in the Slicer.

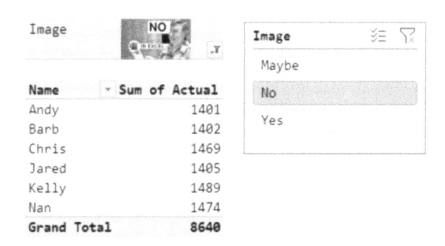

Here is an example of the image being used in the pivot table Rows area.

Image	Name	Sum of Actual
	Hank	1500
Maybe Total		**1500**
	Andy	1401
	Barb	1402
	Chris	1469
	Jared	1405
	Kelly	1489
	Nan	1474
No Total		**8640**
	Diane	1526
	Ed	1507

Here is an example where the lookup value is an image and it returns adjacent text from the lookup table.

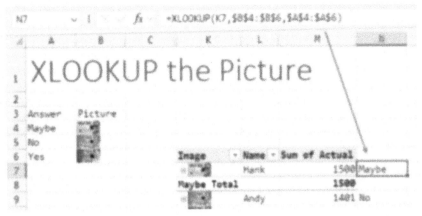

#30 Set Up Your Data for Data Analysis

Make sure to follow these rules when you set up your data for sorting, subtotals, filtering and pivot tables.

- Rule 1: Use only a single row of headings above your data. If you need to have a two-row heading, set it up as a single cell with two lines in the row by using Alt+Enter or Word Wrap as discussed in "Bonus Tip: Use Accounting Underline to Avoid Tiny Blank Columns" on page 64.

- Rule 2: Never leave one heading cell blank. This often happens to me when I set up a temporary column.

- Rule 3: There should be no entirely blank rows or blank columns in the middle of your data. It is okay to have an occasional blank cell, but you should have no entirely blank columns.

- Rule 4: If your heading row is not in row 1, be sure to have a blank row between the report title and the headings. It is fine to make this blank row have a row height of 1 so it is barely visible.

- Rule 5: If you have a total row below your data, leave one blank row above the totals.

- Rule 6: Formatting the heading cells in bold will help the Excel's IntelliSense module understand that these are headings.

  Caution: Following these rules may not help if your data is only two columns wide.

  Tip: To test, select one cell in your data and press Ctrl+* to select the current region. It should include your data and your headings, but not any Title rows or total row or footnotes.

Bonus Tip: Use Accounting Underline to Avoid Tiny Blank Columns

I once had a manager who was obsessed with how heading underlines looked in reports. He couldn't stand the standard underlines like those in row 1—where the underline in cell E1 only stretches as wide as the text. Using a bottom border instead didn't help either, because that created one long, continuous "uni-border" across the row, like in row 6..

	A	B	C	D	E	F
1		Apple	Banana	Cherry	Dill	Total
2	Jan	495	824	298	973	2590
3	Feb	994	574	138	705	2411
4	Mar	306	851	719	598	2474
5						
6		Apple	Banana	Cherry	Dill	Total
7	Jan	495	824	298	973	2590
8	Feb	994	574	138	705	2411
9	Mar	306	851	719	598	2474

To work around this, he added narrow columns between each main column and applied bottom borders to each one. Visually, it looked like separate underlines, but technically they were still borders. The problem? This setup is a data disaster waiting to happen—someone will eventually sort just part of the data and break everything.

	A	B	C	D	E	F	G	H	I	J
1		Apple		Banana		Cherry		Dill		Total
2	Jan	495		824		298		973		2590
3	Feb	994		574		138		705		2411

There's a great solution, but it's not obvious. On the Home tab, the Underline drop-down only shows Single and Double options. However, if you click the dialog launcher in the Font group to open the Format Cells dialog, you'll find more options under the Underline drop-down, including Accounting Underlines. These underlines extend nearly the full width of the cell, but each one is separate—avoiding the long, continuous line issue.

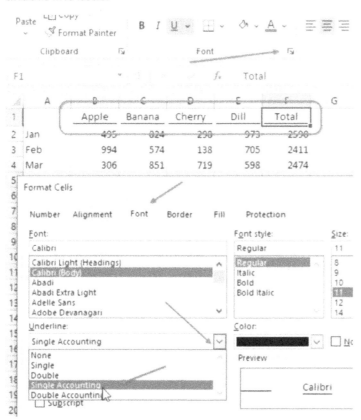

Bonus Tip: Use Alt+Enter to Control Word Wrap

The Gross Profit heading in C1 and C2 violates the rule that each heading should be in a single cell.

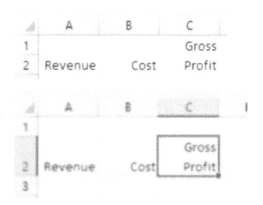

In cell C2, type Gross. Then press Alt+Enter. Type Profit. Press Enter. Delete the word Gross from row 1. Excel will see C2 as a single cell. All of the intellisense will continue to work.

Why use Alt+Enter instead of turning on Word Wrap? When you have long text that you want to wrap to several lines, the Word Wrap icon frequently wraps at the wrong place.

Bonus Tip: Someone went crazy and used Alt+Enter Too Much

Alt-Enter is a great trick until someone uses it in hundreds of cells. I've seen people treat a single cell as if it were Microsoft Word. Pressing Alt+Enter inserts a Character Code 10 in the cell. You might be tempted to fix this by using =SUBSTITUTE(A1,CHAR(10),"").

However, the simple solution is to use Data, Text to Columns. In Step 1, choose Delimited. In Step 2, choose Other. Click into the Other box and press Ctrl+J. You won't see anything in the box, but typing Ctrl+J in this dialog or in the Find & Replace dialog will insert a character 10.

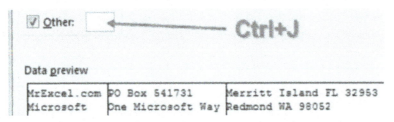

#31 Sort East, Central, and West Using a Custom List

At my last day job, we had three sales regions: East, Central, and West. The company headquarters was in the East, and so the rule was that all reports were sorted with the East region first, then Central, then West. Well, there is no way to do this with a normal sort.

Sort AZ, and you will have Central at the top.

Region	Customer	Revenue
Central	Excel Design Solutions Ltd	810475
Central	Excelerator BI	243675
Central	WSLCB	1116175
East	Budget Wand	692375
East	Deloitte Canada	805775
East	New Hope Laundry	507200
East	SkyWire, Inc.	616200
West	Access Analytic	956425
West	DataSolverz.com	332375
West	Harvest Consulting	437600

Sort the data ZA, and you will have West at the top.

Region	Customer	Revenue
West	Access Analytic	956425
West	DataSolverz.com	332375
West	Harvest Consulting	437600
West	MySpreadsheetLab	651825
West	The Lab with Leo Crew	243925
East	Budget Wand	692375
East	Deloitte Canada	805775
East	New Hope Laundry	507200
East	SkyWire, Inc.	616200
Central	Excel Design Solutions Ltd	810475

I actually went to my manager to ask if he would rename the Central region. "To what?" he asked incredulously. I replied that I didn't care, as long as it started with F through V. Perhaps "Middle"? John shook his head no and went on with his day.

So, over and over, I would sort the report, then Ctrl+X to cut the East region records and paste them before the Central region. If only I had known this trick.

The first thing to do is to set up a custom list with the regions in the correct order: East, Central, West. (See "Teach the Fill Handle a New List" on page 12 for instructions on setting up a custom list.)

Once the custom list is defined, open the Sort dialog by using the Sort icon on the Data tab. Choose to sort by Region. Open the Order dropdown. Choose Custom List….

Choose the East, Central, West custom list.

One you've chosen that custom list, you can either sort it East, Central, West or West, Central, East.

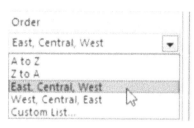

The result: an easy way to sort a list into a nonstandard sequence.

Region	Customer	Revenue
East	Deloitte Canada	805775
East	Budget Wand	692375
East	SkyWire, Inc.	616200
East	New Hope Laundry	507200
Central	WSLCB	1116175
Central	Excel Design Solutions Ltd	810475
Central	Excelerator BI	243675
West	Access Analytic	956425
West	MySpreadsheetLab	651825
West	Harvest Consulting	437600
West	DataSolverz.com	332375
West	The Lab with Leo Crew	243925

Product lines often won't sort correctly: PTC-610, PTC-710, PTC-860, PTC-960, PTC-1100 is the desired order. But PTC-1100 always sorts first in a text sort. A custom list would solve this problem as well.

Thanks to @NeedForExcel for suggesting this tip.

#32 Sort Left to Right

Every day, your IT department sends you a file with the columns in the wrong sequence. It would take them two minutes to change the query, but they have a six-month backlog, so you are stuck rearranging the columns every day.

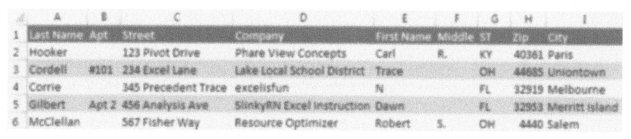

You can reorder the columns with a left-to-right sort.

Add a new row above the data. Type numbers to represent the correct sequence for the columns.

Select Data, Sort. In the Sort dialog, click the Options… button and choose Sort Left to Right. Click OK.

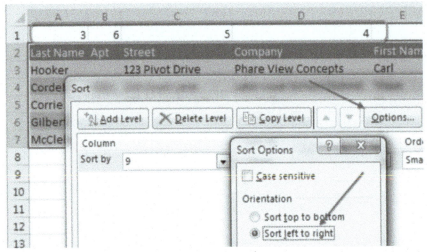

Specify Row 1 in the Sort By dropdown. Click OK.

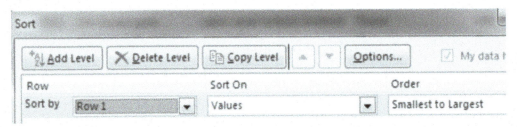

The problem: The column widths do not travel with the columns.

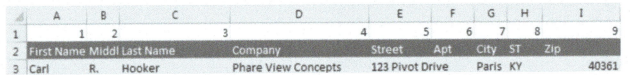

But it is easy to select the data and Press Alt+O, C, A or select Home, Format, Column, AutoFit.

#33 Sort Subtotals

This tip is from my friend Derek Fraley in Springfield, Missouri. I was doing a seminar in Springfield, and I was showing my favorite subtotal tricks.

For those of you who have never used subtotals, here is how to set them up.

Start by making sure your data is sorted. The data below is sorted by customers in column C.

	A	B	C	D	E	F	G	H
1	Sales Rep	Date	Customer	Quantity	Product	Revenue	Profit	Cost
424	Geoffrey G Lilley	12/1/2019	Open Sky Martial Arts	900	Gizmo	22887	9198	13689
425	Geoffrey G Lilley	12/2/2019	Open Sky Martial Arts	600	Gizmo	13290	6132	7158
426	Kevin J Sullivan	1/25/2018	Spain Enterprise	1000	Widget	20770	8470	12300
427	Kevin J Sullivan	2/8/2018	Spain Enterprise	100	Widget	1817	847	970

From the Data tab, choose Subtotals. The Subtotal dialog box always wants to subtotal by the leftmost column. Open the At Each Change In dropdown and choose Customer. Make sure the Use Function box is set to Sum. Choose all of the numeric fields, as shown here.

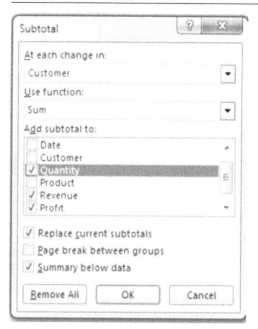

When you click OK, Excel inserts a subtotal below each group of customers. But, more importantly, it adds Group and Outline buttons to the left of column A.

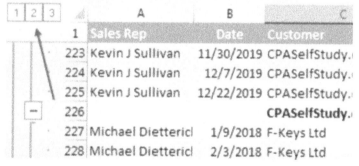

When you click the #2 Group and Outline button, the detail rows are hidden, and you are left with only the subtotal rows and the grand total. This is a beautiful summary of a detailed data set. Of course, at this point, the customers appear in alphabetic sequence. Derek from Springfield showed me that when the data is collapsed in the #2 view, you can sort by any column. In the figure below, a Revenue column cell is selected, and you are about to click the ZA sort button.

f_x =SUBTOTAL(9,F2:F37)

C	D	E	F	G	H
Customer	Quantity	Product	Revenue	Profit	Cost
Association for Computers & Taxation Total	20200		430540	190598	239942
Blockhead Data Consultants Total	21500		460086	206861	253225
BradEdgar.com Total	24700		546662	243117	303545
Clarity Consultancy Services Ltd Total	17400		369567	164599	204968
Construction Intelligence & Analytics, Inc. Total	17800		374497	169684	204813

The top customer, Mike's Dog Store, comes to the top of the data set. But it does not come to row 2. Behind the hidden rows, Excel actually sorted a chunk of records. All of the Mike's detail rows moved along with the subtotal row.

	C	D	E	F	G	H
1	Customer	Quantity	Product	Revenue	Profit	Cost
49	Mike's Dog Store, San Antonio Total			606128	273935	332193
91	BradEdgar.com Total			546662	243117	303545
133	CPASelfStudy.com Total			505279	221591	283688
172	F-Keys Ltd Total			490827	218470	272357
222	Hybrid Software Total			486697	215678	271019
259	Blockhead Data Consultants Total			460086	206861	253225
295	Open Sky Martial Arts Total			448241	196403	251838
332	Association for Computers & Taxation Total			430540	190598	239942
371	Hartville Marketplace & Flea Market Total			410118	181689	228429
408	SurtenExcel.com Total			375472	164413	211059
439	Construction Intelligence & Analytics, Inc. Total			374497	169684	204813
469	Spain Enterprise Total			373852	163926	209926
505	Clarity Consultancy Services Ltd Total			369567	164599	204968
533	The Salem Historical Society, Salem, Ohio Total			329597	145571	184026
559	Juliet Babcock-Hyde CPA, PLLC Total			295018	131416	163602
580	IMA Houston Chapter Total			205231	90443	114788
581	Grand Total			6707812	2978394	3729418

If you go back to the #3 view, you will see the detail records that came along with the subtotal row. Excel did not rearrange the detail records; they remain in their original sequence.

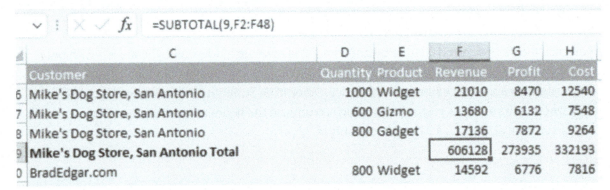

fx	=SUBTOTAL(9,F2:F48)					
	C	D	E	F	G	H
	Customer	Quantity	Product	Revenue	Profit	Cost
6	Mike's Dog Store, San Antonio	1000	Widget	21010	8470	12540
7	Mike's Dog Store, San Antonio	600	Gizmo	13680	6132	7548
8	Mike's Dog Store, San Antonio	800	Gadget	17136	7872	9264
9	Mike's Dog Store, San Antonio Total			606128	273935	332193
0	BradEdgar.com	800	Widget	14592	6776	7816

To me, this is astounding on two fronts. First, I am amazed that Excel handles this correctly. Second, it is amazing that anyone would ever try this. Who would have thought that Excel would handle this correctly? Clearly, Derek from Springfield.

Bonus Tip: Fill in a Text Field on the Subtotal Rows

Say that each customer in a data set is assigned to a single sales rep. It would be great if you could bring the sales rep name down to the subtotal row. Here are the steps:

1. Collapse the data to the #2 view.

2. Select all sales rep cells from the first to last subtotal—skip the Grand Total. At this point, you have both the visible and hidden rows selected. You need just the blank rows or just the visible rows.

3. Go to Home > Find & Select > Go To Special > Blanks and click OK.

4. Now only the blank subtotal cells are selected. Note the active cell is A49. You need a formula here to point one cell up. Type =A48. Instead of pressing Enter, press Ctrl+Enter to enter a similar formula in all of the subtotal rows. It brings the sales rep from the previous row down.

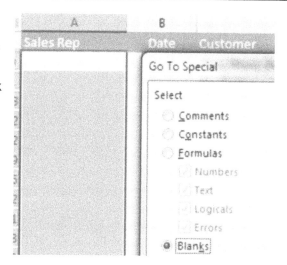

The results: The subtotal rows show the sales rep name in addition to the numeric totals.

	A	B	C
1	Sales Rep	Date	Customer
49	Geoffrey G Lilley		Mike's Dog Store, San Antonio Total
91	Geoffrey G Lilley		BradEdgar.com Total
133	Kevin J Sullivan		CPASelfStudy.com Total

Bonus Tip: An Easier Way to Fill in a Text Field on Subtotal Rows

Kimberly in Oklahoma City and Sarah in Omaha combined to provide a faster solution to getting the sales rep to appear on the Subtotal rows. Provided you only need the data in the #2 Summary View, this works amazingly well:

1. Click the #3 group and outline button to see all rows.

2. Select the first sales rep in A2.

3. Press Ctrl++ and press Enter. In other words, while holding down Ctrl, press the plus sign. This opens the Insert Cells dialog with "Shift Cells Down" selected. Pressing Enter is like pressing OK. This moves all of the sales reps down one row and leaves an ugly gap in A2 and the first row of every other customer.

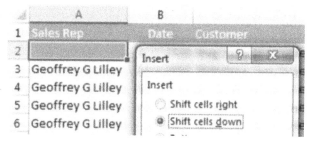

But when you go back to the #2 view, the gaps disappear and the report is correct!

		A	C
	1	Sales Rep	Customer
+	49	Geoffrey G Lilley	Mike's Dog Store, San Antonio Total
+	91	Geoffrey G Lilley	BradEdgar.com Total
+	133	Kevin J Sullivan	CPASelfStudy.com Total
+	172	Michael Dietterid	F-Keys Ltd Total

Bonus Tip: Format the Subtotal Rows

It is a little odd that Subtotals only bolds the customer column and not anything else in the subtotal row. Follow these steps to format the subtotal rows:

1. Collapse the data to the #2 view.

2. Select all data from the first subtotal to the grand totals.

3. Press Alt+; or select Home, Find & Select, Go To Special, Visible Cells Only.

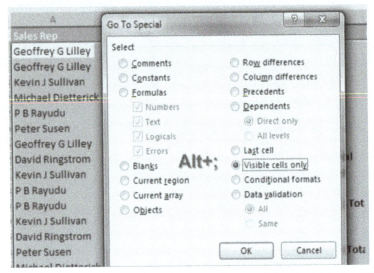

4. Click OK. Format the subtotal rows by applying bold and a fill color.

Now, when you go back to the #3 view, the subtotal rows will be easy to spot.

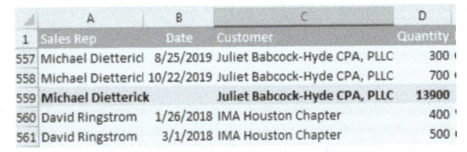

Bonus Tip: Copy the Subtotal Rows

Once you've collapsed the data down to the #2 view, you might want to copy the subtotals to a new worksheet. If so, select all the data. Press Alt+; to select only the visible cells. Press Ctrl+C to copy. Switch to a new workbook and press Ctrl+V to paste. The pasted subtotal formulas are converted to values.

Thanks to Patricia McCarthy for suggesting to select visible cells. Thanks to Derek Fraley for his suggestion from row 6.

#34 Sort and Filter by Color or Icon

Conditional formatting got a lot of new features in Excel 2007, including icon sets and more than three levels of rules. This allows for some pretty interesting formatting over a large range. But once you format the cells, you might want to quickly see all the ones that are formatted a particular way. In Excel 2007, sorting and filtering were also updated to help you do just that!

This book analysis table has some highlighted rows to flag interesting books and an icon next to the price if the book is in the top 25% of prices in the list.

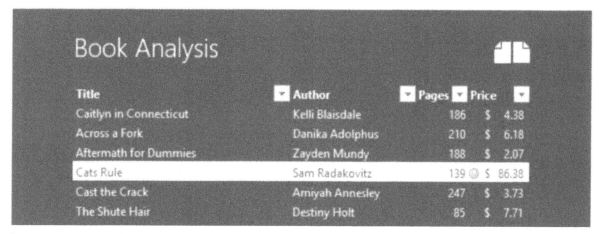

If you want to quickly view all the highlighted rows or cells that have icons, just drop down the filter for the column and choose Filter by Color (or Sort by Color to bubble them to the top).

Then you can pick the formatting you want to sort or filter by! This doesn't just work for conditional formatting; it also works for manually coloring cells. It is also available on the right-click menu of a cell under the Filter or Sort flyout, and in the Sort dialog.

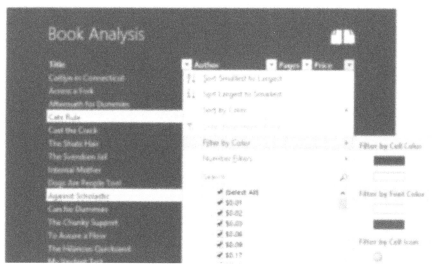

This tip is from Sam Radakovitz, a project manager on the Excel team. He is more fond of cats than dogs

#35 Consolidate Quarterly Worksheets

There are two ancient consolidation tools in Excel.

To understand them, say that you have three data sets. Each has names down the left side and months across the top. Notice that the names are different, and each data set has a different number of months.

Name	Jan	Feb	Mar
James WSLCB Tallman	75	75	69
Michael Seeley	98	90	83
David Colman	62	53	88
P B Rayudu	71	86	93
Fr. Tony Azzarto	71	84	70
Erik Svensen	62	91	81

Name	Apr	May	Jun	Jul	Aug
Michael Seeley	62	56	83	78	98
David Colman	92	58	83	81	67
P B Rayudu	84	97	69	58	60
Erik Svensen	71	69	65	91	68
Michael Karpfen	52	80	89	83	73
Victor E. Scelba II	93	70	54	90	81
Emily Mathews	80	57	51	62	69

Name	Sep	Oct	Nov	Dec
Michael Seeley	94	79	86	92
P B Rayudu	75	83	85	90
Erik Svensen	81	79	87	97
Michael Karpfen	78	86	93	91
Emily Mathews	64	93	92	90
Robert Mika	99	84	93	99
David Ringstrom	71	80	93	94

Illustration: Cartoon Bob D'Amico

You want to combine these into a single data set.

The first tool is the Consolidate command on the Data tab. Choose a blank section of the workbook before starting the command. Use the RefEdit button to point to each of your data sets and then click Add. In the lower left, choose Top Row and Left Column.

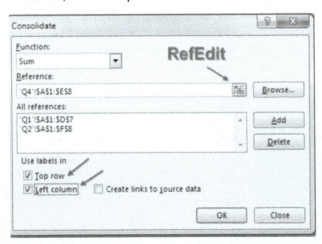

When you click OK, a superset of all three data sets is produced. The first column contains any name in any of the three data sets. Row 1 contains any month in any data set.

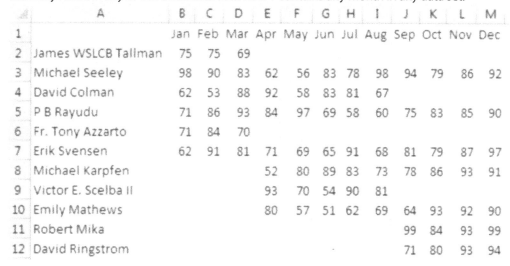

	A	B	C	D	E	F	G	H	I	J	K	L	M
1		Jan	Feb	Mar	Apr	May	Jun	Jul	Aug	Sep	Oct	Nov	Dec
2	James WSLCB Tallman	75	75	69									
3	Michael Seeley	98	90	83	62	56	83	78	98	94	79	86	92
4	David Colman	62	53	88	92	58	83	81	67				
5	P B Rayudu	71	86	93	84	97	69	58	60	75	83	85	90
6	Fr. Tony Azzarto	71	84	70									
7	Erik Svensen	62	91	81	71	69	65	91	68	81	79	87	97
8	Michael Karpfen				52	80	89	83	73	78	86	93	91
9	Victor E. Scelba II				93	70	54	90	81				
10	Emily Mathews				80	57	51	62	69	64	93	92	90
11	Robert Mika									99	84	93	99
12	David Ringstrom				.					71	80	93	94

In the above figure, notice three annoyances: Cell A1 is always left blank, the data in A is not sorted, and if a person was missing from a data set, then cells are left empty instead of being filled with 0.

Filling in cell A1 is easy enough. Sorting by name involves using Flash Fill to get the last name in column N. Here is how to fill blank cells with 0:

1. Select all of the cells that should have numbers: B2:M11.

2. Press Ctrl+H to display Find & Replace.

3. Leave the Find What box empty, and type a zero in the Replace With: box.

4. Click Replace All.

The result: a nicely formatted summary report, as shown below.

Name	Jan	Feb	Mar	Apr	May	Jun	Jul	Aug	Sep	Oct	Nov	Dec
Fr. Tony Azzarto	71	84	70	0	0	0	0	0	0	0	0	0
David Colman	62	53	88	92	58	83	81	67	0	0	0	0
Michael Karpfen	0	0	0	52	80	89	83	73	78	86	93	91
Emily Mathews	0	0	0	80	57	51	62	69	64	93	92	90

The other ancient tool is the Multiple Consolidation Range pivot table. Follow these steps to use it:

1. Press Alt+D, P to invoke the Excel 2003 Pivot Table and Pivot Chart Wizard.

2. Choose Multiple Consolidation Ranges in step 1 of the wizard. Click Next.

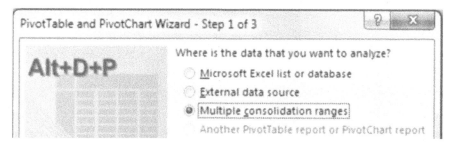

3. Choose I Will Create the Page Fields in step 2a of the wizard. Click Next.

4. In Step 2b of the wizard, use the RefEdit button to point to each table. Click Add after each.

5. Click Finish to create the pivot table, as shown below.

Sum of Value	C ▼					
Row ▼	Jan	Feb	Mar	Apr	May	Jun
David Colman	62	53	88	92	58	83
David Ringstrom						
Emily Mathews				80	57	51
Erik Svensen	62	91	81	71	69	65
Fr. Tony Azzarto	71	84	70			

Thanks to CTroy for suggesting this feature.

#36 Create Your First Pivot Table

Pivot tables let you summarize tabular data to a one-page summary in a few clicks. Start with a data set that has headings in row 1. It should have no blank rows, blank columns, blank headings or merged cells.

	A	B	C	D	E	F	G	H	I	J
1	Region	Market	Rep	Date	Customer	Quantity	Product	Revenue	Cost	Profit
2	West	NoCal	Symons	1/7/2032	www.ExcelTricks.de	1,000	Gizmo	$22,810	$12,590	$10,220
3	South	Houston	Kazmdav	1/8/2032	ABSN Adventures	100	Gadget	$2,257	$1,273	$984
4	Northeast	New York	McGunigal	1/10/2032	Harlem Globetrotters	400	Gizmo	$9,152	$5,064	$4,088
5	Midwest	Cleveland	aBoBoBool	1/10/2032	Serving Brevard Realty	800	Gadget	$18,552	$10,680	$7,872

Select a single cell in your data and choose Insert, Pivot Table.

Excel will detect the edges of your data and offer to create the pivot table on a new worksheet. Click OK to accept the defaults.

Excel inserts a new blank worksheet to the left of the current worksheet. On the right side of the screen is the Pivot Table Fields pane. At the top, a list of your fields with checkboxes.

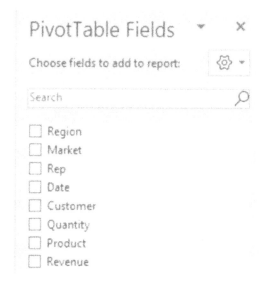

At the bottom are four drop zones with horrible names and confusing icons. Any fields that you drag to the Columns area will appear as headings across the top of your report. Any fields that you drag to the Rows area appear as headings along the left side of your report. Drag numeric fields to the Values area.

You can build some reports without dragging the fields. If you checkmark a text field, it will automatically appear in the Rows area. Checkmark a numeric field and it will appear in the Values area. By choosing Region and Revenue, you will create this pivot table:

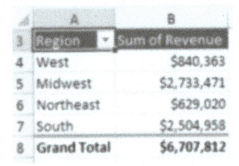

Region	Sum of Revenue
West	$840,363
Midwest	$2,733,471
Northeast	$629,020
South	$2,504,958
Grand Total	$6,707,812

To get products across the top of the report, drag the Product field and drop it in the Columns area:

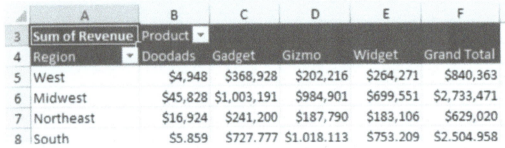

Sum of Revenue	Product				
Region	Doodads	Gadget	Gizmo	Widget	Grand Total
West	$4,948	$368,928	$202,216	$264,271	$840,363
Midwest	$45,828	$1,003,191	$984,901	$699,551	$2,733,471
Northeast	$16,924	$241,200	$187,790	$183,106	$629,020
South	$5.859	$727.777	$1.018.113	$753.209	$2.504.958

Note: your first pivot table might have the words "Column Labels" and "Row Labels" instead of headings like Product and Region. If so, choose Design, Report Layout, Show in Tabular Form. Later, in "#41 Specify Defaults for All Future Pivot Tables" on page 90, you will learn how to make Tabular Form the default for your pivot tables.

Bonus Tip: Rearrange fields in a pivot table

The power of pivot tables is the ability to rearrange the fields. If your manager decides you should put Regions across the top and products down the side, it is two drags to create the new report. Drag product to Rows. Drag Region to Columns.

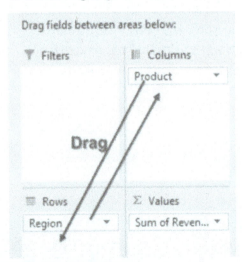

You will have this report:

	A	B	C	D	E	F
3	Sum of Revenue	Region				
4	Product	West	Midwest	Northeast	South	Grand Total
5	Doodads	$4,948	$45,828	$16,924	$5,859	$73,559
6	Gadget	$368,928	$1,003,191	$241,200	$727,777	$2,341,096
7	Gizmo	$202,216	$984,901	$187,790	$1,018,113	$2,393,020
8	Widget	$264,271	$699,551	$183,106	$753,209	$1,900,137
9	Grand Total	$840,363	$2,733,471	$629,020	$2,504,958	$6,707,812

To remove a field from the pivot table, drag the field tile outside of the Fields pane, or simply uncheck the field in the top of the Fields pane.

Bonus Tip: Pivot Table Inherits Number Formatting from the Grid!

In the first half of 2025, an amazing change happened to pivot tables. Say that your source data has thousands separators for Quantity and Currency for Revenue, COGS, and Profit.

E	F	G	H	I
Customer	Quantity	Revenue	COGS	Profit
Southwest Airlines	100	$2,257	$984	$1,273
Merck	800	$18,552	$7,872	$10,680
Texaco	400	$9,152	$4,088	$5,064
Cummins Inc.	1,000	$22,810	$10,220	$12,590
State Farm	1,000	$21,730	$9,840	$11,890
General Motors	400	$8,456	$3,388	$5,068

Create a pivot table from this data. Add Quantity and Revenue to the pivot table. Amazingly, the formatting from the grid is automatically applied to the pivot table!

Sector	Sum of Quantity	Sum of Revenue
Communications	29,400	$634,361
Energy	35,000	$738,723
Financial	52,900	$1,130,961
Healthcare	1,900	$42,316
Manufacturing	128,000	$2,734,175
Retail	48,100	$1,036,298
Transportation	18,600	$390,978
Grand Total	313,900	$6,707,812

Excellers have been asking for this for 30 years. Previous Excel Project Managers would say it could never happen. In 2025, a new project manager took over pivot tables and it was the first thing she did.

Note: The formatting only happens when the pivot table is created. If you later change the formatting of the source data, it does not retroactively change the existing pivot table.

Bonus Tip: Format a Pivot Table

The Design tab has a gallery with 84 built-in formats for pivot tables. Choose a design from the gallery and the colors change.

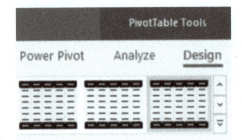

Bonus Tip: Format One Cell in a Pivot Table

This is new in Microsoft 365 starting in 2018. You can right-click any cell in a pivot table and choose Format Cell. Any formatting that you apply is tied to that data in the pivot table. In the figure below, Florida Figs have a yellow fill color.

3	Sum of Sales	Region		
4	**Product**	**California**	**Florida**	**N**
5	Apple	8479	6235	
6	Banana	8287	2635	
7	Cherry	4373	3590	
8	Date	3004	1496	
9	Elderberry	2307	0	
10	Fig	0	9683	
11	Cucumber	1881	9512	
12	**Grand Total**	**28331**	**33151**	
13				

If you change the pivot table, the yellow formatting follows the Florida Fig.

	A	B	C
3	**Product**	**Region**	**Sum of Sales**
26	**Elderberry**	Texas	1381
27	**Elderberry**	Washington	5901
28	**Elderberry Total**		**19679**
29	⊟**Fig**	Florida	9683
30	**Fig**	Missouri	7531
31	Fig	New York	5650

If you add a new inner field, then multiple cells for Florida Fig will have the fill color.

	A	B	C	D
3	**Product**	**Region**	**Rep**	**Sum of Sales**
49	⊟**Fig**	⊟**Florida**	Sonny	6137
50	**Fig**	**Florida**	Fred	3546
51	**Fig**	**Florida Total**		**9683**
52	**Fig**	⊟**Missouri**	Lewis	7531

The formatting will persist if you remove Florida or Fig due to a filter. If you filter to vegetables, Fig is hidden. Filter to fruit and Fig will still be formatted. However, if you completely remove either Product or Region from the pivot table, the formatting will be lost.

Bonus Tip: Fill in the Blanks in the Annoying Outline View

If your pivot table is in Tabular or Outline Form and you have more than one row field, the pivot table defaults to leaving a lot of blank cells in the outer row fields:

3	Region ▼	Market ▼	Sum of Revenue
4	⊟West	NoCal	521,373
5		SoCal	318,990
6	West Total		840,363
7	⊟Midwest	Chicago	520,176
8		Cincinnati	512,391
9		Cleveland	559,826

Starting in Excel 2010, use Design, Report Layout, Repeat all Item Labels to fill in the blanks in column A:

3	Region ▼	Market ▼	Sum of Revenue
4	⊟West	NoCal	521,373
5	West	SoCal	318,990
6	West Total		840,363
7			
8	⊟Midwest	Chicago	520,176
9	Midwest	Cincinnati	512,391
10	Midwest	Cleveland	559,826

Bonus Tip: Replace Blank Values Cells With Zero

There is another way to have blanks in the Values area of a pivot table. Say that you have a product which is only sold in a few regions. If there are no Doodad sales in Atlanta, Excel will leave that cell empty instead of putting a zero there. Right-click the pivot table and choose Pivot Table Options. On the Layout & Format tab, find the box For Empty Cells, Show: and type a zero.

Or, as Hunstville Excel Consultant Andrew Spain discovered, you can simply clear the checkbox to the left of For Empty Cells, Show:

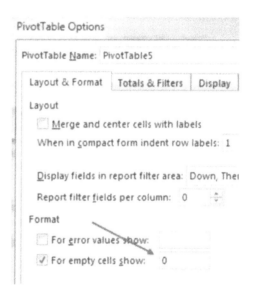

Bonus Tip: Rearrange Fields Pane

Howie Dickerman was the Project Manager in charge of pivot tables at Microsoft. He inherited the product and suggests some of the defaults could have been different. For one, he suggests using the gear at the top right of the PivotTable Fields pane and changing the view to Fields Section and Areas Section side-by-side.

#37 Show Details Behind Any Value Cell

In 2025, the Excel team improved the Show Details feature in pivot tables. This features lets you drill down and see all of the detail records behind any cell in the Values area of a pivot table. Select any number in a pivot table. On the PivotTable Analyze tab, click the new Show Details icon.

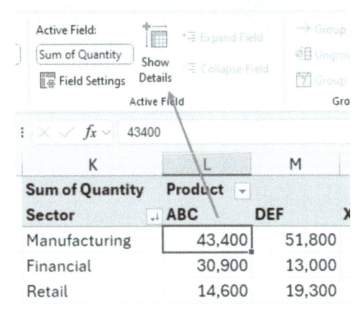

A new worksheet will appear to the left of the current worksheet. It will show all of the data records that make up the 43,400. A heading will indicate that this is Details for Sum of Quantity - Sector: Manufacturing, Product: ABC

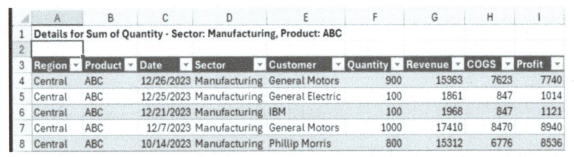

	Region	Product	Date	Sector	Customer	Quantity	Revenue	COGS	Profit
1	Details for Sum of Quantity - Sector: Manufacturing, Product: ABC								
2									
3	Region	Product	Date	Sector	Customer	Quantity	Revenue	COGS	Profit
4	Central	ABC	12/26/2023	Manufacturing	General Motors	900	15363	7623	7740
5	Central	ABC	12/25/2023	Manufacturing	General Electric	100	1861	847	1014
6	Central	ABC	12/21/2023	Manufacturing	IBM	100	1968	847	1121
7	Central	ABC	12/7/2023	Manufacturing	General Motors	1000	17410	8470	8940
8	Central	ABC	10/14/2023	Manufacturing	Phillip Morris	800	15312	6776	8536

Previously, if you wanted to dig into a number in your PivotTable, you'd just double-click a value cell. That still works. You can also right-click any value and choose Show Details.

Notes:

- You can Show Details again on any other cell. Each time you use Show Details, a new worksheet is added.
- If you Show Details, look at the data, and then press Ctrl+Z to Undo, the sheet will be deleted.
- If you discover a mistake in the Show Details sheet, correct that mistake in the original data source.
- The title in cell A1 is new in 2025.
- If you're using an external data source like a data model, Show Details will still work—but it's limited to showing just the first 1,000 rows.

What Happened to Drill Down and Drill Up?

You might notice that the Drill Down and Drill Up buttons are missing from the PivotTable Analyze tab. You can still find them and add them to the Quick Access Toolbar. These buttons only work with Hierarchies defined in external data sources. For a demo, see: https://mrx.cl/hiervid. Thanks to @Sheet1

#38 Create a Year-over-Year Report in a Pivot Table

Let's say you have two years' worth of detail records. Each record has a daily date. When you build a pivot table from this report, you will have hundreds of rows of daily dates in the pivot table. This is not much of a summary.

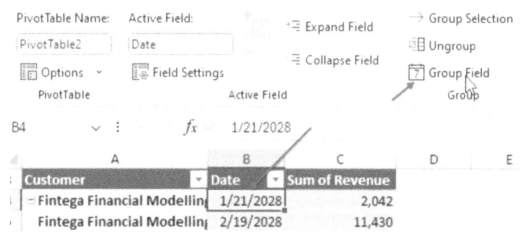

Choose one of those date cells in the pivot table. From the Analyze tab in the Ribbon, choose Group Field.

Because you are on a date field, you get *this* version of the Grouping dialog. In it, deselect Months and select Years.

The daily dates are rolled up to years. Move the Years field from Rows to Columns.

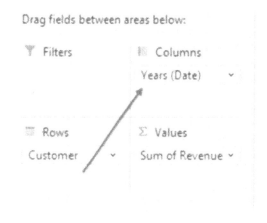

Instead of a grand total in column D, you probably want a percentage variance. To get rid of the Grand Total column, right-click on the Grand Total heading and choose Remove Grand Total.)

To build the variance column as shown below, you need to write a formula outside the pivot table that points inside the pivot table. Do not touch the mouse or arrow keys while building the formula, or the often-annoying GETPIVOTDATA function will appear. Instead, simply type =C5/B5-1 and press Enter.

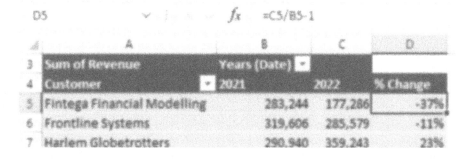

Bonus Tip: Grouping one Pivot Table groups them all

Imagine you have two pivot tables from the same data source. You want on grouped by Years and another grouped by Week. When you group the first pivot table by Year, they are all grouped by Year.

The grouping affects all pivot tables that share the same pivot cache. If you want each pivot table to have different grouping, you need to force the pivot table to use a different cache.

Delete the existing second pivot table. Start the second pivot table again by using Alt+D P. This is the legacy keyboard shortcut for the old PivotTable Wizard dialog box. Alternatively, you can customize the QAT and find the command called PivotTable and PivotChart Wizard.

When you start a pivot table with the Wizard, the wizards says you are in Step 1 of 3. Choose PivotTable and Click Next.

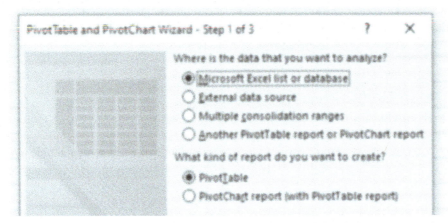

Step 2 shows you the range of data you are using. Click Next. An extra dialog appears asking you to Save Memory by clicking Yes. If you want each pivot table to have different groupings, you need to click No here.

Bonus Tip: Another Way to Calculate Year-Over-Year

Instead of creating a formula outside of the pivot table, you can do this inside the pivot table.

Start from the image above and clear column D. Drag Revenue a second time to the Values area.

Look in the Columns section of the Pivot Table Fields panel. You will see a tile called Values that appears below Date. Drag that tile so it is below the Date field. Your pivot table should look like this:

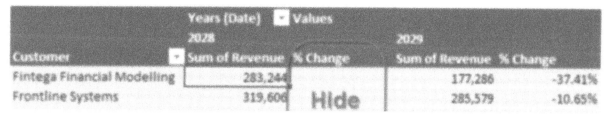

Customer	Years (Date)	Values		2029	
	2028				
	Sum of Revenue	% Change		Sum of Revenue	% Change
Fintega Financial Modelling	283,244			177,286	-37.41%
Frontline Systems	319,606	Hide		285,579	-10.65%

Double-click the Sum of Revenue2 heading in D4 to display the Value Field Settings dialog. Click on the tab for Show Values As. Change the drop-down menu to % Difference From. Change the Base Field to Date. Change the Base Item to (Previous Item). Type a better name than Sum of Revenue2 - perhaps % Change. Click OK.

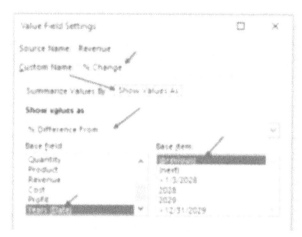

You will have a mostly blank column D (because the pivot table can't calculate a percentage change for the first year. Right-click the D and choose Hide.

Thanks to Tobias Ljung for this method.

#39 Change the Calculation in a Pivot Table

Pivot tables offer a myriad of calculations in the Field Settings dialog box. Here is a faster way to change a calculation:

1. Drag Revenue to the Values area twice.

2. Double-click on the heading Sum of Revenue2. Excel opens the Value Field Settings dialog.

3. Click on Show Values As and select % of Column Total from the dropdown.

4. Type a new name in the Custom Name field, such as % of Total.

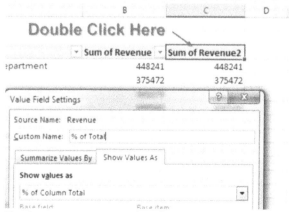

Thanks to Александр Воробьев for suggesting this tip.

#40 Find the True Top Five in a Pivot Table

Pivot tables offer a Top 10 filter. It is cool. It is flexible. But I hate it, and I will tell you why.

Here is a pivot table that shows revenue by customer. The revenue total is $6.7 million. Notice that the largest customer, More4Apps, is 11.46% of the total revenue.

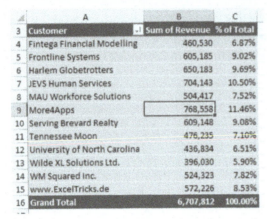

	A	B	C
3	Customer	Sum of Revenue	% of Total
4	Fintega Financial Modelling	460,530	6.87%
5	Frontline Systems	605,185	9.02%
6	Harlem Globetrotters	650,183	9.69%
7	JEVS Human Services	704,143	10.50%
8	MAU Workforce Solutions	504,417	7.52%
9	More4Apps	768,558	11.46%
10	Serving Brevard Realty	609,148	9.08%
11	Tennessee Moon	476,235	7.10%
12	University of North Carolina	436,834	6.51%
13	Wilde XL Solutions Ltd.	396,030	5.90%
14	WM Squared Inc.	524,323	7.82%
15	www.ExcelTricks.de	572,226	8.53%
16	Grand Total	6,707,812	100.00%

What if my manager has the attention span of a goldfish and wants to see only the top five customers? To start, open the dropdown in A3 and select Value Filters, Top 10.

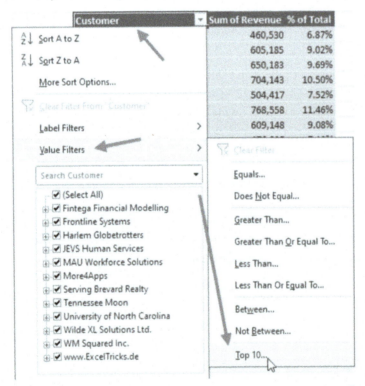

The super-flexible Top 10 Filter dialog allows Top/Bottom. It can do 10, 5, or any other number. You can ask for the top five items, top 80%, or enough customers to get to $5 million.

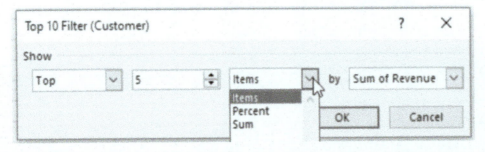

But here is the problem: The resulting report shows five customers and the total from those customers instead of the totals from everyone. More4Apps, who was previously 11% of the total is 23% of the new total. I have two different solutions to this problem.

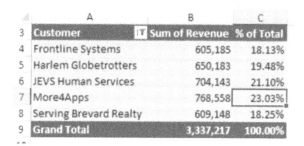

	A	B	C
3	Customer	Sum of Revenue	% of Total
4	Frontline Systems	605,185	18.13%
5	Harlem Globetrotters	650,183	19.48%
6	JEVS Human Services	704,143	21.10%
7	More4Apps	768,558	23.03%
8	Serving Brevard Realty	609,148	18.25%
9	Grand Total	3,337,217	100.00%

But First, a Few Important Words About AutoFilter

I realize this seems like an off-the-wall question. If you want to turn on the Filter dropdowns on a regular data set, how do you do it? Here are three really common ways:

- Select one cell in your data and click the Filter icon on the Data tab or press Ctrl+Shift+L.

- Select all of your data with Ctrl+* and click the Filter icon on the Data tab.

- Press Ctrl+T to format the data as a table.

These are three really good ways. As long as you know any of them, there is absolutely no need to know another way. But here's an incredibly obscure but magical way to turn on the filter:

- Go to your row of headers and then go to the rightmost heading cell. Move one cell to the right. For some unknown reason, when you are in this cell and click the Filter icon, Excel filters the data set to your left. I have no idea why this works. It really isn't worth talking about because there are already three really good ways to turn on the Filter dropdowns. I call this cell the magic cell. (See 2nd image below)

And Now, Back to Pivot Tables

There is a rule that says you cannot use AutoFilter when you are in a pivot table. See below? The Filter icon is grayed out because I've selected a cell in the pivot table.

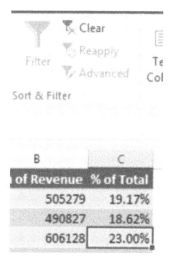

B	C
of Revenue	% of Total
505279	19.17%
490827	18.62%
606128	23.00%

I don't know why Microsoft grays this out. It must be something internal that says AutoFilter and a pivot table can't coexist. So, there is someone on the Excel team who is in charge of graying out the Filter icon. That person has never heard of the magic cell. Select a cell in the pivot table, and the Filter gets grayed out. Click outside the pivot table, and Filter is enabled again.

But wait. What about the magic cell I just told you about? If you click in the cell to the right of the last heading, Excel forgets to gray out the Filter icon!

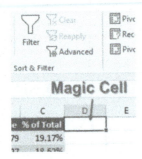

Caution: Clearly, you are tearing a hole in the fabric of Excel with this trick. If you later change the underlying data and refresh your pivot table, Excel will not refresh the filter because, as far as Microsoft knows, there is no way to apply a filter to a pivot table!

Note: Our goal is to keep this a secret from Microsoft because it is a pretty cool feature. It has been "broken" for quite some time, so there are a lot of people who might be relying on it by now.

Sure enough, Excel adds AutoFilter dropdowns to the top row of your pivot table. And AutoFilter operates differently than a pivot table filter. Go to the Revenue dropdown and choose Number Filters, Top 10….

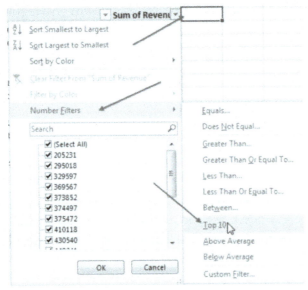

In the Top 10 AutoFilter dialog, choose Top 6 Items. That's not a typo…if you want five customers, choose 6. If you want 10 customers, choose 11.

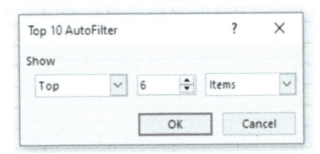

To AutoFilter, the grand total row is the largest item in the data. The top five customers are occupying positions 2 through 6 in the data.

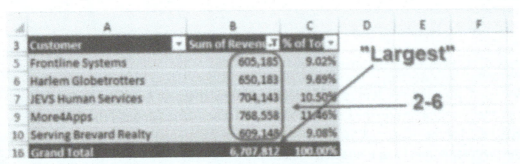

A Completely Legal Solution Using the Data Model

If you want a pivot table showing you the top five customers but the total from all customers, you have to

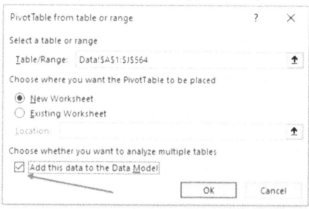

move your data outside Excel. If you have Excel 2013 or newer running in Windows, there is a very convenient way to do this. To show you this, I've deleted the original pivot table. Choose Insert, Pivot Table. Before clicking OK, select the check-box Add This Data To The Data Model.

Build your pivot table as normal. Use the drop-down in A3 to select Value Filters, Top 10, and ask for the top five customers. With one cell in the pivot table selected, go to the Design tab in the Ribbon and open the Subtotals dropdown. The final choice in the dropdown is Include Filtered

Items in Totals. Normally, this choice is grayed out. But because the data is stored in the Data Model instead of a normal pivot cache, this option is now available.

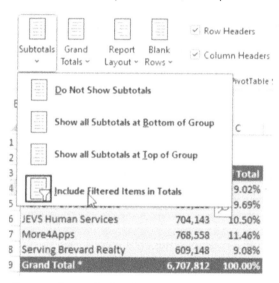

Choose the Include Filtered Items in Totals option, and your Grand Total now includes an asterisk and the total of all of the data, as shown below.

Customer	Sum of Revenue	% of Total
Frontline Systems	605,185	9.02%
Harlem Globetrotters	650,183	9.69%
JEVS Human Services	704,143	10.50%
More4Apps	768,558	11.46%
Serving Brevard Realty	609,148	9.08%
Grand Total *	6,707,812	100.00%

This magic cell trick originally came to me from Dan in my seminar in Philadelphia and was repeated 15 years later by a different Dan from my seminar in Cincinnati. Thanks to Miguel Caballero for suggesting this feature.

#41 Specify Defaults for All Future Pivot Tables

It took me six years, but I finally convinced the Excel team that a lot of people prefer Tabular layout for pivot tables to the Compact layout that became the default layout in Excel 2007. If you have Microsoft 365, you now have the ability to specify pivot table defaults.

Go to File, Options, Data. Click Edit Default Layout….

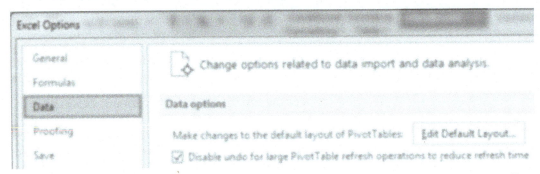

Change the Report Layout to Show in Tabular Form and choose the checkbox Repeat All Item Labels.

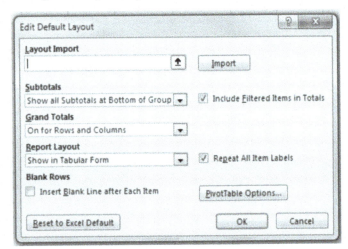

> **Tip**: There are other settings that you can specify as the default. You can either click Pivot Table Options… and specify them or find a pivot table where you've already set up your favorite settings. Select one cell in that pivot table and click Import.

If you don't have Microsoft 365 and don't have access to pivot table defaults, you can get similar functionality by buying Pivot Power Premium from Debra Dalgleish at Contextures.com: mrx.cl/pppdebra.

Bonus Tip: Change What Drives You Crazy About Excel

I've managed to lobby the Excel team to get a few changes into Excel. It isn't always easy. It took me eight years of lobbying to get the Repeat All Item Labels feature added to Excel 2010. It took seven years to get the Pivot Table Defaults feature added.

The old Excel.UserVoice.com site has been migrated to feedbackportal.microsoft.com. Search for Excel and then filter the Platform to Windows or Mac. If you have a great idea of what would make Excel easier, write up a short post here. And then get your friends and co-workers to vote for your idea. The great news is that the Excel team is listening to ideas. They key to getting the Excel team to respond is 20 votes. But I managed 200–300 votes for my Pivot Table Defaults before they started working on the feature.

Add more records to your pivot table source data and you have to visit the Change Data Source dialog. To prevent this step, many people select A:C - the entire column as the source. This avoids having to change the data source. Instead, you can simply Refresh. But there is a better way by using a Ctrl+T table.

When you choose your data set and select Format as Table by using Ctrl+T, the pivot table source will grow as the table grows. You can even do this retroactively, after the pivot table exists.

This figure shows a data set and a pivot table. The pivot table source is A1:C16.

Say that you want to be able to easily add new data below the pivot table, as shown here. Select one cell in the data and press Ctrl+T. Make sure that My Table Has Headers is checked in the Create Table dialog and click OK.

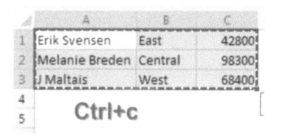

You have some new records to add to the table. Copy the records.

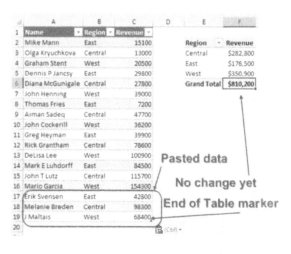

Go to the blank row below the table and paste. The new records pick up the formatting from the table. The angle-bracket-shaped End-of-Table marker moves to C19. But notice that the pivot table has not updated yet.

Click the Refresh button in the Pivot Table Tools Analyze tab. Excel adds the new rows to your pivot table.

Region	Revenue
Central	$381,100
East	$219,300
West	$419,300
Grand Total	$1,019,700

Bonus Tip: Use Ctrl+T with VLOOKUP and Charts

In this figure, the VLOOKUP table is in E5:F9. Item A106 is missing from the table, and the VLOOKUP is returning #N/A. Conventional wisdom says to add A106 to the middle of your VLOOKUP table so you don't have to rewrite the formula.

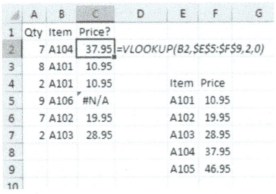

Instead, use Ctrl+T to format the lookup table. Note that the formula is still pointing to E5:F9; nothing changes in the formula.

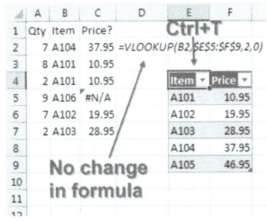

But when you type a new row below the table, it becomes part of the table, and the VLOOKUP formula automatically updates to reflect the new range.

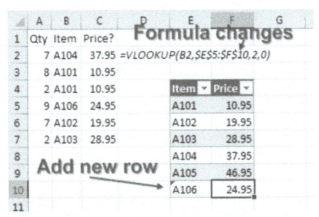

The same thing happens with charts. Format your chart data by pressing Ctrl+T. Add a new row. The row is automatically added to the chart.

It is fairly cool that you can use Ctrl+T after setting up the pivot table, VLOOKUP, or chart, and Excel still makes the range expand.

When I asked readers to vote for their favorite tips, tables were popular. Thanks to Peter Albert, Snorre Eikeland, Nancy Federice, Colin Michael, James E. Moede, Keyur Patel, and Paul Peton for suggesting this feature. Four readers suggested using OFFSET to create expanding ranges for dynamic charts: Charley Baak, Don Knowles, Francis Logan, and Cecelia Rieb. Tables now do the same thing in most cases.

#43 Replicate a Pivot Table for Each Rep

The pivot table below shows products across the top and customers down the side. The pivot table is sorted so the largest customers are at the top. The Sales Rep field is in the report filter. If you open the Rep dropdown, you can filter the data to any one sales rep.

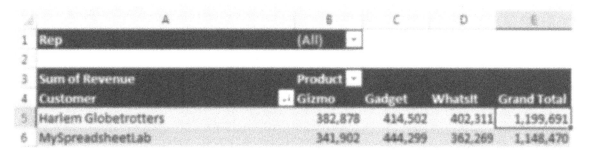

The Excel team has hidden a feature called Show Report Filter Pages. Select any pivot table that has a field in the report filter. Go to the Analyze tab. On the far left side is the large Options button. Next to the large Options button is a tiny dropdown arrow. Click this dropdown and choose Show Report Filter Pages….

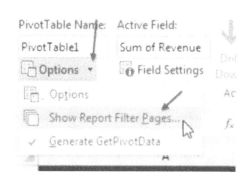

Excel asks which field you want to use. Select the one you want (in this case the only one available) and click OK.

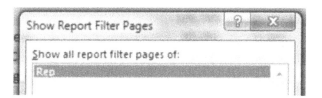

Over the next few seconds, Excel starts inserting new worksheets, one for each sales rep. Each sheet tab is named after the sales rep. Inside each worksheet, Excel replicates the pivot table but changes the name in the report filter to this sales rep. You end up with a report for each sales rep.

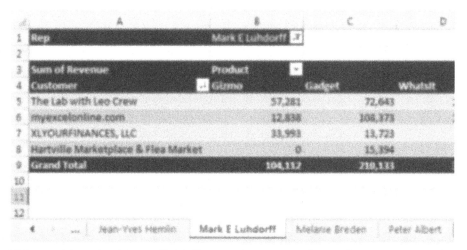

This would work with any field. If you want a report for each customer, product, vendor, or something else, add it to the report filter and use Show Report Filter Pages.

Thanks to Szilvia Juhasz for showing me this feature during a seminar I was teaching at the University of Akron many years ago. For the record, Szilvia was in row 1.

#44 Use a Pivot Table to Compare Lists

When you think of comparing lists, you probably think of VLOOKUP. If you have two lists to compare, you need to add two columns of VLOOKUP. In the figure below, you are trying to compare Tuesday to Monday and Wednesday to Tuesday and maybe even Wednesday to Monday. It is going to take a lot of VLOOKUP columns to figure out who was added to and dropped from each list.

You can use pivot tables to make this job far easier. Combine all of your lists into a single list with a new column called Source. In the Source column, identify which list the data came from. Build a pivot table from the combined list, with Name in rows, RSVP in values, and Source in columns. Turn off the Grand Total row, and you have a neat list showing a superset from day to day, as shown below.

Sum of RSVP	Source		
Name	Monday	Tuesday	Wednesday
Andrew Spain		3	3
Carl Hjortsjö	2		
Caroline Bonner	2	2	
Dawn Kosmakos	2	1	
Jean-Yves Hemlin			1
Jeff Long	1		
Jeffrey P. Coulson			2
John Durran			1
Kathryn Sullivan		2	1
Kevin Lehrbass			1
M.R. Rosenkrantz	1	1	2
Martin Lucas	2	2	1
Melissa Esquibel		2	2
Michael Karpfen		2	2
Paul Hannelly	2		
Peter Harvest		2	1
Roger Fisher	1	1	1
Sabine Hanschitz	1	1	2
Ute Simon	2	2	2
Yesenia Garcia	2	2	
Grand Total	18	23	22

Bonus Tip: Compare Two Lists by Using Go To Special

This tip is not as robust as using a Pivot Table to Compare Two Lists, but it comes in handy when you have to compare one column to another column.

In the figure below, say that you want to find any changes between column A and column D.

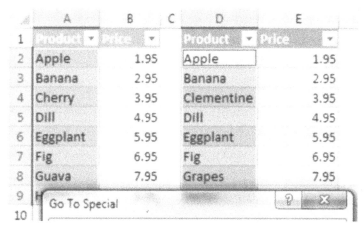

Select the data in A2:A9 and then hold down the Ctrl key while you select the data in D2:D9.

Select, Home, Find & Select, Go To Special. Then, in the Go To Special dialog, choose Row Differences. Click OK.

Only the items in column A that do not match the items in column D are selected. Use a red font to mark these items, as shown below.

Caution: This technique works only for lists that are mostly identical. If you insert one new row near the top of the second list, causing all future rows to be offset by one row, each of those rows is marked as a row difference.

Thanks to Colleen Young for this tip.

#45 Build Dashboards with Sparklines and Slicers

New tools debuted in Excel 2010 that let you create interactive dashboards that do not look like Excel. This figure shows an Excel workbook with two slicers, Region and Line, used to filter the data. Also in this figure, pivot charts plus a collection of sparkline charts illustrate sales trends.

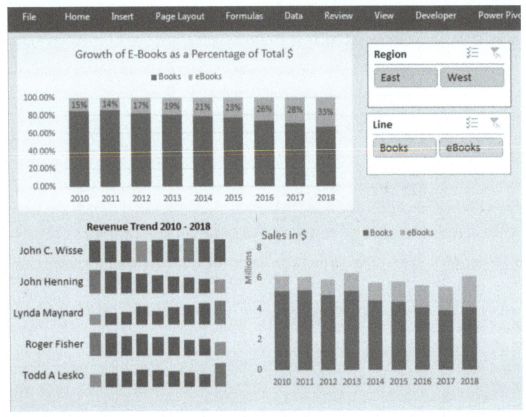

You can use a setup like this and give your manager's manager a touch screen. All you have to do is teach people how to use the slicers, and they will be able to use this interactive tool for running reports. Touch the East region and the Books line. All of the charts update to reflect sales of books in the East region.

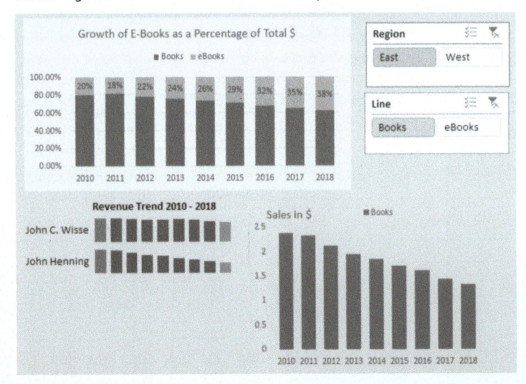

Switch to eBooks, and the data updates.

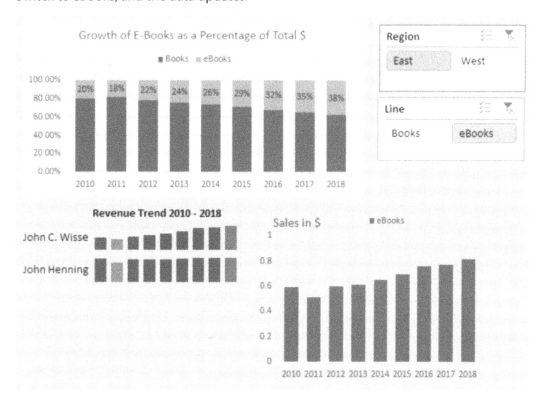

Pivot Tables Galore

Arrange your charts so they fit the size of your display monitor. Each pivot chart has an associated pivot table that does not need to be seen. Those pivot tables can be moved to another sheet or to columns outside of the area seen on the display.

> **Note**: This technique requires all pivot tables share a pivot table cache. I have a video showing how to use VBA to synchronize slicers from two data sets at http://mrx.cl/syncslicer.

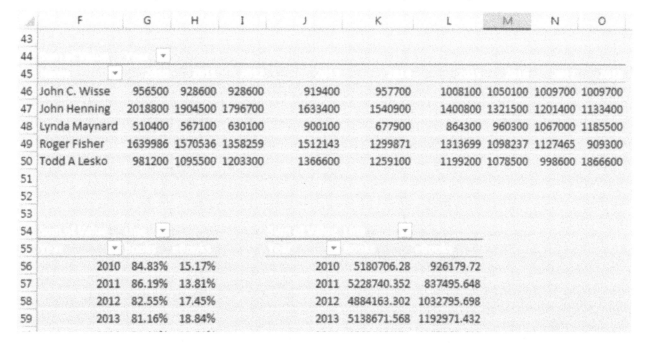

	F	G	H	I	J	K	L	M	N	O
43										
44										
45										
46	John C. Wisse	956500	928600	928600	919400	957700	1008100	1050100	1009700	1009700
47	John Henning	2018800	1904500	1796700	1633400	1540900	1400800	1321500	1201400	1133400
48	Lynda Maynard	510400	567100	630100	900100	677900	864300	960300	1067000	1185500
49	Roger Fisher	1639986	1570536	1358259	1512143	1299871	1313699	1098237	1127465	909300
50	Todd A Lesko	981200	1095500	1203300	1366600	1259100	1199200	1078500	998600	1866600
51										
52										
53										
54										
55										
56		2010	84.83%	15.17%		2010	5180706.28	926179.72		
57		2011	86.19%	13.81%		2011	5228740.352	837495.648		
58		2012	82.55%	17.45%		2012	4884163.302	1032795.698		
59		2013	81.16%	18.84%		2013	5138671.568	1192971.432		

Filter Multiple Pivot Tables with Slicers

Slicers provide a visual way to filter. Choose the first pivot table on your dashboard and select Analyze, Slicers. Add slicers for region and line. Use the Slicer Tools tab in the Ribbon to change the color and the number of columns in each slicer. Resize the slicers to fit and then arrange them on your dashboard.

Initially, the slicers are tied to only the first pivot table. Select a cell in the second pivot table and choose Filter Connections. Indicate which slicers should be tied to this pivot table. In many cases, you will tie each pivot table to all slicers. But not always. For example, in the chart showing how Books and eBooks add up to 100%, you need to keep all lines. The Filter Connections dialog box choices for that pivot table connect to the Region slicer but not the Line slicer.

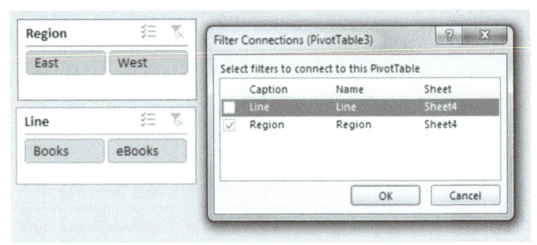

Thanks to John Michaloudis from MyExcelOnline.com for the connecting multiple pivot tables to one slicer idea.

Bonus Tip: Replace a Long Slicer with a Filter Drop-Down

Slicers can get too large if there are too many tiles. This figure shows a slicer with 146 items. The Slicer is already too big, and you aren't seeing all of the tiles nor all of the text in the tiles.

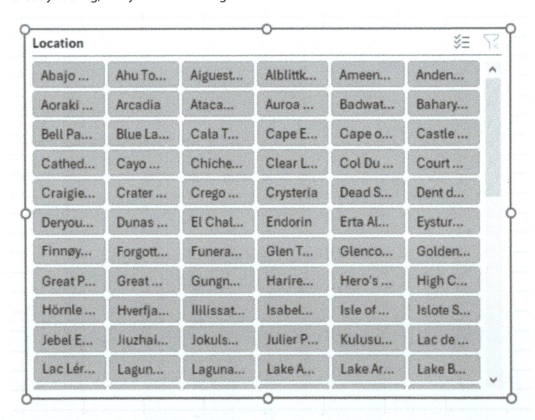

Create the slicer shown above but hide it out of view. Create another pivot table that is connected to this slicer. In the pivot table, put the Location field in the Filters area. This gives you two cells as shown here:

When you open the drop-down in B1 and choose a Location, the Slicer also updates. Any pivot tables connected to the Slicer will update.

With careful planning, you can hide column A. Then, it will appear that you have a single drop-down cell that filters all of the pivot tables. This takes up much less space than a slicer.

Thanks to Tine Ozimič for this idea.

Sparklines: Word-Sized Charts

Professor Edward Tufte introduced sparklines in his 2007 book *Beautiful Evidence*. Excel 2010 implemented sparklines as either line, column, or win/loss charts, where each series fills a single cell.

Personally, I like my sparklines to be larger. In this example, I changed the row height to 30 and <gasp> merged B14:D14 into a single cell to make the charts wider. The labels in A14:A18 are formulas that point to the first column of the pivot table.

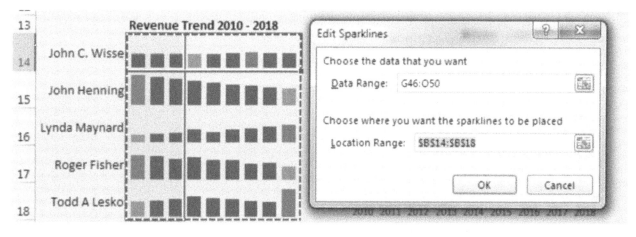

To change the color of the low and high points, choose these boxes in the Sparkline Tools tab:

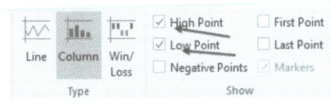

Then change the color for the high and low points:

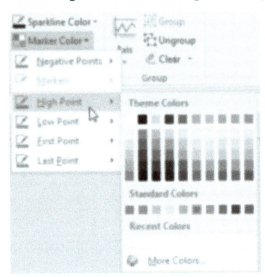

By default, sparklines are scaled independently of each other. I almost always go to the Axis settings and choose Same for All Sparklines for Minimum and Maximum. Below, I set Minimum to 0 for all sparklines.

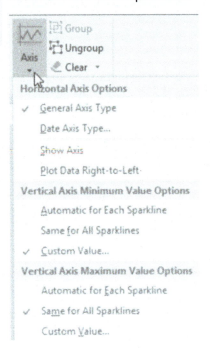

Make Excel Not Look Like Excel

Did you notice that many of the dashboards shown in the previous topics don't look like Excel? With several easy settings, you can make a dashboard look less like Excel:

- Select all cells and apply a light fill color to get rid of the gridlines.
- On the View tab, uncheck Formula Bar, Headings, and Gridlines.

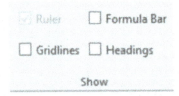

- Collapse the Ribbon: at the right edge of the Ribbon, use the ^ to collapse. (You can use Ctrl+F1 or double-click the active tab in the Ribbon to toggle from collapsed to pinned.)
- Use the arrow keys to move the active cell so it is hidden behind a chart or slicer.
- Hide all sheets except for the dashboard sheet.
- In File, Options, Advanced, hide the scroll bars and sheet tabs.

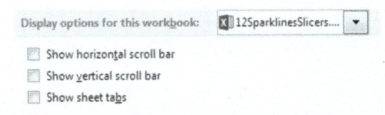

Bonus Tip: Line Up Dashboard Sections with Different Column Widths

If you are anything like me, you often need to fit a lot of data into a small area in a dashboard. What if columns in one dashboard tile don't line up with columns in another tile? Using a linked picture will solve the problem. In the figure below, the report in A1:M9 requires 13 columns. But the report in Rows 11:13 needs that same space to be two columns. I am rarely one to recommend merged cells, so let's not broach that evil topic.

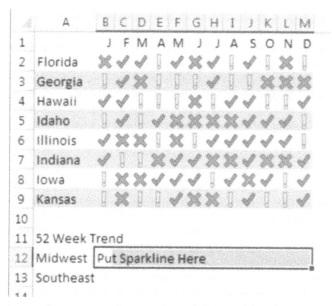

Instead, go to another section of the workbook and build the report tile. Copy the cells that encompass the tile.

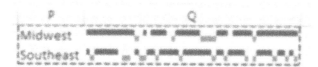

Select where you want the tile to appear. On the Home tab, click on the lower half of the Paste dropdown to open the paste options. The last icon is Paste Picture Link. Click that icon. A live picture of the other cells appears.

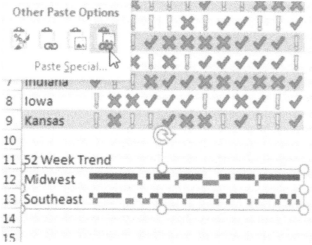

Thanks to Ghaleb Bakri for suggesting a similar technique using dropdown boxes. Ryan Wilson suggested making Excel not look like Excel. Jon Wittwer of Vertex42 suggested the sparklines and slicers trick.

Bonus Tip: Report Slicer Selections in a Title

Slicers are great, but they can take up a lot of space in your report.

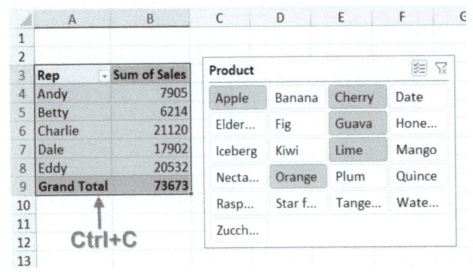

Here is an awesome way to get the selected slicers in a single cell. First, select your entire pivot table and copy with Ctrl+C.

Then, paste a new pivot table somewhere outside of your print range. Copying and pasting makes sure that both pivot tables react to the slicer. Change the pivot table so you have the slicer field in the Row area. Right-click the Grand Total and choose Remove Grand Total. You should end up with a pivot table that looks like this:

The list of products starts in I4 and might potentially extend to I26. Use the new TEXTJOIN function to join all of the selected products in a single cell. The first argument of TEXTJOIN is the delimiter. I use a comma followed by a space. The second argument tells Excel to ignore empty cells. This makes sure that Excel does not add a bunch of commas to the end of your formula result.

	A	B	C	D
1	Report for Apple, Cherry, Guava, Lime, Orange			
2	="Report for "&TEXTJOIN(", ",TRUE,I4:I26)			
3	Rep ⌄	Sum of Sales		
4	Andy	7905		
5	Betty	6214		
6	Charlie	21120		
7	Dale	17902		
8	Eddy	20532		
9	Grand Total	73673		
10				

#46 See Why GETPIVOTDATA Might Not Be Entirely Evil

Most people first encounter GETPIVOTDATA when they try to build a formula outside a pivot table that uses numbers in the pivot table. For example, this variance percentage won't copy down to the other months due to Excel inserting GETPIVOTDATA functions.

fx =GETPIVOTDATA("Sales",$B$3,"Date",1,
"Years",2029)/GETPIVOTDATA("Sales",$B$3,
"Date",1,"Years",2028)-1

Date	2028	2029	% Change
Jan	80772	84640	4.8%
Feb	161924	77381	4.8%
Mar	81695	84963	4.8%
Apr	80774	77705	4.8%

Excel inserts GETPIVOTDATA any time you use the mouse or arrow keys to point to a cell inside the pivot table while building a formula outside the pivot table.

By the way, if you don't want the GETPIVOTDATA function to appear, simply type a formula such as =D5/C5-1 without using the mouse or arrow keys to point to cells. That formula copies without any problems.

fx =D5/C5-1

Date	2028	2029	% Change
Jan	80772	84640	4.8%
Feb	161924	77381	-52.2%
Mar	81695	84963	4.0%
Apr	80774	77705	-3.8%
May	81827	85673	4.7%

Here is a data set that contains one plan number per month per store. There are also actual sales per month per store for the months that are complete. Your goal is to build a report that shows actuals for the completed months and plan for the future months.

	Store	Month	Type	Sales
1		Month	Type	Sales
1727	Fair Oaks Mall	Dec	Plan	123700
1728	Bellevue Square	Dec	Plan	140500
1729	U Village	Dec	Plan	126600
1730	Park Place	Jan	Actual	13475
1731	Kierland Commons	Jan	Actual	11708
1732	Scottsdale Fashion Square	Jan	Actual	12415
1733	Chandler Fashion Center	Jan	Actual	12848

Build a pivot table with Store in Rows. Put Month and Type in Columns. You get the report shown below, with January Actual, January Plan, and the completely nonsensical January Actual+Plan.

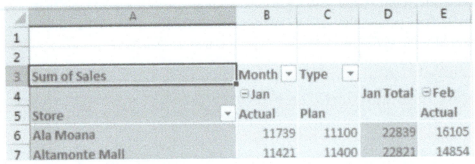

If you select a month cell and go to Field Settings, you can change Subtotals to None.

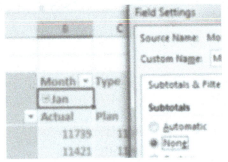

This removes the useless Actual+Plan. But you still have to get rid of the plan columns for January through April. There is no good way to do this inside a regular pivot table.

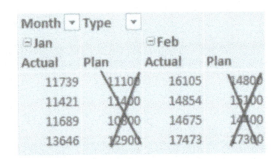

Note: Pivot tables based on external data have a featured called a Set based on Columns. You could run your data through the Data Model and then build a set to remove certain columns. But this would have to be edited every month. The GetPivotData solution will be easier to maintain going forward.

So, your monthly workflow becomes:

1. Add the actuals for the new month to the data set.

2. Build a new pivot table from scratch.

3. Copy the pivot table and paste as values so it is not a pivot table anymore.

4. Delete the columns that you don't need.

There is a better way to go. The following very compressed figure shows a new Excel worksheet added to the workbook. This is all just straight Excel, no pivot tables. The only bit of magic is an IF function in row 4 that toggles from Actual to Plan, based on the date in cell P1.

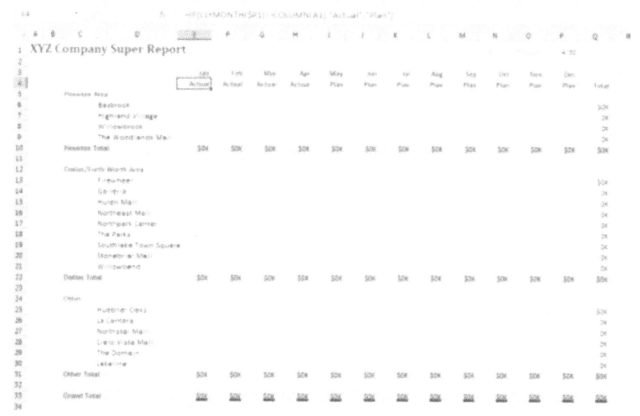

The very first cell that needs to be filled in is January Actual for Baybrook. Click in that cell and type an equal sign.

Using the mouse, navigate back to the pivot table. Find the cell for January Actual for Baybrook. Click on that cell and press Enter. As usual, Excel builds one of those annoying GETPIVOTDATA functions that cannot be copied.

But this time, let's study the syntax of GETPIVOTDATA.

The first argument below is the numeric field "Sales". The second argument is the cell where the pivot table resides. The remaining pairs of arguments are field name and value. Do you see what the auto-generated formula did? It hard-coded "Baybrook" as the name of the store. That is why you cannot copy these auto-generated GETPIVOTDATA formulas. They actually hard-code names into formulas. Even though you can't copy these formulas, you can edit them. In this case, it would be better if you edited the formula to point to cell $D6.

The figure below shows the formula after you edit it. Gone are "Baybrook", "Jan", and "Actual". Instead, you are pointing to $D6, E$3, and E$4.

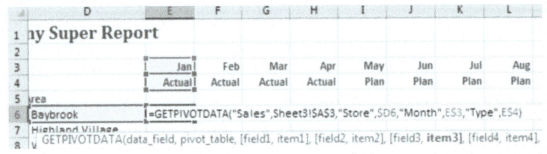

Copy this formula and then choose Paste Special, Formulas in all of the other numeric cells.

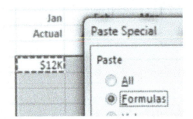

Now here's your monthly workflow:

1. Build an ugly pivot table that no one will ever see.

2. Set up the report worksheet.

Each month, you have to:

1. Paste new actuals below the data.

2. Refresh the ugly pivot table.

3. Change cell P1 on the report sheet to reflect the new month. All the numbers update.

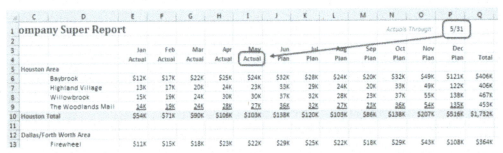

You have to admit that using a report that pulls numbers from a pivot table gives you the best of both worlds. You are free to format the report in ways that you cannot format a pivot table. Blank rows are fine. You can have currency symbols on the first and last rows but not in between. You get double-underlines under the grand totals, too.

Thanks to @iTrainerMX for suggesting this feature.

#47 Eliminate VLOOKUP or XLOOKUP with the Data Model

Say that you have a data set with product, date, customer, and sales information.

1	Product	Date	Customer	Quantity	Revenue	Profit
560	Gizmo	12/24/2033	Association for Computers	200	4690	2044
561	Gadget	12/26/2033	University of North Carolin.	700	14560	6888
562	Gizmo	12/26/2033	More4Apps Toolbox	500	11680	5110

The IT department forgot to put sector in there. Here is a lookup table that maps customer to sector. Time for a VLOOKUP, right?

There is no need to do VLOOKUPs to join these data sets.

In both the original data set and the lookup table, use Home, Format as Table. On the Table Tools tab, rename the table from Table1 to something meaningful. I've used Data and Sectors.

Do you see a Power Pivot tab in the ribbon? It would be after the Help tab. If you do not, go to File, Options, Data, and choose "Enable Data Analysis Add-ins: Power Pivot and 3D Map". It is the 4th checkbox. While you are in Excel Options, go to Customize Ribbon and ensure Power Pivot is selected.

Select one cell in the Data table. On the Power Pivot tab, choose Add to Data Model. A Data Model window will open. Close that window for now. Select one cell in the Sectors table. Choose Add to Data Model. Close the Data Model window again.

On the Data tab, open the Data Model drop-down and choose Relationships.

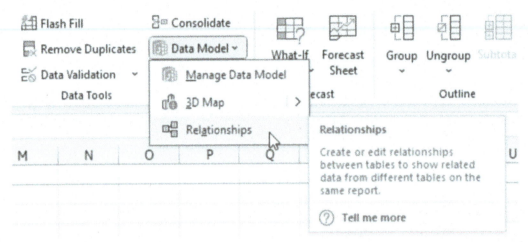

In the Relationships dialog, click New... in the top right. To build a relationship, you specify the field in common between the two tables. In this case, the field is Customer.

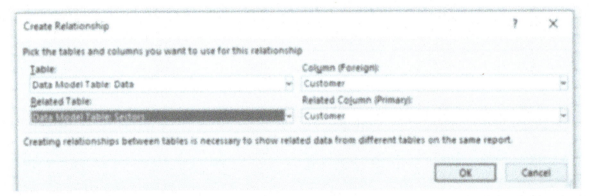

Go to a blank section of the worksheet where you want the pivot table to appear. From the Insert tab, choose Pivot Table, from Data Model.

The PivotTable Fields pane will show both the Data and the Sectors table. Expand the Sectors table and choose Sector. Expand the Data table and choose Revenue. The resulting pivot table is a mash up of the original data and the data in the lookup table. No VLOOKUPs required.

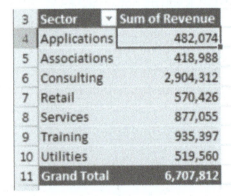

Sector	Sum of Revenue
Applications	482,074
Associations	418,988
Consulting	2,904,312
Retail	570,426
Services	877,055
Training	935,397
Utilities	519,560
Grand Total	6,707,812

Bonus Tip: Count Distinct

To see an annoyance with pivot tables, drag the Customer column from the Data table to the VALUES area. The field says Count of Customer, but it is really a count of the invoices belong to each sector. What if you really want to see how many unique customers belong to each sector?

	Sector	Sum of Revenue	Count of Customer
3			
4	Applications	482,074	44
5	Associations	418,988	32
6	Consulting	2,904,312	238
7	Retail	570,426	49
8	Services	877,055	79
9	Training	935,397	75
10	Utilities	519,560	46
11	Grand Total	6,707,812	563

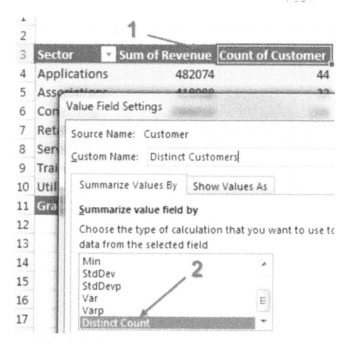

Double-click the Count of Customer heading. At first, the Summarize Values By offers choices such as Sum, Average, and Count. Scroll down to the bottom. Because the pivot table is based on the Data Model, you now have Distinct Count.

After you select Distinct Count, the pivot table shows a distinct count of customers for each sector. This was very hard to do in regular pivot tables.

Sector	Revenue	Distinct Customers
Applications	482,074	6
Associations	418,988	5
Consulting	2,904,312	30
Retail	570,426	5
Services	877,055	10
Training	935,397	11
Utilities	519,560	6
Grand Total	6,707,812	73

Thanks to Colin Michael and Alejandro Quiceno for suggesting Power Pivot.

#48 Pivot Table with Sum and Average Total Rows (MDX)

Check out this impossible pivot table. Details for Sum of Sales. Total for Sum of Sales. Then, without any details for Average of Sales, a Total row for Average of Sales. Notice that there are no hidden rows between row 11 and 12.

In the past, I've done this using a Data Model pivot table and a Set. This fragile method will break if a new product is introduced. The MDX method below is better.

	Values	Product	
4	Values	Product	
5	Sum of Sales	Apple	$47,323
6		Banana	$4,440
7		Cherry	$2,878
8		Elderberry	$4,570
9		Fig	$2,229
10		Guava	$3,020
11	Total Sum of Sales		$64,460
12	Total Average of Sales		$1,572.20

1. Select a cell in your data and press Ctrl+T to convert it to a table. Make sure "My Data Has Headers" is checked. Rename the table to "Data" in the Table Tools Design tab.

2. From inside the Data table, choose Insert, Pivot Table. In the Pivottable dialog box, choose Add This Data To The Data Model. This setting enables MDX to work.

3. Drag Product to the Rows area of the pivot table. Drag Sales to the Values area. Drag Sales a second time to the Values area. Change the second Sum of Sales to show Average, and update the custom name to Average of Sales.

4. Drag the "Sigma Values" tile from the Columns area and drop it **above** the Product tile in the Rows area. If you did this correctly, your pivot table now has 6 rows of Sum followed by 6 rows of Average, followed by two grand total rows.

5. In the sample workbook, copy this MDX set from the red text box::

```
{
([Measures].[Sum of Sales],[Data].[Product].Children),
([Measures].[Sum of Sales],[Data].[Product].[All]),
([Measures].[Average of Sales],[Data].[Product].[All])}
```

6. On the PivotTable Analyze tab, open the drop-down for Fields Items and Sets. Choose Manage Sets.

7. In the Set Manager dialog, open the drop-down for New and choose Create Set from MDX.

8. Paste the four lines of MDX code from above. Click Test MDX to make sure it is valid.

9. At the bottom of the dialog, choose Recalculate Set With Every Update. Click OK. Click Close.

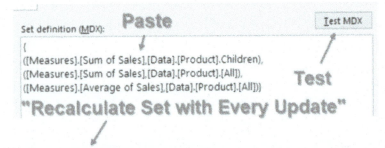

10. You will now see a new checkbox at the top of the PivotTable Fields pane for Set 1. Uncheck Product and Sales from the PivotTable Fields pane. Choose Set 1. Your pivot table will now look like the pivot table at the beginning of this topic.

#49 Compare Budget Versus Actual via Power Pivot

Budgets are done at the top level – revenue by product line by region by month. Actuals accumulate slowly over time – invoice by invoice, line item by line item. Comparing the small Budget file to the voluminous Actual data has been a pain forever. I love this trick from Rob Collie, aka PowerPivotPro.com.

To set up the example, you have a 54-row budget table: 1 row per month per region per product.

The invoice file is at the detail level: 422 rows so far this year.

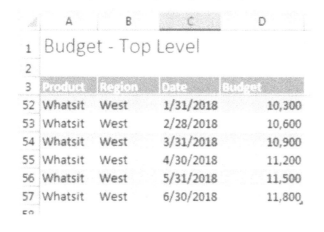

	A	B	C	D
1	Budget - Top Level			
2				
3	Product	Region	Date	Budget
52	Whatsit	West	1/31/2018	10,300
53	Whatsit	West	2/28/2018	10,600
54	Whatsit	West	3/31/2018	10,900
55	Whatsit	West	4/30/2018	11,200
56	Whatsit	West	5/31/2018	11,500
57	Whatsit	West	6/30/2018	11,800

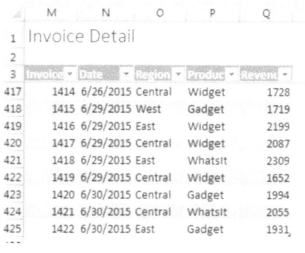

	M	N	O	P	Q
1	Invoice Detail				
2					
3	Invoice	Date	Region	Product	Revenue
417	1414	6/26/2015	Central	Widget	1728
418	1415	6/29/2015	West	Gadget	1719
419	1416	6/29/2015	East	Widget	2199
420	1417	6/29/2015	Central	Widget	2087
421	1418	6/29/2015	East	Whatsit	2309
422	1419	6/29/2015	Central	Widget	1652
423	1420	6/30/2015	Central	Gadget	1994
424	1421	6/30/2015	Central	Whatsit	2055
425	1422	6/30/2015	East	Gadget	1931

There is no VLOOKUP in the world that will ever let you match these two data sets. But, thanks to Power Pivot (aka the Data Model in Excel 2013+), this becomes easy.

You need to create tiny little tables that I call "joiners" to link the two larger data sets. In my case, Product, Region, and Date are in common between the two tables. The Product table is a tiny four-cell table. Ditto for Region. Create each of those by copying data from one table and using Remove Duplicates.

Illustration: George Berlin

"Joiners"

Product	Region	Date	Month
Gadget	Central	1/2/2018	2018-01
Whatsit	East	1/5/2018	2018-01
Widget	West	1/6/2018	2018-01
		1/7/2018	2018-01
		1/8/2018	2018-01
		1/9/2018	2018-01

The calendar table on the right was actually tougher to create. The budget data has one row per month, always falling on the end of the month. The invoice data shows daily dates, usually weekdays. So, I had to copy the Date field from both data sets into a single column and then remove duplicates to make sure that all dates are represented. I then used =TEXT(J4,"YYYY-MM") to create a Month column from the daily dates.

If you don't have the full Power Pivot add-in, you need to create a pivot table from the Budget table and select the checkbox for Add This Data to the Data Model.

Choose whether you want to analyze multiple tables

☑ Add this data to the Data Model

As discussed in the previous tip, as you add fields to the pivot table, you will have to define six relationships. While you could do this with six visits to the Create Relationship dialog, I fired up my Power Pivot add-in and used the diagram view to define the six relationships.

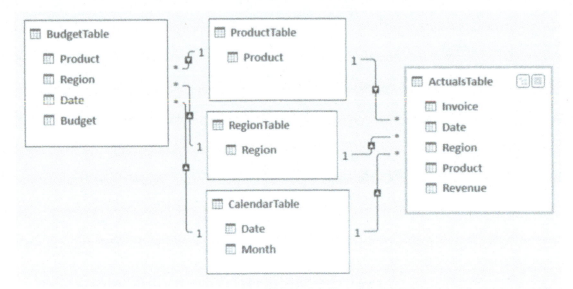

> **Aha**: Here is the key to making all of this work: You are free to use the numeric fields from Budget and from Actual. But if you want to show Region, Product, or Month in the pivot table, they must come from the joiner tables!

Here is a pivot table with data coming from five tables. Column A is coming from the Region joiner. Row 2 is coming from the Calendar joiner. The Product slicer is from the Product joiner. The Budget numbers come from the Budget table, and the Actual numbers come from the Invoice table.

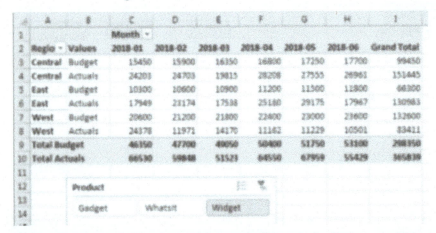

This works because the joiner tables apply filters to the Budget and Actual table. It is a beautiful technique and shows that Power Pivot is not just for big data.

Bonus Tip: Portable Formulas

You can use the DAX formula language to create new calculated fields. From the Power Pivot tab in the Ribbon, choose Measures, New Measure. If you don't have the Power Pivot tab in the Ribbon, you can right-click the Table name in the PivotTable Fields pane and choose Add Measure.

Give the field a name, such as Variance. When you go to type the formula, type =[. As soon as you type the square bracket, Excel gives you a list of fields to choose from.

Note that you can also assign a numeric format to these calculated fields. Wouldn't it be great if regular pivot tables brought the numeric formatting from the underlying data?

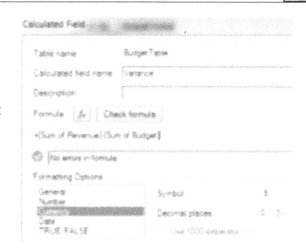

In the next calculation, VariancePercent is reusing the Variance field that you just defined.

So far, you've added several calculated fields to the pivot table, as shown below.

Region	Values	Month 2018-01	2018-02
Central	Sum of Budget	7730	7950
Central	Sum of Revenue	10539	13909
Central	Variance	$2,809	$5,959
Central	VariancePercent	36.3 %	75.0 %

But you don't have to leave any of those fields in the pivot table. If your manager only cares about the variance percentage, you can remove all of the other numeric fields.

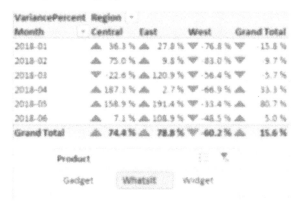

Note that the DAX in this bonus tip is barely scratching the surface of what is possible. If you want to explore Power Pivot, you need to get a copy of *Supercharge Power BI* by Matt Allington.

Thanks to Rob Collie for teaching me this feature. Find Rob at www.PowerPivotPro.com.

Bonus Tip: Text in the Values of a Pivot Table

Another amazing use for a measure in a Data Model pivot table is to use the CONCATENATEX function to move text into the values area of a pivot table.

In this data set, there is an original and revised value for each sales rep.

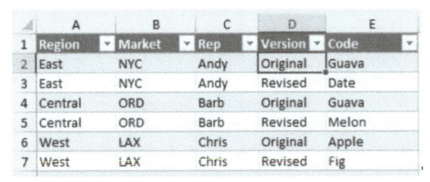

	A	B	C	D	E
1	Region	Market	Rep	Version	Code
2	East	NYC	Andy	Original	Guava
3	East	NYC	Andy	Revised	Date
4	Central	ORD	Barb	Original	Guava
5	Central	ORD	Barb	Revised	Melon
6	West	LAX	Chris	Original	Apple
7	West	LAX	Chris	Revised	Fig

Insert a pivot table and check the box for Add This Data To The Data Model. Drag Rep to the Rows and Version to Columns.

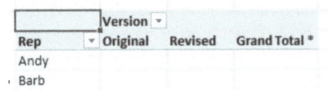

	Version		
Rep	Original	Revised	Grand Total *
Andy			
Barb			

The Grand Totals get really ugly, so you should remove them now. On the Design tab, use Grand Totals, Off For Rows and Columns.

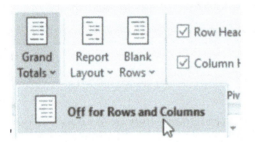

In the Pivot Table Fields panel, right-click the Table name and choose Add Measure.

The formula for the measure is =CONCATENATEX(Values(Table1[Code]),Table1[Code],", "). The VALUES function makes sure that you don't get duplicate values in the answer.

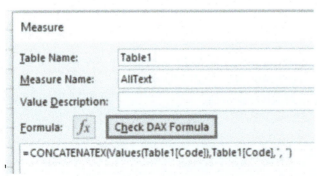

Measure	
Table Name:	Table1
Measure Name:	AllText
Value Description:	
Formula: f_x	Check DAX Formula

=CONCATENATEX(Values(Table1[Code]),Table1[Code],", ")

After defining the measure, drag the measure to the Values area. In this case, each cell only has one value.

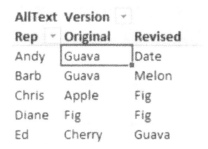

AllText Version		
Rep	Original	Revised
Andy	Guava	Date
Barb	Guava	Melon
Chris	Apple	Fig
Diane	Fig	Fig
Ed	Cherry	Guava

However, if you rearrange the pivot table, you might have multiple values joined in a cell.

AllText Version		
Market	Original	Revised
ATL	Fig, Cherry	Fig, Orange
LAX	Apple, Elderberry	Fig, Lime
MSP	Date, Cherry	Guava, Date
NYC	Guava	Date
ORD	Guava, Banana	Melon, Banana
PHL	Date, Fig	Date, Fig
SFO	Honeydew, Elderberry	Honeydew, Iceberg

Caution: A cell may not contain more than 32,768 characters. If you have a large data set, it is possible that this Grand Total of this measure will be more than 32,768 characters. The Excel team never anticipated that a pivot table cell would contain more than this many characters, but thanks to DAX and CONCATENATEX, it can happen. When it does happen, Excel can not draw the pivot table. But - there is no error message - the pivot table simply stops updating until you get rid of the Grand Total or somehow make the largest cell be less than 32,768 characters.

#50 Slicers for Pivot Tables From Two Data Sets

Say that you have two different data sets. You want a pivot table from each data set and you want those two pivot tables to react to one slicer.

This really is the holy grail of Excel questions. Lots of Excel forums have many complicated ways to attempt to make this work. But the easiest way is loading all of the data into the workbook data model.

Both of the tables have to have one field in common. Make a third table with the unique list of values found in either column.

Store Name	Sum of Sales 2019	Store Name	Sum of
Brea Mall	309467	Brea Mall	
Corona Del Mar Plaza	325574	Chino Hills Shoppes	
Fashion Valley	307504	Corona Del Mar Plaza	
Irvine Spectrum	254090	Dos Lagos Center	
Jordan Creek Mall	246447	Fashion Valley	

If the two tables are shown above, the third table has to have Store Names that are found in either table: Brea, Chino Hills, Corona Del Mar, Dos Lagos, Fashion Valley, Irvine, and so on.

Format all three of your tables using Ctrl+T.

Use the Relationships icon on the Data tab to set up a relationship from each of the two original tables to the third table.

If you have access to the Power Pivot grid, the diagram view would look like this:

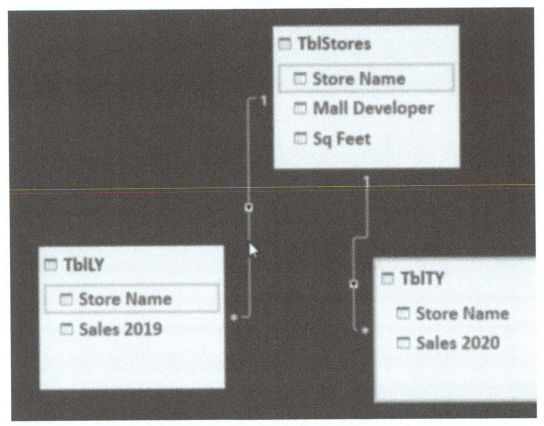

If not, the Relationships diagram should show two relationships, although certainly not as pretty as above.

From either pivot table, choose Insert Slicer. Initially, that slicer will only show one table. Click on the All tab and choose Mall Developer from your third table.

Try and choose a few items from the slicer. Watch your hopes get dashed as only one pivot table reacts. Once you recover, click on the Slicer. In the Slicer Tools Design tab of the Ribbon, choose Report Connections. Add the other pivot table to this slicer:

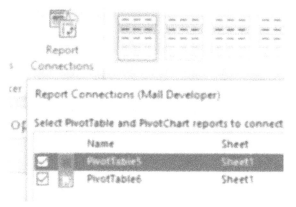

Finally, both pivot tables will react to the slicer.

Store Name	Sum of Sales 2019		Store Name	Sum of Sales 2020
Paseo	310198		Paseo	341218
Simi Valley Town Center	317889		Simi Valley Town Center	349678
The Galleria Edina	271106		The Galleria Edina	298217
Victoria Gardens	328199		Victoria Gardens	361019
Grand Total *	**1227392**		**Grand Total ***	**1350132**

Mall Developer			
Caruso Affiliated ...	Developers Divers...	Forest City Manag...	Gabbert & Gabbe...
Investec	Irvine Retail Group	Poag & McEwen L...	Shops At Chino Hi...
Simon Property G...	Westfield	General Growth P...	

#51 Using Python in Excel

In 2023, Microsoft added Python support to Excel. Everyone has access to basic Python. People who will use Python frequently can sign up for Premium Python.

This section of the book will talk about Python from an Exceller's perspective. In a few chapters, you will see how Copilot automates writing Python. This topic gives you a solid foundation of how Python works in Excel..

Python is a data science language. Ten years ago, I bought my first Python book. Flipping through the chapters, I found a technique called k-Means clustering that seemed interesting. So then I went back to the beginning of the book and attempted to get Python installed. That put an end to my Python journey. Installing Python requires several steps in a Command Prompt run as an Administrator. I could not figure it out. Five years ago, I donated the dusty book to the thrift store.

In 2023, Python comes to Excel as a preview. All of the setup disappeared. You can start writing Python on Day 1 without ever going to a command prompt.

Funny but true: I re-bought the same Python book that I had purchased ten years ago. Not for a dollar at the thrift store, but at full price.

Also funny and also true. After I ran into a few limitations in the Excel version of Python, I decided I wanted to install Python on my computer. My friend sent me a video with the 45 steps detailed in all their glory. I still haven't gotten through it. I am happy enough with the Python in Excel.

Here are some basics:

Python can be written in any cell. You can put a bunch of lines of Python code in one cell. The code in cell 2 can re-use the variables set up in cell 1. The Python statements are processed in Row Major Order, which means A1 first, then B1, then C1, out to XFD1, followed by A2, B2, ... XFD1048576.

To type Python in a cell, press Ctrl+Alt+Shift+P or use Formulas, Insert Python, Python in Excel.

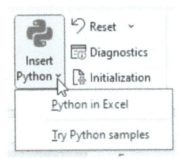

When you press Ctrl+Alt+Shift+P, the formula bar shows a green PY on the left side. You will also see a new drop-down menu to the left of the Formula Bar where you can decide to have this Python cell return values to the grid or simply return a Python object that can be used by later Python cells.

What you and I would call a Range in Excel is called a Data Frame in Python. Every example that you encounter on the web will use the variable df to refer to a Data Frame. You can use any variable name that you want. PetHelpful.com suggests great names for a pet snake include Buttercup, Raven, Yoshi or Zuke. But rather than Zuke = xl("A5:C151", headers=True) I am going to be boring and use df = xl("A5:C151", headers=True) just like every other Python tutorial. Just remember that "df" stands for Data Frame, which is a name for a range.

That is just enough to get you started. Follow these steps:

1. Grab any Excel data. It should have headers. And some numeric columns. Paste to cell A1 of new workbook.

2. Go to a cell to the right of your data.

3. Press Ctrl+Alt+Shift+P to turn your cell into a Python cell. You will see a green PY to the left of the Formula Bar.

4. You want to load your Excel data into a Data Frame with the name df. Type **df =** and then, using your mouse, drag to select your data. Excel will fill in the rest of the line of code: df = xl("A1:C16", headers=True) Congratulations - you have now loaded your Excel data into Python.

5. A python cell usually contains multiple lines of code. Press Ctrl+F2 to move your editing from in-cell to the formula bar.

6. Press Ctrl+Shift+U to make the Formula Bar taller.

7. To go to a new line in the Python code, press Enter.

8. Type the next line of code: df.describe()

9. Look to the left of the Formula bar. There are two possible icons. The "stack of squares laying on their side" stands for "Return a Python Object". The "123 with curved arrow" stands for return values to Excel. In this example, you want to return values to Excel. If you are currently seeing the Stack of Squares icon, press Ctrl+Alt+Shift+M to toggle to return values.

10. Press Ctrl+Enter to commit the code. In 10-15 seconds, you will see statistics about your data. Congratulations, you are now a Python coder!

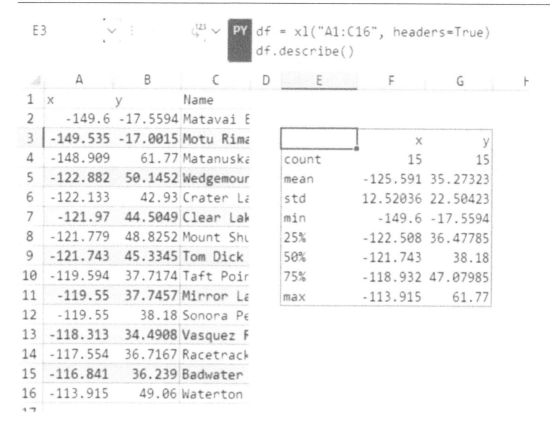

Bonus Tip: Excel Pre-Loads Many Python Libraries

As you begin your Python journey and look for code online or from Chat-GPT, you will see that the first several lines of Python is often loading the various libraries needed for a particular analysis. Excel pre-loads several libraries for you.

Go to Formulas, Python, Initialize for a current list of which libraries are loaded. Any of the lines of code that you find on the Internet that are already in the following screenshot can be skipped.

Initialization

```
# The following import statements are pre-loaded.
import numpy as np
import pandas as pd
import matplotlib.pyplot as plt
import statsmodels as sm
import seaborn as sns
import excel
import warnings

warnings.simplefilter('ignore')

# Set default conversions for the xl() function.
excel.set_xl_scalar_conversion(excel.convert_to_scalar)
excel.set_xl_array_conversion(excel.convert_to_dataframe)
```

As of July 2025, standard Python is free in Excel. After too many Python calls in a month, Excel will slow your Python results. If your I.T. department has a license from Microsoft, they can assign you Premium Python, which is faster. It also allows you to select Formulas, Calculation Options, Partial which will make less calls to Python.

#52 Python for K-Means Clustering of Excel Data

I recently had a puzzle to visit 146 locations in a VR headset. This seems simple enough - I sorted the latitude and longitude to arrange the data from west to east, starting in Tahiti and going through California, England, Europe, Australia and ending up at Aurora Point New Zealand. During this virtual journey, I noticed one day where the tour went from Utah in the western United States, down to Easter Island in the South Pacific, and then back to Colorado in the western United States.

It struck me that this was not an efficient way to travel the world. Here is a scatter plot showing the path.

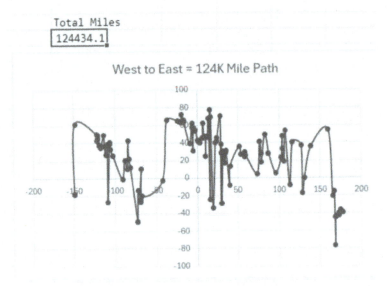

My first attempt to improve the route was a macro to find the next-closest point that had not been visited.

But then, I ran the data set through Python in Excel using K-Means Clustering. With this tool, you ask Python to find similar groups of customers. In this code, the important variable is in the 4th line, where you specify Clusters=6. I randomly tried different numbers until the clusters visually made sense.

```
from sklearn.cluster import KMeans

df=xl("A5:C151", headers=True)
df_cluster = df[['x', 'y']]
kmeans = KMeans(n_clusters=6, n_init=10)
kmeans.fit(df_cluster)

plt.scatter(df_cluster.x, df_cluster.y, c=kmeans.labels_, cmap='viridis')
centers = kmeans.cluster_centers_
plt.scatter(centers[:, 0], centers[:, 1], c='red', s=300, alpha=0.5)
# plt.show()

# Add the Cluster Label back to df
df["Cluster"] = kmeans.labels_
df
```

You get to specify how many groups. With the 148 locations, I tried 12 groups, then 10 groups, then 6 groups. Each attempt produced a new chart returned to a cell in Excel.

The data for six clusters looked pretty good. My code added the cluster number as a new column in the Data Frame. I then used a simply bit of python in a new cell that simply says "df" to return the new Data Frame to Excel.

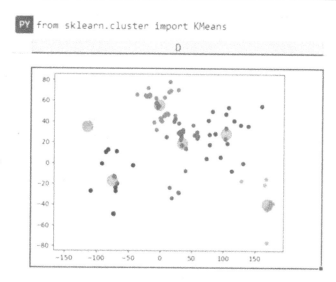

```
PY  from sklearn.cluster import KMeans
```

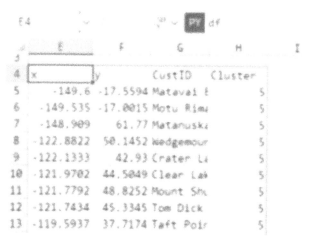

Arranging the data in clusters and then using the macro to find the next closest point resulted in a path that was only 86K miles.

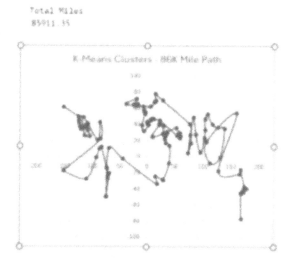

This is just one example of what you can do with Python.

Tip: While you can still write code in the Formula Bar, the new Python Editor is a better experience. See "#66 View all Python Code in the Python Editor" on page 142.

#53 Ask OpenAI Questions from Excel Using Excel Labs

A team of Microsoft researchers in Cambridge England have developed a free add-in for Excel called Excel Labs. At press time, there are three tools in the add-in: The Advanced Formula Environment, a function called LABS.GENERATIVEAI, and a Python Editor.

I recently had a hobby project where I needed to look up the year that 3400 music songs were recorded. I thought of using the Spotify API, but because songs are often remastered, it may not be accurate. The Excel database included columns for artist and song title. Using a concatenation formula, I added a column with 3400 questions similar to "In what year did Benny Goodman originally record the song "Sing, Sing, Sing "?". In this example, the question is in cell C9.

Using the Excel Labs add-in, I then added a column with =LABS.GENERATIVEAI(C9).

It took 10-15 seconds but the answer in C9 eventually came back and said Benny Goodman originally recorded the song "Sing, Sing, Sing" in 1937. This answer is not particularly useful. But with a formula in E9 of =LEFT(RIGHT(D9,5),4)+0, I was able to extract 1937 from the answer.

C9			f_x	="In what year did "&A9&" originally record the song """&B9&"""?"		

	A	B	C	
9	Benny Goodman	Sing, Sing, Sing	In what	Benny Goodman originally recorded the song "Sing, Si
10	Count Basie An Topsy		In what	Count Basie And His Orchestra originally recorded th
11	Ella Fitzgerald A-Tisket, A-Tasket		In what	Ella Fitzgerald and Chick Webb And His Orchestra ori
12	Louis Armstrong Jeepers Creepers		In what	Louis Armstrong originally recorded the song "Jeeper

I waited until I could leave the computer for a few hours. On the Formulas tab, I changed the Calculation Mode to Manual. Then I copied the formula down to all 3400 rows. Finally, I clicked Calculate Now and walked away. When I returned a few hours later, all 3400 questions had been answered.

To avoid asking the same 3400 questions again, copy the results and paste as values.

D9			f_x	=LABS.GENERATIVEAI(C9)	

	C	D	E
9	In what	Benny Goodman originally recorded the song "Sing, Sing, Sing" in 1936.	1936
10	In what	Count Basie And His Orchestra originally recorded the song "Topsy" in th	1937
11	In what	Ella Fitzgerald and Chick Webb And His Orchestra originally recorded the	1938
12	In what	Louis Armstrong originally recorded the song "Jeepers Creepers" in the y	1938
13	In what	Count Basie And His Orchestra originally recorded the song "Shorty Georg	1939
14	In what	Judy Garland and Ray Bolger originally recorded the song "We're Off To S	1939
15	In what	Ray Bolger and Judy Garland originally recorded the song "If I Only Had	1939

Here are some important points about this task. (1) It is a hobby project. (2) There was no summer intern I could pay to go look up 3400 facts. (3) If I did not use OpenAI, the project would not have gotten done. (4) No one is going to die if the answers were wrong 10% of the time.

Given those points, it was a perfect way to make progress on a project that otherwise would not have been possible. As I am writing this in January 2024, the chat-bots are still notorious for hallucinating facts. You have to be willing to accept that the answers will be wrong or made up 1 out of 10 times.

My Accounting 101 professor Ward would be spinning in his grave if I offered to rely on something that is wrong 10% of the time. But there are times when 90% accuracy is good enough.

Before you use the LABS.GENERATIVEAI the first time, you need to go through some pre-requisites.

1. On the Home tab in Excel, go to Add-Ins and search for Excel Labs. Install the add-in.

2. Click on the new Excel Labs icon on the far right side of the Home tab. Open the section for LABS. GENERATIVEAI.

3. Follow the instructions for getting an API Key from OpenAI. The first 30 days of use will be free and you will need a credit card after that. As of January 2024, the fees for OpenAI are ridiculously inexpensive. The 3,400 calls to the API cost me sixty six cents. That works out to one penny for every 50+ calls to the service. By changing to calculation to Manual, you can perform all the calls once with a single Calculate Now and then paste the answers as values.

4. While the questions are queued up, you will see a circle icon and the word BUSY! in the cell.

There are a number of settings in the task pane where you can customize how OpenAI should respond. You can override some of these settings using optional arguments in the formula.

Before using the LABS.GENERATIVEAI function, you need to create an account at OpenAI.com and generate an API key.

Hover over each of these settings found in the Excel Labs pane to control the answers that you might get back from the questions.

Excel Labs ⌄

LABS.GENERATIVEAI ☰

The function sends the "prompt" argument to a remote generative AI model and returns the response.

Keep in mind >

Configure API key ⌄

To use the LABS.GENERATIVEAI function, you must register an OpenAI account and enter your account key in the following OpenAI API key field.

This OpenAI account key is stored in your machine's local Excel settings and is shared across workbooks on your machine, but it's not saved in the workbook or shared with other users who open the workbook.

OpenAI API key

•••••••••••••••••••••••••••••••••••...

Get your API key here ⟵

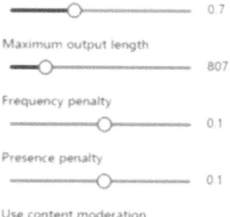

Settings

The following settings are the defaults across the workbook. The settings can be overridden by individual calls to LABS.GENERATIVEAI

Model

gpt-3.5-turbo-16k

The model that generates the result. Learn about OpenAI models.

Temperature

———————○——————— 0.7

Maximum output length

——○———————————— 807

Frequency penalty

—————————○————— 0.1

Presence penalty

—————————○————— 0.1

Use content moderation

● Moderation disabled

#54 Ask Excel's A.I. a Question About Your Data

A Natural Language Query feature started rolling out to Microsoft 365 in late 2019. The feature uses artificial intelligence to answer questions about your data.

The Analyze Data feature can be found towards the right side of the Home tab. The feature has the potential to help millions of people, but it is hard to discover.

Anyone can perform advanced data analysis by simply asking questions by typing a sentence. Your data set can be up to 250,000 cells. Select one cell in your data. Use the Analyze Data icon on the right side of the Home tab.

A box says to Ask A Question About Your Data and it gives you a few sample questions.

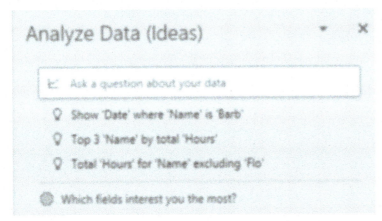

Type a question such as "Top 3 Products by 'Sales' where Category is "Bikes"". Excel restates your question and shows you a thumbnail of the report.

If this is the correct analysis, you can use the +Insert Pivot Table icon to insert the results into a new worksheet in your workbook.

Sometimes the feature will give you a chart when you want a table. Try adding "as table" to the end of your sentence.

The "Is this helpful?" link in the lower right is not being used. The original idea was to use Machine Learning to suggest better reports in the future. But the reality is that Microsoft is taking privacy very seriously and they can't learn without retaining your data.

New for 2021 is the "Which Fields Interest You the Most?". This can be used to tell Excel that they should never offer to sum fields such as Year, Part Number, or Cost Center. You can choose to Sum or Average numeric fields. Or you can uncheck the field to make sure it is not in any of the suggestions.

Even before you type a question, Excel will offer you 5-10 suggested reports and a link to load up to 30 more reports. If you aren't sure what you are looking for, it is sometimes interesting to read through these suggested reports.

My one complaint about the feature is shown in the following chart. Ideas was able to find some outliers in this data and offers to create a chart with those points called out in orange. For this chart to work correctly, Excel would have to support conditional formatting in charts and it does not. That means that the pivot chart will always call out these three points, even if the underlying data changes and new outliers emerge. You would have to re-run Ideas and hope that a similar result is offered.

PASTE HERE

#55 Introduction to Copilot in June 2025

Copilot is the broad term for Artificial Intelligence at Microsoft. The pace of innovation is so fast. I guarantee that Copilot will change between when I am writing this and when you read it. However, it is important to document where the feature is now.

Bonus Tip: There Are Many Entry Points to Copilot

A lot of Copilot in Excel happens in the Copilot task pane. You can get there through the Copilot icon on the far right side of the Home tab or through the (annoying) Copilot skittle that floats just above and to the right of the active cell. But new entry points are emerging:

- There are Copilot templates in File, New
- Data, Clean Data leads to a feature powered by Copilot. Messages in the yellow information bar will also get you to the Clean Data experience.
- If you create a new blank Excel document, the Start With Copilot floating window uses Copilot.
- Go to OneDrive in a web browser. Copilot icons are available for each file.

Bonus Tip: The Copilot Task Pane offers Four Different Experiences

Originally, Copilot could add new columns of formulas, add conditional formatting, Sort, Filter, or create pivot tables. But half way through 2024, Microsoft introduced the ability for Copilot to write Python code. This feature is currently called "Advanced Analysis", "Advanced" or "Think Deeper". The results from Copilot writing Python are far more reliable than traditional Copilot. In Q2 of 2025, Copilot includes text processing, with the ability to calculate sentiment for large amounts of text.

Bonus Tip: Much of Copilot Requires AutoSave to be On

I hate AutoSave. The Excel team made an early decision that Copilot would require AutoSave to be on to use Copilot. This a huge disadvantage to anyone using Windows or Mac versions of Excel.

At Microsoft, everyone is required to use Excel Online (they call it "eating your own dogfood"). That creates an environment where everyone is forced to have AutoSave On, all the time. So, when the Excel team realized they could bring Copilot to the product faster if they required AutoSave, I am sure it was not a big deal to them. But outside of Microsoft, where practically no one uses Excel Online, have to switch on AutoSave is hideous.

My secret: I will temporarily switch on AutoSave, use Copilot, then turn AutoSave off.

Bonus Tip: Artificial Intelligence is Unpredictable, On Purpose

Copilot, Chat-GPT, Deep Seek, Claude - all of these are Large Language Models or LLMs.

Working with accountants, I know that we love predictability. If I enter the same formula 100 times, getting the same answer 100 times is what I expect.

I was giving a live seminar at the UCF Accounting Conference. They ask me to give the same talk in two consecutive sessions. I started noticing that the formulas offered by Copilot at 9:45 AM were completely different from the formulas offered at 11 AM. Sometimes, both formulas worked. Sometimes, one was wrong. Sometimes, Copilot would say it could not come up with an answer,

Microsoft says that Copilot is "Non-Deterministic". This means the same question will give you different answers.

This is simplified: At every word/token, the model predicts a probability distribution of the next likely word. Instead of always picking the top choice, it samples from that distribution. That sampling process means multiple runs can take different valid paths. This makes responses feel more natural and creative. It avoids repetitive or robotic answers. It can be helpful in use cases like brainstorming or writing where variety matters.

I hate it.

But here is what I hate more. I understand that the creative answer provided by Copilot will be different. But after that answer, I always want the "Insert to New Sheet" button to be there. But it is not always there. It seems random. One time, I get Insert to New Sheet. The next 5 times, I have to use the Copy icon and paste it myself. Then, Copilot will tell me that it can't do something. Even though it just did the exact same thing six times in a row. It is maddening.

WIth Chat-GPT, you can say "Temperarture = 0" to lessen the creativity. But that is not in Copilot yet.

This following section of the book follows this path:

- Starting from a blank sheet: Start with Copilot. Research and Download data. Templates for fake data, Upload Photo from Phone and extract text.

- Clean Data

- Copilot task pane for traditional tasks

- Copilot task pane for Python. Think Deeper. Text Analysis

- Creating a Custom Agent for use in the Copilot task pane

- Using Copilot outside of Excel: Financial Ratio Analysis, YouTube video summary

By the time you are reading this, this is undoubtedly more. Watch my MrExcel.com YouTube channel for breaking developments.

#56 Hide the Floating Copilot Icon and "Start With Copilot" Prompt

Microsoft *really* wants you to try Copilot.

They are putting Copilot in your face a little too often. In particular, as of June 2025, these are the items I am thinking about.

- The floating Copilot icon that follows just above and to the right of the active cell. If you move your mouse away, it temporarily disappears. If you click the icon, there is an option to dismiss it for the rest of the day for this workbook only.

- Every time you start a new blank workbook, the Start With Copilot window appears covering the bottom half of your screen. I am a fan of this feature. But I don't want it there all the time. In theory, if you just start typing something in cell A1, it will automatically disappear. But here is my problem. Press Ctrl+N to start a new workbook. Immediately start typing Hello. You will see the "H" and the "e" disappear. But the act of rendering the Start with Copilot window takes a fraction of a second, and the two "L"s that you type will never make it into the keyboard buffer. So, now, Microsoft is expecting me to start a new workbook and then pause briefly while they show the floating box I don't need? Sorry, but that is obnoxious.

- Clean Data is great at finding misspelled customers, numbers stored as text, and invisible trailing spaces. But when I am working on Sheet1 and it finds a problem on Sheet3, the yellow information bar keeps asking me to go and fix the other sheet. "Not now!" I think.

The good news: there is now an option to turn off the floating Copilot icon and the big Start with Copilot window. For the Clean Data message, you need to dismiss the message three times in one day and then Excel will pause showing you the message for 30 days.

In Excel, go to File, Options. In the left-hand navigation, select Copilot—it's the fifth item down.

The top checkbox is "Show Copilot Icon Only For Highly Relevant Suggestions". Choose this to stop the floating icon from following the active cell.

The second checkbox is Turn Off Auto-Start For Copilot. Choose this to stop the Start with Copilot window from appearing.

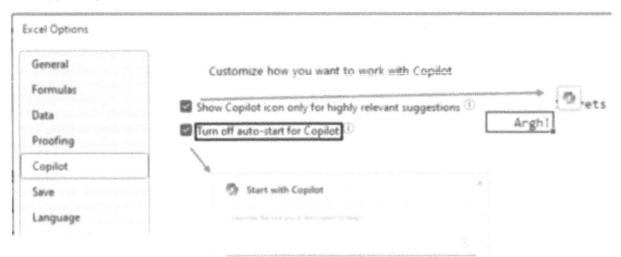

Note: By the time you are reading this, Microsoft will have introduced new annoying Copilot entry points. Those entry points will initially have no way to turn them off. People will complain. Then they will add a new option to the File, Options or some other method.

#57 Explore "Start With Copilot" – Excel's New Way to Launch

For those of us who've stared at a blank spreadsheet wondering, "What now?", Microsoft's new Start With Copilot feature is a welcome addition. It gives you a head start building your spreadsheet—even before you type your first value.

You'll see it whenever you go to File > New or press Ctrl+N to open a blank workbook. Think of it as a smarter, friendlier version of Excel's old templates, and it's designed to compete directly with Google Sheets' "Create a Table" prompt—but it's faster and more flexible.

Getting Started With Start With Copilot

1. Press Ctrl+N or choose File > New.

2. You'll see a floating prompt: Start With Copilot.

3. Enter a natural language prompt like "Create a personal monthly budget" or "Project tracker with due dates and priority".

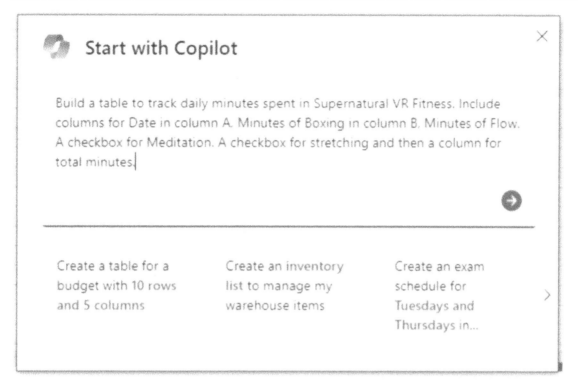

4. Click Go, and Copilot generates a prebuilt table with columns, formulas, and even sample data.

	A	B	C	D	E	F
	F2			fx	=[@[Minutes of Boxing]]+[@[Minutes of Flow]]	
1	Date	Minutes of Boxing	Minutes of Flow	Meditation Done	Stretching Done	Total Minutes
2	2025-06-15	30	25	☑	☐	55
3	2025-06-16	20	35	☐	☑	55
4	2025-06-17	40	20	☑	☑	60
5	2025-06-18	25	30	☐	☐	55
6	2025-06-19	35	15	☑	☐	50
7	2025-06-20	28	32	☑	☑	60
8	2025-06-21	22	38	☐	☑	60
9	2025-06-22	31	29	☑	☐	60
10	2025-06-23	27	33	☑	☑	60
11	2025-06-24	24	36	☐	☐	60

This works even without AutoSave turned on—which is a promising sign for future features.

> Tip for Pros: Ignore It and Move On If you're a spreadsheet veteran and find this intrusive—don't worry. You don't need to click the X. Just start typing, pasting data, or building your spreadsheet, and the Copilot prompt will quietly vanish.

The table that is generated by Start with Copilot might have: Headers, Sample Data, Formulas, Conditional Formatting. The one weakness is that Start With Copilot always creates a Ctrl+T table. Those tables have real trouble with Running Total formulas. If you need a formula that has to look back at previous rows, the Start With Copilot will fail.

Use the "Keep It" Button

If you like the result you get, click "Keep It" to lock in the layout. Pressing the refresh icon will discard the current design and offer something different. If you like the original option better, use the arrow buttons in the top left of the dialog to switch between results..

Advanced Follow-Up with Full Copilot

If you turn on AutoSave, you unlock the real power of Copilot. After Copilot builds the table, you can then use the full Copilot assistant to: Create summaries, Filter for specific rows, like overdue tasks, add more calculation columns, add more conditional formatting.

Start With Copilot is an impressive first step—especially for beginners or those looking to build a quick model. It doesn't yet do everything, but it's heading in the right direction. Let Copilot get you started and then you can continue adding new rows.

#58 Copilot Can Search the Web and Download Data

Copilot isn't just for summarizing or formatting data you already have—it can go out and find new data for you and drop it straight into your spreadsheet. Think of it like Excel with its own research assistant.

Make sure AutoSave is turned on. Open the Copilot task pane using the Copilot icon near the right side of the Home tab. In the chat box, type a prompt like: "Search the Internet. Download data for each US State. Get total population and area in square miles." Click Send.

Copilot goes out, finds the data (usually from reliable sources like the U.S. Census Bureau), and summarizes it. Once the results are ready, you'll see a confirmation that the data was found and parsed.

When the preview looks good, click Insert to New Sheet—and just like that, the live data is embedded into your workbook.

It even includes source links at the bottom, so you can verify or cite where the numbers came from.

Bonus Tip: Use Your Voice with Copilot

On devices with microphone support, you can even speak your questions to Copilot. For example:

"What is the Excel shortcut key for Flash Fill?"

Copilot will return the answer:

"The shortcut key for Flash Fill in Excel is CONTROL + E."

You can even have Copilot read the answer aloud.

You're no longer limited to whatever data you already have. Need country populations? Market trends? Historical weather? As long as it's public, Copilot can pull it in and let you work with it inside Excel—without needing to copy and paste from your browser.

#59 Use Copilot to Extract Data From an Image

Getting data into Excel from a picture used to be painful—especially if you tried using the old "Data From Picture" feature. But now with Copilot, there's a faster and more reliable method that even works with your phone.

Step-by-Step: Upload an Image From Your Phone

1. Make sure AutoSave is on.

2. Select Home > Copilot.

3. At the bottom of the Copilot pane, to the left of the chat box, there is an icon of a plus sign. Click this icon. Choose Add An Image. Then choose Add Image From Phone.

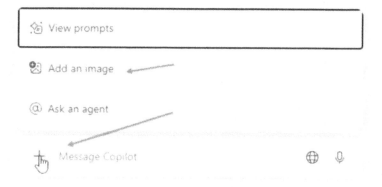

4. A QR code appears on your screen.

5. Use your phone's camera or scanner app on the QR Code.

6. On your phone, choose Take a Photo or Select an Image from Your Library.

7. Select the image.

8. Tap Done, and your phone will say "Image Sent."

9. In a few seconds, a thumbnail of the image appears in the Copilot pane, just above the chat box.

10. One you see the thumbnail, send a prompt of "Extract data from this image. There should be three columns of data."

11. Copilot will analyze the image, detect the tabular structure, and preview the data.

12. Click Insert to New Sheet, and the data is placed right into your workbook.

This new image-to-Excel workflow with Copilot is light-years ahead of the old "Data From Picture" tool. It's especially handy for receipts, reports, invoices—anything where retyping would be a pain. Snap a pic, upload from your phone, and let Copilot do the rest.

#60 Generate Fake Data with Python in Excel

Sometimes you need a bunch of fake data. Perhaps for demos, testing formulas, or just exploring a spreadsheet idea. Thanks to Microsoft's new Python integration in Excel, generating that data is now just a few clicks away.

Open Excel and go to File, New.

In the template search box, type "Python".

As of June 2025, the two choices are Random Data Generator and QR Code Generator.

New

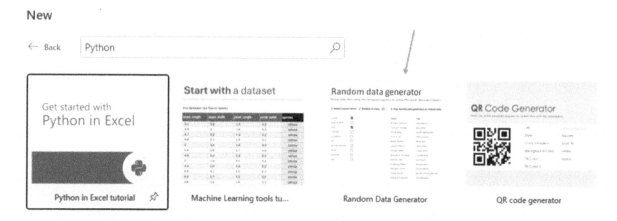

Select "Random Data Generator" and click Create. The left side of the workbook lets you choose which columns and enter how many rows. The data in H7 will automatically recalculate.

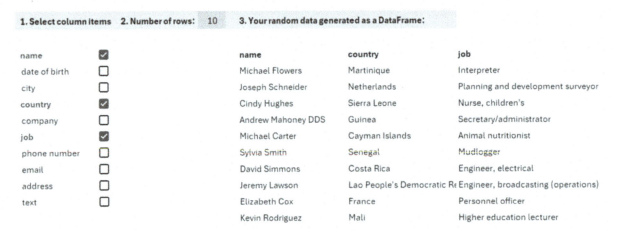

Random data generator

Please note that using this template requires an active Microsoft 365 subscription.

1. Select column items	2. Number of rows:	10	3. Your random data generated as a DataFrame:

		name	country	job
name	☑	Michael Flowers	Martinique	Interpreter
date of birth	☐	Joseph Schneider	Netherlands	Planning and development surveyor
city	☐	Cindy Hughes	Sierra Leone	Nurse, children's
country	☑	Andrew Mahoney DDS	Guinea	Secretary/administrator
company	☐	Michael Carter	Cayman Islands	Animal nutritionist
job	☑	Sylvia Smith	Senegal	Mudlogger
phone number	☐	David Simmons	Costa Rica	Engineer, electrical
email	☐	Jeremy Lawson	Lao People's Democratic Re	Engineer, broadcasting (operations)
address	☐	Elizabeth Cox	France	Personnel officer
text	☐	Kevin Rodriguez	Mali	Higher education lecturer

Tip: If addresses look truncated, it is because there is a line feed in the cell. Turn off Wrap Text or make the rows taller to see the complete address.

Explore the Python Code

Want to see how it works? You can! Column A is usually hidden. Unhide it to inspect the control logic.

Then, unhide the Imports and Functions worksheet. Expand the formula bar and you can see all four cells containing Python code.

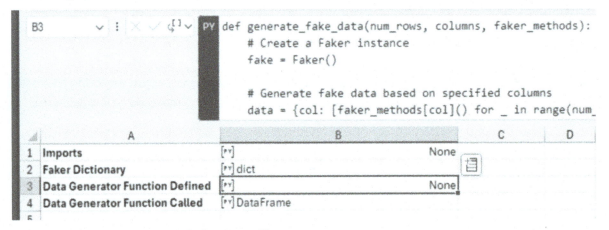

```
B3          v  :  X ✓  ∢[]v  PY  def generate_fake_data(num_rows, columns, faker_methods):
                                      # Create a Faker instance
                                      fake = Faker()

                                      # Generate fake data based on specified columns
                                      data = {col: [faker_methods[col]() for _ in range(num_
```

	A	B		C	D
1	Imports	[▾]	None		
2	Faker Dictionary	[▾] dict			
3	Data Generator Function Defined	[▾]	None		
4	Data Generator Function Called	[▾] DataFrame			
5					

#61 Clean Data with Copilot

Excel's Clean Data tool is finally showing up on the Win32 desktop app, after being in Excel Online since late 2024. You can find it on the Data tab, just to the right of Text to Columns.

It's an exciting idea: use AI to detect inconsistencies across a huge dataset (up to 100 columns, 50,000 rows) and offer a one-click cleanup.

Start with a dataset that's been imported or manually typed—something that's a bit messy. Select any part of it, and choose Data, Clean Data.

Make sure AutoSave is turned on, or you'll get a cryptic error message telling you to try again in a few minutes.

Suggestions will appear in the Clean Data with Copilot pane.

Here are some things Clean Data nailed:

- Identified DEF, D.E.F., and D E F as variations of the same product
- Merged United Airlines and UA
- Highlighted numbers stored as text in an otherwise numeric column
- Found trailing spaces and interior duplicated spaces and offered to remove them.

If there are three or more mistakes on a worksheet, the yellow information bar will appear on the grid, inviting you to use Clean Data. If you close this information bar three times in a day, the bar will be paused for some days. I recently had a workbook with 7 worksheets. I was giving a webinar about Copilot. I planned to talk about Clean Data later in the hour when I arrived at Sheet4. But the whole time that I was talking about Sheet1 through Sheet3, the Clean Data yellow bar kept appearing.

This is a version 1 feature. There are inconsistencies. Once it found Southwest Airlines and SWA and South West Airlines, but many times it does not. G.E. and General Electric are sometimes found and other times not. If you find data that you think should have been called out by Clean Data, use the button at the bottom of the pane for "Tell Us What You Think About Clean Data".

Thanks to Danielle Rifinski Fainman

#62 Regular Copilot in Excel

Copilot is a broad term for several features at Microsoft. Each of the apps Excel, Word, PowerPoint, Outlook and Teams have different functionality. There is also a Business Chat feature in Copilot that uses a Large Language Model along with data in your calendar, e-mails, chats, documents, meetings and contacts to perform tasks. The descriptions below are of the Copilot tools in Excel.

To use Copilot, your data has to be stored in OneDrive and AutoSave must be turned on.

You will see a Copilot icon on the right side of the Home tab.

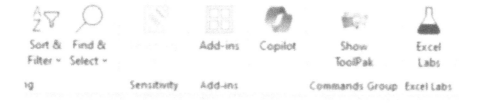

Click the icon and a Copilot pane will open on the right. Six sample prompts will appear at the top. These prompts are generic and are not based on your data. Other smaller prompts will appear just above the chat box. These change based on the data available. There is a refresh icon near the bottom prompts. Click Refresh to generate a new set of sample prompts at the bottom.

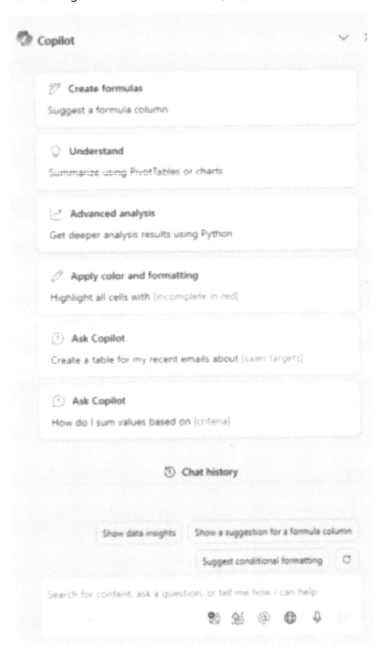

This figure shows a sample data set. There are columns for Revenue, COGS and Profit.

Region	Product	Date	Sector	Customer	Quantity	Revenue	COGS	Profit
Central	ABC	1/1/2032	Transportation	Southwest Airlines	100	$2,257	$984	$1,273
East	ABC	1/1/2032	Healthcare	Merck	800	$18,552	$7,872	$10,680
Central	XYZ	1/1/2032	Energy	Texaco	400	$9,152	$4,088	$5,064
East	DEF	1/1/2032	Manufacturing	Cummins Inc.	1,000	$22,810	$10,220	$12,590
East	DEF	1/4/2032	Financial	State Farm	1,000	$21,730	$9,840	$11,890
East	ABC	1/4/2032	Manufacturing	General Motors	400	$8,456	$3,388	$5,068

Say that you want to add a column to calculate Gross Profit Percent. In my company, this is generally abbreviated as GP%. I click in the Copilot prompt box and type "Add a calculation for GP%" and press Enter.

REGULAR COPILOT IN EXCEL

Excel takes tens of seconds to process the question. There are various status updates where it says it is working on understanding the question, then understanding the data.

It eventually comes back with the figure below. They've suggested a valid formula to calculate gross profit percent. If you try this on the same data, there is a good chance you will get a different formula.

Add a calculation for GP%

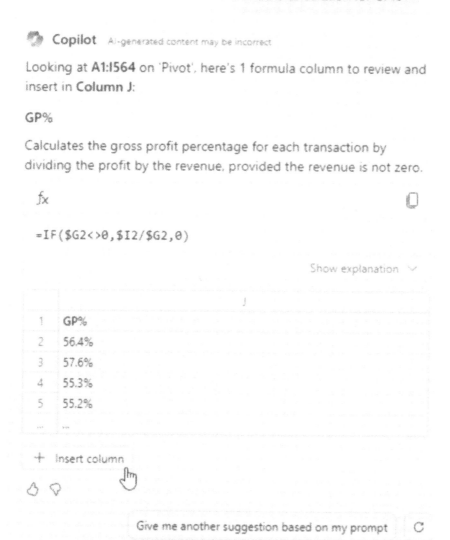

Copilot AI-generated content may be incorrect

Looking at **A1:I564** on 'Pivot', here's 1 formula column to review and insert in **Column J**:

GP%

Calculates the gross profit percentage for each transaction by dividing the profit by the revenue, provided the revenue is not zero.

fx

=IF($G2<>0,$I2/$G2,0)

Show explanation ⌄

	J
1	GP%
2	56.4%
3	57.6%
4	55.3%
5	55.2%
...	...

+ Insert column

Give me another suggestion based on my prompt ↻

Read the explanation and the formula. If you hover over Insert Column, a preview will appear in the grid with the formula results. Click Insert Column and the formula is added to the grid.

J2   ⌄ ⁝   *fx* ⌄   =IF($G2<>0,$I2/$G2,0)

	F	G	H	I	J
1	**Quantity**	**Revenue**	**COGS**	**Profit**	**GP%**
2	100	$2,257	$984	$1,273	56.4%
3	800	$18,552	$7,872	$10,680	57.6%
4	400	$9,152	$4,088	$5,064	55.3%
5	1,000	$22,810	$10,220	$12,590	55.2%

In the Copilot pane they report that they added the column. There are also feedback buttons where you can report back to Microsoft if the answer worked or not. When you send negative feedback, someone at Microsoft will read that daily. If you choose to include your e-mail address, you will often get a reply from someone on the Excel team.

Here are some other prompts that work:

- Highlight all cells where the GP% is in the top 20% - Copilot applies conditional formatting.
- Running total for revenue: `=SUMIFS($G$2:$G$564, $C$2:$C$564,"<="&$C2)`
- Calculate a bonus of 2% of revenue if the Product is ABC and the GP% is in the top 20%:
  `=IF(AND($B2="ABC",$J2>=PERCENTILE($J$2:$J$564,0.8)),$G2*0.02,0)`

- Sort by product within region
- Highlight all dates in the month of February
- Format Revenue as Currency with 2 decimal places
- How many customers are there?
- What is the total revenue for the Central region?
- Which customer has the highest revenue?

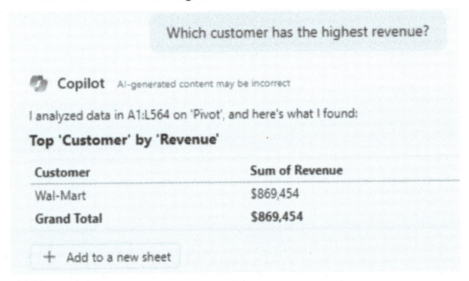

Here are some prompts that did not work:

- Calculate a $100 bonus if the Quantity is a prime number:
  `=IF($F2>1,IF(SUM(--(MOD($F2,SEQUENCE($F2-1,1,2))=0))=0,100,0),0)`
- Highlight the revenue amount that is the maximum revenue for each customer. Copilot said it could not apply the right conditional formatting but then told me how to do it.

Although it is not perfect, the feature is still in preview and shows a lot of promise. As the team at Microsoft gets feedback from the big companies in the preview, they will be able to improve the results.

#63 Let Copilot Write Python Code for You in Excel

Python in Excel used to be something for coders and data pros. But now—with Copilot's Advanced Analysis—you don't have to write a single line of Python to unlock its power. Copilot will do it for you.

Whether you're running clustering algorithms or building word clouds, Excel's Copilot makes Python approachable and useful.

Follow these steps:

LET COPILOT WRITE PYTHON CODE FOR YOU IN EXCEL

1. Open the data file for this chapter.

1. Save your file to OneDrive and make sure AutoSave is ON.

2. Go to the Home tab and click Copilot. You need to switch Copilot over to Advanced Analysis or Think Deeper. One easy way is to write your prompt and add the words "with Python" to the end of the prompt. The other way is to find the suggested prompt with any of the words "advanced", "python", or "deeper".

3. Use a prompt like: "Create K-means clustering from this data with six clusters. using Python."

> Note: K-means clustering is a way to group similar items together based on patterns in the data. It helps you find natural groupings—like which customers behave alike—so you can better understand or target them.

The Copilot pane will tell you that "I can use Advanced Analysis for that". It tells you that it will insert a new worksheet to hold the Python data frame and the Python code. You need to confirm this plan by clicking the green Start button. (For more about the Start with Think Deeper button, see the next topic.

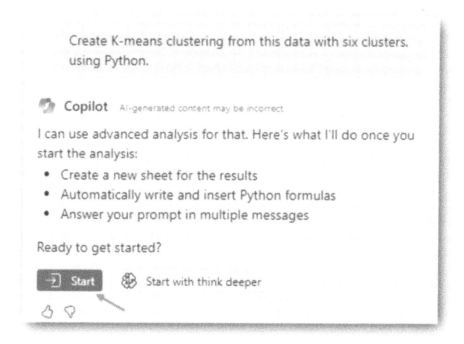

Copilot will insert a new worksheet. Cell A5 will contain a dataframe pointing to your original data. A preview of the data frame will show the first five records and the last five records.

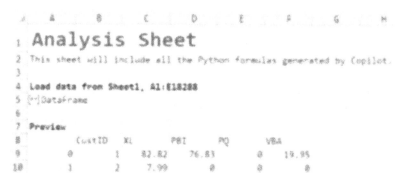

This is the first step every time you start Advanced Analysis or Think Deeper.

After the data frame is defined, Copilot will then begin writing code for your specific task. Cell A22 contains several lines of Python code. The new Cluster assignment has been added as a new column on the right side of the data frame.

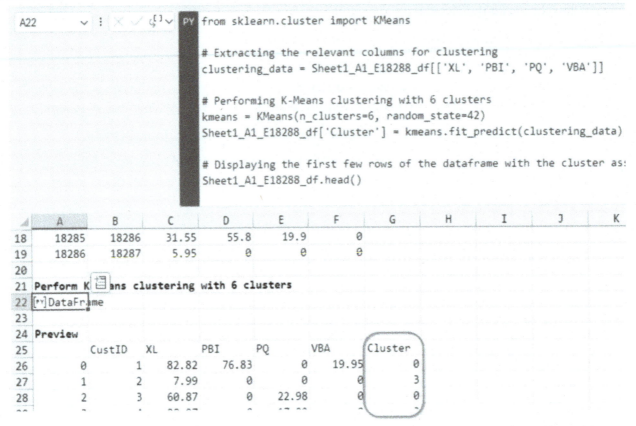

```
A22          v  :  X  ✓  ⌗¹ v  PY  from sklearn.cluster import KMeans

                                  # Extracting the relevant columns for clustering
                                  clustering_data = Sheet1_A1_E18288_df[['XL', 'PBI', 'PQ', 'VBA']]

                                  # Performing K-Means clustering with 6 clusters
                                  kmeans = KMeans(n_clusters=6, random_state=42)
                                  Sheet1_A1_E18288_df['Cluster'] = kmeans.fit_predict(clustering_data)

                                  # Displaying the first few rows of the dataframe with the cluster as:
                                  Sheet1_A1_E18288_df.head()
```

	A	B	C	D	E	F	G	H	I	J	K
18	18285	18286	31.55	55.8	19.9	0					
19	18286	18287	5.95	0	0	0					
20											
21	Perform K Means clustering with 6 clusters										
22	[·] DataFrame										
23											
24	Preview										
25		CustID	XL	PBI	PQ	VBA	Cluster				
26		0	1	82.82	76.83	0	19.95	0			
27		1	2	7.99	0	0	0	3			
28		2	3	60.87	0	22.98	0	0			

Note: Python starts counting with the number zero. If it creates six clusters, the cluster names will be 0, 1, 2, 3, 4, and 5.

Tip: Python code is shown in the Formula Bar and it is almost always more than one line tall. Use Ctrl+Shift+U to expand the formula bar. If you need the expanded Formula Bar to be taller, hover between the formula bar and the grid until you see a white arrow that points up and down. Click and drag to change the height of the formula bar.

Python code can either return a Python object (as shown above) or it can return all of the data to the grid. If you plan on using Python to create more visuals of your data, it is fine to leave it as an object with the preview. But, if you want to use Excel to analyze your data, open the drop-down menu to the left of the formula bar and choose Excel Value instead of Python Object.

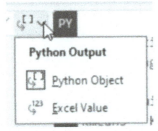

Isn't this amazing? You just describe what you want, and Copilot handles writing the Python code. You can even tweak the code. For example, if you want to change the number of clusters or variables used, just edit the Python directly.

Bonus Tip: Create a Word Cloud with One Prompt

Here's another awesome example: Word Clouds.

Let's say you have 3,000 rows of product titles or user feedback. You want to see the most common words—but ignore "the," "and," "of," and other filler words.

Start Advanced Analysis in Copilot.

Try this prompt: "Create a word cloud from the Title column. Exclude stop words."

Generate a clean, customizable word cloud

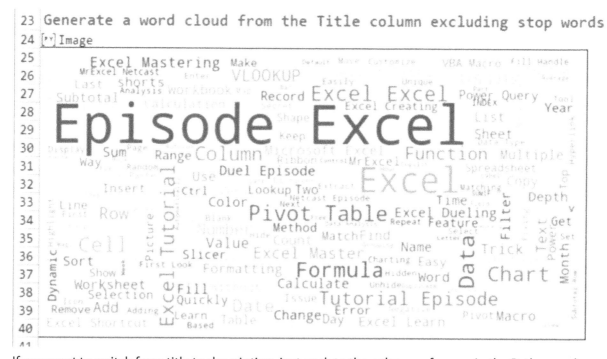

If you want to switch from title to description, just update the column reference in the Python code:

titles = Sheet1_A1_F2469_df['Description']

Finish editing the cell with Ctrl+Enter. And boom—updated word cloud.

Exporting the Visual

Right-click the word cloud image and choose Save As Picture to export it for reports or presentations.

You can also tweak dimensions, fonts, or colors by editing the Python settings—Copilot gives you a clean starting point.

These Python tools used to be reserved for data scientists. Now, Copilot writes the code for you. Whether you're clustering customers or visualizing feedback, it's all built right into Excel.

#64 Regular Copilot Tasks Do Not Work in Advanced Analysis

Once Copilot is in Think Deeper or Advanced Analysis, it will use Python to solve everything. If you want to use Copilot for non-Python tasks, they will fail in Advanced Analysis mode. Look near the bottom of the Copilot pane for a link to "Stop Advanced Analysis". Click this to return to regular Copilot.

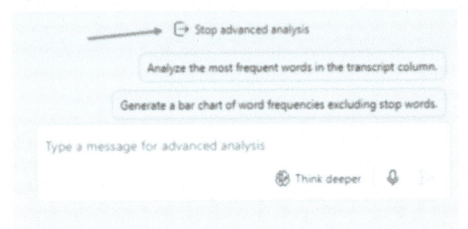

Caution: This distinction is very subtle and gave me heartburn for months. Some days, Copilot worked great. Other days, Copilot would say it had no idea how to solve my problem. How could it be that you can't solve this problem when you just solved it yesterday. There are two different Copilots. The Copilot for Advanced Analysis does not know how to solve things that the regular Copilot can do.

Thanks to David Monroy

#65 Create 10 Visualizations with "Think Deeper"

The example above where Copilot used Python to create a Word Cloud is called Advanced Analysis. In 2025, Microsoft added a new feature called Think Deeper. One prompt will generate multiple steps of analysis and Python code.

Click the Copilot chiclet, then choose Get Deeper Analysis Results using Python.

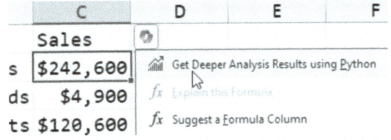

But don't choose "Start Advanced Analysis"—we want Start With Think Deeper. Even though the pane still says "Start Advanced Analysis," you'll know you're in Think Deeper because it explains: "With Think Deeper, I take longer to respond with more in-depth answers for complex tasks." That's what we want.

Get Deeper Analysis Results using Python

 Copilot AI-generated content may be incorrect

I can use advanced analysis for that. Here's what I'll do once you start the analysis:

- Create a new sheet for the results
- Automatically write and insert Python formulas
- Answer your prompt in multiple messages

Ready to get started?

 Start Start with think deeper

Try a prompt like this: "Create 10 charts or visualizations for a sales trend dashboard using bright colors. Show how the seasonality is different for each of the three products. Identify the underlying sales trend after each product has been adjusted to remove seasonality."

Copilot will respond with a detailed plan. Here is an example of the plan they show in the Copilot pane:

Here is the complete data analysis plan:

Data Preparation and Overview: Ensure that the Date column is in datetime format and sort data chronologically. Verify that sales for all three products (Snowmobiles, Paddleboards, Hiking Boots) are correctly identified.

Feature Engineering: Create time-based features such as month and day-of-week to help identify seasonal effects. Aggregate sales data on different time levels (daily, monthly) to support multiple visualizations.

Chart 1: Daily Sales Trend by Product: Create a line chart for each product showing daily sales over time, using bright distinct colors, to visualize overall sales dynamics.

Chart 2: Monthly Sales Aggregation: Generate a bar chart that aggregates monthly sales for all products, highlighting differences in volume and revealing periodic patterns.

... Charts 3 through 8 omitted for space considerations.

Chart 9: Combined Seasonal Patterns: Create a multi-panel plot that aligns seasonal patterns across products, showcasing the differences in seasonality among the three product lines.

Chart 10: Residual Analysis: Plot the residual components from all three seasonal decompositions to review any remaining patterns or noise after adjustment.

Final Adjustments and Aesthetics: Ensure a bright color palette is used for all visualizations to enhance readability and impact. Add clear titles, labels, legends, and tooltips as needed to make the dashboard intuitive.

Then it actually builds those visualizations—all from that one prompt!

If I have one complaint: Each chart is shown both in the grid and in the Copilot pane. The Copilot pane also includes a narrative for every chart. It explains what the chart is telling you. When you save the workbook, all of the charts in the grid are saved. Very little of the task pane is saved. It feels like you are losing a lot of the explanatory text.

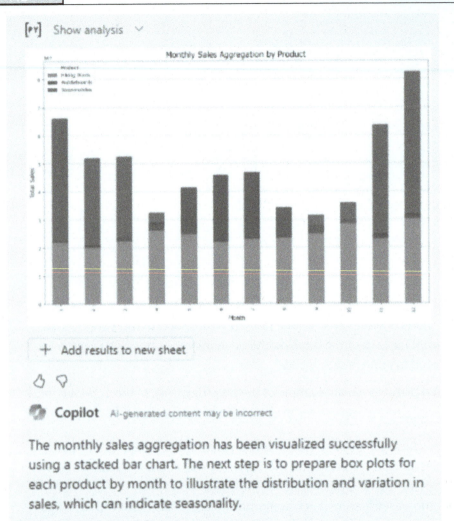

The monthly sales aggregation has been visualized successfully using a stacked bar chart. The next step is to prepare box plots for each product by month to illustrate the distribution and variation in sales, which can indicate seasonality.

The system generates a running commentary alongside the Python cells. You'll see explanations for each visualization. Why it was chosen. What trend or insight it reveals.

#66 View all Python Code in the Python Editor

If you've just used "Think Deeper," there's a good chance Excel Copilot has generated several Python cells for you. In the past, the only way to inspect that code was to select each Python cell and expand the formula bar—not ideal.

Thanks to the Microsoft Labs team in Cambridge, we now have the Python Editor. Go to the Formulas tab, find the Python group, and choose PY Editor.
A task pane will appear on the right with all of the Python code from the workbook. You can drag the left edge of this pane to widen it, making it easier to read. The code is color-coded like you'd see in a modern IDE.

You can edit the code directly in this pane and then click the little Save icon to update the worksheet. Below each code block, there's a preview area. Click Preview to see the result of your updated code.

The funny thing is, with how powerful Think Deeper has become, you're probably not writing much Python by hand anymore. Copilot does the heavy lifting. But it's good to know that if you ever want to tweak something, the PY Editor is just a click away.

Python Editor

∇ All Python cells ∨

Analysis1

```
1    #Seasonal decomposition for Hiking Boots
2    #Seasonal decomposition for Hiking Boots
3    # Filter Hiking Boots data
4    hiking_boots_data = Deeper_A1_C5479_df[Deeper_A1_C5479_df['Product'] == 'Hiking
     Boots']
5
6    # Set Date as index for time series analysis
7    hiking_boots_data.set_index('Date', inplace=True)
8
9    # Perform seasonal decomposition
10   result_hiking_boots = seasonal_decompose(hiking_boots_data['Sales'],
     model='additive', period=12)
11
12   # Plot the decomposed components
13   result_hiking_boots.plot()
14   plt.suptitle('Seasonal Decomposition of Hiking Boots Sales', fontsize=16)
15   plt.tight_layout()
16   plt.show()
```

PngImageFile ∨

Seasonal Decomposition of Hiking Boots Sales

#67 Your Chat History is Barely Available, and Only to You

When you save the workbook, the Chat History is hidden for anyone else who opens the workbook. They can see what was inserted in the grid, but they can not see the Chat History.

Microsoft claims that they save the Chat History for the author of the workbook. Originally, Chat History was hidden where no one would find it. They've taken great steps to make the Chat History visible. But the amount of Chat History that is being saved is less than 10% of the Chat History generated by Think Deeper.

Consider the paragraph at the bottom of the previous figure. When using Think Deeper, there was a plan, 10 charts with paragraphs, a summary, and then some follow-up questions. When you close the workbook, then re-open and access Chat History, I am finding only some of the follow-up questions are available. There is no way to scroll further back.

How to Access Chat History - Version A

After re-opening the workbook, open the Copilot Chat pane.

Six prompts appear. Just below the last prompt is a link to Chat History.

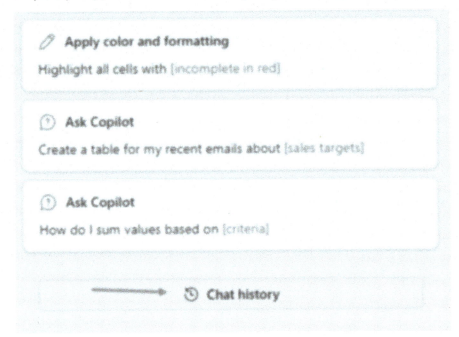

When you click on Chat History, there is a list of dates and discussions. When you hover over a chat, there is an option for deleting that chat history. Or, click the Chat to open the chat history.

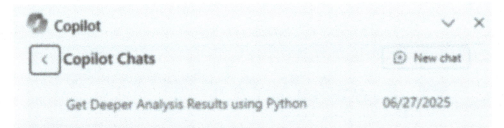

To delete Chat History, hover over one chat and click the Trash icon.

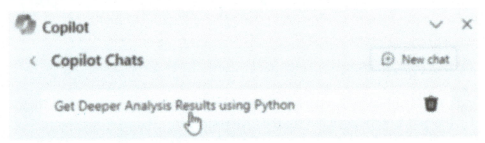

Or, at the bottom of the pane, there is an option to Delete All Copilot History.

How to Access Chat History - Version B

If you do not see the Chat History in the main Copilot pane, then use the 3-Lines menu at the top left.

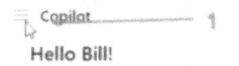

Hello Bill!

Here are some ideas to get you started.

Chat History is hidden all the way at the bottom of this pane.

#68 Using Copilot for Text Sentiment Analysis

Copilot now supports impressive text analytics using Python—especially when you're working with long-form text comments. In this example, we'll walk through how Think Deeper helps uncover sentiment trends and actionable insights from over 17,000 user comments.

Step 1: Load a Dataset of Long Comments. I am starting with a large table: 17,000 rows of comments. The key column here is Comment Text, a freeform field containing everything from short reactions to full-length paragraphs.

Step 2: Start Copilot and ask for "Analyze sentiment of the Comment Text field using Python." Copilot will offer you the choice to Start or Use Think Deeper. Choose Think Deeper.

Think Deeper will create a Python data frame and apply a sentiment score to each comment. The range of scores is negative 1 for very negative, to 1 for very positive. Think of these as percentages. -100% is someone who hates your company. -50% is a somewhat negative comment. +20% is slightly on the positive side of neutral.

In my example, I was shown a summary grouping the comments.

```
Sentiment_Level      Proportion
Very Positive           52.9%
Somewhat Positive       24.9%
Neutral                 14.7%
Somewhat Negative        5.8%
Very Negative            1.8%
```

Bonus Tip: Find Products with an overall Negative Sentiment

Ask Think Deeper: "Figure out the average sentiment per Product. Which Products have a negative average sentiment?"

It will return a table listing all Products where the average comment sentiment is below zero. To make this list editable in Excel: Click the dropdown next to the Formula Bar. Choose Excel Values instead of Python Object. Now you can sort, filter, or copy the list.

#69 Create a Custom Agent For Use in Excel

You can train a custom agent to use in Copilot for Excel! It requires no programming code. You can probably set it up in less than ten minutes. The agent is available in Copilot Studio, but also in the Word Copilot pane and the Excel Copilot pane.

Start at Copilot Studio. Currently, this is https://m365.cloud.microsoft/chat. Along the left navigation bar, look for All Agents - Create an Agent.

CREATE A CUSTOM AGENT FOR USE IN EXCEL

At the top of the page, you have two options:

- Describe: you will provide a series of prompts
- Configure: You will out a form with six fields. I prefer this method.

Click the Configure tab.

1. Provide a small icon for your agent. It should be roughly square, in PNG format and under 1 MB.

2. Give your agent a name. This is how it will appear in the Copilot pane.

3. Give your agent a short description.

4. The Instructions box is the most important. This is where you teach your agent what you want it to do. My prompt for one agent is "You are a librarian of a collection of 2,400 YouTube videos about Microsoft Excel. Every row in the Knowledge workbook is a video. The user of this agent will give you a concept, such as "Multiple Consolidation". You will search the columns for Title, Description, and Transcript. The search should be case-insensitive. Present a list of matching videos with the Title, Published date, and URL in a table that can be inserted into Excel."

5. The Knowledge section is optional, but it was important here. I had an existing Excel workbook with the data that needed to be searched. I copied the workbook from OneNote to my SharePoint site. Using the Cloud icon to the right of the Search box, I could specify my knowledge file.

6. Scroll down some more and you will see a Suggested Prompt section. This is how the person using your Agent will ask the question. For me, the Message is "Find all videos with this keyword".

Once you have everything filled out, you can test the agent on the right side of the screen.

But until you click Publish at the top right, you agent will not be available to Excel or Word. While publishing, you can choose if the Agent is only for you or for others in your company.

> ## Your agent was updated successfully!
>
> ×Default-f8797441-f2c6-4e71-8843-d68573fb54bc&source=embedded-builder 〇
>
> The link works for **only you**. Change sharing settings
>
> **Go to agent**   Dismiss

After your Agent has been published, restart Excel. Open a workbook that has AutoSave On. Open the Copilot pane. I've seen the Copilot Agent in one of two places.

Use the 3-Line Menu at the Top Left of the Pane. A list of custom agents will appear there.

On a different computer, the custom agents are found using a Search icon in the chat window:

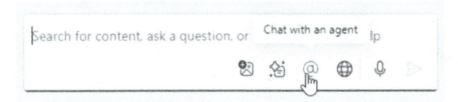

When you start using the Agent, your Suggested Prompts will be available. I clicked on "Find all videos with this keyword" and then typed RANDBETWEEN. Click Send. A half a minute later, the Agent has searched the Knowledge file and returned three matches.

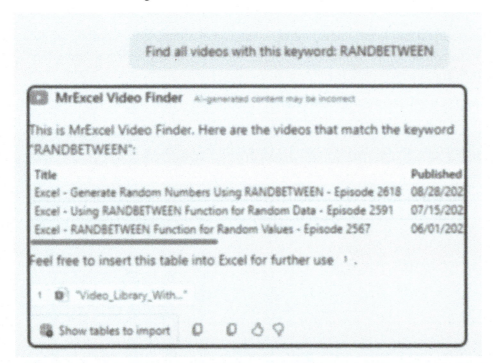

Note that for the Footnote with the source, they offer my entire Excel workbook. This is great for me, but maybe not something I would want to share with others.

Sometimes, the results include a Insert to New Worksheet icon. Other times, you need to use the Copy icon and then paste to Excel.

#70 Use Copilot to Instantly Summarize any YouTube Video

Have you ever wanted to rewatch one of your favorite Excel tutorials—but dreaded sitting through the entire video to find the one tip you needed? Thanks to Microsoft Copilot in Edge, you'll never have to watch a whole YouTube video again.

For example, starts at https://mrx.cl/gpt - this is a page that lets anyone find MrExcel videos on any topic. Let's say I vaguely remember doing a video on how to place people on a bell curve. Just type that into the search box, and you'll get a list of matching videos. Click the link to open the video in Edge.

Here's the magic: if you're using Microsoft Edge and you have Copilot 365 installed, you'll see a Copilot icon in the upper-right corner of the browser. Click it, and then choose: Generate video highlights. Copilot reads the video's transcript and instantly provides a summary.

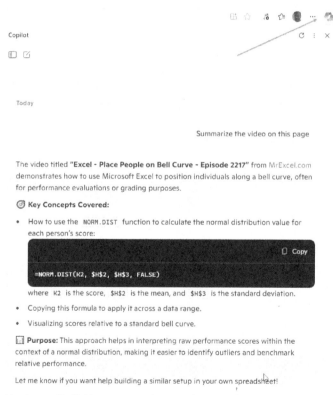

No intro fluff. No outro sales pitch. Just the good stuff.

#71 Copilot in OneDrive to Analyze Financial Statements

I downloaded financial statements for one company from SEC Edgar data. I had to clean up merged cells and other messy data. But I ended up with an Excel workbook that had the Income Statement, followed by the Balance Sheet, followed by Statement of Cash Flows. I saved this workbook to OneDrive.

When I hover over the file in OneDrive, a Copilot icon appears:

Click the Copilot icon and you can ask a question.

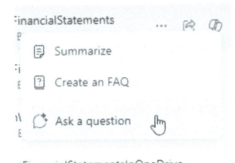

Both of these prompts work:

- Give me a financial summary and outlook for this company based on these three financial statements.
- Calculate key financial ratios from this set of financial statements.

The following screenshot is just a tiny portion of the ratios provided. Notice there is some unusual encoding errors that sometimes appear.

Liquidity Ratios:

1. Current Ratio:
- 2023: (\frac{26732}{23571} = 1.13)
- 2022: (\frac{22591}{19724} = 1.14)

2. Quick Ratio:
- 2023: (\frac{26732 - 4424}{23571} = 0.95)
- 2022: (\frac{22591 - 4233}{19724} = 0.93)

Leverage Ratios:

1. Debt to Equity Ratio:
- 2023: (\frac{35547}{25941} = 1.37)
- 2022: (\frac{36377}{24105} = 1.51)

When I first saw a demo like this, I was fairly amazed. Copilot inside of Excel could not perform any analysis like this and Copilot in Word or OneDrive was able to do it.

#72 Fixing Excel Functions Without Breaking the Past

For decades, the Excel team faced a dilemma: they couldn't fix known issues in legacy functions without risking compatibility across millions of existing worksheets. Mathemeticians have pointed out that certain functions (particularly those that came from the old Analysis TookPak) misbehave in edge cases. If the Excel team rewrote an old function, then old worksheets might start producing different answers.

In the past, the Excel team would have to release a new function, such as CEILING.MATH so they would not break people who had already adjusted formulas that used CEILING.

That ends now. With the new Function Compatibility Version setting, Microsoft can finally improve functions—fixing edge-case errors—without breaking existing workbooks.

Why does this matter? It's a foundational shift in how Excel evolves: Old workbooks stay safe: By default, all files continue using the original behavior (Compatibility Version 1). If you are creating a new workbook, you can opt in to the latest calculation logic.

The Excel team is now free to modernize functions, correct obscure bugs, and align better with evolving standards It's a win-win: backward compatibility and progress.

A Simple Example: Emoji and LEN

Let's illustrate the concept with a small but telling example: In cell A1, type three emojis using Windows + Period. Use =LEN(A1) to count the characters. Excel returns 6 because each emoji consists of two underlying characters. While this is technically accurate, people who were using emoji expected a length of 3.

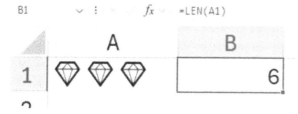

Go to Formulas, Calculation Options, Compatability Versions. By default, it's set to Version 1 (Recommended). Change the setting to Version 2 (Latest).

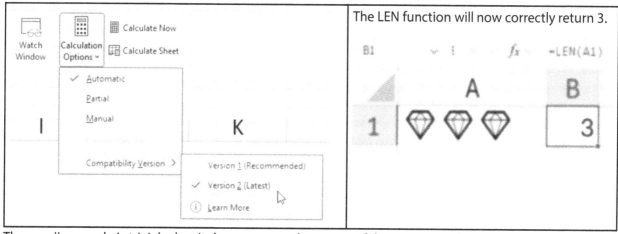

The LEN function will now correctly return 3.

The emoji example is trivial—but it demonstrates the power of this system. In the future, dozens of other functions will benefit from similar corrections.This is about freeing Excel from 40 years of function baggage. Going forward, the Excel team can tackle all sorts of long-standing quirks—without fear of breaking your existing workbooks. That's a big deal.

#73 TRIMRANGE or Dot Notation for Dynamic Ranges

2025 brings a new way to create expanding, dynamic ranges using either a new function or a new short-hand syntax with dots. If you've ever resorted to referencing entire columns just to make your formula included enough rows—this update is for you. In this image, a 6-row lookup table points to all 1.1 million rows due to the formula using F:G.

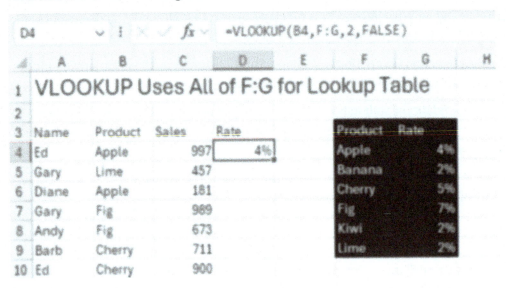

Meet the New TRIMRANGE Function

This new function trims a range down to just the rows with data. Here's the syntax:

```
=TRIMRANGE(range, [row_trim_mode], [column_trim_mode])
```

For either mode argument, you can use:

- 1 for leading blanks
- 2 for trailing blanks
- 3 for both (default)

With your lookup table in F:G but you only want the non-blank rows:

```
=VLOOKUP(B4,TRIMRANGE(F:G),2,FALSE)
```

Try the Dot Notation

Want something shorter? Excel now supports dot notation:

B:.B — trims trailing blanks

B.:B — trims leading blanks

B.:.B — trims both

So instead of using TRIMRANGE, you can use:

```
=VLOOKUP(B4,(F.:.G),2,FALSE)
```

in Data Validation, you can use this dot notation to define a growing list. For example, use =A2:.A30.

Note that these ranges partially work in Pivot Tables. (The Range gets hard-coded.) As of June 2025, it is not working with Charts (yet).

#74 Use F4 for Absolute Reference or Repeating Commands

The mighty F4 key should be in your Excel arsenal for two completely different reasons:

- Use F4 to add dollar signs in formula references to make them absolute, mixed, or relative.

- When you are not editing a formula, use F4 to repeat the last command.

Illustration: Cartoon Bob D'Amico

Make a Reference Absolute

In the following figure, the tax in C2 is B2 times F1.

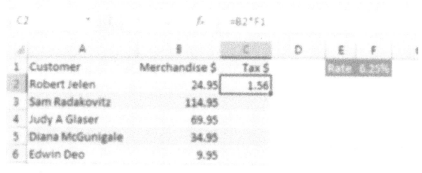

But when you copy this formula down, none of the sales tax calculations are working. As you copy the formula down the column, the B2 reference automatically changes to B3, B4, and so on. That is what you want. But unfortunately, the reference to the sales tax in F1 is changing as well. That is not what you want.

	A	B	C	D	E	F	G
1	Customer	Merchandise $	Tax $		Rate 6.25%		
2	Robert Jelen	24.95	1.56				
3	Sam Radakovitz	114.95	0.00				
4	Judy A Glaser	69.95	0.00				
5	Diana McGunigale	34.95	=B5*F4				
6	Edwin Deo	9.95	0.00				
7	Mario Garcia	189.95	0.00				
8	Anne Troy	129.95	0.00				

4

The solution? Edit the original formula and press F4. Two dollar signs are added to the final element of the formula. The $F$1 says that no matter where you copy this formula, that part of the formula always needs to point to F1. This is called an absolute reference. Pressing F4 while the insertion point is touching the F1 reference is a fast way to add both dollar signs.

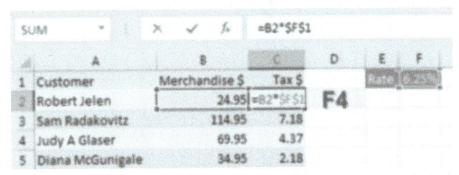

There are other times when you need only part of the reference to be locked. In the following example, you need to multiply H2 by A3 by C1. The H1 will always point to H1, so you need both dollar signs in $H$1. The A3 will always point back to column A, so you need $A3. The C1 will always point to row 1, so you need C$1.

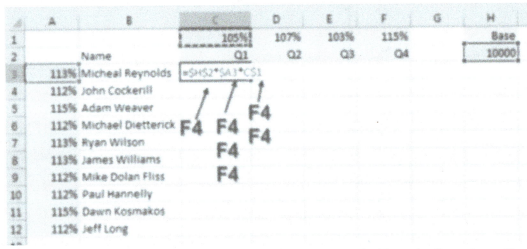

To enter the above formula, you would press F4 once after clicking on H1, three times after clicking on A3, and twice after clicking on C1. What if you screw up and press F4 too many times? Keep pressing F4: It will toggle back to relative then absolute, then row absolute, then column absolute.

The result? A single formula that can be copied to C3:F12.

F12						f_x	=$H$2*$A12*F$1			

⫿	A	B	C	D	E	F	G	H
1			105%	107%	103%	115%		Base
2		Name	Q1	Q2	Q3	Q4		10000
3	113%	Micheal Reynolds	11865	12091	11639	12995		
4	112%	John Cockerill	11760	11984	11536	12880		
5	115%	Adam Weaver	12075	12305	11845	13225		
6	110%	Michael Dietterick	11550	11770	11330	12650		
7	113%	Ryan Wilson	11865	12091	11639	12995		
8	113%	James Williams	11865	12091	11639	12995		
9	114%	Mike Dolan Fliss	11970	12198	11742	13110		
10	112%	Paul Hannelly	11760	11984	11536	12880		
11	115%	Dawn Kosmakos	12075	12305	11845	13225		
12	112%	Jeff Long	11760	11984	11536	12880		

Tip: If you forget to put dollar signs in the formula, you can edit the formula, click inside any cell reference and press F4 the appropriate number of times. If you have a cell reference such as C3:C12, select the colon with the mouse and press F4 to change both C3 and C12 to $C$3:$C$12.

Caution: There is a special type of reference called an Expanding Range. In this instance, you might lock down the start of the range using F$3 but let the end of the range be relative. The reference starts out as F$3:F3 but will expand as you copy it down, such as F$3:F12. Using F4 will never toggle through an expandable reference. You have to click inside the first F3 in the formula bar and press F4 to change just that part of the reference. See an Expanding Range in use in "#87 Preview What Remove Duplicates Will Remove" on page 184

Repeat the Last Command

Keyboard shortcuts are great. For example, Alt+E, D, C Enter deletes a column. But even if you are really fast at doing Alt+E, D, C Enter, it can be a pain to do this many times in a row.

	A	B	C	D	E	F	G	H	I
1	Name			Q1		Q2		Q3		Q4
2	Jeffrey P. Coulson			161		153		136		163
3									
4	Robert Phillips			150		143		198		161
5									
6	Peter Harvest			132		185		167		150
7		Alt+EDC							
8	Trace Cordell			149		140		167		176
9									

After deleting column B, press the Right Arrow key to move to the next column that needs to be deleted. Instead of doing Alt+E, D, C Enter again, simply press F4. This beautiful command repeats the last command that you invoked.

	A	B	C	D	E
1	Name		Q1	Q2	
2	Jeffrey P. Coulson		161	153	
3					
4	Robert Phillips		150	143	
5					
6	Peter Harvest		132	185	
7					

Rt Arrow
F4

To delete the remaining columns, keep pressing Right Arrow and then F4.

	A	B	C	D	E	F	G
	Name		Q1	Q2	Q3		Q4
	Jeffrey P. Coulson		161	153	136		163
	Robert Phillips		150	143	198		161
	Peter Harvest		132	185	167		150

Rt Arrow
F4

4

Next, you need to delete a row, so use Alt+E, D, R Enter to delete the row.

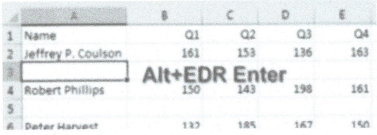

To keep deleting rows, press the Down Arrow key followed by F4 until all the blank rows are gone.

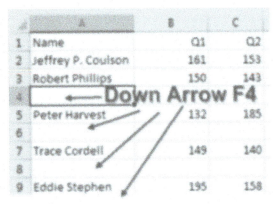

The F4 trick works for a surprising number of commands. Perhaps you just built a custom format to display numbers in thousands: #,##0,K. If you see a few more cells that need the same format, select the cells and press F4. Annoyingly, a few commands do not work with F4. For example, going into Field Settings in a pivot table and changing the number format and calculation is one that would be nice to repeat. But it does not work.

Bonus Tip: Use a Named Range Instead of Absolute References

If you want to avoid using $ in references to make them absolute, you can use named ranges instead. Select the tax rate cell in F1 and click in the name box to the left of the formula bar.

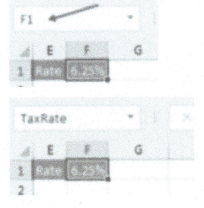

Type a name for this cell or range of cells. You cannot use spaces in the name, but TaxRate (or Tax_Rate) will work.

When you type the formula, use =B2*TaxRate.

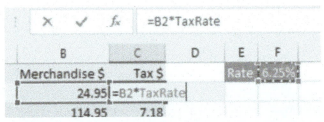

Tip: To see all of the named ranges in a worksheet, reduce the zoom to 39% or lower.

Thanks to Myles Arnott, Glen Feechan, Shelley Fishel, Colin Legg, and Nathan Zelany for suggesting this feature. Bob Umlas sent in the tip about seeing names below 39% zoom.

#75 Quickly Convert Formulas to Values

Converting live formulas to values is a task that can be done many ways. But I will bet that I can teach you two ways that are faster than what you are using now.

The goal is to convert the formulas in column D to values.

You are probably using one of the ways shown below. Note that Ctrl+Shift+V is new since 2022.

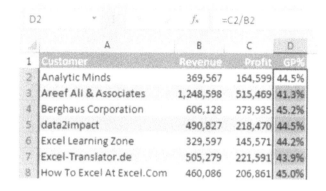

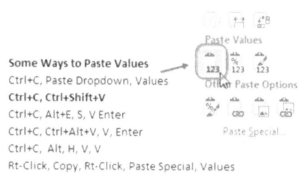

Some Ways to Paste Values

Ctrl+C, Paste Dropdown, Values

Ctrl+C, Ctrl+Shift+V

Ctrl+C, Alt+E, S, V Enter

Ctrl+C, Ctrl+Alt+V, V, Enter

Ctrl+C, Alt, H, V, V

Rt-Click, Copy, Rt-Click, Paste Special, Values

For Those Who Prefer Using the Mouse

If you prefer to use the mouse, nothing is faster than this trick I learned from Dave in Columbus, Indiana. You don't even have to copy the cells using this technique:

1. Select the data.

2. Go to the right edge of the selection box.

3. Hold down the right mouse button while you drag the box to the right.

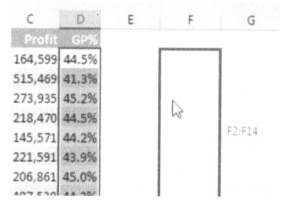

4. Keep holding down the right mouse button while you drag the box back to the original location.

5. When you release the right mouse button, in the menu that pops up, select Copy Here As Values Only.

How does anyone ever randomly discover right-click, drag right, drag left, let go? It is not something that you would ever accidentally do.

It turns out the menu is called the Alternate Drag-and-Drop menu. You get this menu any time you right-drag a selection somewhere.

In this case, you want the values to cover the original formulas, so you have to drag right and then back to the left.

For Those Who Prefer Using Keyboard Shortcuts

I love keyboard shortcuts. I can Ctrl+C, Alt+E, S, V, Enter faster than you can blink. Starting in 2022, Ctrl+Shift+V will paste values. Back in Excel 2010, there is a faster way. Look at the bottom row of your keyboard. To the left of the Spacebar, you usually have Ctrl, Windows, Alt. To the right of the Spacebar is Alt, *Something*, and Ctrl.

What is that key between the right Alt and the right Ctrl? It has a picture of a mouse pointer and a pop-up menu. Its official name is the Application key. I've heard it called the Program key, the Menu key, the Context Menu key, and the Right-Click key. I don't care what you call it, but here is a picture of it:

Here is the fastest keyboard shortcut for copying and pasting values. Press Ctrl+C. Press and release the Program/Application/Right-Click key. Press V. And, if you have a Lenovo laptop, it is likely that you don't even have this key. On a keyboard without this key, you can press Shift+F10 instead.

Bonus Tip: Skip Blanks While Pasting

A mysterious part of the Paste Special dialog is the Skip Blanks feature. What does it do? Say that you have a list of existing values. In another column, you have updates for some of those values but not all of them. In the next figure, select D2:D10 and Copy.

◢	A	B	C	D
1	State	Rate		Updated Rate
2	Alabama	92		87
3	Alaska	51		
4	Arizona	10		14
5	Arkansas	13		
6	California	21		
7	Colorado	17		16
8	Connecticut	51		
9	Delaware	39		
10	Florida	20		15

The 87 in D2 overwrites the 92 in B2, but Excel does not clear out the 51 in B3.

◢	A	B
1	State	Rate
2	Alabama	87
3	Alaska	51
4	Arizona	14
5	Arkansas	13
6	California	21
7	Colorado	16
8	Connecticut	51
9	Delaware	39
10	Florida	15

Select the original values in B2:B10. Do a Paste Special and select Skip Blanks.

Operation
- ◉ N**o**ne
- ○ A**d**d
- ○ **S**ubtract

☑ Skip **b**lanks

Thanks to Ed Bott, Ken McLean, Melih Met, and Bryony Stewart-Seume for suggesting this feature. Laura Lewis suggested the Skip Blanks trick.

#76 See All Formulas at Once

You inherit a spreadsheet from a former co-worker and you need to figure out how the calculations work. You could visit each cell, one at a time, and look at the formula in the formula bar. Or you could quickly toggle between pressing F2 and Esc to see the formula right in the cell.

	A	B	C	D
1	Vendor	Last Year	Growth	Next Year
2	adaept information management	190,716	7%	204,100
3	Orange County Health Department	188,874	8%	204,000
4	MrExcel.com	188,173	5%	197,600
5	Access Analytic	177,972	7%	190,400
6	Excelerator BI	185,529	4%	193,000
7	MyOnlineTrainingHub.com	181,901	6%	192,800
8	Cambia Factor	153,609	6%	162,800
9	data2impact	154,605	8%	117,000
10	Blockhead Data Consultants	121,751	8%	131,500
11	Bits of Confetti	100,308	8%	108,300
12	Total	1,643,438		1,701,500

But there is a faster way. On most U.S. keyboards, just below the Esc key is a key with two accent characters: the tilde from Spanish and the grave accent from French. It is an odd key. I don't know how I would ever use this key to actually type piñata or frère .

Esc

Ctrl+ ~ `

If you hold down Ctrl and the grave accent, you toggle into something called Show Formulas mode. Each column gets wider, and you see all of the formulas.

B	C	D
Last Year	Growth	Next Year
190716	=RANDBETWEEN(4,8)/100	=ROUND(B2*(1+C2),-2)
188874	=RANDBETWEEN(4,8)/100	=ROUND(B3*(1+C3),-2)
188173	=RANDBETWEEN(4,8)/100	=ROUND(B4*(1+C4),-2)
177972	=RANDBETWEEN(4,8)/100	=ROUND(B5*(1+C5),-2)
185529	=RANDBETWEEN(4,8)/100	=ROUND(B6*(1+C6),-2)
181901	=RANDBETWEEN(4,8)/100	=ROUND(B7*(1+C7),-2)
153609	=RANDBETWEEN(4,8)/100	=ROUND(B8*(1+C8),-2)
154605	=RANDBETWEEN(4,8)/100	=ROUND(B9*(1+C9),-2)-50000
121751	=RANDBETWEEN(4,8)/100	=ROUND(B10*(1+C10),-2)
100308	=RANDBETWEEN(4,8)/100	=ROUND(B11*(1+C11),-2)
1643438		=SUM(D2:D11)

This gives you a view of all the formulas at once. It is great for spotting "plug" numbers (D9) or when someone added the totals with a calculator and typed the number instead of using =SUM(). You can see that the co-worker left RANDBETWEEN functions in this model.

Note: Here is another use for the Tilde key. Say you need to use the Find dialog to search for a wildcard character (such as the * in "Wal*Mart" or the ? in "Hey!?" Precede the wildcard with a tilde. Search for Wal~*Mart or Hey!~?.

Tip: To type a lowercase n with a tilde above, hold down Alt while pressing 164 on the number keypad. Then release Alt.

Bonus Tip: Highlight All Formula Cells

If you are going to be auditing the worksheet, it would help to mark all of the formula cells. Here are the steps:

1. Select any blank cell in the worksheet.

4

2. Choose Home, Find & Select, Formulas.

3. All of the formula cells will be selected. Mark them in a different font color, or, heck, use Home, Cell Styles, Calculation.

To mark all of the input cells, use Home, Find & Select, Go To Special, Constants. I prefer to then uncheck Text, Logical, and Errors, leaving only the numeric constants. Click OK in the Go To Special dialog.

Bonus Tip: Trace Precedents to See What Cells Flow into a Formula

If you need to see which cells flow into a formula, you can use the Trace Precedents command in the Formula Auditing group on the Formulas tab. In the following figure, select D6. Choose Trace Precedents. Blue lines will draw to each cell referenced by the formula in D6.

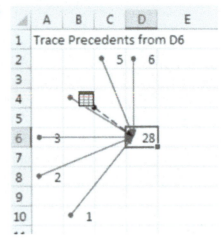

The dotted line leading to a symbol in B4 means there is at least one precedent on another worksheet. If you double-click the dotted line, Excel shows you a list of the off-sheet precedents.

If you stay in cell D6 and choose Trace Precedents a few more times, you will see the second-level precedents, then the third-level precedents, and so on. When you are done, click Remove Arrows.

Bonus Tip: See Which Cells Depend on the Current Cell

Sometimes you have the opposite problem: You want to see which cells rely on the value in the current cell. Choose any cell and click Trace Dependents to see which cells directly refer to the active cell.

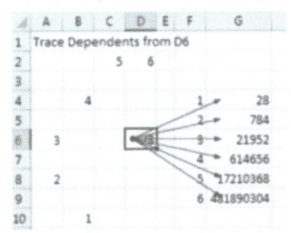

#77 Audit a Worksheet With Spreadsheet Inquire

Spreadsheet Inquire is a tool you probably have but have never activated. Inquire was developed by a company called Prodiance that offered the slick Spreadsheet Compare tool for $145 per person per year. The Excel team liked it so much that Microsoft bought out Prodiance and gave the tool for free to anyone who is on Pro Plus, Professional Plus, or Enterprise Level E3 or above.

In classic Microsoft fashion, they kept the tool hidden so even if you have it, you don't know that it is there. If you've ever seen a Power Pivot tab in your Ribbon, you likely have Inquire. It is at least worth the minute to figure out if you have it.

If you have the Developer tab in the Ribbon, click the COM Add-Ins button and continue to step 3 below. Otherwise, follow these steps:

1. Go to File, Options. In the left bar of Excel Options, choose Add-ins (near the bottom of the list).

2. Go all the way to the bottom of the dialog, next to Manage. Open the dropdown and change from Excel Add-Ins to COM Add-ins. After choosing COM Add-ins, click Go....

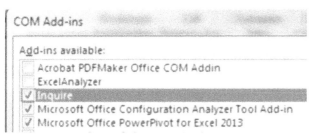

3. If you have Inquire in the list, check the box next to it, click OK, and keep reading. If you don't have Inquire in your list, jump ahead to "#78 Discover New Functions by Using fx" on page 162.

Once you enable Inquire, you have a new tab in the Ribbon called Inquire that provides the following options.

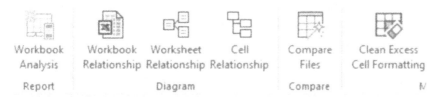

- The Workbook Analysis takes from a few seconds to a few minutes to build a report about your worksheet. It tells you the number of formulas, hidden sheets, linked workbooks, external data connections, and array formulas, as well as how many formulas result in errors. Click any category for a list of the various items.

- The next three icons allow you to draw diagrams showing relationships between workbooks, worksheets, or cells. The diagram below shows all inbound and outbound dependencies for cell D6. You can see the second-level precedents. Each node can be collapsed or expanded.

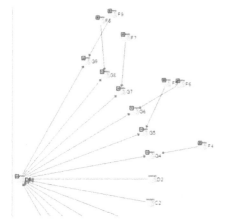

- Compare Files helps you find all changes between two open files. It does a really good job. You can foil most comparison tools by deleting a row in the second file. But Inquire detects that row 8 was deleted and keeps comparing row 9 in one file to row 8 in the other file.

- Clean Excess Cell Formatting locates the last non blank cell in a worksheet and deletes all conditional formatting beyond that cell. You might want to do this, for example, if someone selects an entire row or column and applies conditional formatting.

Thanks to Ron Armstrong, Olga Kryuchkova, and Sven Simon for suggesting this feature.

#78 Discover New Functions by Using fx

There are 509 functions in Excel. I have room for only 155 tips this book, so there is no way I can cover them all. But instead of taking 450 pages to describe every function, I am going to teach you how to find the function that you need.

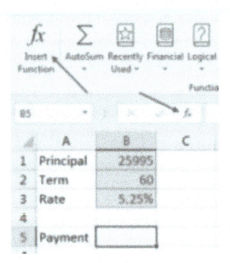

The Excel 2007 formulas tab introduced a huge *fx* Insert Function icon. But you don't need to use the one on the Formulas tab; the same icon has been to the left of the formula bar ever since I can remember.

If you are trying to figure out how to calculate a loan payment, the Insert Function dialog will help. Click the icon next to the formula bar. In the Search for a Function box, type what you are trying to do. Click Go. The Select a Function box shows functions related to your search term. Click on a function in that box to see the description at the bottom of the dialog.

> **Caution**: A change in Excel Help caused the search to return less results starting in 2019.

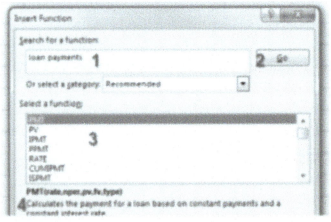

When you find the correct function and click OK, Excel takes you into the Function Arguments dialog. This is an amazing tool when you are new to a function. As you click in each argument box, help appears at the bottom of the window, with specifics on that argument.

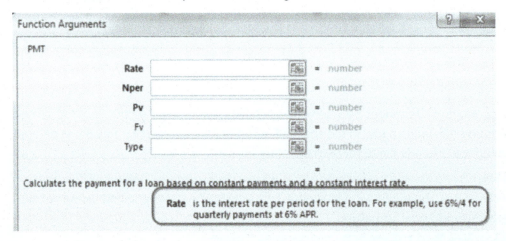

Personally, I could never get the PMT function to work correctly because I always forgot that the rate had to be the interest rate per period. Instead of pointing to the 5.25% in B3, you have to point to B3/12. Below, the help for Nper explains that it is the total number of payments for the loan, also known as the term, from B2.

PV is the loan amount. Since I never write a check for negative $493, I want the answer from PMT to be positive instead of negative. That is why I always use –B1 for the PV argument. If you use B1 instead, you will get the correct $493.54065 answer, but it will appear as negative in your worksheet. Think of the original $25,995 as money leaving the bank; that is why the PV is negative.

Notice in the above figure that three argument names are bold. These are the required arguments. Once you finish the required arguments, the Function Arguments dialog shows you the answer in two places. I always use this as a sanity check. Does this answer sound like a typical car payment?

This one topic really covered three things: how to calculate a loan payment, how to use the *fx* icon to discover new functions, and how to use the Function Arguments dialog to get help on any function.

If you are in a situation where you remember the function name but still want to use the Function Arguments dialog, type =PMT(with the opening parenthesis and then press Ctrl+A. If you press Ctrl+Shift+A, Excel will insert the names of the arguments into the formula.

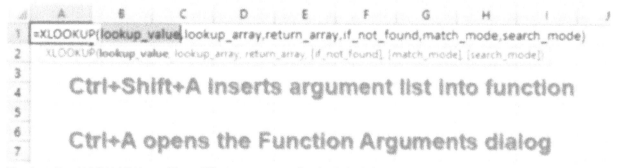

Thanks to Excel MVP Nabil Mourad from OfficeInstructor.com for the Ctrl+Shift+A technique.

4

#79 Use Function Arguments for Nested Functions

The Function Arguments dialog shown above is cool, but in real life, when you have to nest functions, how would you use this dialog? Say that you want to build a formula to do a two-way lookup:

```
=INDEX(B2:E16,MATCH(G2,A2:A16,0),MATCH(H2,B1:E1,0))
```

	A	B	C	D	E	F	G	H	I
1		Jan	Feb	Mar	Apr		Acct	Month	Result
2	C221	4	6	8	10		E106	Apr	20
3	C236	6	9	12	15				
4	E106	8	12	16	20				
5	C116	10	15	20	25				

You would start out using the Function Arguments dialog box for INDEX. In the Row_num argument box, type MATCH(. Using the mouse, go up to the formula bar and click anywhere inside the word MATCH.

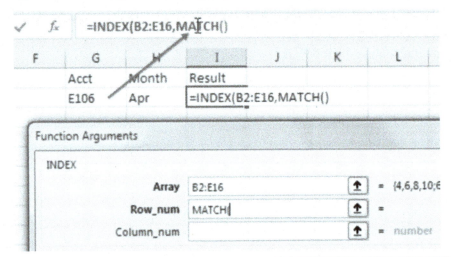

Caution: Don't click the formula in the cell. You have to click the formula in the formula bar.

The Function Arguments dialog switches over to MATCH. When you are finished building the MATCH function, go up to the formula bar and click anywhere in the word INDEX.

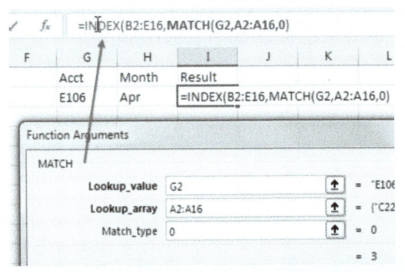

Repeat these steps to build the MATCH in the third argument of INDEX. Make sure to click back in the word INDEX in the formula bar when you are done with the second MATCH.

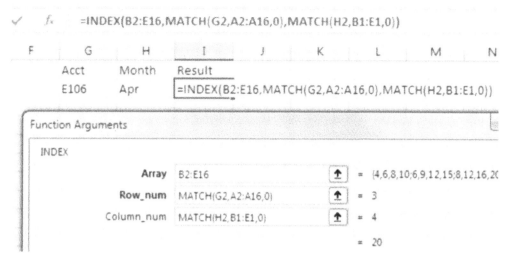

It turns out that the Function Arguments dialog can be fooled into building an invalid function. Type a well-formed but nonsensical function in the formula bar. Using the mouse, click inside the fake function name in the formula bar and click the fx icon.

Thanks to Tony DeJonker, Cat Parkinson, & Geoff in Huntsville for suggesting the Function Arguments dialog trick.

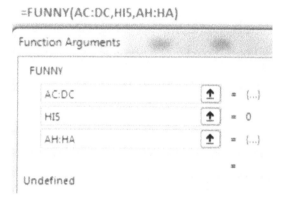

#80 Calculate Nonstandard Work Weeks

In my live Power Excel seminars, I show how to right-click the Fill Handle, drag a date, and then choose Fill Weekdays. This fills Monday through Friday dates. I ask the audience, "How many of you work Monday through Friday?" A lot of hands go up. I say, "That's great. For everyone else, Microsoft clearly doesn't care about you." Laughter.

It certainly seems that if you work anything other than Monday through Friday or have a year ending any day other than December 31, a lot of things in Excel don't work very well. However, two functions in Excel show that the Excel team does care about people who work odd work weeks: NETWORKDAYS.INTL and WORKDAY.INTL.

But let's start with their original Monday–Friday antecedents. The following figure shows a start date in column B and an end date in column C. If you subtract =C5-B5, you will get the number of days between the two dates. To figure out the number of weekdays, you use =NETWORKDAYS(B2,C2).

E2				fx	=NETWORKDAYS(B2,C2)

	A	B	C	D	E
1	Name	Start	End	Days	Work Days
2	Aaron Culbertson	5/1/2024	5/9/2024	8	7
3	Celine Loos	5/1/2024	5/16/2024	15	12
4	Rob Collie	5/1/2024	6/1/2024	31	23
5	Mike Dolan Fliss	5/1/2024	6/12/2024	42	31
6	Cecelia Rieb	5/1/2024	7/17/2024	77	56
7	Todd A Lesko	5/1/2024	7/28/2024	88	63
8	Micheal Reynolds	5/1/2024	8/14/2024	105	76

Note: If you subtract Monday August 14 from Friday August 18, Excel will tell you that there are 4 days between the two dates. Excel does not count the end date. But, NETWORKDAYS counts both the first and last date in the range.

It gets even better. NETWORKDAYS allows for an optional third argument where you specify work holidays. In the next figure, the list of holidays in H2:H13 allows the Work Days Less Holidays calculation in column F.

F2		f_x	=NETWORKDAYS(B2,C2,$H$2:$H$13)				
	B	C	D	E	F	G	H
1	Start	End	Days	Work Days	Work Days less Holidays		Holidays
2	5/1/2024	5/9/2024	8	7	7		5/27/2024
3	5/1/2024	5/16/2024	15	12	12		6/19/2024
4	5/1/2024	6/1/2024	31	23	22		7/4/2024
5	5/1/2024	6/12/2024	42	31	30		9/2/2024
6	5/1/2024	7/17/2024	77	56	53		10/14/2024
7	5/1/2024	7/28/2024	88	63	60		11/11/2024

In Excel 2007, Microsoft added INTL versions of both functions with a new Weekend argument. This argument allowed for any two consecutive days as the weekend and also allowed for a one-day weekend.

Working Saturdays

Work Days less Holidays		
8	=NETWORKDAYS.INTL(B4,C4,11	
15	NETWORKDAYS.INTL(start_date, end_date, [weekend], [holidays])	
31	27	(...) 2 - Sunday, Monday
42	36	(...) 3 - Monday, Tuesday
77	64	(...) 4 - Tuesday, Wednesday
88	73	(...) 5 - Wednesday, Thursday
105	88	(...) 6 - Thursday, Friday
155	130	(...) 7 - Friday, Saturday
185	155	(...) 11 - Sunday only
		(...) 12 - Monday only
		(...) 13 - Tuesday only

However, there are still cases where the weekend does not meet any of the 14 weekend definitions added in Excel 2007.

For example, in northeast Ohio, the Hartville Marketplace is open Monday, Thursday, Friday, and Saturday. That means their weekend is Tuesday, Wednesday, and Sunday.

Starting in Excel 2010, in addition to using 1-7 or 11-17 as the weekend argument, you can pass 7-digit binary text to indicate whether a company is open or closed on a particular day. It seems a bit unusual, but you use a 1 to indicate that the store is closed for the weekend and a 0 to indicate that the store is open. After all, 1 normally means On and 0 normally means Off. But the name of the argument is Weekend, so 1 means it is a day off, and 0 means you don't have the day off.

Thus, for the Monday, Thursday, Friday, Saturday schedule at the Hartville Marketplace, you would use "0110001". Every time I type one of these text strings, I have to silently say in my head, "Monday, Tuesday, Wednesday…" as I type each digit.

Marion Coblentz at the Hartville Marketplace could use the following formula to figure out how many Marketplace days there are between two dates.

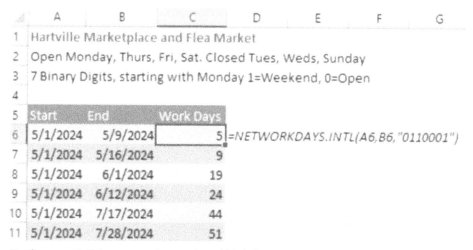

By the way, I did not use the optional Holidays argument above because Memorial Day, July 4, and Labor Day are the biggest customer days in Hartville.

If you are ever in northeastern Ohio, you need to stop by Hartville to see the 100% American-Made house inside of the Hartville Hardware and to try the great food at the Hartville Kitchen.

Bonus Tip: Use WORKDAY.INTL for a Work Calendar

While NETWORKDAYS calculates the work days between two dates, the WORKDAY function takes a starting date and a number of days, and it calculates the date that is a certain number of work days away.

One common use is to calculate the next work day. In the following figure, the start date is the date on the previous row. The number of days is always 1. To generate a class schedule that meets on Monday, Wednesday, and Friday, specify a weekend of "0101011".

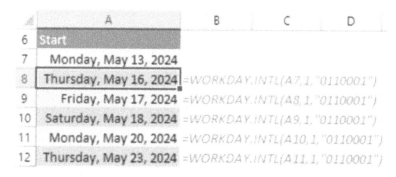

4

#81 Turn Data Sideways with a Formula

Someone built this lookup table sideways, stretching across C1:N2. I realize that I could use HLOOKUP instead of VLOOKUP, but I prefer to turn the data back to a vertical orientation.

Copy C1:N2. Right-click in A4 and choose the Transpose option under the Paste Options. Transpose is the fancy Excel word for "turn the data sideways."

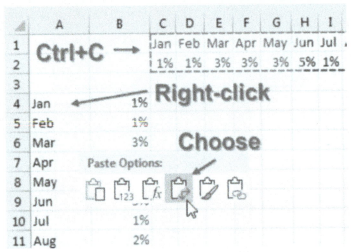

I transpose a lot. But I use Alt+E, S, E, Enter to transpose instead of the right-click.

There is a problem, though. Transpose is a one-time snapshot of the data. What if you have formulas in the horizontal data? Is there a way to transpose with a formula? Yes, using the TRANSPOSE function. In the following image, use =TRANSPOSE(C2:N2). The new =WRAPCOLS(C2:N2,1) will also produce the same result.

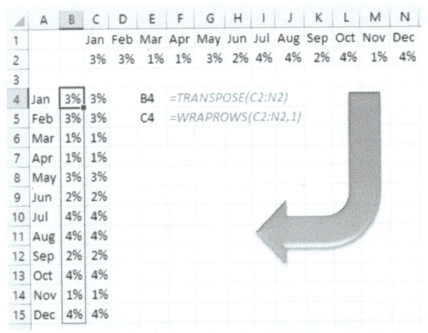

If you don't have Microsoft 365 and you don't have access to the dynamic array formulas, you can use a combination of INDEX and ROW, as shown in the figure below. =ROW(1:1) is a clever way of writing the number 1. As you copy this formula down, the row reference changes to 2:2 and returns a 2.

The INDEX function says you are getting the answers from C2:N2, and you want the *n*th item from the range.

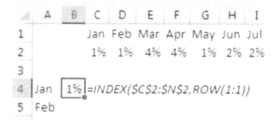

Bonus Tip: Protect Rows with an Old-Style Array Formula

Here is an odd use for an array formula: Say that you don't want anyone to delete or insert any rows in one section of a worksheet. Scroll far to the right, off the screen, and build an array in those rows. Select Z1:Z9. Type =2 and press Ctrl+Shift+Enter. You can use any number, =0, =1, =2, and so on.

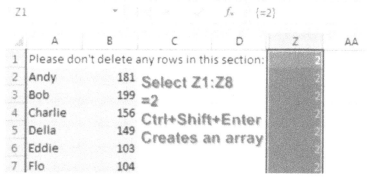

If someone tries to delete a row, Excel prevents it and shows a cryptic message about arrays, shown below.

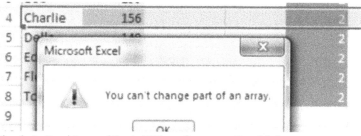

Thanks to Excel Ace and Tracia Williams for suggesting this feature.

#82 Handle Multiple Conditions in IF

4

When you need to do a conditional calculation, the IF function is the answer. It works like this: If <something is true>, then <this formula>; otherwise <that formula>. In the following figure, a simple IF calculates a bonus for your sales of more than $20,000.

D4		f_x	=IF(B4>=20000,0.02*B4,0)	

	A	B	C	D	E
1	Pay a 2% bonus for sales > 20000				
2					
3	Sales Rep	Revenue	GP%	Bonus	
4	Richard B Lanza	22810	45.9%	456.2	
5	David Haggarty	2257	54.0%	0	
6	Anthony J. LoBello Jr.	18552	46.3%	0	
7	Jon Higbed	9152	50.5%	0	
8	David Colman	8456	46.1%	0	
9	Eddie Stephen	21730	54.4%	434.6	

But what happens when two conditions need to be met? Most people will nest one IF statement inside another, as shown below:

But this nesting gets out of hand if you have many conditions that have to be met. Use the AND function to shorten and simplify the formula. =AND(Test,Test,Test,Test) is True only if all of the logical tests evaluate to True. The following example shows a shorter formula with the same results.

	A	B	C	D
1	Bonus for sales > 20000 + GP%>50%			
2	=IF(AND(B4>20000,C4>0.5),0.02*B4,0)			
3	Sales Rep	Revenue	GP%	Bonus
4	Richard B Lanza	22810	45.9%	0
5	David Haggarty	2257	54.0%	0
6	Anthony J. LoBello Jr.	18552	46.3%	0
7	Jon Higbed	9152	50.5%	0
8	David Colman	8456	46.1%	0
9	Eddie Stephen	21730	54.4%	434.6
10	Mike excelisfun Girvii	16416	48.2%	0

If you like AND, you might find a use for OR and NOT. =OR(Test,Test,Test,Test) is True if any one of the logical tests are True. NOT reverses an answer, so =NOT(True) is False, and =NOT(False) is True. If you ever have to do something fancy like a NAND, you can use NOT(AND(Test,Test,Test,Test)).

Caution: Although Excel 2013 introduced XOR as an Exclusive Or, it does not work the way that accountants would expect. =XOR(True,False,True,True) is True for reasons that are too complicated to explain here. XOR counts whether you have an odd number of True values. Odd. Really odd.

Bonus Tip: Use Boolean Logic

I always cover IF in my seminars. And I always ask how people would solve the two-conditions problem. The results are often the same: 70–80% of people use nested IF, and 20–30% use AND. Just one time, in Virginia, a person from Price Waterhouse offered the formula shown below:

	A	B	C	D
1	Bonus for sales > 20000 + GP%>50%			
2	=B4*0.02*(B4>20000)*(C4>0.5)			
3	Sales Rep	Revenue	GP%	Bonus
4	Richard B Lanza	22810	45.9%	0
5	David Haggarty	2257	54.0%	0
6	Anthony J. LoBello Jr.	18552	46.3%	0
7	Jon Higbed	9152	50.5%	0
8	David Colman	8456	46.1%	0
9	Eddie Stephen	21730	54.4%	434.6
10	Mike excelisfun Girvii	16416	48.2%	0

It works. It gives the same answer as the other formulas. Calculate the bonus .02*B4. But then multiply that bonus by logical tests in parentheses. When you force Excel to multiply a number by True or False, the True becomes 1, and the False becomes 0. Any number times 1 is itself. Any number times 0 is 0. Multiplying the bonus by the conditions ensures that only rows that meet both conditions are paid.

It is cool. It works. But it seems confusing when you first see it. My joke in my seminar is, "If you are leaving your job next month and you hate your co-workers, start using this formula."

#83 Pattern Matching with RegEx

RegEx—short for Regular Expressions—has arrived in Excel. It unlocks a whole new level of pattern-matching possibilities. If you've ever used RegEx in programming, Python, JavaScript, or even Adobe InDesign (where they call it GREP), you know how powerful it is. Now we have it built right into the grid—with three new functions, and integration into XLOOKUP and XMATCH.

Meet the New RegEx Functions

Excel adds three new worksheet functions:

- REGEXTEST(text, pattern)
- REGEXEXTRACT(text, pattern, [return_mode], [match_mode])
- REGEXREPLACE(text, pattern, replacement, [match_mode])

REGEXTEST — Does it match? Want to know if a cell contains a digit? Use:

```
=REGEXTEST(A2, "\d")
```

It returns `TRUE` if the pattern is found. Combine with `FILTER` to return rows with matching patterns.

	A	B	C	D
2	**Test for a pattern of characters**			
3	=REGEXTEST(text,pattern,case_sensitivity)			
4				
5		Text	=REGEXTEST(B6,"[0-9]")	
6		12 Apples	TRUE	
7		Six Bananas	FALSE	
8		39 Cherries	TRUE	
9		101 Dalmations	TRUE	
10		Too many Schnauzers	FALSE	
11		2 Mini Schnauzers	TRUE	
12		23 Skidoo	TRUE	
13		Beverly Hills 90210	TRUE	

REGEXEXTRACT — Pull specific data from a match. Need to pull out the first number from a string?

```
=REGEXEXTRACT(A2, "\d+")
```

Here, `\d` means a digit, and `+` means one or more digits.

Want to extract two different parts from a string like "1280x720"? Use parentheses to define capture groups:

```
=REGEXEXTRACT(A2, "(\d+)x(\d+)", 2)
```

Set return_mode to 2 for "capture all groups."

B4			fx	=REGEXEXTRACT(A4,$B$3,2)	
	A		**B**	**C**	
1	Returning Two Groups				
2			=REGEXEXTRACT(A4,$B$3,2)		
3			(\d+)x(\d+)		
4	This monitor is 1280x720		1280	720	
5	The resolution size 1920x1600		1920	1600	
6	Projector supports 1024x768		1024	768	

REGEXREPLACE — Obscure or clean up text. Let's say you need to mask part of a Social Security Number:

=REGEXREPLACE(A2, "\d{3}-\d{2}", "***-**")

	A	**B**	**C**	**D**	**E**
1	Fake Data	\d{3}-\d{2}			
2	551-52-4337	***-**-4337	=REGEXREPLACE(A2,$B$1,"***-**")		
3	404-87-8362	***-**-8362			
4	952-68-1275	***-**-1275			
5	916-12-3507	***-**-3507			

It's that easy to scrub sensitive data.

Bonus Tip: Learn the Basics of RegEx Patterns

You don't need to be a programmer to learn RegEx. Here's a crash course with Excel-specific examples:

Wildcards: `.` matches any character; `\.` matches a literal period.

Character sets: `[abc]` matches a, b, or c; `[A-Z]` matches any uppercase letter.

Start and end: ^the matches strings starting with "the"; `end$` matches strings ending with "end".

Quantifiers:

- `*` = zero or more
- `+` = one or more
- `?` = optional
- `{3}` = exactly three
- `{2,4}` = between two and four

Use `\d` for digits, `\w` for letters/digits, `\s` for any whitespace (including non-breaking spaces from web data), and capital versions (`\D`, `\W`, `\S`) for "not".

Bonus Tip: A Real-World Fix: Replace Non-breaking Spaces

Web-scraped data often includes invisible non-breaking spaces (ASCII 160). These mess up Excel's `TRIM()` function. Use this formula to clean them up. Save this one—it's worth gold when cleaning messy data.

```
=REGEXREPLACE(A2, "\s", " ")
```

Selective Extraction with Capture Groups

Want just the filename from a path like `"report.pdf"`?

```
=REGEXEXTRACT(A2, "(.*)(?=\.pdf)", 2)
```

Or maybe you want to split into filename and extension:

```
=REGEXEXTRACT(A2, "(.*)\.(xls[xm]?)", 2)
```

Use return_mode 2 to get both groups, and TRANSPOSE() if needed.

Bonus Tip: RegEx Now Works in XLOOKUP and XMATCH!

This takes XLOOKUP from powerful to *wildly flexible*. Use a new match mode option 3 for RegEx.

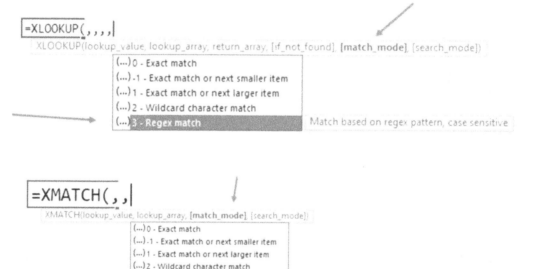

New Options for XLOOKUP and XMATCH

Example: You have a product and only the zip code, but not the full city/state. You want to find the correct record by matching partial zip patterns.

Create RegEx patterns dynamically. For example:

- Match Los Angeles zip codes (900xx to 918xx)
- Match San Diego zips (919xx or 92xxx)
- Build these with help from CHOOSE() or lookup tables

Use word boundaries (`\b`) and optional segments (`?`) to fine-tune the match. Even `zip+4` variations work.

> Tip: Excel's RegEx support is one of the most powerful updates in years. You can clean, extract, replace, and now even lookup using patterns. Yes, it's a new language to learn—but once you get the hang of it, you'll find it indispensable. And now that RegEx works inside XLOOKUP? You've got superpowers.

4

#84 Troubleshoot VLOOKUP

Until XLOOKUP replaced it, VLOOKUP was my favorite function in Excel. If you can use VLOOKUP, you can solve many problems in Excel. But there are things that can trip up a VLOOKUP. This topic talks about a few of them.

But first, the basics of VLOOKUP in plain English.

The data in A:C came from the IT department. You asked for sales by item and date. They gave you item number. You need the item description. Rather than wait for the IT department to rerun the data, you find the table shown in column F:G.

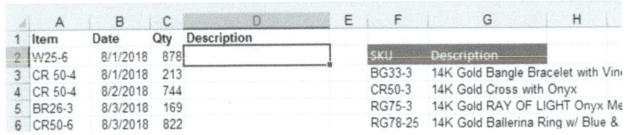

You want VLOOKUP to find the item in A2 while it searches through the first column of the table in $F$3:$G$30. When VLOOKUP finds the match in F7, you want VLOOKUP to return the description found in the second column of the table. Every VLOOKUP that is looking for an exact match has to end in False (or zero, which is equivalent to False). The formula below is set up properly.

| D2 | | | | f_x | =VLOOKUP(A2,$F$3:$G$30,2,FALSE) | |

	A	B	C	D	E	F
1	Item	Date	Qty	Description		
2	W25-6	8/1/2018	878	18K Italian Gold Women's Watch		SKU	Descri
3	CR 50-4	8/1/2018	213	14K Gold Onyx Cross		BG33-3	14K G
4	CR 50-4	8/2/2018	744	14K Gold Onyx Cross		CR50-3	14K G
5	BR26-3	8/3/2018	169	18K Italian Gold Men's Bracelet		RG75-3	14K G

Notice that you use F4 to add four dollar signs to the address for the lookup table. As you copy the formula down column D, you need the address for the lookup table to remain constant. There are two common alternatives: You could specify the entire columns F:G as the lookup table. Or, you could name F3:G30 with a name such as ItemTable. If you use =VLOOKUP(A2,ItemTable,2,False), the named range acts like an absolute reference.

Any time you do a bunch of VLOOKUPs, you need to sort the column of VLOOKUPs. Sort ZA, and any #N/A errors come to the top. In this case, there is one. Item BG33-9 is missing from the lookup table. Maybe it is a typo. Maybe it is a brand-new item. If it is new, insert a new row anywhere in the middle of your lookup table and add the new item.

	A	B	C	Sort ZA	E	F
1	Item	Date	Qty	Description		
2	BG33-9	8/19/2018	37	#N/A		SKU
3	W25-6	8/1/2018	878	18K Italian Gold Women's Watch		BG33-3
4	W25-6	8/21/2018	254	18K Italian Gold Women's Watch		CR50-3
5	W25-6	8/22/2018	832	18K Italian Gold Women's Watch		RG75-3
6	W25-6	8/29/2018	581	18K Italian Gold Women's Watch		RG78-25
7	BR26-3	8/3/2018	169	18K Italian Gold Men's Bracelet		W25-6
8	BR26-3	8/5/2018	541	18K Italian Gold Men's Bracelet		BR26-3
9	BR26-3	8/6/2018	849	18K Italian Gold Men's Bracelet		BR15-3
10	BR26-3	8/10/2018	881	18K Italian Gold Men's Bracelet		BG33-8
11	BR26-3	8/12/2018	737	18K Italian Gold Men's Bracelet		BG33-17

It is fairly normal to have a few #N/A errors. But in the figure below, exactly the same formula is returning nothing but #N/A. When this happens, see if you can solve the first VLOOKUP. You are looking up the BG33-8 found in A2. Start cruising down through the first column of the lookup table. As you can see, the matching value clearly is in F10. Why can you see this, but Excel cannot see it?

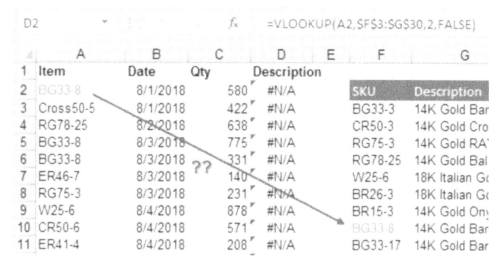

Go to each cell and press the F2 key. This figure shows F10 in Edit mode. Note that the insertion cursor appears right after the 8.

This figure shows cell A2 in Edit mode. The insertion cursor is a couple of spaces away from the 8. This is a sign that at some point, this data was stored in an old COBOL data set. Back in COBOL, if the Item field was defined as 10 characters and you typed only 6 characters, COBOL would pad it with 4 extra spaces.

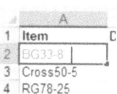

The solution? See "#61 Clean Data with Copilot" on page 132. Or, use look up TRIM(A2).

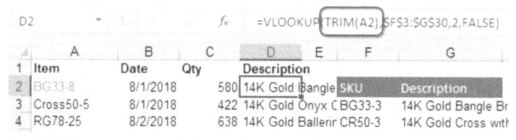

The TRIM() function removes leading and trailing spaces. If you have multiple spaces between words, TRIM converts them to a single space. In the figure below there are spaces before and after both names in A1. =TRIM(A1) removes all but one space in A3.

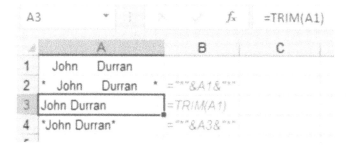

4

By the way, what if the problem had been trailing spaces in column F instead of column A? Add a column of TRIM() functions to E, pointing to column F. Copy those and paste as values in F to make the lookups start working again.

The other very common reason that VLOOKUP won't work is shown here. Column F contains real numbers. Column A holds text that looks like numbers.

Select all of column A. Press Alt+D, E, F. This does a default Text to Columns operation and converts all text numbers to real numbers. The lookup starts working again.

If you want the VLOOKUP to work without changing the data, you can use =VLOOKUP(1*A2,...) to handle numbers stored as text or =VLOOKUP(A2&"",...) when your lookup table has text numbers.

#85 Use a Wildcard in VLOOKUP or XLOOKUP

You can use a wildcard in VLOOKUP or XLOOKUP. If you aren't sure if your lookup table will contain Apple, Apple Computer, or Apple Computer Inc, you can use =VLOOKUP("Apple*",Table,2,False), and Excel will find the first item in the lookup table that starts with Apple. For XLOOKUP, you have to explicitly ask for a wildcard searching using a 2 as the 5th argument =XLOOKUP("Apple*",A,B,,2) (Thanks to -Khalif John Clark)

Bonus Tip: VLOOKUP to Two Tables

You want to try to find a match in Table1. If a match is not found, then do a lookup to Table2. You can use =IFNA(Formula,Value if NA). =IFNA(VLOOKUP(A2,Table1,3,False),VLOOKUP(A2,Table2,3,False)). With XLOOKUP, the IF_NA is the 4th argument so =XLOOKUP(A2,A,B,XLOOKUP(A2,C,D)).

VLOOKUP was suggested by Rod Apfelbeck, Patty Hahn, John Henning, @ExcelKOS, and @tomatecaolho. Thanks to all of you.

#86 Twelve Benefits of XLOOKUP

The new XLOOKUP function is rolled out to Microsoft 365 starting in November 2019. Joe McDaid of the Excel team designed XLOOKUP to unify the people who use VLOOKUP and the people who use INDEX/MATCH. This section will discuss the 12 benefits of XLOOKUP:

1. Exact match is the default.

2. Integer-based third argument of VLOOKUP is now a proper reference.

3. IFNA is built-in to handle missing values.

4. XLOOKUP has no problem going to the left.

5. Find next-smaller or next-larger match without sorting the table.

6. XLOOKUP can do HLOOKUP.

7. Find the last match by searching from the bottom.

8. Wildcards are "off" by default, but you can enable them, or switch to RegEx.

9. Return all 12 months in a single formula.

10. Can return a cell reference if the XLOOKUP is next to a colon such as XLOOKUP():XLOOKUP()

11. Can do a two-way match like INDEX(,MATCH,MATCH) can do.

12. Can sum all lookups in a single formula like LOOKUP could do.

Here is the syntax:

=XLOOKUP(Lookup_Value, Lookup_Array, Results_Array, [if_not_found], {match_mode}, [search_mode]).

XLOOKUP Benefit 1: Exact Match by Default

99% of my VLOOKUP formulas end in ,FALSE or ,0 to indicate an exact match. If you always use the exact match version of VLOOKUP, you can start leaving the match_mode off of your XLOOKUP function.

In the following figure, you are looking up W25-6 from cell A4. You want to look for that item in L8:L35. When it is found, you want the corresponding price from column N. There is no need to specify False as the match_mode because XLOOKUP defaults to an exact match.

	A	B	C	D	K	L	M	N	O
1	**XLOOKUP Benefit #1: Exact Match is Automatic**								
2						where to look		what to return	
3	Item	Date	Qty	Price					
4	W25-6	8/1/2019	878	=XLOOKUP(A4,$L$8:$L$35,$N$8:$N$35)					
5	CR 50-4	8/1/2019	213	14.95					
6	CR 50-4	8/2/2019	744	14.95					
7	BR26-3	8/3/2019	169	39.95		SKU	Description	Price	Category
8	CR50-6	8/3/2019	822	19.95		BG33-3	14K Gold Bangle Bracelet	29.95	Wrist
9	ER46-14	8/3/2019	740	15.95		CR50-3	14K Gold Cross with Ony	19.95	Charm
10	RG78-25	8/3/2019	638	89.95		RG75-3	14K Gold RAY OF LIGHT	79.95	Ring
11	BR15-3	8/4/2019	817	39.95		RG78-25	14K Gold Ballerina Ring w	89.95	Ring
12	Cross50-5	8/4/2019	871	19.95		W25-6	18K Italian Gold Women's	69.95	Wrist
13	CR50-2	8/4/2019	686	14.95		BR26-3	18K Italian Gold Men's Br	39.95	Wrist
14	BR26-3	8/5/2019	541	39.95		BR15-3	14K Gold Onyx Men's Bra	39.95	Wrist
15	ER41-4	8/5/2019	208	15.95		BG33-8	14K Gold Bangle Bracelet	39.95	Wrist

4

XLOOKUP Benefit 2: the Results_Array is a reference instead of an integer

Think about the VLOOKUP formula that you would use before XLOOKUP. The third argument would've been a 3 to indicate that you wanted to return the 3rd column. There was always a danger that a clueless co-worker would've inserted (or deleted) a column in your table. With an extra column in the table, the VLOOKUP that had been returning a price would start returning a description. Because XLOOKUP was pointing to a cell reference, the formula rewrites itself to keep pointing to the price that is now in column O.

	A	B	C	D	K	L	M	N	O	P
2						=VLOOKUP(A4,L8:P35,3,FALSE) **breaks!**				
3	Item	Date	Qty	Price		18K Italian Gold Women's Watch				
4	W25-6	8/1/2019	878	=XLOOKUP(A4,$L$8:$L$35,$O$8:$O$35)				**keeps**		
5	CR 50-4	8/1/2019	213	14.95						
6	CR 50-4	8/2/2019	744	14.95				**working!**		
7	BR26-3	8/3/2019	169	39.95		SKU		Description	Price	Category
8	CR50-6	8/3/2019	822	19.95		BG33-3		14K Gold Bar	29.95	Wrist
9	ER46-14	8/3/2019	740	15.95		CR50-3	x	14K Gold Cro	19.95	Charm
10	RG78-25	8/3/2019	638	89.95		RG75-3		14K Gold RA	79.95	Ring
11	BR15-3	8/4/2019	817	39.95		RG78-25	x	14K Gold Bal	89.95	Ring

XLOOKUP Benefit 3: IFNA is built in as an optional argument

The dreaded #N/A error is returned when your lookup value is not found in the table. In the past, to replace #N/A with something else, you would have to use IFERROR or IFNA wrapped around the VLOOKUP.

	A	B	C	D
3	Item	Date	Qty	Price
4	W25-6	8/1/2019	878	69.95
5	CR 50-4	8/1/2019	213	14.95
6	X999	8/2/2019	744	#N/A
7	BR26-3	8/3/2019	169	39.95
8	CR50-6	8/3/2019	822	19.95
9	ER46-14	8/3/2019	740	15.95
10	X999	8/3/2019	638	#N/A

Thanks to a suggestion from Rico S. on my YouTube channel, the Excel team incorporated an optional fourth argument for if_not_found. If you want to replace those #N/A errors with zero, simply add ,0 as the fourth argument. Or, you could use some text, such as "Value not found".

| MID | ▼ | : | × | ✓ | f_x | =XLOOKUP(A4,$L$8:$L$35,$N$8:$N$35,0 |

	A	B	C	D	K	L	M
3	Item	Date	Qty	Price			
4	W25-6	8/1/2019	878	=XLOOKUP(A4,$L$8:$L$35,$N$8:$N$35,0			
5		XLOOKUP(lookup_value, lookup_array, return_array, [if_not_found], [match_mode], [search_mode])					
6	X999	8/2/2019	744	0			
7	BR26-3	8/3/2019	169	39.95		SKU	Description
8	CR50-6	8/3/2019	822	19.95		BG33-3	14K Gold Bangle Brace
9	ER46-14	8/3/2019	740	15.95		CR50-3	14K Gold Cross with Or
10	X999	8/3/2019	638	0		RG75-3	14K Gold RAY OF LIGH
11	BR15-3	8/4/2019	817	39.95		RG78-25	14K Gold Ballerina Ring

XLOOKUP Benefit 4: No problem looking to the left of the key field

VLOOKUP can not look to the left of the key field without resorting to VLOOKUP(A4, CHOOSE({1,2}, G7:G34,F7:F34),2,False). With XLOOKUP, there is no problem having the Results_array to the left of the Lookup_array.

⬚	A	B	C	D	E	F	G
3	Item	Date	Qty	Category?			
4	W25-6	8/1/2019	878	=XLOOKUP(A4,$G$7:$G$34,$F$7:$F$34)			
5	CR 50-4	8/1/2019	213	Charm			
6	CR 50-4	8/2/2019	744	Charm		Category	Item
7	BR26-3	8/3/2019	169	Wrist		Wrist	BG33-3
8	CR50-6	8/3/2019	822	Charm		Charm	CR50-3

XLOOKUP Benefit 5: Next-smaller or next-larger match without sorting

By default, XLOOKUP looks for an exact match. Using the 5th argument for match_mode allows you to look for the exact value or just smaller or the exact value or just larger.

Before XLOOKUP, VLOOKUP was able to do the just smaller. For just larger, you had to use MATCH. But both of those obsolete functions required the lookup table to be sorted. With XLOOKUP, the table does not have to be sorted.

XLOOKUP's optional fifth argument match_mode uses these values:

- -1 finds the value equal to or just smaller
- 0 find an exact match
- 1 finds the value equal to or just larger.
  Caution: The 1 and -1 here are opposite of MATCH. These make more sense than MATCH.

Below, a match_mode of -1 find the next-smaller item.

⬚	Amount	Bonus				Reservation	Passengers	Recon
ole	12835	=XLOOKUP(C4,$F$7 $F$11,$G$7 $G$11,,-1					2	Car
ly	19634	XLOOKUP(lookup_value, lookup_array, return_array, [if_not_found], [match_mode], [search_m						
ole	898	0		Sale	Bonus			
:tor	7747	5		0	0			
ly	6239	5		5000	5			
y	19867	12		10000	12	A100	2 Car	
ly	27537	100		20000	50	A107	20 Bus	
e	679	0		25000	100	A108	40 Bus	
	24240	50				A100	12 Tour V	

Match mode dropdown shown:
- 0 - Exact match
- -1 - Exact match or next smaller item
- 1 - Exact match or next larger item
- 2 - Wildcard character match

Here, a match_mode of 1, finds what vehicle is needed depending on the number of people in the party. Note that the lookup table is not sorted by passengers and the vehicle name is to the left of the key.

⬚	I	J	K	L	M	N
3	Reservation	Passengers	Recommended			
4	A101	2	=XLOOKUP(J4,$N$6 $N$10,$M$6 $M$10,,1)			
5	A102	5	Van		Vehicle	Capacity
6	A103	12	Tour Van		Bus	64
7	A104	1	Motorcycle		Car	4
8	A105	11	Tour Van		Motorcycle	1
9	A106	2	Car		Tour Van	12
10	A107	20	Bus		Van	6
11	A108	40	Bus			
12	A109	12	Tour Van			

XLOOKUP Benefit 6: Sideways XLOOKUP replaces HLOOKUP

The lookup_array and results_array can be horizontal with XLOOKUP, making it simple to replace HLOOKUP.

⊿	A	B	C	D	E	F	G	H	I
3						Jan	Feb	Mar	Apr
4	Item	Month	Sales	Bonus		1.5%	2.4%	3.0%	1.2%
5	BG33-8	Jan	17753	=XLOOKUP(B5,$F$3:$Q$3,$F$4:$Q$4)					
6	Cross50-5	Feb	16500	2.4%					
7	RG78-25	Mar	26648	3.0%					
8	BG33-8	Oct	10564	1.6%					

XLOOKUP Benefit 7: Search from the bottom for latest match

I have an old video on YouTube answering a question from a British horse farm. They had a fleet of vehicles. Every time a vehicle came in for fuel or service, they logged vehicle, date, and mileage in a spreadsheet. They wanted to find the latest known mileage for each vehicle. While the Excel-2017 era MAXIFS might solve this today, the solution many years ago was an arcane formula using LOOKUP and involved division by zero.

Today, XLOOKUP's optional sixth argument lets you specify that the search should start from the bottom of the data set.

F6	▼ : ⤫ ✓	fx	=XLOOKUP(E6,$A$4:$A$18,$C$4:$C$18,,,-1)			

⊿	A	B	C	D	E	F	G
3	Vehicle	Date	Mileage				
4	Red Ford Truck	1/3/22	80020		Find the latest mileage reading		
5	Blue Chevy Truck	1/22/22	70210				
6	Black Van	4/3/22	30920		Red Ford Truck	83250	
7	Red Ford Truck	4/27/22	81160		Blue Chevy Truck	73350	
8	Blue Chevy Truck	5/2/22	71210		Black Van	32220	
9	Red Ford Truck	5/14/22	81330				
10	Black Van	5/15/22	31340				
11	Red Ford Truck	5/21/22	81400		1 - Search first-to-last		
12	Black Van	6/15/22	31650		-1 - Search last-to-first		
13	Blue Chevy Truck	6/24/22	71740		2 - Binary search (sorted ascending order)		
14	Black Van	7/19/22	31990		-2 - Binary search (sorted descending order)		
15	Black Van	8/11/22	32220				
16	Blue Chevy Truck	8/29/22	72400				
17	Red Ford Truck	11/22/22	83250				
18	Blue Chevy Truck	12/2/22	73350				
19							

Note: While this is a great improvement, it only lets you find the first or last match. Some people hoped this would let you find the second or third match, but that is not the intention of the search_mode argument.

Caution: The figure above shows that there are search modes using the old binary search. Joe McDaid advises against using these. First, the improved lookup algorithm from 2018 is fast enough that there is no significant speed benefit. Second, you run the risk of a clueless co-worker sorting the lookup table and introducing wrong answers.

XLOOKUP Benefit 8: Wildcards are "turned off" by default

Most people did not realize that VLOOKUP is treating asterisk, question mark, and tilde as wildcard characters as described in "#85 Use a Wildcard in VLOOKUP or XLOOKUP" on page 176. With XLOOKUP, wildcards are turned off by default. If you want XLOOKUP to treat these characters as a wildcard, use 2 as the Match_Mode.

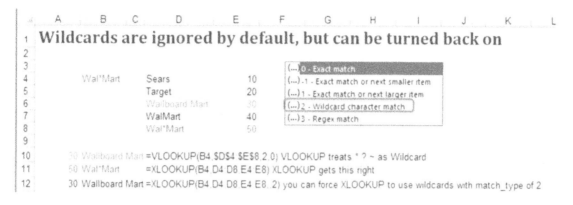

XLOOKUP Benefit 9: Return All 12 Months in a Single Formula!

This is really a benefit of Dynamic Arrays, but it is my favorite reason to love XLOOKUP. When you have to return all 12 months in a lookup, a single formula entered in B6 with a rectangular return_array will return multiple results. Those results will spill into adjacent cells.

In the figure below, a single formula entered in B7 returns all 12 answers shown in B7:M7.

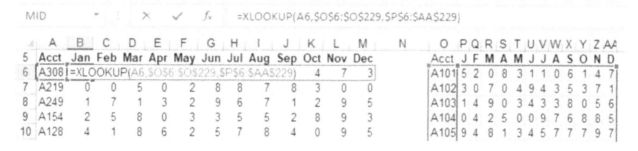

XLOOKUP Benefit 10: One Formula Performs All XLOOKUP

A single formula can perform an entire column of XLOOKUP. In the figure below, one formula in C4 replaces 11 XLOOKUP formulas. You can **not** combine benefit #9 and #10 to return many rows of many columns because Excel won't currently return an array of arrays..

C4   fx =XLOOKUP(B4:B14,E4:E12,F4:F12)

	A	B	C	D	E	F	G	H
1	**One formula performs all XLOOKUP**							
2								
3	Shift	Name	Rate		Name	Rate		
4	AM Manager	Ed	120		Barb	96		
5	AM Asst	Barb	96		Diane	72		
6	AM Grill	Kelly	80		Ed	120		
7	AM Grill	Jared	78		Flo	72		
8	AM Front	Gary	56		Gary	56		
9	AM Front	Flo	72		Hank	72		
10	PM Manager	Ed	120		Ike	70		
11	PM Grill	Diane	72		Jared	78		
12	PM Grill	Ike	70		Kelly	80		
13	PM Front	Gary	56					
14	PM Front	Hank	72					

Benefit 11: XLOOKUP Can Return a Cell Reference If Adjacent to Colon

This one is complex but beautiful. In the past, there were seven functions that would change from returning a cell value to returning a cell reference if the function was touching a colon. For an example, see "#113 Use A2:INDEX() as a Non-Volatile OFFSET" on page 217. XLOOKUP is the eighth function to offer this behavior, joining CHOOSE, IF, IFS, INDEX, INDIRECT, OFFSET, and SWITCH.

Consider the following figure. Someone select Cherry in E4 and Fig in E5. You want a formula that will sum everything from B6 to B9.

▲	A	B	C	D	E	F	G	H	I
4	Apple	5		From:	Cherry				
5	Banana	10		To:	Fig				
6	Cherry	15							
7	Date	20		90	=SUM(XLOOKUP(E4,A4:A29,B4:B29):XLOOKUP(E5,A4:A29,B4:B29))				
8	Elderberry	25							
9	Fig	30		15	=XLOOKUP(E4,A4:A29,B4:B29)				
10	Guava	35		30	=XLOOKUP(E5,A4:A29,B4:B29)				

In the figure above, you can see that an XLOOKUP of E4 will return the 15 from cell B6. An XLOOKUP of E5 will return the 30 from B9. However, if you take the two XLOOKUP functions from cells D9 and D10 and put them together with a colon in-between, the behavior of XLOOKUP changes. Instead of returning 15, the first XLOOKUP returns the cell address B6!

To prove this, I've selected D7 and use Formulas, Evaluate Formula. After pressing Evaluate two times, the next part to be calculated is XLOOKUP("Cherry",A4:A29,B4:B29), as shown here.

Evaluate Formula   ?

Reference: Evaluation:
Reference!$D$7   =   SUM(XLOOKUP("Cherry",A4:A29,B4:B29):XLOOKUP(E5,A4:A29,
                              B4:B29))

Press Evaluate again and amazingly, the XLOOKUP formula returns $B$6 instead of the 15 stored in B6. This happens because there is a colon immediately following this XLOOKUP formula.

Evaluation:
=   SUM($B$6:XLOOKUP(E5,A4:A29,B4:B29))

Press Evaluate two more times, and the interim formula will be =SUM(B6:B9).

▲	A	B	C	D	E	F	G
4	Apple	5		From:	Cherry		
5	Banana	10		To:	Fig		
6	Cherry	15					
7	Date	20		90	=SUM(XLOOKUP(E4,A4:A29,B4:B29		
8	Elderberry	25					
9	Fig	30		Evaluate Formula			
10	Guava	35		Reference:		Evaluation:	
11	Honeydew	40		Reference!$D$7	=	SUM($B$6:$B$9)	
12	Iceberg	45					

This is amazing behavior that most people don't know about. Excel MVP Charles Williams tells me that it can be triggered with any of these three operators next to XLOOKUP: Colon, Space (Intersection operator), or a Comma (Union operator).

For all of my VLOOKUP friends, the INDEX/MATCH people have been waiting to see if XLOOKUP can handle a two-way match. The great news: it can do it. The bad news: the methodology is a little different than the INDEX/MATCH fans would expect. It might be a little over their heads. But I am sure they can come around to this method.

For a two-way match, you want to find which row contains the account number A621 shown in J3. So, the XLOOKUP starts out easy enough: =XLOOKUP(J3,A5:A15. But then you have to provide a results_array. You can use the same trick as in "XLOOKUP Benefit 9: Return All 12 Months in a Single Formula!" on page 181, but use it to return a vertical vector. An inner XLOOKUP looks for the J4 month in the month headings in B4:G4. The return_array is specified as B5:G15. The result is that the inner XLOOKUP returns an array like the one shown in I10:I20 below. Since A621 is found in the fifth cell of the lookup_array and 104 is found in the fifth cell of the results_array, you get the correct answer from the formula. Below, J6 shows the old way. J7 returns the new way.

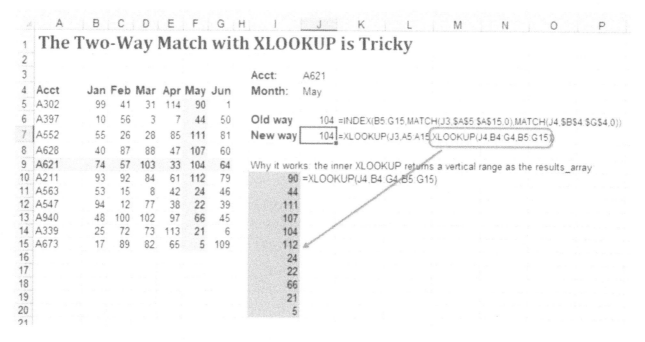

Bonus Tip: What about a Twisted LOOKUP?

Excel MVP Mike Girvin often shows a trick of the LOOKUP function where the Lookup_Vector is vertical and the Result_Vector is horizontal. XLOOKUP will not natively support this trick. But, if you cheat a little bit and wrap the results_array in the TRANSPOSE function, you can manage a twisted lookup.

#87 Preview What Remove Duplicates Will Remove

The Remove Duplicates tool added in Excel 2010 was a nice addition.

Data Tools

However, the tool **does** remove the duplicates. Sometimes, you might want to see the duplicates before you remove them. And the Home, Conditional Formatting, Highlight Cells, Duplicate Values marks both instances of Andy instead of just the one that will be removed. The solution is to create a conditional formatting rule using a formula. Select A2:B14. Home, Conditional Formatting, New Rule, Use a Formula. The formula should be: `=COUNTIF($A$1:$A1,$A2)>0`.

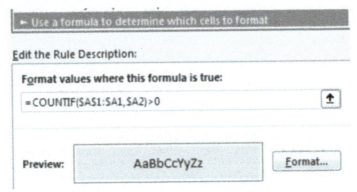

It is hard to visualize why this will work. Notice that there is a dollar sign missing from $A$1:$A1. This creates an expanding range. In English the formula says "Look at all of the values from A1 to A just above the current cell and see if they are equal to the current cell". Only cells that return >0 will be formatted.

I've added the formula to column C below so you can see how the range expands. In Row 5, the COUNTIF checks how many times Andy appears in A1:A4. Since there is one match, the cell is formatted.

	A	B	C
1	Name	Amount	Formula
2	Andy	36.80	=COUNTIF($A$1:$A1,$A2)>0
3	Barb	36.90	=COUNTIF($A$1:$A2,$A3)>0
4	Chris	92.25	=COUNTIF($A$1:$A3,$A4)>0
5	Andy	85.15	=COUNTIF($A$1:$A4,$A5)>0
6	Diane	85.65	=COUNTIF($A$1:$A5,$A6)>0
7	Ed	78.35	=COUNTIF($A$1:$A6,$A7)>0
8	Chris	69.75	=COUNTIF($A$1:$A7,$A8)>0
9	Hank	62.90	=COUNTIF($A$1:$A8,$A9)>0
10	Gary	95.60	=COUNTIF($A$1:$A9,$A10)>0
11	Chris	47.25	=COUNTIF($A$1:$A10,$A11)>0
12	Flo	91.80	=COUNTIF($A$1:$A11,$A12)>0
13	Flo	94.35	=COUNTIF($A$1:$A12,$A13)>0
14	Hank	61.90	=COUNTIF($A$1:$A13,$A14)>0

#88 Replace Nested IFs with a Lookup Table

A long time ago, I worked for the vice president of sales at a company. I was always modeling some new bonus program or commission plan. I became pretty used to commission plans with all sorts of conditions. The one shown in this tip is pretty tame.

The normal approach is to start building a nested IF formula. You always start at either the high end or the low end of the range. "If sales are over $500K, then the discount is 20%; otherwise,...." The third argument of the IF function is a whole new IF function that tests for the second level: "If sales are over $250K, then the discount is 15%; otherwise,...."

These formulas get longer and longer as there are more levels. Once you get past a few levels, it is easier to move the logic to a lookup table.

Rather than use the nested IF function, try using the XLOOKUP function. In the formula below, all of the discount rules are shown in the table in E12:G18.

The Match_Mode argument with -1 will find the value just less than the search value. In the past with VLOOKUP and MATCH, your lookup table would have to be sorted. The following example shows that the XLOOKUP can perform an approximate match even if the table is not sorted.

Consider the table below. In cell C10, Excel will be looking for a match for $550,000 in the table. When it can't find 550,000, Excel will return the discount associated with the value that is just less—in this case, the 20% discount for the $500K level.

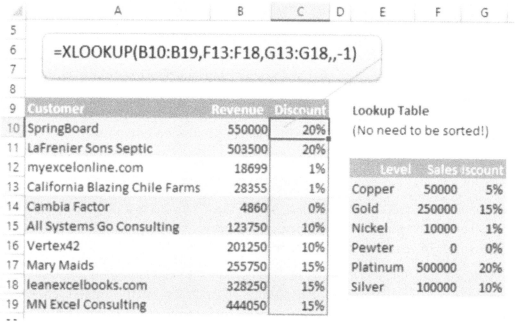

What if your manager wants a self-contained formula and does not want to see the bonus table off to the right? Select the C10 cell. Click in the formula bar and select the characters F13:F18. Press F9 and Excel will replace the cell reference with an array constant. Repeat for the characters G13:G18. Press Enter. You can now delete the lookup table.

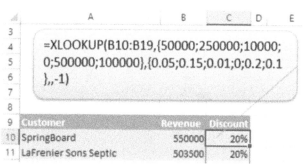

Bonus Tip: Match the Parentheses

Excel cycles through a variety of colors for each new level of parentheses. While Excel reuses the colors, it uses black only for the opening parenthesis and for the matching closing parenthesis. As you are finishing the formula below, just keep typing closing parentheses until you type a black parenthesis.

	A	B	C	D
1	Next Year Discount Level Rules			
2	Based on last year's revenue:			
3	Anyone over $500K: 20% discount		=IF(B10>500000,20%,	
4	Anyone over $250K: 15% discount		IF(B10>250000,15%,	
5	Anyone over $100K: 10% discount		IF(B10>100000,10%,	
6	Anyone over $50K: 5% discount		IF(B10>50000,5%,	
7	Anyone over $10K: 1% Discount		IF(B10>10000,1%,0)))))	
9	Customer	Revenue	Future Discount	
10	SpringBoard	550000	20%	
11	LaFrenier Sons Septic	503500	20%	

Tip: In Microsoft 365, you could use the following formula to solve the discount presented above:
=IFS(B10>500000,20%,B10>250000,15%,B10>100000,10%,B10>50000,5%,B10>10000,1%,TRUE,0)

Thanks to Mike Girvin for teaching me about the matching parentheses. The lookup table technique was suggested by Danny Mac, Boriana Petrova, Andreas Thehos, and @mvmcos.

#89 Suppress Errors with IFERROR

Formula errors are common. If you have a data set with hundreds of records, a divide-by-zero and an #N/A errors are bound to pop up now and then.

In the past, preventing errors required Herculean efforts. Nod your head knowingly if you've ever knocked out =IF(ISNA(VLOOKUP(A2,Table,2,0)),"Not Found",VLOOKUP(A2,Table,2,0)). Besides being really long to type, that solution requires twice as many VLOOKUPs. First, you do a VLOOKUP to see if the VLOOKUP is going to produce an error. Then you do the same VLOOKUP again to get the non-error result.

Excel 2010 introduced the greatly improved =IFERROR(Formula,Value If Error). I know that IFERROR sounds like the old ISERROR, ISERR, and ISNA functions, but it is completely different.

This is a brilliant function: =IFERROR(VLOOKUP(A2,Table,2,0),"Not Found"). If you have 1,000 VLOOKUPs and only 5 return #N/A, then the 995 that worked require only a single VLOOKUP. Only the 5 VLOOKUPs returned #N/A that need to move on to the second argument of IFERROR.

Oddly, Excel 2013 added the IFNA() function. It is just like IFERROR but only looks for #N/A errors. One might imagine a strange situation where the value in the lookup table is found, but the resulting answer is a division by 0. If you want to preserve the divide-by-zero error for some reason, you can use IFNA() to do this.

B4   =IFNA(VLOOKUP(A4,Table,4,0),"Not Found")

	A	B		D	E	F	G
1	Handle	Average					
2	Bluefeather8989	539		Handle	Qty	Revenue	Avg Price
3	MikeAsHimself	582		aBoBoBook	895	521785	583
4	MrExcel	#DIV/0!		Bluefeather8989	989	533071	539
5	ExcelisFun	Not Found		INDZARA	1124	611456	544
6	Bluefeather8989	539		Kazmdav	1019	507462	498
7	McGunigales	527		McGunigales	921	485367	527
8				MikeAsHimself	843	490626	582
9				MrExcel	0	0	#DIV/0!
10				Symons	972	562788	579

Of course, the person who built the lookup table should have used IFERROR to prevent the division by zero in the first place. In the figure below, the "n.m." is a former manager's code for "not meaningful."

		f_x	=IFERROR(F9/E9,"n.m.")	

D	E	F	G
Handle	Qty	Revenue	Avg Price
aBoBoBook	895	521785	583
Bluefeather8989	989	533071	539
INDZARA	1124	611456	544
Kazmdav	1019	507462	498
McGunigales	921	485367	527
MikeAsHimself	843	490626	582
MrExcel	0	0	n.m.
Symons	972	562788	579

Thanks to Justin Fishman, Stephen Gilmer, and Excel by Joe.

#90 Handle Plural Conditions with SUMIFS

Did you notice the "S" that got added to the end of SUMIF starting in Excel 2007? While SUMIF and SUMIFS sound the same, the new SUMIFS can run circles around its elder sibling.

The old SUMIF and COUNTIF have been around since Excel 97. In the figure below, the formula tells Excel to look through the names in B2:B22. If a name is equal to the name in F4, then sum the corresponding cell from the range starting in D2:D22. (While the third argument could be the first cell of the sum range D2, it will make the function volatile, causing the worksheet to calculate more slowly.)

G4					f_x	=SUMIF($B$2:$B$22,F4,$D$2:$D$22)			

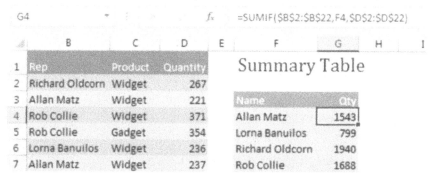

SUMIF and COUNTIF were great with only one condition. But with two or more things to check, you had to switch over to SUMPRODUCT, as shown below. (I realize most people would replace my multiplication signs with commas and add a double-minus before the first two terms, but my version works, too.)

G4					f_x	=SUMPRODUCT(($B$2:$B$22=$F4)*($C$2:$C$22=G$3)*($D$2:$D$22))				

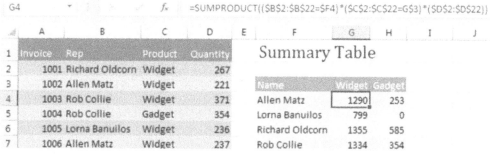

SUMIFS allows for up to 127 conditions. Because you might have an indeterminate number of conditions in the function, the numbers that you are adding up move from the third argument to the first argument.

In the following formula, you are summing D2:D22, but only the rows where column B is Allen Matz and column C is Widget. The logic of "Sum this if these conditions are true" is logical in SUMIFS.

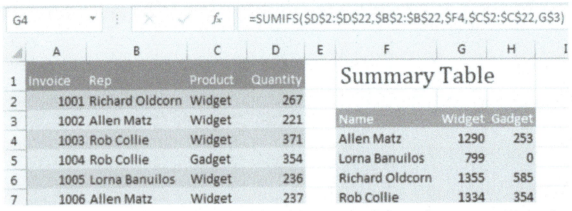

Excel 2007 also added plural versions of COUNTIFS and AVERAGEIFS. In February 2017, Microsoft 365 added MAXIFS and MINIFS. All these "S" functions are very efficient and fast.

> **Caution:** The first argument of these functions must be a range. It can not be a calculation. If you need a calculation for the first argument, enter that calculation in the grid.

Thanks to Nathi Njoko, Abshir Osman, Scott Russell, and Ryan Sitoy.

#91 Geography, Exchange Rate & Stock Data Types in Excel

In the past, Excel did not really handle data types. Yes, you could format some cells as Date or Text, but the new data types provide a whole new entry point for new data types now and in the future.

Start with a column of City names. For large cities like Madison Wisconsin, you can just put Madison. For smaller towns, you might enter Madison, FL.

From the Data tab, select Geography.

Excel searches the Internet and finds a city for each cell. A folded map appears next to each cell. Notice that you lose the state that was in the original cell.

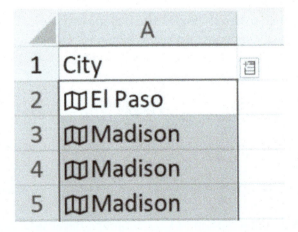

If you look in the Formula Bar, you will see a Value Token. This shows an icon plus white text on a grey background. The Value Token was introduced in April 2025 and is used to indicate that the cell contains more than a single value.

Click on the Map icon and a data card appears with information about the city.

The best part: for any data in the card, you can use a formula to pull that data into a cell. Enter =A2.Population in cell B2 and Excel returns the population of El Paso. Double click the Fill Handle in B2 and Excel returns the population for each city.

	A	B
1	City	Population
2	🗺 El Paso	683,080
3	🗺 Madison	2,853
4	🗺 Madison	47,959
5	🗺 Madison	2,853
6	🗺 Paris	9,840
7	🗺 Springfield	167,319
8	🗺 Houston	2,303,482

Caution: These new formulas might return a #FIELD! error. This means, Excel (or more correctly Bing), does not know the answer to this yet, but it may do so at some time in the future. It is not an error with the formula or the table, just a lack of knowledge currently.

Here is a great tip: Excel uses the context of other cells around the value to try to figure out ambiguous entries. In the following image, because Madison is in the middle of other Wisconsin cities, Excel will automatically choose Madison Wisconsin.

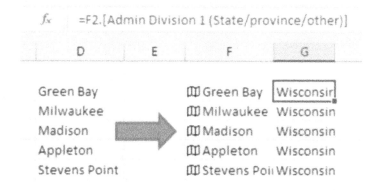

If you type Madison in a column that has Florida cities, Excel will correctly figure out that you want Madison Florida, even though it is smaller than the capital city of Wisconsin.

4

Miami		Miami	Florida	463,347
Orlando		Orlando	Florida	280,257
Jacksonville		Jacksonville	Florida	880,619
Madison	→	Madison	Florida	2,853
Christmas		Christmas	Florida	1,146
Daytona Beach		Daytona Beach	Florida	66,645

If you simply type Madison in a cell without any other values above or below it, Excel won't choose any of the towns named Madison. Instead of a map icon, you will have a circled question mark. The Data Selector pane will appear to allow you to choose which Madison you want.

The Geography and Stock data types have extra features if you format as a table using Ctrl+T.

A new Add Data icon appears to the right of the heading. Use this drop-down menu to add fields without having to type the formulas. Clicking the icon will enter the formula for you.

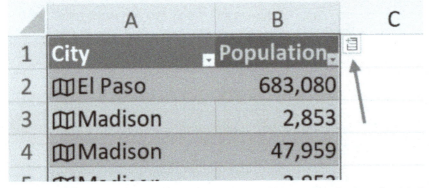

You can also sort the data by any field, even if it is not in the Excel grid. Open the drop-down menu for the City column. Use the new Display Field drop-down to choose Longitude.

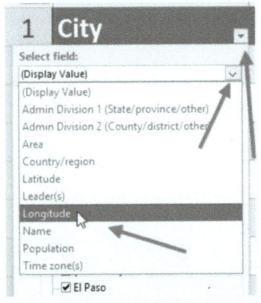

With Longitude selected, choose sort Smallest to Largest.

The result: data is sorted west to east.

	A	B	C	D
1	City	Population	Admin Div	Admin Division 2 (Co
2	🗺 El Paso	683,080	Texas	El Paso County
3	🗺 Houston	2,303,482	Texas	Harris County
4	🗺 Springfield	167,319	Missouri	Greene County
5	🗺 Madison	252,551	Wisconsin	Dane County
6	🗺 Madison	47,959	Alabama	Madison County
7	🗺 Paris	9,840	Kentucky	Bourbon County
8	🗺 Madison	2,853	Florida	Madison County

Support for exchange rates appeared in early 2019. While it initially was accessed by using the Stocks icon, it now has it's own Currency icon in the gallery. Enter currency pairs such as USD-CAD for U.S. Dollar to Canadian Dollar. Use the Price field for the current exchange rate.

4

	Y	Z	AA	AB	AC	AD
			Currency	Price	52-Week Low	52-Week High
	USD-CAD		🏛 USD/CAD	$ 1.35	$ 1.31	$ 1.39
	CAD-USD		🏛 CAD/USD	$ 0.74	$ 0.72	$ 0.76
	USD-EUR		🏛 USD/EUR	$ 0.92	$ 0.89	$ 0.96
	EUR-USD		🏛 EUR/USD	$ 1.09	$ 1.04	$ 1.13
	USD-GBP		🏛 USD/GBP	$ 0.79	$ 0.76	$ 0.85
	GBP-USD		🏛 GBP/USD	$ 1.27	$ 1.18	$ 1.31
	USD-AUD		🏛 USD/AUD	$ 1.52	$ 1.40	$ 1.59
	AUD-USD		🏛 AUD/USD	$ 0.66	$ 0.63	$ 0.72
	USD-BTC		🏛 USD/BTC	$ 0.0000244	$ 0.00	$ 0.00
	BTC-USD		🏛 BTC/USD	$ 41,051.58	$ 18,707.63	$ 49,051.33

Bonus Tip: Use Data, Refresh All to Update Stock Data

Another data type available is Stock data. Enter some publicly held companies:

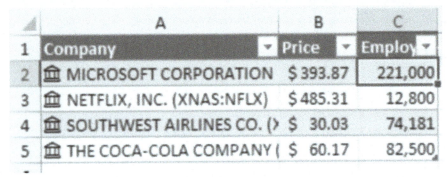

Choose, Data, Stocks. An icon of a building with Roman columns should appear next to each company You can add fields such as Number of Employees, Price, Volume, High, Low, Previous Close.

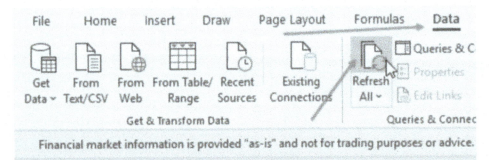

In contrast to Geography, where population might only be updated once a year, the stock price will be constantly changing throughout the trading day. Rather than go out to the Internet with every recalc, Excel will only updated the data from these Linked Data Types when you choose Refresh.

One easy way to update the stock prices is to use the Refresh All icon on the Data tab.

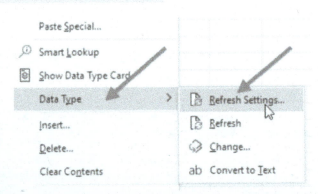

As the name implies, Refresh All will update everything in your workbook, including any Power Query data connections which might take a long time to update. If you want to only refresh the current block of linked data, right-click on A2, choose Data Types, Refresh. At some point in 2021, a new setting will allow Stock Data Types to update every five minutes. Right-click any cell with a Stock Data Type. Choose Data Type, Refresh Settings.

In the Data Types Refresh Settings, click the Stocks chevron to open the options. Select Automatically Update Every 5 Minutes.

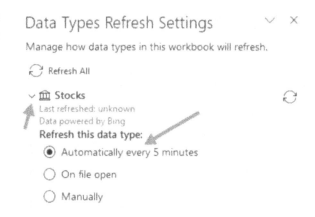

> **Note**: Yes, the choices here are limited. What if you want to refresh every one minute or every 10 minutes? Too bad. Getting the choice to refresh every five minutes is better than the two years when you had to manually refresh.

The Stock data type only delivers the current day's stock price. For stock history, see the STOCKHISTORY function, discussed next.

#92 Get Historical Stock History from STOCKHISTORY

In June 2020, Microsoft 365 added the new STOCKHISTORY function. It will pull historical stock data after the market has closed. The syntax is as follows:

=STOCKHISTORY(stock,start_date,end_date,interval,headers,properties1,...)

For the stock, use any ticker symbol. The start date can be a cell containing a date or text such as "1-1-2021". The end date is assumed to be today, or you can enter another date.

For the interval, use 0 for daily, 1 for weekly, 2 for monthly.

The headers argument can be 0 for no headers, 1 for a single row of headers or 2 for the stock name and then headers.

Properties1 through Properties6 specify which fields and the order they should appear: 0 is Date, 1 is Close, 2 is Open, 3 is High, 4 is Low, 5 is Volume. You can specify from 1 to 6 properties in any order. ...

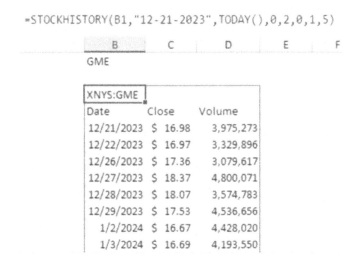

Note that the stock data is updated once a day, a few hours after the market closes.

In the following image, the interval is set to weekly. All six properties are shown and in the numerical order.

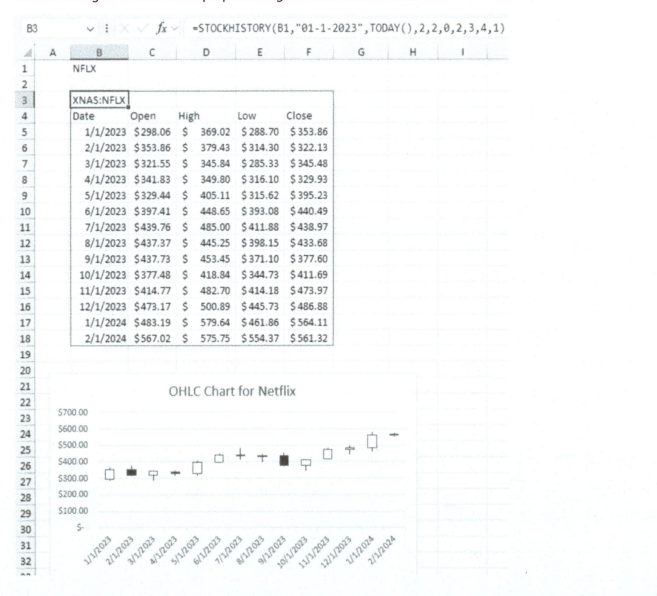

| B3 | | | fx | =STOCKHISTORY(B1,"01-1-2024",TODAY(),1,2,0,1,2,3,4,5) | | | | | |

	A	B	C	D	E	F	G	H	I	J
1		PG								
2										
3		XNYS:PG								
4		Date	Close	Open	High	Low	Volume			
5		1/2/2024	$147.42	$ 146.36	$149.41	$146.31	27,297,898			
6		1/8/2024	$150.60	$ 147.91	$151.30	$147.65	38,977,638			
7		1/16/2024	$147.57	$ 150.15	$151.50	$146.92	29,035,899			
8		1/22/2024	$156.14	$ 146.97	$156.40	$146.28	60,487,635			
9		1/29/2024	$158.09	$ 156.68	$159.60	$155.40	41,191,414			
10		2/5/2024	$157.42	$ 158.17	$159.83	$156.96	32,427,150			

You might need the columns to appear in a different sequence. For example, the built-in Open-High-Low-Close chart needs the data to have Date, Open, High, Low, Close.

You can change the order of the properties arguments as shown here:

| B3 | | | fx | =STOCKHISTORY(B1,"01-1-2023",TODAY(),2,2,0,2,3,4,1) | | | | |

	A	B	C	D	E	F	G	H	I
1		NFLX							
2									
3		XNAS:NFLX							
4		Date	Open	High	Low	Close			
5		1/1/2023	$298.06	$ 369.02	$288.70	$353.86			
6		2/1/2023	$353.86	$ 379.43	$314.30	$322.13			
7		3/1/2023	$321.55	$ 345.84	$285.33	$345.48			
8		4/1/2023	$341.83	$ 349.80	$316.10	$329.93			
9		5/1/2023	$329.44	$ 405.11	$315.62	$395.23			
10		6/1/2023	$397.41	$ 448.65	$393.08	$440.49			
11		7/1/2023	$439.76	$ 485.00	$411.88	$438.97			
12		8/1/2023	$437.37	$ 445.25	$398.15	$433.68			
13		9/1/2023	$437.73	$ 453.45	$371.10	$377.60			
14		10/1/2023	$377.48	$ 418.84	$344.73	$411.69			
15		11/1/2023	$414.77	$ 482.70	$414.18	$473.97			
16		12/1/2023	$473.17	$ 500.89	$445.73	$486.88			
17		1/1/2024	$483.19	$ 579.64	$461.86	$564.11			
18		2/1/2024	$567.02	$ 575.75	$554.37	$561.32			

OHLC Chart for Netflix

#93 Create Your Own Data Types

Data types sound great, but wouldn't you like to have your own company data as a data type? Imagine if you had your company product list in a data type. You could store the SKU in a column and then extract item information using XLOOKUP or dot formulas such as =A2.Country.

There have been three solutions from Microsoft that allow you to do this. Power Query was first. Then Power BI. Then a Javascript API. I've tried them all. I want these to work just like real data types do. Here is my wish list and how PQ (Power Query), PBI (Power BI), and API (JavaScript API).

The Quest for a Perfect Custom Data Type

Wish List Item	PQ	PBI	API
1) Type plain text and convert to a data type	✗	✓	!
1b) From the same gallery as other Data Types	✗	✓	✗
2) From the card for the data type, return an array of entities (such as all the people in Bob Marley and the Wailers music act.)	✗	✗	✓
3) Have those fields returned from the Data Card be Data Types as well, so you can drill down and get more information about the sub-entity	✗	✗	✓
4) The data type should be able to return an image from an Image URL	✗	✓	✓
5) The data type should be able to return a clickable hyperlink.	✗	✗	✗
6) It would be nice if the little icon for the data type was customizable.	✗	✗	✗

So far, the best experience is JavaScript API. Here are three videos, one for each method.

Power Query	Power BI	JavaScript API
https://youtu.be/z-WDstDUzyA	https://youtu.be/B5Kg-5XCWZA	https://youtu.be/iAajH_Nkr_s

Yes!!! Define Your Own Linked Data Types in Excel! Episode 2378

MrExcel.com • 9.4K views • 1 year ago

It is like the Christmas where you got almost every thing you asked for. The Excel team has given us almost everything I asked for with the new data types. You can now create your own data...

CC

Excel Custom Data Types From Power BI - 2450

MrExcel.com • 1.4K views • 3 months ago

The data types gallery with Geography, Stocks, Currency, and Wolfram is mildly interesting. But I think the real goal is to get your own company data in the Data Type. I want it to be a very...

CC

Wow! Excel Custom Data Types From JavaScript API - 2451

MrExcel.com • 2.9K views • 3 months ago

How to create your own custom data types in Excel using ScriptLab and the Javascript API. Important Links: Try out the workbook with my custom data types: https://1drv.ms/x/s!As7G72S!487JliYRn...

CC

#94 TRANSLATE and DETECTLANGUAGE

Ever stumbled across text in a spreadsheet that wasn't in your language? Thanks to two new functions, TRANSLATE and DETECTLANGUAGE, you can now break the language barrier right in the grid—no more copying and pasting into online translators.

Start with a simple scenario: you have text in English and want to translate it to German. Let's say A2 contains the English phrase. In the adjacent cell, enter the formula: =TRANSLATE(A2, , "de"). You can leave the source language blank (Excel assumes it's English), and "de" is the language code for German.

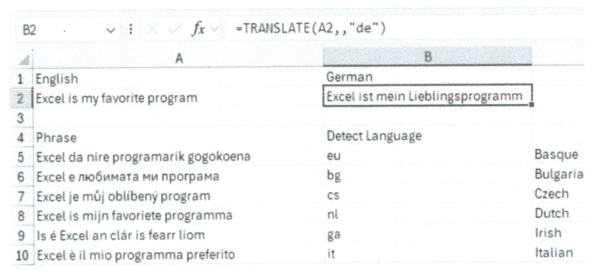

The DETECTLANGUAGE function identifies the language code of any text. =DETECTLANGUAGE(A2) will return a language code, like "es" for Spanish or "fr" for French. You can combine this with TRANSLATE to convert unknown languages into English:

#95 Dynamic Arrays Can Spill

Introduced in 2019, the new Dynamic Arrays represent a major change to the Excel calculation engine. While the old Ctrl+Shift+Enter array formulas could return several results into a pre-selected range, these new formulas do not require Ctrl+Shift+Enter and you don't have to pre-select the range.

For example, let's say you type =B2:B8*C1 into cell C2. In the past, this formula would have required dollar signs around $C$1. You would copy the formula to all 7 cells and something called implicit intersection would make sure the numbers were correct.

	A	B	C	
1	Product	Amount	10%	
2	Apple	5460	=B2:B8*C1	
3	Banana	4370		
4	Cherry	1520		
5	Date	1410		
6	Elderberry	5470		
7	Fig	1620		
8	Guava	2330		
9				

But now, with Dynamic Arrays, one formula in cell C2 will spill over and return results into many cells.

C2 f_x =B2:B8*C1

▲	A	B	C	D
1	Product	Amount	10%	
2	Apple	2060	206	
3	Banana	1530	153	
4	Cherry	2560	256	
5	Date	2760	276	
6	Elderberry	4450	445	
7	Fig	4790	479	
8	Guava	3940	394	
9				

When you select any cell from C2:C8, a blue outline appears around the cells to let you know that the values are the result of a single formula. That single formula only exists in C2. If you select any other cell in the range, the formula appears in the formula bar, but it is greyed out.

If the range B2:B8 grows (by someone inserting rows in the middle), the spilled results will grow as well. However, simply typing new values in A9:B9 will not cause the formula to extend, unless you format the whole range with Ctrl+T before adding values.

f_x =B2:B8*C1

B	C	D
Amount	10%	
2060	206	
1530	153	
2560	256	

What if a formula can not spill? What if there are non-empty cells in the way? Rather than return partial results, the formula will return the new #SPILL! error.

B	C
Amount	10%
1 ! 0	#SPILL!
2420	
2060	stuff
4030	in
4740	the
1490	way

Open the yellow dropdown to the left of the error and you can select the obstructing cells.

B	C	D
ount	10%	
1 ! ▾	#SPILL!	
2	Spill range isn't blank	
2	Help on this Error	
4	Select Obstructing Cells	
4	Show Calculation Steps...	
1	Ignore Error	
3	Edit in Formula Bar	
	Error Checking Options...	

Once you clear the obstructing cells, the answers will appear again.

#96 Sorting with a Formula

Sorting data in Excel is easy. Unless, you are building a dashboard for your manager's manager. You can't ask that person to select C3, go to the Data tab and click the AZ button every time they want an updated report. The new SORT and SORTBY functions allow you to easily sort with a formula.

You can pass three arguments to the SORT function. The first is the range to be sorted. Leave the headings out of this argument. Next, which column do you want to sort by. If your data is in B:D and you want to sort by column D, you would specify column 3 as the sort column. The third argument is a 1 for ascending or -1 for descending.

In this figure, the data is sorted by Amount descending:

| F3 | | | f_x | =SORT(B3:D9,3,-1) | | |

	A	B	C	D	E	F	G	H
1	**Sort by Amount (column 3), descending (-1)**							
2		Product	Team	Amount				
3		Apple	Red	1220		Elderberry	Red	4740
4		Banana	Blue	2420		Lime	Blue	4030
5		Cherry	Red	2060		Guava	Red	3890
6		Elderberry	Red	4740		Banana	Blue	2420
7		Fig	Blue	1490		Cherry	Red	2060
8		Guava	Red	3890		Fig	Blue	1490
9		Lime	Blue	4030		Apple	Red	1220

What if you want to do a two-level sort? You can specify an array constant for both the second and third argument. In this case, the data is sorted by Team ascending and Amount descending. For the sort column, specify {2;3}. For the sort order, specify {1;-1}.

| F3 | | | f_x | =SORT(B3:D9,{2;3},{1;-1}) | | |

	A	B	C	D	E	F	G	H
1	**Sort by Team ascending and Amount descending**							
2		Product	Team	Amount				
3		Apple	Red	1220		Lime	Blue	4030
4		Banana	Blue	2420		Banana	Blue	2420
5		Cherry	Red	2060		Fig	Blue	1490
6		Elderberry	Red	4740		Elderberry	Red	4740
7		Fig	Blue	1490		Guava	Red	3890
8		Guava	Red	3890		Cherry	Red	2060
9		Lime	Blue	4030		Apple	Red	1220

The Excel Calc team also gave you the SORTBY function. Say you want to return a list of products but not the associated amounts. You want the products to be sorted by the amount. The formula below says to return the products from B3:B9 sorted descending by the amounts in D3:D9.

F3			f_x	=SORTBY(B3:B9,D3:D9,-1)			

	A	B	C	D	E	F	G	H
1	Sort products by amount, but only show products							
2		Product	Team	Amount				
3		Apple	Red	1220		Elderberry		
4		Banana	Blue	2420		Lime		
5		Cherry	Red	2060		Guava		
6		Elderberry	Red	4740		Banana		
7		Fig	Blue	1490		Cherry		
8		Guava	Red	3890		Fig		
9		Lime	Blue	4030		Apple		

Bonus Tip: Sort into a Random Sequence

Why would you need to sort randomly? Perhaps you are picking the lucky winner of a free Thanksgiving turkey. Or the unlucky winner of the quarterly drug screening. Use SORTBY and specify the list of employees as the first argument. For the second argument, use RANDARRAY(N) where N is the number of employees. Every time you press F9, the results in column D will sort again.

D3			f_x	=SORTBY(B3:B10,RANDARRAY(8))	

	A	B	C	D	E	
1						
2		Employee		Winner		
3		Andy		Andy		
4		Barb		Ed		
5		Chris		Gary		
6		Diane		Diane		
7		Ed		Barb		
8		Flo		Flo		
9		Gary		Chris		
10		Hank		Hank		
11						

4

#97 Filter with a Formula

The FILTER function is new as part of the dynamic arrays feature. There are three arguments: array, include, and an optional [if empty].

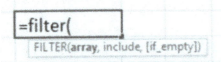

=filter(

FILTER(**array**, include, [if_empty])

Say you want to be able to enter a team name in G1 and extract all of the records for that team. Use a formula of =FILTER(B3:E9,C3:C9=G1).

| G3 | | | fx | =FILTER(B3:E9,C3:C9=G1) | | | | |

	A	B	C	D	E	F	G	H	I	J
1	**Filter to Red Team**						Red			
2		Product	Team	Status	Amount					
3		Apple	Red	O	1220		Apple	Red	O	1220
4		Banana	Blue	C	2420		Cherry	Red	C	2060
5		Cherry	Red	C	2060		Elderberry	Red	O	4740
6		Date	Blue	O	4030		Guava	Red	C	3890
7		Elderberry	Red	O	4740					
8		Fig	Blue	C	1490					
9		Guava	Red	C	3890					
10										

If cell G1 changes from Red to Blue, the results change to show you the blue team records.

F	G	H	I	J
	Blue			
	Banana	Blue	C	2420
	Date	Blue	O	4030
	Fig	Blue	C	1490

In the above examples, the optional [If Empty] argument is missing. If someone is allowed to enter the wrong team name in G1, then you will get a #CALC! error.

=FILTER(B3:E9,C3:C9=G1)

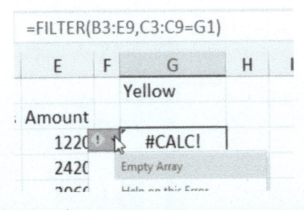

E	F	G	H	I
		Yellow		
Amount				
1220		#CALC!		
2420		Empty Array		
2060		Help on this Error		

To avoid the #CALC! error, add a third argument.

=FILTER(B3:E9,C3:C9=G1,"None Found")

E	F	G	H	I
		Yellow		
Amount				
1220		None Found		
2420				

You can specify an array constant for the third argument if you want to fill each column of the answer array.

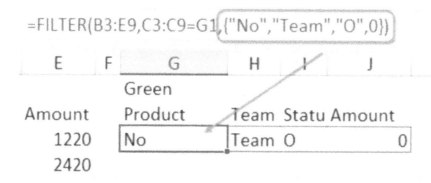

=FILTER(B3:E9,C3:C9=G1,{"No","Team","O",0})

E	F	G	H	I	J
		Green			
Amount		Product	Team	Statu	Amount
1220		No		Team	O	0
2420					

To filter to records where multiple conditions are met, multiply the conditions together.

G3 f_x =FILTER(B3:E9,(C3:C9=G1)*(D3:D9="O"),"None

▲	A	B	C	D	E	F	G	H	I	J
1	Filter to Red Team & Status=O						Red			
2		Product	Team	Status	Amount					
3		Apple	Red	O	1220		Apple		Red	O	122(
4		Banana	Blue	C	2420		Elderberry	Red	O	474(
5		Cherry	Red	C	2060					
6		Date	Blue	O	4030					
7		Elderberry	Red	O	4740					
8		Fig	Blue	C	1490					
9		Guava	Red	C	3890					

Bonus Tip: Understanding Array Constants

You've just seen a few examples that included an array constant. Here is a simple way to understand them. A comma inside an array constant means to move to the next column. A semi-colon means to move to the next row. How do you remember which is which? The semi-colon on your keyboard is located near the Enter or Return key which also goes to the next row.

When you see an array constant with a mix of commas and semi-colons, remember that each semi-colon moves to a new row.

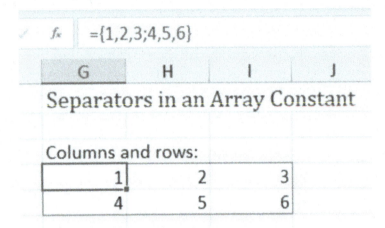

#98 Formula for Unique or Distinct

The UNIQUE function will provide either a list of unique or distinct values.

If you ask me for the list of unique values from this list: Apple, Apple, Banana, Cherry, Cherry, I would tell you that the list of unique values is Apple, Banana, Cherry. If you ask 100 accountants, about 92 of them would agree with me. But there is a segment of the population who disagrees and says that the only unique thing in the list is Banana because it is the only item that appears once.

This unusual definition of "unique" comes from the SQL Server world, where database pros would say that "Apple, Banana, Cherry" is a list of distinct values and Banana is the only unique value.

The new UNIQUE function will return either list. If you simply ask for =UNIQUE(R5:R9), you get my definition of all values that occur one or more times. But, if you are a database pro or Casey Kasem, then you can put a True as the third argument.

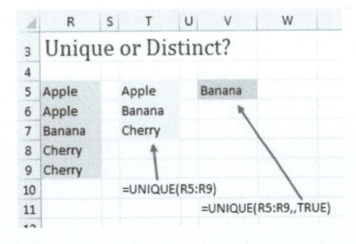

Here is a list of all the Billboard Top 10 Hits from 1979 - 1993.   To get a list of genres, use =UNIQUE()

Bonus Tip: Use # "The Spiller" to Refer to All Array Results

In the previous screenshot, the UNIQUE function is in cell F5. You never really know how many results that formula will return. To refer to "the entire array returned by the formula in F5", you would write F5#. There is no official name for this notation, so I am using an idiom coined by Excel MVP Ingeborg Hawighorst: The Spiller.

#99 Other Functions Can Now Accept Arrays as Arguments

Once you see the list of genres, you might want to know how frequently each genre appears. That would normally require a series of COUNTIF or COUNTIFS formulas. For example, =COUNTIF(D$4:D$6132,"Rock") would count how many songs were in the Rock genre. But rather than entering a bunch of COUNTIF functions, you could enter a single COUNTIF function and pass an array as the second argument. The formula below uses The Spiller syntax to ask Excel to repeat the COUNTIF for each answer in the UNIQUE function in F5.

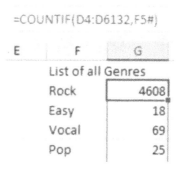

#100 One Hit Wonders with UNIQUE

For me, I can't imagine why I would ever need a list of items that have been sold exactly once. My only example is the One-Hit Wonders segment on Casey Kasem's American Top 40 radio show.

To get a list of artists who had exactly one hit, use =UNIQUE(B4:B6132..True). In the figure below, the UNIQUE function is wrapped in a SORT function so the resulting list is alphabetical.

To get the titles in column J, a VLOOKUP uses an array as the first argument. This is pretty wild - one VLOOKUP formula is actually doing over 1000 lookups and returning all 1000 results.

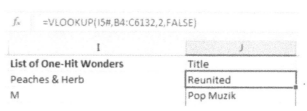

4

Another approach is to use a FILTER function combined with IFERROR and MATCH.

```
=FILTER(A4:D6132,
IFERROR(MATCH(B4:B6132,
UNIQUE(B4:B6132,FALSE,TRUE),0),FALSE))
```

L	M	N	O	P
	1979_004	Peaches & Herb	Reunited	Rock

#101 SEQUENCE inside of other Functions such as IPMT

After SORT, SORTBY, FILTER, and UNIQUE, the SEQUENCE and RANDARRAY functions seem pretty tame. SEQUENCE will generate a sequence of numbers.

	A	B	C	D
1	=SEQUENCE(			
2	SEQUENCE(**rows**, [columns], [start], [step])			

It does not seem like this is very interesting. Who needs to generate a list of numbers?

	A	B	C	D
1	=SEQUENCE(5)		=SEQUENCE(5,2,3,9)	
2				
3	1		3	12
4	2		21	30
5	3		39	48
6	4		57	66
7	5		75	84

Try putting SEQUENCE inside other functions. Here, IPMT calculates the interest in the 7th month of a loan:

	G	H	I
1	How much interest will be paid		
2	during month 7 of this loan?		
3	Principal	250000	
4	Term	60	
5	Rate	5%	
6			
7	($948.80)	=IPMT(H5/12,7,H4,H3)	

Thanks to SEQUENCE, this formula calculates the interest paid during 12 months starting in month 7:

	G	H	I	J	K	L
1	How much interest will be paid					
2	during months 7-18 of this loan?					
3	Principal	250000				
4	Term	60				
5	Rate	5%				
7	($10,334.60)	=SUM(IPMT(H5/12,SEQUENCE(12,1,7),H4,H3))				
8						
9	**12 numbers starting with 7**					

Two formulas create a forward-looking calendar:

	A	B	C	D	E	F	G
1	Tue	Wed	Thu	Fri	Sat	Sun	Mon
2	Jan-29	Jan-30	Jan-31	Feb-1	Feb-2	Feb-3	Feb-4
3	Feb-5	Feb-6	Feb-7	Feb-8	Feb-9	Feb-10	Feb-11
4	Feb-12	Feb-13	Feb-14	Feb-15	Feb-16	Feb-17	Feb-18
5	Feb-19	Feb-20	Feb-21	Feb-22	Feb-23	Feb-24	Feb-25
6	Feb-26	Feb-27	Feb-28	Mar-1	Mar-2	Mar-3	Mar-4

7 A1: =TEXT(A2:G2,"DDD")   B1: =SEQUENCE(5,7,TODAY())

=SEQUENCE(52,1,TODAY(),-7) would produce a list of the past 52 weeks.

#102 Generating Random Numbers in Excel

The RAND function generates a random decimal between 0 and 1, not including 1. The RANDBETWEEN function generates a random integer between 2 numbers. The new RANDARRAY function products an array of random numbers. Specify the numbers of rows, columns, minimum, maximum, and if you only want integers.

If you ask for =RANDARRAY(14,1,50,150,True), you will get a scatttershot of numbers from 50 to 150. In some models, it might make more sense to have the numbers in a bell curve with a mean of 100 and a standard deviation of 25. Use =SORT(NORM.INV(RANDARRAY(14),100,25)) to generate random numbers that tend to be closer to 100.

	A	B	C
1	=SORT(RANDARRAY(14,1,50,150,TRUE))		=SORT(NORM.INV(RANDARRAY(14),100,25))
2		60	51.64264294
3		77	79.86079349
4		80	86.85789406
5		87	88.31196404
6		93	88.55331803
7		108	90.47847136
8		115	102.937622
9		125	105.3442696
10		126	106.8438722
11		128	107.7499518
12		129	109.1756321
13		133	109.776343
14		148	124.5987151
15		150	132.4923299

4

#103 Create a Summary Table With the GROUPBY Function

The GROUPBY function debuted in late 2023. It makes it very easy to create a summary array. The optional arguments for the function provide flexibility.

The syntax of the function is:
=GROUPBY(row_fields,values,function,[field_headers],[total_depth],[sort_order],[filter_array])

Let's start with a simple data set like this one:

	A	B	C	D
4	Category	Product	Sales	Cost
5	Fruit	Apple	1275	689
6	Vegetables	Asparagus	4864	2335
7	Fruit	Banana	3809	1828
8	Herbs	Basil	8088	3640
9	Vegetables	Broccoli	3943	2090
10	Vegetables	Cabbage	2653	1353
11	Fruit	Cherry	9936	5365
12	Herbs	Cilantro	3967	2142
13	Fruit	Dill	9855	5223
14	Fruit	Elderberry	2768	1439
15	Vegetables	Endive	7164	3725
16	Herbs	Fennel	9514	4376
17	Fruit	Fig	9028	4965
18	Fruit	Guava	5385	2854
19	Herbs	Oregano	7262	3341
20	Herbs	Parsley	3540	1628
21	Vegetables	Peppers	85560	39360
22				

Say that you want total sales for each category in column A. The Row Fields argument is A4:A21. The Values argument is C4:C21. The Function is the word "Sum". A simple formula provides this summary:

	F	G	H
5	=GROUPBY(A4:A21,C4:C21,SUM)		
6	Fruit	42056	
7	Herbs	32371	
8	Vegetables	104184	
9	Total	178611	
10			

In the next example, both the Sales and Costs column are the Values argument. The optional Headers argument is 3 for "Yes, and Show".

	F	G	H
11	=GROUPBY(A4:A21,C4:D21,SUM,3)		
12	Category	Sales	Cost
13	Fruit	42056	22363
14	Herbs	32371	15127
15	Vegetables	104184	48863
16	Total	178611	86353
17			

In the next example, the Row Fields are both Category and Product. The optional Total Depth argument now comes into play. A value of 2 says you want grand totals and subtotals as well. The optional Sort Order argument is -3. The 3 indicates that Excel should sort by the 3rd column of the array. The negative sign indicates that the values are sorted descending. The optional Filter Array removes any herbs from the results.

Check out the sorting closely. You've asked for the report to be sorted by descending sales. That means Vegetables with 104K in sales will be at the top. Within the Vegetables, Peppers are at the top with the largest sales.

	F	G	H	I	J
18	=GROUPBY(A4:B21,C4:D21,SUM,3,2,-3,A4:A21<>"Herbs")				
19	Category	Product	Sales	Cost	
20	Vegetables	Peppers	85560	39360	
21	Vegetables	Endive	7164	3725	
22	Vegetables	Asparagus	4864	2335	
23	Vegetables	Broccoli	3943	2090	
24	Vegetables	Cabbage	2653	1353	
25	Vegetables		104184	48863	
26	Fruit	Cherry	9936	5365	
27	Fruit	Dill	9855	5223	
28	Fruit	Fig	9028	4965	
29	Fruit	Guava	5385	2854	
30	Fruit	Banana	3809	1828	
31	Fruit	Elderberry	2768	1439	
32	Fruit	Apple	1275	689	
33	Fruit		42056	22363	
34	Grand Total		146240	71226	

Here are many details on the various arguments.

- The third argument is called Function. You can put any LAMBDA function in this spot. The Excel team gave us 16 new Eta-Lambdas specifically for GROUPBY and PIVOTBY. Those functions are: SUM, PERCENTOF, AVERAGE, MEDIAN, COUNT, COUNTA, MAX, MIN, PRODUCT, ARRAYTOTEXT, CONCAT, STDEV.S, STDEV.P, VAR.S, VAR.P, and MODE.SNGL. These Eta-Lambdas are a shorthand way to simplify your formulas. Where you might have had to use LAMBDA(x,SUM(x)) in the past, you can now just specify SUM.

  Tip: Eta-Lambda is pronounced like Etta James married Joe Lambda.

- These Eta-Lambdas can be used inside of functions BYROW, BYCOL, SCAN, REDUCE, and MAKEARRAY.
- The choices for the Field Headers argument are 0=No, 1=Yes But Don't Show, 2=No but generate, 3=Yes and Show.
- The choices for Total Depth are 0=No Totals, 1=Grand Totals at Bottom, 2=Grand Totals and Subtotals at Bottom, -1=Grand Totals at Top, -2=Grand Totals and Subtotals at Top.
- The Sort Order is the integer column number of the sort column. Positive 2 will sort by the second column in ascending sequence. Negative 2 will sort by the second column in descending sequence. You can sort by two columns with {3;-4}.
- The Filter Array can be used to remove rows that match a criteria.
- To show multiple functions (for example both a Sum and Average), wrap those functions in HSTACK.

```
=GROUPBY(A4:A21,C4:C21,HSTACK(COUNT,SUM,PERCENTOF))
```

	F	G	H	I	J

USE HSTACK FOR MULTIPLE FUNCTIONS

	COUNT	SUM	PERCENTOF
Category	Sales	Sales	Sales
Fruit	7	42056	41.4%
Herbs	5	32371	31.9%
Vegetables	5	27180	26.8%
Total	17	101607	100.0%

4

Bonus Tip: Counting with GROUPBY

The previous example was similar to using UNIQUE to get a list of items and then SUMIFS to total the columns. What if you essentially need to use COUNTIFS? This can happen easily with GROUPBY.

To count how many of each item appear in the data, you use the COUNTA function. In the following example, you are asking for every unique combination of columns A & B and then counting column B.

	A	B	C	D	E
1	INT_NAME	WOTYPE			
2	Medium	Box	=GROUPBY(A2:B503,B2:B503,COUNTA)		
3	Medium	Box	High	Box	45
4	Low	Box	High	Flow	110
5	Low	Flow	Low	Box	35
6	Medium	Flow	Low	Flow	115
7	Medium	Flow	Meditation	Meditate	14
8	Medium	Flow	Medium	Box	58
9	Low	Flow	Medium	Flow	125
10	High	Flow	Total		502
11	High	Box			

#104 Moving from GROUPBY to PIVOTBY

Once you are familiar with GROUPBY as described in the previous pages, it is easy to move on to the PIVOTBY function.

The PIVOTBY function adds three new arguments to the GROUPBY arguments to allow for column fields. The three arguments are Col_Fields, Col_Total_Depth, and Col_Sort_Order. They work just like Row_Fields, Total_Depth and Sort_Order in GROUPBY, but they apply to the Columns fields in the resultant array.

The following image shows a simple PIVOTBY with one row field and one column field.

	A	B	C	D	E	F	G	H	I	J	K
1	=PIVOTBY(row_fields,col_fields,values,function,[field_headers],										
2		[row_total_depth],[row_sort_order],									
3			[col_total_depth],[col_sort_order],[filter_array])								
4											
5	Region	Rep	Category	Product	Sales	Cost					
6	East	Ed	Fruit	Apple	1275	638	=PIVOTBY(C5:C39,A5:A39,E5:E39,SUM,3)				
7	West	Flo	Fruit	Apple	1782	820		Region			
8	East	Ed	Vegetables	Asparagus	4864	2189	Category	East	West	Total	
9	West	Hank	Vegetables	Asparagus	3158	1547	Fruit	42056	24351	66407	
10	East	Andy	Fruit	Banana	3809	2095	Herbs	32371	15982	48353	
11	West	Hank	Fruit	Banana	3627	1668	Vegetables	27180	11199	38379	
12	East	Ed	Herbs	Basil	8088	4044	Total	101607	51532	153139	
13	West	Hank	Herbs	Basil	4618	2401					

Why do you need PIVOTBY when you could just as easily create a pivot table? Because the PIVOTBY formula will automatically recalculate. You won't have to rely on the person using the workbook to click Refresh. Are pivot tables dead? No - there are still plenty of pivot features that are not possible with PIVOTBY. For example, all of the Show Values As choices are not supported in PIVOTBY.

#105 Calculate Percent of Total with PERCENTOF Function

When the Excel team created PIVOTBY, they wanted to be able to show percent of total within the pivot table. One of the side benefits is that you get a new PIVOTBY function.

The syntax is simple: =PERCENTOF(data_subset,data_all)

In this image, the formula in D6 is asking for the 3809 divided by the total of sales in C4:C9.

D6		fx	=PERCENTOF(C6,$C$4:$C$9)			
	A	B	C	D	E	F	G
1	=PERCENTOF(data_subset,data_all)						
2							
3	Category	Product	Sales	Percent			
4	Fruit	Apple	1275	5.2%			
5	Vegetable	Asparagu	4864	19.7%			
6	Fruit	Banana	3809	15.5%			
7	Herb	Basil	8088	32.8%			
8	Vegetable	Broccoli	3943	16.0%			
9	Vegetable	Cabbage	2653	10.8%			
10							

Bonus Tip: Replace Ctrl+Shift+Enter with Dynamic Arrays.

Before dynamic arrays, people would use these crazy Ctrl+Shift+Enter formulas.

Say that you have a friend who is superstitious about Friday the 13th. You want to illustrate how many Friday the 13ths your friend has lived through. Before Dynamic Arrays, you would have to use the formula below.

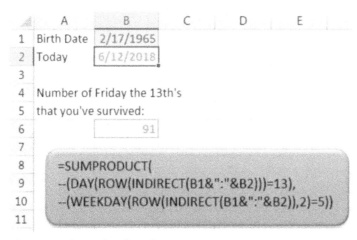

The same formula after dynamic arrays is still complicated, but less intimidating:

B5		fx	=SUMPRODUCT(				
			(DAY(SEQUENCE(B4,,B3))=13)*				
			(WEEKDAY(SEQUENCE(B4,,B3),2)=5))				
	A	B	C	D	E	F	G
1	Start	2/17/1965					
2	End	6/12/2018					
3	Start as a number	23790					
4	# of Days	19474 =B2-B1+1					
5	# Friday the 13ths	91					
6							

4

Another example from Mike Girvin's Ctrl+Shift+Enter book is to get a unique list.

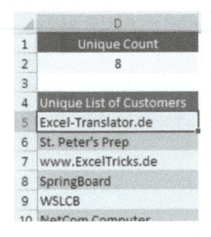

Here is the formula. I won't try to explain it to you.

```
{=IF(ROWS(D$5:D5)>$D$2,"",
INDEX($B$2:$B$146,
SMALL(IF(FREQUENCY(IF($B$2:$B$146<>"",
MATCH($B$2:$B$146,$B$2:$B$146,0)),
ROW($B$2:$B$146)-1),
ROW($B$2:$B$146)-1),
ROWS(D$5:D5)))))}
```

The replacement formula with dynamic arrays is =UNIQUE(B2:B146).

#106 Dependent Validation using Dynamic Arrays

The Data Validation feature lets you choose from a dropdown list in Excel. It works great until someone wants to have two lists. The items in the second list are dependent on what is chosen in the first list. This is called dependent validation.

In the figure below, the items for the first dropdown list appear in **D4#**, thanks to **=SORT(UNIQUE(B4:B23))**. The validation in **H3** points to **=D4#**. The list for the second validation appears in **E4#** because of the formula **=SORT(FILTER(A4:A23,B4:B23=H3,"Choose Class First"))**. The validation in **H5** uses **=E4#**.

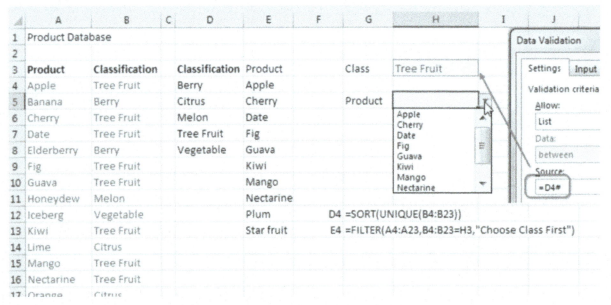

#107 Complex Validation Using a Formula

The method above is fine if you have Dynamic Arrays. But a lot of people running perpetual versions of Excel won't have Dynamic Arrays for years. Other published methods for Dependent Validation require a new named range for every possible choice in the first and second drop-down.

I was doing a seminar in Mobile, Alabama and several people there wanted to set up a three-level valida-tion, but they did not care about having drop-downs to choose from. "I just want to validate that people are typing the correct values."

Rather than use the option to allow a list, you can set up custom validation using a formula. Say that you have a table with hundreds of valid selections.

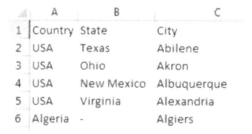

	A	B	C
1	Country	State	City
2	USA	Texas	Abilene
3	USA	Ohio	Akron
4	USA	New Mexico	Albuquerque
5	USA	Virginia	Alexandria
6	Algeria	-	Algiers

If you think that your list will grow over time, format it as a Table using Ctrl+T.

Set up a named range for each of the three columns. This step is necessary so you can refer to each column and the names will grow as the table grows.

Select A2:A551. In the Name Box, type cCountry and press enter.

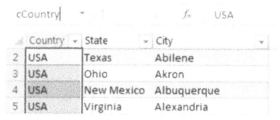

cCountry			f_x	USA

	Country	State	City	
2	USA	Texas	Abilene	
3	USA	Ohio	Akron	
4	USA	New Mexico	Albuquerque	
5	USA	Virginia	Alexandria	

Name B2:B551 as cState. Name C2:C551 as cCity.

Here is the area where you want people to type a Country, State, and City.

It is always easier to build and test your formulas for conditional formatting and validation in a cell first. Take a look at the formulas shown below to test each of the entries.

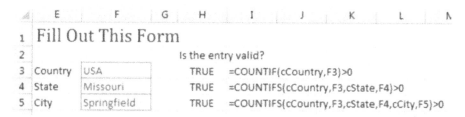

	E	F	G	H	I	J	K	L	M
1	Fill Out This Form								
2				Is the entry valid?					
3	Country	USA		TRUE	=COUNTIF(cCountry,F3)>0				
4	State	Missouri		TRUE	=COUNTIFS(cCountry,F3,cState,F4)>0				
5	City	Springfield		TRUE	=COUNTIFS(cCountry,F3,cState,F4,cCity,F5)>0				

Once those formulas are working, edit cell H3. Using the mouse, select the characters in the formula bar and press Ctrl+C to copy. Select F3 and press Alt+D L to open the Data Validation drop-down. In the Allow box, choose Custom. This will reveal a Formula box. Paste your formula in that box.

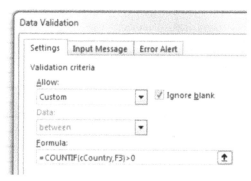

4

Optionally, fill out an Input Message and Error Alert. Repeat to put the H4 formula as the validation for F4 and the H5 formula for validation for F5. The result: it will prevent a wrong entry.

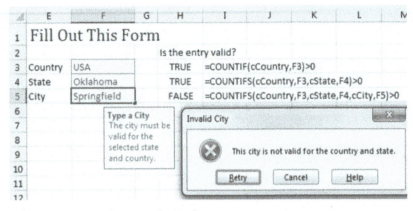

#108 Stack Multiple Arrays

If you need to combine multiple arrays into a single array, you can stack multiple arrays vertically using VSTACK. Stack multiple arrays horizontally using HSTACK.

In the figure below, one array formula is returning the headings in A2:D2. A second array formula is returning the numbers in A3:D3. These are two separate arrays. If you needed to stack them into a single array, you could use =VSTACK(A2#,A3#).

A5			fx	=VSTACK(A2#,A3#)
	A	B	C	D	E
2	Q1	Q2	Q3	Q4	
3	1350	1362	1380	1800	
4					
5	Q1	Q2	Q3	Q4	
6	1350	1362	1380	1800	
7					

Caution: If the arrays being stacked have different number of columns, Excel will fill the shorter arrays with #N/A. To prevent this, use the EXPAND function. =EXPAND(array, rows, columns, pad with). In the figure below, there are only 3 numbers in A3# and this causes the #N/A in D6. By using =VSTACK(A2#,EXPAND(A3#,1,4,"")) you can prevent the #N/A.

A5			fx	=VSTACK(A2#,A3#)
	A	B	C	D	E
2	Q1	Q2	Q3	Q4	
3	1350	1362	1380		
4					
5	Q1	Q2	Q3	Q4	
6	1350	1362	1380	#N/A	
7					
8	=EXPAND(A3#,1,4,"")				
9	1350	1362	1380		

Tip: These examples are only stacking two arrays. You can stack up to 254 arrays.

#109 Dropping, Taking, or Choosing from an Array

Say that you have an array in A1# that includes 1 row of headings, 10 rows of numbers and 1 row of totals. If you want to remove the headers, you could =DROP(A1#,1) to drop the top row.

=DROP(A1#, 2) will drop the top two rows.

The function syntax is DROP(array, rows, [columns]).

Any time that you use a negative number for Rows or Columns, Excel will drop from the bottom or right edge of the array.

=DROP(A1#,-1) will remove the bottom row.

=DROP(A1#,,-1) will remove the right-most column.

=DROP(A1#,-1,-1) will remove the bottom row and right-most column.

A13				f_x	=DROP(A1#,-1,-1)
	A	B	C	D	E	F

	A	B	C	D	E	F
1	Name	Apple	Banana	Cherry	Dill	Total
2	Andy	98	21	47	48	214
3	Barb	45	94	29	41	209
4	Chris	59	50	82	53	244
5	Diane	94	21	79	40	234
6	Ed	53	56	84	85	278
7	Flo	56	94	15	52	217
8	Gary	99	13	53	48	213
9	Hank	68	82	31	18	199
10	Total	572	431	420	385	1808
11						
12	Remove Totals					
13	Name	Apple	Banana	Cherry	Dill	
14	Andy	98	21	47	48	
15	Barb	45	94	29	41	
16	Chris	59	50	82	53	
17	Diane	94	21	79	40	
18	Ed	53	56	84	85	
19	Flo	56	94	15	52	
20	Gary	99	13	53	48	
21	Hank	68	82	31	18	
22						

If you wanted to remove the top row and bottom row, you can not specify both 1 and -1 in the same DROP function. But you could use two DROP functions, like this: =DROP(DROP(A1#,1),-1).

While DROP is designed to remove rows or columns from the start or end of an array, the TAKE function will keep only the beginning or ending rows or columns from an array. =TAKE(Array, Rows, [Columns]). If you =TAKE(A1#,1), you will get the top row of the array. Negative numbers will take from the end of the array. To get the Total column, you could use =TAKE(A1#,,-1).

DROP and TAKE are oddly specific, in that they only point to the first or last rows/columns of an array. In contrast, CHOOSEROWS and CHOOSECOLS will let you specify any number of rows or columns. If you wanted to get the first and last rows of the array in A1#, you could use =CHOOSEROWS(A1#,1,-1).

If you wanted to get all of the odd numbered columns in an array, you could use =CHOOSECOLS(A1#, SEQUENCE(5,1,1,2)).

A13			⌄ ✕ ✓	*fx*	=CHOOSEROWS(A1#,1,-1)	
	A	B	C	D	E	F
1	Name	Apple	Banana	Cherry	Dill	Total
2	Andy	98	21	47	48	214
3	Barb	45	94	29	41	209
4	Chris	59	50	82	53	244
5	Diane	94	21	79	40	234
6	Ed	53	56	84	85	278
7	Flo	56	94	15	52	217
8	Gary	99	13	53	48	213
9	Hank	68	82	31	18	199
10	Total	572	431	420	385	1808
11						
12	Get top row and last row with CHOOSEROWS					
13	Name	Apple	Banana	Cherry	Dill	Total
14	Total	572	431	420	385	1808

My question: when would you use DROP or TAKE versus CHOOSEROWS or CHOOSECOLS? Here is my early thoughts on this. DROP or TAKE only work on the rows or columns at the edge of the array. The one benefit of DROP or TAKE is that you can simultaneously remove a total row and total column.

You can DROP or TAKE multiple rows or columns, but only from one side of the array at a time. For example, you can remove the top 3 rows: =DROP(A1#,3) or the bottom 4 rows: =DROP(A1#,-4). But you can not remove the top row and bottom row without nesting two DROP functions.

The downside to CHOOSEROWS and CHOOSECOLS is that you can select only rows or only columns. But you can select any number of either: =CHOOSEROWS(A1#,1,2,5,6,9,10,11).

#110 Reshaping an Array to a Vector and Back

You can unwind a rectangular range or array into a single column using TOCOL or a single row using TOROW. Each function can take an array or a range as the first argument. The optional Ignore argument can have Excel skip empty cells. The optional Scan_By_Column argument will control if values are read row-by-row (the default) or column-by-column.

Here are three ways to run TOCOL on the array in A2:B6, which includes an empty cell in B6. Using =TOCOL(A2:B6) in D2 returns a zero for the empty cell (D11). To exclude empty cells, use =TOCOL(A2:B6,1) as in E2—note there's no zero.

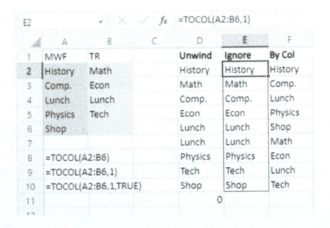

Both D and E read data by rows: History (A2), Math (B2), Comp. (A3), and so on. To read by columns instead, add TRUE as the third argument, as in F2. This returns History, Comp, Lunch, Physics, Shop from column A, followed by Math, Econ, Lunch, Tech from column B.

What if you did not want Lunch in the results? Since Lunch is in the 3rd row of both columns, you could use =TOCOL(CHOOSEROWS(A2:B6,1,2,4,5)).

Once you have your results in a single column or row, you might like to rearrange it to a rectangular range. This can be done with WRAPCOLS or WRAPROWS. For a detailed walk-through, see the topic about shuffling a deck of cards on the next page.

#111 Getting the UNIQUE of a Rectangular Range

Getting all of the unique values from a rectangular range was previously very complicated. Today, using a combination of UNIQUE and TOCOL, it is easy. The figure below adds in a SORT function to make sure the results are sorted alphabetically.

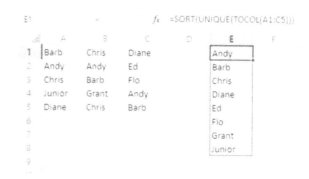

#112 Shuffling and Dealing a Deck of Cards

Take a look at the figure below. The 13 playing card values are in A5:A17. The four playing card suits are in B4:E4. A simple =A5:A17&B4:E4 in cell B5 generates a 13-row by 4-column array of all 52 playing cards.

To rearrange those into a single column, use =TOCOL(B5#) in cell G5.

To sort the 52 cards randomly, =SORTBY(G5#,RANDARRAY(52)). Every time that the worksheet recalculates, you will get a new shuffle of the deck of cards.

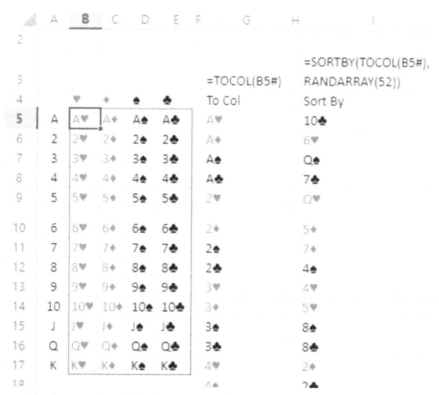

> **Tip**: Arrays are still bad at copying formatting. The red for diamonds and hearts is achieved through conditional formatting rules applied to the entire worksheet.

Now that you have the 52 cards arranged in a random sequence, you can deal them using WRAPCOLS or WRAPROWS. In the figure below, cards are dealt to 6 players. Avoid an #N/A error for the last two cards by using "" for Pad_With argument.

fx   =WRAPCOLS(I5#,L2,"")

WRAPCOLS(vector,wrap_count,[pad_with])

	# Players	6								
		=WRAPCOLS(I5#,L2,"")								
Sort By	Player 1	K♠	10♥	2♣	Q♥	9♣	5♠	2♥	2♦	K♦
K♠	Player 2	7♦	3♣	7♠	A♥	10♣	Q♠	6♣	4♥	5♥
7♦	Player 3	3♦	9♥	6♦	Q♦	J♠	2♠	8♠	4♣	Q♣
3♦	Player 4	9♠	7♥	8♣	J♦	8♦	8♥	3♥	7♣	A♠
9♠	Player 5	6♥	10♣	10♦	5♦	J♣	9♦	3♠	K♥	
6♥	Player 6	5♣	A♦	4♠	6♠	4♦	J♥	K♣	A♣	

WRAPROWS(vector,wrap_count,[pad_with])

	# Cards	8							
5♣		=WRAPROWS(I5#,L11,"")							
10♥		C 1	C 2	C 3	C 4	C 5	C 6	C 7	C 8
3♣		K♠	7♦	3♦	9♠	6♥	5♣	10♥	3♣
9♥		9♥	7♥	10♠	A♦	2♣	7♠	6♦	8♣
7♥		10♦	4♠	Q♥	A♥	Q♦	J♦	5♦	6♠
10♠		9♣	10♣	J♠	8♦	J♣	4♦	5♠	Q♠
A♦		2♠	8♥	9♦	J♥	2♥	6♣	8♠	3♥
2♣		3♠	K♣	2♦	4♥	4♣	7♣	K♥	A♠
7♠		K♦	5♥	Q♣	A♣				
6♦									
8♣									

Typically, in a card game, you would be dealing one card to each player and then a second card to each player. If you would want to deal the first 8 cards into a single pile, use WRAPROWS as shown above.

The next figure shows some interesting alternatives. The formula shown in L22 uses TOCOL, SORTBY, RANDARRAY and WRAPCOLS to perform the shuffle and deal in a single formula.

The formula shown in L24 and the results in L25:P28 use TAKE to make sure that each player only receives 5 cards.

	K	L	M	N	O	P	Q	R	S	T	U
21		All in one formula									
22		=WRAPCOLS(SORTBY(TOCOL(B5#),RANDARRAY(52)),L11,"")									
23		Only deal five cards to each player									
24		=TAKE(WRAPCOLS(I5#,4),,5)									
25	Player 1	K♠	6♥	9♥	2♣	10♦					
26	Player 2	7♦	5♣	7♥	7♠	4♠					
27	Player 3	3♦	10♥	10♠	6♦	Q♥					
28	Player 4	9♠	3♣	A♦	8♣	A♥					

#113 Use A2:INDEX() as a Non-Volatile OFFSET

There is a flexible function called OFFSET. It can point to a different-sized range that is calculated on-the-fly. In the image below, if someone changes the # Qtrs dropdown in H1 from 3 to 4, the fourth argument of OFFSET will make sure that the range expands to include four columns.

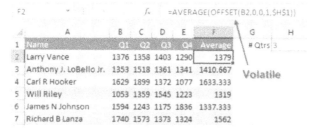

Spreadsheet gurus hate OFFSET because it is a volatile function. If you go to a completely unrelated cell and enter a number, all of the OFFSET functions will calculate—even if that cell has nothing to do with H1 or B2. Most of the time, Excel is very careful to only spend time calculating the cells that need to calculate. But once you introduce OFFSET, all of the OFFSET cells, plus everything downline from the OFFSET, starts calculating after every change in the worksheet.

In the formula below, there is a colon before the INDEX function. Normally, the INDEX function shown below would return the 1403 from cell D2. But when you put a colon on either side of the INDEX function, it starts returning the cell address D2 instead of the contents of D2. It is wild that this works.

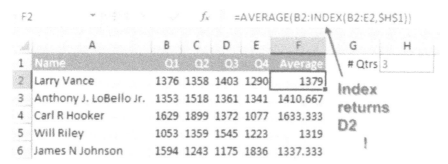

Why does this matter? INDEX is not volatile. You get all of the flexible goodness of OFFSET without the time-sucking recalculations over and over.

I first learned this tip from Dan Mayoh at Fintega. Thanks to Access Analytic for suggesting this feature.

#114 Number the Visible Rows in a Filtered Data Set

You've applied a filter to a data set and would like to number the visible rows. Two functions that can ignore rows hidden by a filter are SUBTOTAL and AGGREGATE. The key to this solution is to use the COUNTA version of SUBTOTAL for every cell from the Heading row to the current row. This number will always be one too high due to the heading, so subtract 1.

In this data set, notice how row 38 gets a row number of 1 because it is the first row visible from the filter.

#115 Unhide Multiple Worksheets

This is a great improvement introduced near the end of 2020 for Microsoft 365 subscribers. In the past, you could hide multiple worksheets at once, but you had to unhide them one at a time. With the change, you right-click any sheet tab and choose Unhide….

Excel now lets you multi-select which worksheets to unhide. The first time you use the feature, a guide appears telling you how to multi-select.

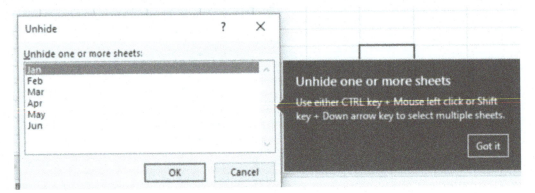

#116 Write Your Data with the Action Pen

The new Action Pen on the Draw tab of the Ribbon lets you hand-write data in a cell. After a moment, Excel converts the drawing to text or numbers as if you had typed the characters.

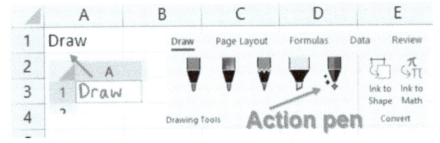

#117 Draw Perfect Shapes Using the New Draw-and-Hold Gesture

If you've ever tried sketching a circle or square in Excel using your mouse or stylus, you know the struggle is real. Jagged lines, wobbly edges—it's not great. But now, thanks to the Draw and Hold feature (borrowed from OneNote), you can sketch a rough shape and have Excel recognize and replace it with a perfect one.

First - make sure you have a Draw tab in the ribbon. If you don't already see a Draw tab in the ribbon:

1. Right-click anywhere on the ribbon.

2. Choose Customize the Ribbon.

3. Check the box for Draw.

4. Click OK.

Use the Draw and Hold Gesture

1. Go to the Draw tab.

2. Select a pen (you can choose from different ink colors and thicknesses).

3. Using your mouse or stylus, draw a shape in one fluid motion—square, circle, triangle, etc.

4. Hold the mouse or stylus at the end of the stroke (don't let go!).

If Excel recognizes the shape, it will clean up your rough drawing and replace it with a perfect version.

Resize or Rotate While Holding

If you continue holding after the shape appears, Excel enters a special mode: Drag out to resize the shape. Rotate by moving your cursor in a circular motion. Most people instinctively let go once the shape appears (guilty!), but hang on just a second longer and you can tweak the result before dropping it.

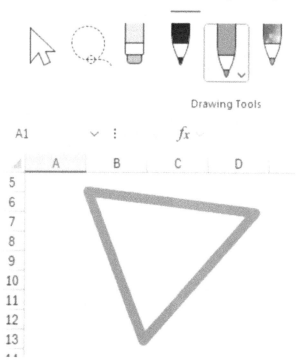

After some tests, it recognizes: Squares, rectangles, circles, ovals, stars, triangles. Hearts are tricky but possible.

How Is This Different From Insert > Shapes?

You can still go to Insert > Shapes to add precise geometry, but that process requires extra formatting (no fill, thicker outlines, etc.). The Draw and Hold method feels more natural and faster for casual or creative work. Shapes from Insert have detailed format controls and names like "Star, Five Points". Shapes from Draw are labeled "Ink" and lack some formatting options.

#118 Many Task Panes Now Collapse into a Tab Strip

There are several features in Excel that open a task pane on the right side of Excel. Sometimes, you would end up with 2, 3, or even 4 task panes open and it would cover your entire screen.

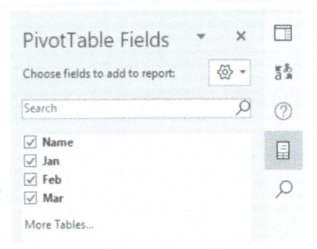

In February 2020, Microsoft 365 started collapsing task panes when more than 1 is open. A tab strip on the right side holds all the open task panes.

In the figure here, five task panes are available. The fourth is highlighted in grey and is the currently open PivotTable Fields task pane.

Click the icon to collapse the currently open task pane.

> **Note**: It is possible to collapse and open the task panes using the right arrow key to collapse and the left arrow key to open. In this state, you can move up and down the task panes using the arrow keys. However, it is also possible for focus to get stuck in the task pane strip and you can't use your arrows to navigate around the grid. In this case, press the F6 key three times to return focus to the grid.

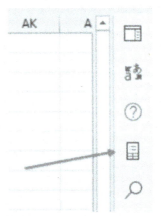

Tip: What if you like having two task panes open at the same time? Grab the title of a task pane and drop it on the grid. Or grab the title of a task pane and drag it off the left side of the worksheet. This will dock the task pane on the left. Anything docked on the left will never collapse. You could even dock four task panes on the left if you needed to.

#119 How to Provide Usable Feedback to the Excel Team

If you encounter a bug in Excel, here is the best way to get it fixed quickly. On the Help tab in the Ribbon, choose the Feedback icon. This opens a Feedback pane on the right side. Follow all of these steps:

1. Choose "Report a Problem". No one reads the "Send a Compliment" submissions.

2. Type a description of the problem.

3. Choose "Include Screenshot"

4. Choose "You can contact me about this feedback" and provide an e-mail address.

If you don't do all four of these, no one reads your feedback. But if you complete all four steps, a live person from the Excel team reads it and often a fix is sent out in a week.

How can you report a crash? Re-open Excel. Immediately send Feedback. In step 2, type "Excel crashed on the last session". The logs from step 3 will help pinpoint the problem.

> **Caution**: In 2021, Microsoft gave your I.T. department the ability to prevent you from including your e-mail in feedback. This is an unfortunate decision, as it prevents Microsoft from acting on any feedback or bugs from your entire organization. Maybe you can show this topic to your Microsoft 365 Admin and they can alter the settings to allow you to report a bug so it can get fixed.

#120 Date Tricks in Excel

Column C in the figure below shows several cool date formulas. Given a date in B1, you can use EOMONTH to get to the end or start of the month. You can break out the YEAR, MONTH, DAY and then put it back together using the DATE function.

You can use the TEXT function to isolate the weekday name or month name. The WORKDAY and NETWORKDAYS in row 9 and 13 are similar to "Thanks to Tony DeJonker, Cat Parkinson, & Geoff in Huntsville for suggesting the Function Arguments dialog trick." on page 165.

	A	B	C
1	Date	4/15/2024	*Formula to achieve result*
2	End of this month	4/30/2024	=EOMONTH(B1,0)
3	Start of this month	4/1/2024	=EOMONTH(B1,-1)+1
4	Year	2024	=YEAR(B1)
5	Month	4	=MONTH(B1)
6	Day	15	=DAY(B1)
7	3 Months Later	7/15/2024	=DATE(YEAR(B1),MONTH(B1)+3,DAY(B1))
8	18 Months Later	10/15/2025	=DATE(YEAR(B1),MONTH(B1)+18,DAY(B1))
9	30 Workdays Later	5/27/2024	=WORKDAY(B1,30)
10	Weekday Name	Monday	=TEXT(B1,"DDDD")
11	Weekday Abbrev.	Mon	=TEXT(B1,"DDD")
12	Month Name	April	=TEXT(B1,"MMM")
13	Fridays between B1 & B8	78	=NETWORKDAYS.INTL(B1,B8,"1111011")

#121 Use the LET Function to Re-Use Variables in a Formula

The LET function debuted during 2020 for Microsoft 365 Subscribers. There are all sorts of calculations in Excel that can benefit from re-using an intermediate calculation.

> **Note**: The actual problem presented in this topic is not important. This is just a problem that is representative of the kind of problem that LET will make easier.

Someone e-mailed me and needed a formula to find the next-to-last word in a series of phrases stored in column A. Each cell might have anywhere from 5 to 10 words. I know that I can solve this type of problem, but I know the solution will have a lot of parts. So – my strategy is to insert a bunch of columns and work it out, piece by piece.

The solution requires me to count the words by taking the LEN of the phrase and then the LEN of the phrase with the spaces removed. Once you know the number of words, you can change the correct space to a ^ and then use FIND to isolate the location of the caret. Once you use MID to get the text after the caret, you find the space between the last and next-to-last word and use LEFT. While each step is simple, knowing how to put all of those together is tricky.

In the figure below, I have built the solution using five formulas. It is working and I could likely explain it to anyone who uses Excel 10 hours a week.

▲	A	B	C	D	E	F
1	Find the Second-to-Last Word					
3	**Phrase**	**TRIM**	**Which Word?**	**Add Caret**	**After Caret**	**Answer**
4	hi you airport id	hi you airp	2	hi you^airport id	airport id	airport
5	web do thousands museur	web do th	2	web do^thousands museu	thousands m	thousands
6	second house a do ball	second ho	3	second house a^do ball	do ball	do
7	allowed tax do yesterday s	allowed ta	5	allowed tax do yesterday	classroom lo	classroom
8		B4: =TRIM(A4)				
9		C4: =LEN(B4)-LEN(SUBSTITUTE(B4," ",""))-1			E4 is used twice in F4	
10		D4: =SUBSTITUTE(B4," ","^",C4)			D4 is used four times	
11		E4: =MID(D4,FIND("^",D4)+1,30)			C4 is used four times	
12		F4: =LEFT(E4,FIND(" ",E4)-1)			B4 is used 12 times!	

However, I've also learned that some people just want the formula to solve this, and they don't want to know how it works. Those people want the whole formula to be in a single cell.

At this point, I often try to merge everything into a single formula. The formula in cell F4 refers to the formula in E4 twice. Select E4. Using the mouse in the Formula Bar, carefully select everything after the equals sign and then copy it. Edit the original formula in F4. Select the characters "E4" in the formula and use CTRL+V to paste to replace "E4" with the actual formula from E4. Continue in this fashion until you have a single formula.

The formula keeps growing, and eventually the B4 formula of TRIM(A4) appears a total of 12 times in the final formula. Excel has to perform the TRIM operation 12 times for each cell. Explaining this formula to someone else will be difficult, if not impossible.

```
=LEFT(MID(SUBSTITUTE(TRIM(A4)," ","^",LEN(TRIM(A4))-LEN(SUBSTITUTE(TRIM(A4)," ","")))-1),
FIND("^",SUBSTITUTE(TRIM(A4)," ","^",LEN(TRIM(A4))-LEN(SUBSTITUTE(TRIM(A4)," ","")))-
1))+1,30),FIND(" ",MID(SUBSTITUTE(TRIM(A4)," ","^",LEN(TRIM(A4))-LEN(SUBSTITUTE(TRIM(A4),
" ","")))-1),FIND("^",SUBSTITUTE(TRIM(A4)," ","^",LEN(TRIM(A4))-LEN(SUBSTITUTE(TRIM(A4),
" ","")))-1))+1,30))-1)
```

This is where the LET function helps. The LET function starts out with pairs of arguments where you give a variable name and the definition for that variable. The calculation for the second variable can re-use the logic assigned to the first variable. The final argument in the function is the calculation returned to the cell.

You can plan out your LET function as shown here:

Variable	Stands For	Calculation
T	Trimmed phrase	TRIM(A4)
WW	Which word	LEN(T)-LEN(SUBSTITUTE(T," ",""))-1
CT	Careted Text	SUBSTITUTE(T," ","^",WW)
LastTwo	After Caret	MID(CT,FIND("^",CT)+1,30)
Word	LastTwo up to first space	LEFT(LastTwo,FIND(" ",LastTwo)-1)

And then wrap that logic in the LET function:

```
B4                          fx      =LET(
                                    T,TRIM(A4),
                                    WW,LEN(T)-LEN(SUBSTITUTE(T," ",""))-1,
                                    CT,SUBSTITUTE(T," ","^",WW),
                                    LastTwo,MID(CT,FIND("^",CT)+1,30),
                                    LEFT(LastTwo,FIND(" ",LastTwo)-1)
```

	A	B	C	D	E
1	Find the Second-to-Last Word				
3	Phrase	Penultimate using LET			
4	wondering importance expert yel	go			
5	album guess if found an	found			
6	second house a do ball	do			

The best practice for LET is to use Alt+Enter to go to a new line in the formula bar after each pair of arguments. This makes the formula easier to read.

The LET function will simplify an entire class of problems where you need to repeatedly refer to an earlier component later in the formula.

#122 Store Complex Formula Logic in LAMBDA function

Excel has a great formula language with hundreds of built-in calculations, but it doesn't have functions for every possible calculation. A new research project from Microsoft's Calc Intelligence team in England will allow you to create your own functions.

The new function, LAMBDA, is available for any Microsoft 365 subscribers. It's named after Princeton University mathematician Alonzo Church, who invented lambda calculus in 1936. Church was the doctoral advisor of Alan Turing, the famous mathematician who proposed the Turing machine to perform calculations long before modern computers were invented.

Imagine performing a complex calculation and passing variables to it. The variable names and logic are stored in the LAMBDA function and – after testing in the worksheet – you create a Name and insert the logic into name manager.

In the beta versions of LAMBDA, you were required to add LAMBDA functions to the Name Manager in Excel. This tiny dialog box with a single-row text box for entering the formula was not a fun place to try to edit your formulas.

In early 2021, Microsoft Research released an Advanced Formula Environment that makes LAMBDA easier to use. It is part of the Excel Labs add-in. Here is how to install it.

1. From the Home tab in Excel, select Add-ins. The Office Add-Ins dialog opens.

2. In the Search box, type Excel Labs and press Enter..

3. Click the Add button. Click the Continue button. The Excel Labs icon appear on the right side of the Home tab. Open the Excel Labs add-in. Choose the Open button below the Advanced Formula Environment.

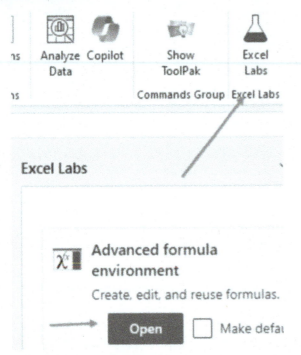

There are three main buttons in the add-in. Click the + icon to define a new LAMBDA. Click the Sync button to save your LAMBDAs to the Name Manager. Click the Import button to import from a GitHub Gist URL.

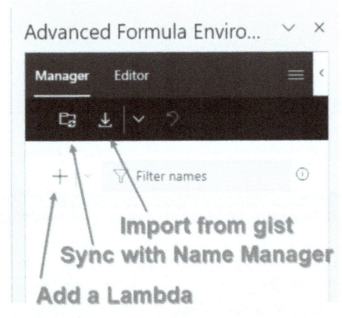

Let's start with a simple example. In a right triangle, the length of the hypotenuse is the square root of A squared plus B squared. To calculate the hypotenuse, you would use a formula such as =LAMBDA(A,B,SQRT(A^2+B^2)).

In this formula, the first two arguments are variables to hold values that will be passed to the function. The final argument is the logic to perform the calculation. You aren't limited to just two input variables. Everything up to the last argument is considered to be a variable. The final argument always holds the calculation logic.

In the Advanced Formula Editor, click the + icon and choose Function. A box will appear where you name your LAMBDA. A second box lets you edit your LAMBDA.

STORE COMPLEX FORMULA LOGIC IN LAMBDA FUNCTION

Give this a name of HYP. Type the formula =LAMBDA(a, b, SQRT(a^2 + b^2)). Click the Add button to add the formula definition. Caution: The formula is not yet available to use. You must first click the Sync button to Sync Names With The Excel Name Manager.

After you sync the new LAMBDA to the Name Manager, you can use the formula in the Excel grid. Excel offers intellisense, just like any other Excel function.

Here is the formula in the AFE panel:

HYP

=LAMBDA(a, b,
    SQRT(a ^ 2 + b ^ 2)
)

The AFE panel is really just a conduit for getting the formula into the Name Manager:

Edit Name

Name: HYP

Scope: Workbook

Comment:

Refers to: = LAMBDA(a,b,SQRT(a^2+b^2))

OK   Cancel

Here are the formulas working in the grid. Notice that the intellisense even shows that the function is expecting two arguments, named a & b.

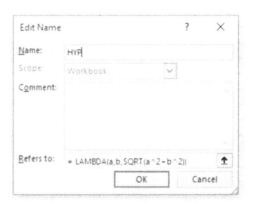

fx =HYP(C7,D7)

B	C	D	E	F

Side 1	Side 2	Hypontenuse
3	4	5
5	12	13
8	15	17
9	12	=HYP(C7,D7)

HYP(a, b)

Before the AFE was available, you would sometimes want to edit and test the formula in the grid before trying to add it to the Name Manager. You could type the formula in the grid, followed by the argument values in parentheses. This still works. =LAMBDA(A,B,SQRT(A^2+B^2))(3,4) would return the answer of 5.

D4 fx =HYP(B4,C4)

	A	B	C	D	E	F
1	Test:		5	=LAMBDA(A,B,SQRT(A^2+B^2))(3,4)		
2						
3		Side A	Side B	Hypotenuse		
4		3	4	5	=HYP(B4,C4)	
5		5	12	13	=HYP(B5,C5)	
6		9	12	15	=HYP(B6,C6)	
7		15	36	39	=HYP(B7,C7)	
8		18	24	30	=HYP(B8,C8)	

Bonus: Importing LAMBDAs from GitHub

The AFE lets you import LAMBDA from a GitHub Gist (pronouced jist). Chris Gross, from the Excel team, made this Gist available on the day the AFE was released. Import it and you will instantly have several LAMBDAs available in the workbook.

1. In the Advanced Formula Environment, click the Import icon.

2. A box appears where you can type a URL. Enter the following: https://gist.github.com/chgrossMSFT/d172fd552cf6893bcdc7942223cb0e55

3. Optionally, you can add these LAMBDAs to a Name Space. If you use a name space of MSFT, then all of the LAMBDAs imported will start with MSFT. This might help you to keep your LAMBDA formulas categorized.

4. After a successful import, you can browse the new LAMBDAs. They won't be available to use until you press the Sync button to add them to the Name Manager.

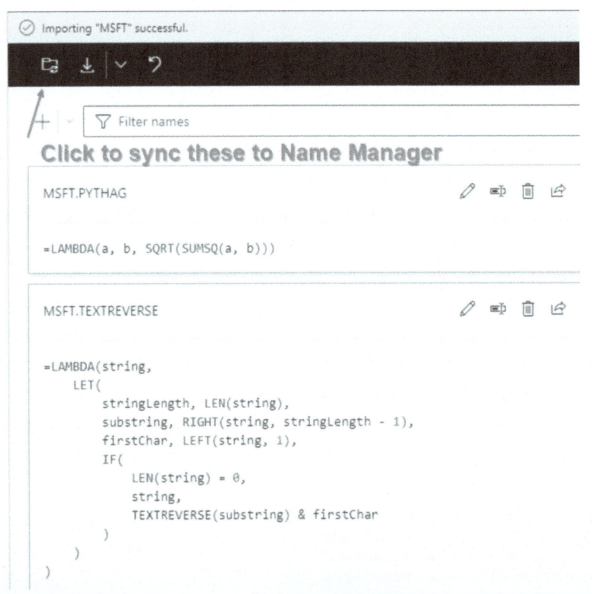

By using a Name Space of MSFT, all of these functions will appear in the Formula AutoComplete when you type =MSFT.

Here is the MSFT.TEXTREVERSE function working in the grid.

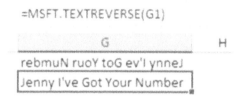

Another great resource is Owen Price's collection of Lambdas. Browse the complete list at https://github.com/ncalm

Transferring LAMBDAs Between Workbooks

A LAMBDA is stored in the Name Manager in the workbook. There is a "bug" in Excel that actually comes in very handy here. Let's say that you have a workbook with many LAMBDAs defined. Insert a new blank worksheet in that workbook. Copy the worksheet to another Excel file. All of the Names defined in the first workbook will be copied to the new workbook. This is usually pretty annoying. But in this, case it is a perfect way to transfer LAMBDAs from one workbook to another.

LAMBDAs Work in More Endpoints than VBA.

In the past, people might have used VBA to write their own user-defined functions. These were fine when everyone was using a PC or a Mac. But slowly, the small percentage of people using Excel on an iPad or Android or Excel Online is growing, and those versions of Excel can't support VBA. LAMBDA functions, however, can be used with Excel online or a mobile device.

Charles Williams and the LAMBDA Explorer

MVP Charles Williams is working on an amazing free add-in called the LAMBDA EXPLORER. It allows you to watch your Lambda functions to calculate in slow motion. Download the beta from http://www.decisionmodels.com/FastExcelLambdaExplorer.htm. Recursive Lambdas are fully evaluated and can be expanded to the next recursion level: the arguments show at each level the progression of the recursion.

#123 Combining Subformulas into a Single Lambda

Often, I will need a complicated formula. It is easier to build that formula in tiny steps. Once the subformulas are working, you can try to combine everything into one complicated formula.

Just as an example, your manager wants you to calculate sales per workday for this spreadsheet of sales in 2028.

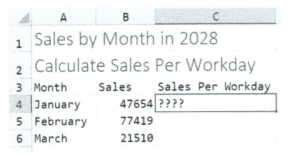

As I start to think about this, I break it down into steps:

	E	F	G
3	Steps to Solve this:		
4	1. Convert text month in A4 to a date at the beginning of the month		
5		1/1/2028	=DATEVALUE(A4&" 1, 2028")
6	2. Use EOMONTH(,0) to get End of Month		
7		1/31/2028	=EOMONTH(F5,0)
8	3. Use NETWORKDAYS to count Monday through Friday Dates		
9		21	=NETWORKDAYS(F5,F7)
10	4. Divide Sales by Net Work Days		
11		2269.2381	=B4/F9

In the distant past, I would end up with one super-formula:

```
=B4/NETWORKDAYS(DATEVALUE(A4&" 1, 2028"),EOMONTH(DATEVALUE(A4&" 1, 2028"),0))
```

In the more recent past, I could re-use formula logic in the LET function:

```
=LET(FirstOfMonth,DATEVALUE(A4&" 1, 2028"),
EndOfMonth,EOMONTH(FirstOfMonth,0),
NumberWorkDays,NETWORKDAYS(FirstOfMonth,EndOfMonth),
B4/NumberWorkDays)
```

But the new Import from Grid functionality in the Excel Labs add-in makes it simple to reduce the formula.

Start with a system of subformulas as shown here:

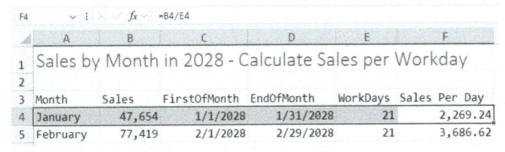

Select the input cell, the subformulas and the final result as shown above.

Install the Excel Labs add-in. Using the icon at the right side of the Home tab, open Excel Labs.

Click on the section for Advanced Formula Environment.

In the Excel Labs task pane, choose Modules and then Import from Grid.

Excel Labs

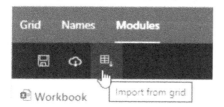

The Excel Labs add-in will detect the output cell and the parameter cells.

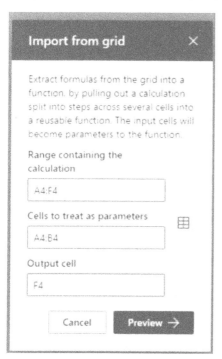

Click Preview and you will see the formula being proposed.

Import from grid

Function name

Sales_Per_Day

Refers to

```
=LAMBDA(Month, Sales,
    LET(
        FirstOfMonth, DATEVALUE(
            Month &
                " 1, 2028"
        ),
        EndOfMonth, EOMONTH(
            FirstOfMonth,
            0
        ),
        WorkDays, NETWORKDAYS(
            FirstOfMonth,
            EndOfMonth
        ),
        Sales / WorkDays
```

Click Create. This adds the formula to the Advanced Formula Environment, but it is not available in the grid until you click the Save icon:

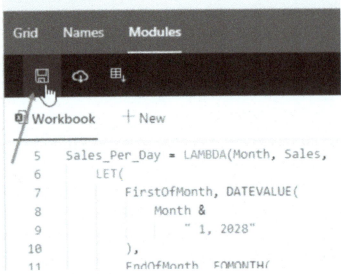

Clicking Save will add the Lambda function to the Name Manager in Excel. You can then use the formula as shown here:

	Month	Sales	Sales Per WorkDay
2			
3	Month	Sales	Sales Per WorkDay
4	January	47,654	=Sales_Per_Day(A4,B4
5	February	77,419	Sales_Per_Day(Month, Sales)
6	March	21,510	
7	April	94,562	

Here is the final result after formatting the cell and copying the formula down.

C4		fx	=Sales_Per_Day(A4,B4)

	A	B	C
1	Sales by Month in 2028		
2	Calculate Sales Per Workday		
3	Month	Sales	Sales Per WorkDay
4	January	47,654	$2,269.24
5	February	77,419	$3,686.62
6	March	21,510	$935.22
7	April	94,562	$4,728.10
8	May	9,093	$395.35
9	June	56,926	$2,587.55
10	July	8,080	$384.76

COMBINING SUBFORMULAS INTO A SINGLE LAMBDA

The logic for Sales_Per_Day is stored in the Name Manager for the workbook. That means anyone who opens the workbook on any computer or in Excel Online will have access to this function. Copy the worksheet to a new workbook and the logic will travel to the new workbook. This is amazing.

Using LAMBDA with Data Types

The team that developed LAMBDA is the same one that created data types and the LET function. That means LAMBDA was designed to work perfectly with Data Types. This enables more complex uses of LAMBDA.

Say that you have city pairs in column A and B. You convert these to Geography data types using the Data Type gallery on the Data tab of the ribbon. The Map icons mean that each cell contains many fields about the city. Two of those fields are Latitude and Longitude.

C2		f_x =MILES(A2,B2)	
	A	B	C
1	From	To	Distance in Miles
2	Cleveland	Orlando	894.54
3	Pago Pago	Timbuktu	11600.38
4	Montvale	Springfield	1063.37
5	Bangor	San Diego	2694.10

```
=LAMBDA(From,To,(3959*2)*
ASIN(SQRT(0.5-COS((To.Latitude-
From.Latitude)*PI()/180)/2+
COS(From.Latitude*PI()/180)*
COS(To.Latitude*PI()/180)*
(1-COS((To.Longitude-From.Longitude)*PI()
/180))/2)))
```

There's a complicated formula for calculating the distance between two cities using their respective latitude and longitude. You start out assuming the radius of the Earth is 3,959 miles. The formula uses functions for arcsine and cosine and is generally one that most people would never remember:

```
=(3959*2)*ASIN(SQRT(0.5-COS((B2.Latitude-A2.Latitude)*PI()/180)/2+COS(A2.
Latitude*PI()/180)*COS(B2.Latitude*PI()/180)*(1-COS((B2.Longitude-A2.
Longitude)*PI()/180))/2)).
```

If you wrap that formula in the LAMBDA function as =LAMBDA(From,To,(3959*2)*ASIN(SQRT(0.5-COS((To.Latitude-From.Latitude)*PI()/180)/2+COS(From.Latitude*PI()/180)*COS(To.Latitude*PI()/180)*(1-COS((To.Longitude-From.Longitude)*PI()/180))/2))) and then store it in the Name Manager with an easy name like MILES, then you can calculate the distance between two cities using a formula as simple as =MILES(A2,B2).

To move that formula from one workbook to another, you simply copy any worksheet from the original workbook to a new workbook, and the names will travel along. With this portability, it's possible to envision a company's accounting department that has a library of custom LAMBDA functions that move from workbook to workbook.

> **Note**: Mathematicians are celebrating that the LAMBDA function makes Excel "Turing Complete" and can solve any mathematical problem.

Bonus Tip: Perform a Loop with a Recursive LAMBDA

A LAMBDA function can also call other LAMBDA functions, and it can recursively call itself. This lets you create a LAMBDA function that keeps calling itself until the task is complete.

These are likely the most complicated topic in the whole book. Let me demonstrate how one LAMBDA can solve a problem that would be pretty difficult with regular Excel functions.

I frequently write articles for MrExcel.com. My full stack developer is Suat Ozgur. When Suat is converting my article to a web page, he puts the title in the URL to help with Search Engine Optimization. Converting a title from "Why I say 'Bazinga!' - my #1 Reason for Using =INDEX(MATCH())!!", to a URL requires certain rules. The only characters that are used in our URLs are the lower case letters a through z and the digits 0 through 9 and a dash. As you scan through any article title, there are 37 characters that can be left alone. Another 26 upper case characters need to be converted to lower case. That leaves 192 other characters that have to be replaced with an dash. (Technically, Suat thinks he only has to check the 31 illegal characters that are on a U.S. keyboard. Because he thinks I am too lazy to type a =CHAR(149) to get a bullet point. But Suat doesn't realize that I can press the Alt key and 7 on the number keypad to get bullet points. ••••••
So he better check all 192 potential bad characters because he never knows when I might surprise him.)

Getting rid of bad characters with SUBSTITUTE would take a long time. To be really safe, you would have to use one SUBSTITUTE function for each of the 192 characters. Since you can not nest more than 64 functions, you would have to break the formula into four columns. Even if you tried to only handle the 31 illegal characters that are on a U.S. keyboard, the problem would be overwhelming.

The process of converting the above phrase to "why-i-say-bazinga-my-1-reason-for-using-index-match-" is called turning the title into a slug. The people who deal with web pages have made word this into a verb, saying that you have to "slugify" next month's article titles.

If you were going to build this in regular Excel formulas, the logic might go like this:

1. Start with character position 1. Store this in a cell column that we will call Index.

2. Convert that character to lowercase using LOWER()

3. See what ASCII code that letter is.

4. If the code for that letter between 48-57 or between 97 to 122? If it is, then use that character. If it is not, then use a hyphen.

5. Take the characters to the left of index, the new character from step 4, and the characters to the right of index. This is the new phrase.

6. Add 1 to the Index.

7. Check to see if the new Index is greater than the number of characters in the title. If it is, then do a final SUBSTITUTE to replace any instances of a double -- with a single hypen. You are done. Stop calculating.

8. But if the Index is not greater than the LEN, go to step 2, this time processing the 2nd character.

It is a crazy worksheet. I managed to convert my article title using just 630 formulas in A3:J65. Here is a tiny fraction of the worksheet.

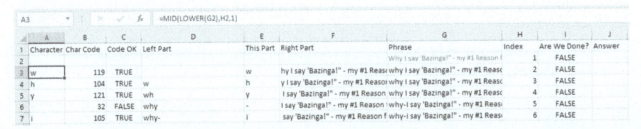

	A	B	C	D	E	F	G	H	I	J
1	Character	Char Code	Code OK	Left Part	This Part	Right Part	Phrase	Index	Are We Done?	Answer
2							Why I say 'Bazinga!' - my #1 Reason	1	FALSE	
3	w	119	TRUE		w	hy I say 'Bazinga!' - my #1 Reaso	why I say 'Bazinga!' - my #1 Reaso	2	FALSE	
4	h	104	TRUE	w	h	y I say 'Bazinga!' - my #1 Reaso	why I say 'Bazinga!' - my #1 Reaso	3	FALSE	
5	y	121	TRUE	wh	y	I say 'Bazinga!' - my #1 Reason	why I say 'Bazinga!' - my #1 Reaso	4	FALSE	
6		32	FALSE	why	-	I say 'Bazinga!' - my #1 Reason	why-I say 'Bazinga!' - my #1 Reas	5	FALSE	
7	i	105	TRUE	why-	i	say 'Bazinga!' - my #1 Reason f	why-I say 'Bazinga!' - my #1 Reas	6	FALSE	

A3   fx   =MID(LOWER(G2),H2,1)

At the end of the worksheet, the index is finally greater than the LEN, and you finally get an answer in cell J65.

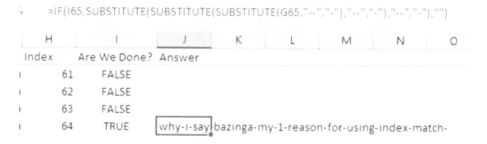

`=IF(I65,SUBSTITUTE(SUBSTITUTE(SUBSTITUTE(G65,"--","-"),"--","-"),"--","-"),"")`

H	I	J	K	L	M	N	O
Index	Are We Done?	Answer					
61	FALSE						
62	FALSE						
63	FALSE						
64	TRUE	why-i-say-bazinga-my-1-reason-for-using-index-match-					

I want us to agree that the above method is pretty ugly and not really reasonable. I don't want to have to explain the formulas that I used above, since we are abandoning that method. However, in case you really want to see the formulas, here they are:

A3	Character	`=MID(LOWER(G2),H2,1)`	Get "this" character
B3	Char Code	`=CODE(A3)`	
C3	Code OK	`=OR(AND(B3>96,B3<123),AND(B3>47,B3<58))`	Check if it is okay
D3	Left Part	`=LEFT(G2,H2-1)`	
E3	This Part	`=IF(C3,A3,"-")`	If it is not okay, use a dash
F3	Right Part	`=RIGHT(G2,LEN(G2)-H2)`	
G3	Phrase	`=CONCAT(D3:F3)`	Put left, this, right back together
H3	Index	`=1+H2`	Add 1 to the index
I3	Are We Done?	`=H3>LEN(G3)`	Are we done?
J3	Answer	`=IF(I3,SUBSTITUTE(SUBSTITUTE(SUBSTITUTE(G3,"--","-"),"--","-"),"--","-"),"")`	

All of the above is ugly. 630 formulas. If the phrase gets longer, you will need more formulas.

It can all be replaced with one LAMBDA function stored in a name called SLUGIFY.

As the author of this book, I am hoping you ignored everything above this. **But I really hope you try and understand everything that follows.** This is the part that shows you how recursive LAMBDAs work.

Start the function with =LAMBDA and name the two arguments that will be passed to it. The first argument is a phrase. The second argument will always be a 1 and will be stored in a variable called "ndx" because this sounds like "index" but is 40% shorter.

> **Tip**: For the VBA programmers reading this, "ndx" is our loop counter. Unlike VBA where you could just create a variable on the fly, for LAMBDA, we have to send a 1 in as an argument. Trust me - it is a small compromise.

Call Slugify by passing a phrase and index of 1

```
=LAMBDA(phrase,ndx,
  IF(ndx <= LEN(phrase),
    Slugify(
      LET(
        char, LOWER(MID(phrase, ndx, 1)),
        charcode, CODE(char),
        LEFT(phrase, ndx - 1) &
        IF(OR(AND(charcode > 96, charcode < 123), AND(charcode > 47, charcode < 58)), char, "-")
        & RIGHT(phrase, LEN(phrase) - ndx) ),
        ndx + 1),
    SUBSTITUTE(TRIM(SUBSTITUTE(phrase, "-", " ")),"  ","-")
  )
)
```

Start off with an IF function that checks to see if we are done. Is the ndx beyond the end of the phrase?.

Have we processed all characters?

```
=LAMBDA(phrase,ndx,
  IF(ndx <= LEN(phrase),
    Slugify(
      LET(
        char, LOWER(MID(phrase, ndx, 1)),
        charcode, CODE(char),
        LEFT(phrase, ndx - 1) &
        IF(OR(AND(charcode > 96, charcode < 123), AND(charcode > 47, charcode < 58)), char, "-")
        & RIGHT(phrase, LEN(phrase) - ndx) ),
        ndx + 1),
    SUBSTITUTE(TRIM(SUBSTITUTE(phrase, "-", " ")),"  ","-")
  )
)
```

The part in the box below is the Value_if_True part of the IF statement. If we aren't done with Slugify, then call Slugify again, but make the Index be 1 more than the last time. The inner logic is described after the figure.

This is the "not done yet" clause of IF

```
=LAMBDA(phrase,ndx,
  IF(ndx <= LEN(phrase),
    Slugify(      ← Call Slugify again(!)
      LET(
        char, LOWER(MID(phrase, ndx, 1)),   These 6 lines calculate the
        charcode, CODE(char),
        LEFT(phrase, ndx - 1) &              phrase for the next call to Slugify
        IF(OR(AND(charcode > 96, charcode < 123), AND(charcode > 47, charcode < 58)), char, "-")
        & RIGHT(phrase, LEN(phrase) - ndx) ),
        ndx + 1),   ← & the index will be 1 more than last time
    SUBSTITUTE(TRIM(SUBSTITUTE(phrase, "-", " ")),"  ","-")
  )
)
```

These six lines are the part of the formula that build the PHRASE for the next call to Slugify. If you use Excel frequently, all of the functions in this part should feel familiar. Use LOWER and MID to isolate this character. Get the CODE of that character. If the CODE is a letter or digit, then use it, otherwise use a hyphen. The phrase for the next time is going to be the left part, the newly fixed character, and the right part.

Isolate *this* character

```
LET(
   char, LOWER(MID(phrase, ndx, 1)),       get the character code
   charcode, CODE(char),
   LEFT(phrase, ndx - 1) &                 text to the left of this character
   IF(OR(AND(charcode > 96, charcode < 123), AND(charcode > 47, charcode < 58)), char, "-")
   & RIGHT(phrase, LEN(phrase) - ndx) ),   text to the right
```

Deep inside the LAMBDA is the one line that really does the work. If we have a letter or a digit, keep it. If it is one of the other 192 bad characters, then use a hyphen.

if char is lower-case letter or a digit   then use char

```
LET(
   char, LOWER(MID(phrase, ndx, 1)),
   charcode, CODE(char),
   LEFT(phrase, ndx - 1) &
   IF(OR(AND(charcode > 96, charcode < 123), AND(charcode > 47, charcode < 58)), char, "-")
   & RIGHT(phrase, LEN(phrase) - ndx) ),
```

otherwise use -

The first time you call Slugify, it will be fixing the first character. The Excel calculation engine will then call Slugify to fix the 2nd character. This keeps going. Eventually, Excel calls Slugify to fix the 64th character, but that's bad because there are only 63 characters in this phrase. So, when ndx is greater than the LEN of the phrase, it is time to finally return the result.

The SUBSTITUTE / TRIM / SUBSTITUTE logic replaces any multiple hyphens with a single hyphen.

Are we done?

```
=LAMBDA(phrase,ndx,
   IF(ndx <= LEN(phrase),          when ndx is beyond end of phrase
      Slugify(
         LET(
            char, LOWER(MID(phrase, ndx, 1)),
            charcode, CODE(char),
            LEFT(phrase, ndx - 1) &
            IF(OR(AND(charcode > 96, charcode < 123), AND(charcode > 47, charcode < 58)), char, "-")
            & RIGHT(phrase, LEN(phrase) - ndx) ),
         ndx + 1),
      SUBSTITUTE(TRIM(SUBSTITUTE(phrase, "-", " "))," ","-")
   )
)
```

then return the phrase, replacing -- with -

Note that up to this point, I've been building the LAMBDA in notepad or in a textbox in Excel.

So, you've written your LAMBDA. You have to give it a name so you can call it. On the Formulas tab, click New Name. Name it Slugify. Paste the formula from the textbox, spaces and all into the Refers To box.

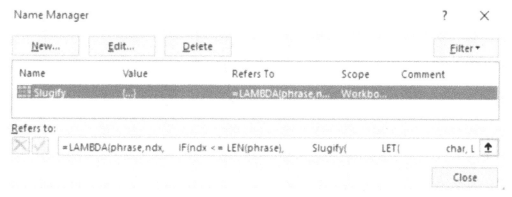

Here is the payoff... you now have a function called SLUGIFY that you can use repeatedly.

	A	B
	B2 ▼ : ✕ ✓ fx =Slugify(A2,1)	
1	Article Title	URL Slug
2	Why I say 'Bazinga!" - my #1 Reason for Using =INDEX(MATCH())!!	why-i-say-bazinga-my-1-reason-for-using-index-match
3	PowerPivot? PowerPoint?	powerpivot-powerpoint
4	Return Zero instead of #N/A	return-zero-instead-of-n-a
5	Bug with Rand() in Excel 2003	bug-with-rand-in-excel-2003
6	Prevent #N/A! in Excel VLOOKUP	prevent-n-a-in-excel-vlookup
7	Convert 11.5 to 11 Minutes and 30 Seconds	convert-11-5-to-11-minutes-and-30-seconds

The rebel in me (and perhaps in you) wonders what would happen if I changed the 1 in the second argument to 5. What do I get with =Slugify(A2,5)? I tried it. It sort of works. It just does not fix any of the first 4 characters.

Before LAMBDA, I would have created this as a VBA user-defined function. That requires you to understand VBA. And it won't ever work in Excel Online. Now, with LAMBDA, you can simply use familiar Excel logic to build a function that loops through all of the characters in a cell.

Bonus Tip: Branching in a LAMBDA

On an earlier version of the previous LAMBDA, I was getting multiple hyphens in the result. I wondered if you could have a second loop to clean those. Could you do the first task - replacing illegal characters with dash, and then have a second task of looping to look for consecutive hyphens.

Later, I realized that replacing - with space, using TRIM, and then replacing space with hyphen solved the problem without the need for a second loop. However, this formula assigned to the name Slugify.Plus is an example of branching, so I am leaving it in.

The following formula offers two routines. The Branch parameter controls which part of the code is used.

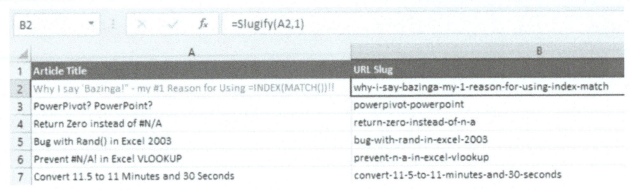

```
=LAMBDA(phrase,ndx,branch,
   IF(branch=1,
                                      ← original slugify logic
     IF(ndx > LEN(phrase),      ←———— Are we done?
       SLUGIFY.PLUS(phrase, 0,2);←———— Call Slugify branch 2
       SLUGIFY.PLUS(
         LET(
           character, LOWER(MID(phrase, ndx, 1)),
           charcode, CODE(character),
           LEFT(phrase, ndx - 1) &
             IF(OR(AND(charcode > 96, charcode < 123), AND(charcode > 47, charcode < 58)), character, "-") &
             RIGHT(phrase, LEN(phrase) - ndx) ),
         ndx + 1, 1 ) ),
   IF(LEN(phrase)-LEN(SUBSTITUTE(phrase, "--", ""))) = 0,
     LET( clearleft, IF(LEFT(phrase, 1)="-", RIGHT(phrase, LEN(phrase)-1), phrase),
       clearright, IF(RIGHT(clearleft, 1)="-", LEFT(clearleft, LEN(clearleft)-1), clearleft),
       clearright),
     SLUGIFY.PLUS(
       SUBSTITUTE(phrase, "--", "-"), 0, 2 ) ) ) )
```

These six lines are Branch 2 - a recursive routine to clean multiple hyphens

Note that the ndx argument is not used in Branch 2. But since LAMBDA arguments are not optional, you have to put something - I chose 0 - when calling branch 2.

Thanks to Suat Ozgur and Richard Simpson for help with Recursion and Branching.

#124 New LAMBDA Helper Functions

About a year after LAMBDA was introduced, Microsoft realized that we needed some helper functions. They gave us MAP, REDUCE, SCAN, MAKEARRAY, BYROW, BYCOL, and ISOMITTED.

- The MAP function runs a LAMBDA on each cell in an array or range and returns an identical-sized array or range.

- The REDUCE function runs a LAMBDA on each cell in an array or range but uses an accumulator variable to return one single answer.

- The SCAN function is sort of a combination of the two. It runs a LAMBDA on each cell of an array or range and returns an array the same size as the input range, showing the accumulator value after each step.

- The MAKEARRAY function will create an array of any size that you specify. You provide a LAMBDA to calculate each cell in the new array.

- The BYROW function forces a LAMBDA to calculate on each row in a range instead of the entire range.

- The BYCOL function forces a LAMBDA to calculate on each column in a range.

- LAMBDAs now support optional arguments. You can test if an optional argument was skipped using the new ISOMITTED function.

Evaluating a LAMBDA for Each Cell in a Range or Ranges

The MAP function will perform a LAMBDA calculation for each cell in a range. In the example below, you are passing two ranges to MAP. Because there are two incoming ranges, your LAMBDA needs two incoming variables A and B. Notice that each of the incoming arrays are 5 rows by 3 columns and the result from MAP is also 5 rows by 3 columns.

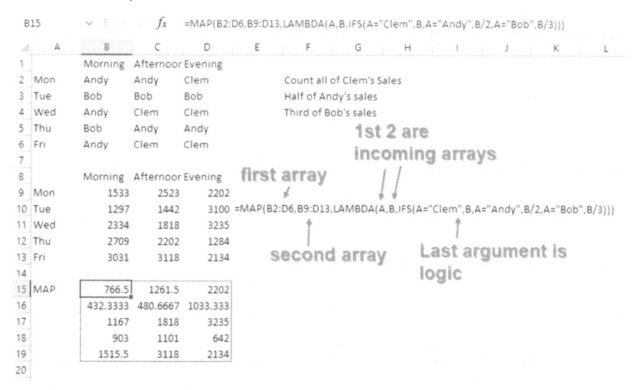

Note that MAP can accept multiple incoming arrays. This is not true for REDUCE, discussed next.

Accumulating a LAMBDA for Each Cell Using REDUCE

With REDUCE, a LAMBDA will be evaluated for each cell in an incoming array or range. On each pass through the logic, the result of the LAMBDA can be added to an accumulator variable. At the end of the calculation, the formula returns the final value of the accumulator variable.

In this image, a REDUCE formula in B8 calculates the total bonus pool after several shifts. The initial value is set to 0. The incoming array is each cell in B2:D6. Inside the LAMBDA, the first two arguments are the variable for the accumulator and for the cell from the incoming array. The last argument in the LAMBDA is the logic. Notice how the logic is adding the previous value of the accumulator to some calculation from this cell of the incoming range.

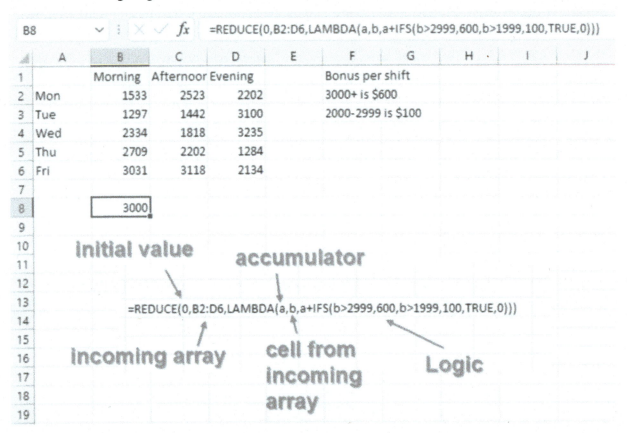

Seeing the Results From Each Step of REDUCE with SCAN

The SCAN function performs the same calculation as REDUCE shown on the previous page. However, instead of returning a single value, it shows each intermediate value along the way.

In the image below, the Monday morning shift with sales of $1533 did not qualify for a bonus, so B8 shows 0. The Monday afternoon shift qualified for a $100 bonus, so C8 shows the total bonus earned so far is $100. The Monday evening shift earned another $100 for the bonus pool, so the total bonus as of the end of Monday is $200 shown in D8. Notice how the $3100 in sales for Tuesday evening kicked the bonus pool up from $200 to $800, with the $800 being shown in D9.

B8   ✓ : fx =SCAN(0,B2:D6,LAMBDA(a,b,a+IFS(b>2999,600,b>1999,100,TRUE,0)))

	A	B	C	D	E	F	G	H	I	J
1		Morning	Afternoor	Evening		Bonus per shift				
2	Mon	1533	2523	2202		3000+ is $600				
3	Tue	1297	1442	3100		2000-2999 is $100				
4	Wed	2334	1818	3235						
5	Thu	2709	2202	1284						
6	Fri	3031	3118	2134						
7										
8		0	100	200						
9		200	200	800						
10		900	900	1500						
11		1600	1700	1700						
12		2300	2900	3000						
13										

Evaluate a LAMBDA for Each Row or Column

Say that you asked for the MAX(A5:D11). You would get one single number that was the largest value in the range. Sometimes, though, it would be good to have MAX run on a column-by-column basis or a row-by-row basis and return the results as a spillable array. The BYCOL and BYROW functions allow you to do this.

A14   ✓ : fx =BYCOL(A5:D11,MAX)

	A	B	C	D	E	F
1	BYCOL and BYROW					
2	=BYCOL(array,LAMBDA(a,logic))					
3	=BYROW(array,LAMBDA(a,logic))					
4						Max each row
5	11	89	48	26		89
6	92	83	32	221		221
7	777	39	24	43		777
8	26	93	554	33		554
9	42	80	89	24		89
10	1	666	2	33		666
11	46	67	18	67		67
12						
13	Max Each Column					
14	777	666	554	221		
15	A14 =BYCOL(A5:D11,MAX)					

Note that the MAX in the above formulas is an Eta-Lambda introduced in November 2023. Before the Eta-Lambdas were introduced, you would use LAMBDA(A,Max(A)).

Make an Array of Any Size

The MAKEARRAY function lets you specify a number of rows and columns for the new array. The third argument is a LAMBDA function with three arguments. The first is the row number. The second is the column number. The third argument is the logic to apply to this cell of the array.

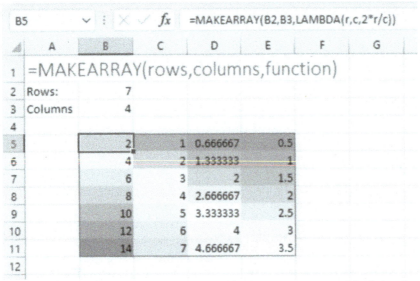

Thanks to Chris Gross and his team in Redmond for these great new LAMBDA helper functions.

#125 Find Largest Value That Meets One or More Criteria

One of the new Microsoft 365 functions added in February 2016 is the MAXIFS function. This function, which is similar to SUMIFS, finds the largest value that meets one or more criteria: You can either hard-code the criterion as in row 7 below or point to cells as in row 9. A similar MINIFS function finds the smallest value that meets one or more criteria.

	A	B	C	D	E	F	G	H
1	Largest	$99,876.41	=MAX($D$12:$D$125)					
2	2nd Largest	$99,588.23	=LARGE($D$12:$D$125,2)					
3	3rd Largest	$98,469.33	=LARGE($D$12:$D$125,3)					
4	3rd Smallest	$14,691.12	=SMALL($D$12:$D$125,3)					
5	2nd Smallest	$14,469.75	=SMALL($D$12:$D$125,2)					
6	Smallest	$13,593.04	=MIN($D$12:$D$125)					
7	Smallest Widget	$13,593.04	=MINIFS($D$12:$D$125,$B$12:$B$125,"Widget")					
8	Choose Criteria:	Widget	Central					
9	Largest with Criteria	$90,861.70	=MAXIFS($D$12:$D$125,$B$12:$B$125,B8,$C$12:$C$125,C8)					
10								
11	Name	Item	Region	Amount				
12	Peter Albert	Gadget	East	$40,292.39				
13	Amy Andrae	Whatzit	Central	$28,872.16				
14	Frank Arendt-Theilen	Gadget	West	$88,640.58				
15	Fr Tony Azzarto	Gadget	East	$49,898.29				
16	Lorna Banuilos	Widget	Central	$90,861.70				

While most people have probably heard of MAX and MIN, but how do you find the second largest value? Use LARGE (rows 2 and 3) or SMALL (rows 4 and 5).

What if you need to sum the top seven values that meet criteria? The orange box below shows how to solve with the new Dynamic Arrays. The green box is the Ctrl+Shift+Enter formula required previously.

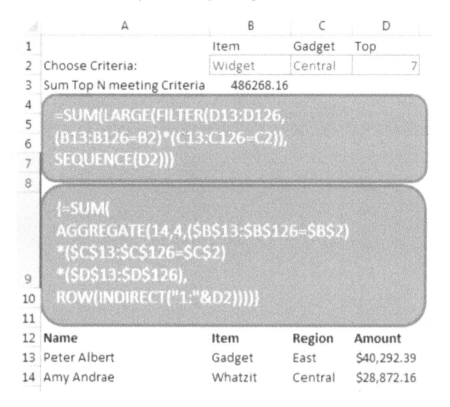

Bonus Tip: Concatenate a Range by Using TEXTJOIN

I love TEXTJOIN. What if you needed to concatenate all of the names in A1:A10? The formula =A1&A2&A3&A4&A5&A6&A7&A8&A9&A10 would jam everyone together like AndyBobCaroleDaleEdFloGloriaHelenIkeJill. By using TEXTJOIN, you can specify a delimiter such as ", ". The second argument lets you specify if blank cells should be ignored. =TEXTJOIN(", ",True,A1:A10) would produce Andy, Bob, Carole, and so on.

Tip: TEXTJOIN works with arrays. The array formula shown in A7 uses a criterion to find only the people who answered Yes. Make sure to hold down Ctrl + Shift while pressing Enter to accept this formula. The alternate formula shown in A8 uses the Dynamic Array FILTER function and does not require Ctrl+Shift+Enter.

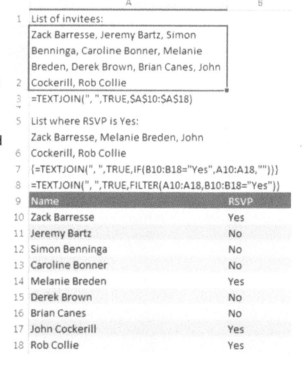

#126 Text Before or After a Specific Delimiter

The new TEXTBEFORE and TEXTAFTER functions debuted on March 16, 2022 for Microsoft 365 Insiders. These functions isolate the text before or after a specific delimiter.

The function syntax requires some text and the delimiter. Optional arguments: instance_num for which delimiter, match_mode for case sensitive, match_end prevents an #N/A if the delimiter is not found. TEXTBEFORE("Cher","") returns #N/A. =TEXTBEFORE("Cher","",,,1) returns Cher.

Note the third argument lets you specify which delimiter. If you use a negative number here, it counts from the right edge of the cell. The formula in F5 finds the last word in a phrase by using -1 as the value for N.

	A	B	C	D	E	F	G
1	=TEXTBEFORE(text,delimiter,instance_num,match_mode,match_end,if_not_found)						
2	=TEXTAFTER(text,delimiter,instance_num,match_mode,match_end,if_not_found)						
3							
4	Part Number	Before	After		Phrase	Last Word	
5	ICH-728	ICH	728		what is the last word	word	
6	ZR-581	ZR	581		how many words	words	
7	HC-872	HC	872		it is different every time	time	
8	DPE-488	DPE	488		Not difficult now	now	
9	HVMR-823	HVMR	823				
10	VT-403	VT	403				
11	BD-768	BD	768	B5	=TEXTBEFORE(A5,"-")		
12	FGNQJ-852	FGNQJ	852	C5	=TEXTAFTER(A5,"-")		
13	GED-153	GED	153	F5	=TEXTAFTER(E5," ",-1)		

#127 Split Text into Words Using TEXTSPLIT

Many people had been asking for TEXTSPLIT. It was one of the most popular requests on the Excel UserVoice site. I often used a three-line User-Defined Function from Excel MVP Brad Yundt to create a function to split text into words.

The version of TEXTSPLIT that made it to Excel is better than the simple UDF. The row_delimiter argument lets you split text into new rows. In the figure below, TEXTSPLIT is used without a column delimiter and has a row delimiter of ". " in order to put each sentence into a new row.

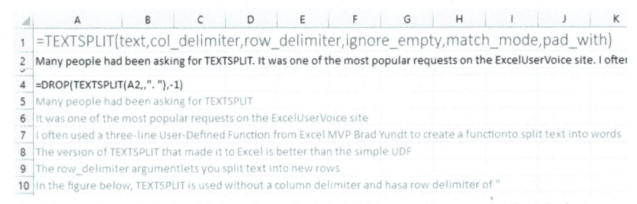

	A	B	C	D	E	F	G	H	I	J	K
1	=TEXTSPLIT(text,col_delimiter,row_delimiter,ignore_empty,match_mode,pad_with)										
2	Many people had been asking for TEXTSPLIT. It was one of the most popular requests on the ExcelUserVoice site. I ofter										
4	=DROP(TEXTSPLIT(A2,,". "),-1)										
5	Many people had been asking for TEXTSPLIT										
6	It was one of the most popular requests on the ExcelUserVoice site										
7	I often used a three-line User-Defined Function from Excel MVP Brad Yundt to create a functionto split text into words										
8	The version of TEXTSPLIT that made it to Excel is better than the simple UDF										
9	The row_delimiter argumentlets you split text into new rows										
10	In the figure below, TEXTSPLIT is used without a column delimiter and hasa row delimiter of "										

The ignore_empty argument will help with text that has multiple spaces between words. In the figure below, cells B3, E3, F3, H3, I3:M3 are empty because the text in A1 has multiple spaces between words. While you could solve this with =TEXTSPLIT(TRIM(A1)," "), you can also tell TEXTSPLIT to ignore empty with =TEXTSPLIT(A1," ",,TRUE). While TRIM removes multiple interior spaces, it is not a suitable solution for other delimiters such as a period or comma.

	A	B	C	D	E	F	G	H	I	J	K	L	M	N
1	this text has			too	many			spaces						
2	=TEXTSPLIT(A1," ")													
3	this			text has					too		many			spaces
4	=TEXTSPLIT(A1," ",,TRUE)													
5	this text has too many spaces													

When you use TEXTSPLIT for both rows and columns, the function fills any empty cells with #N/A errors. Use a Pad_With of "" to prevent the #N/A. Formulas shown below calculate the frequency of all words in the text.

	A	B	C	D	E	F	G	H	I	J	K
1	=TEXTSPLIT(text,col_delimiter,row_delimiter,ignore_empty,match_mode,pad_with)										
2	Many people had been asking for TEXTSPLIT. It was one of the most popular requests on the ExcelUserVoice site. I often use										
4	Many	people	had	been	asking	for	TEXTSPLIT				
5	It	was	one	of	the	most	popular	requests	on	the	ExcelUser s
6	I	often	used	a	three-line	User-Defi	Function	from	Excel	MVP	Brad Y
7	The	version	of	TEXTSPLIT	that	made	it	to	Excel	is	better t
8	The	row_delir	argument	you	split	text	into	new	rows		
9	In	the	figure	below,	TEXTSPLIT is		used	without	a	column	delimiter a
10	"	in	order	to	put	each	sentence	into	a	new	row
11											
12	Many		49	the		6	A4	=TEXTSPLIT(A2," ",".",TRUE,,"")			
13	people	"	2	a		4	A12	=TOCOL(A4#,3)			
14	had	a	4	into		3	B12	=SORT(UNIQUE(A12#))			
15	been	and	1	of		3	C12	=COUNTIFS(A12#,B12#)			
16	asking	argument	1	TEXTSPLIT		3	D12	=DROP(SORT(HSTACK(B12#,C12#),2,-1),1)			
17	for	asking	1	to		3					

#128 Less CSV Nagging

Some people have to create CSV files hundreds of times per day. Excel used to hassle you when you saved a CSV file: "Some features in your workbook might be lost if you save as CSV." People who have to export as CSV understand this and wanted Excel to stop hassling them. Starting in 2017, people with Microsoft 365 are no longer hassled for choosing to save as CSV.

#129 Better AutoComplete

Another small change in Microsoft 365: If you type an equals sign and start to type a function name, the tooltip offers partial matching. Type LOOK, and you will see all three functions that contain the text LOOK.

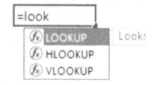

#130 Protect All Formula Cells

The use of worksheet protection in Excel is a little strange. Using the steps below, you can quickly protect just the formula cells in your worksheet.

It seems unusual, but all 16 billion cells on a worksheet start out with their Locked property set to True. You need to unlock all of the cells first:

1. Select all cells by using the icon above and to the left of cell A1.

2. Press Ctrl+1 (that is the number 1) to open the Format Cells dialog.

3. In the Format Cells dialog, go to the Protection tab. Uncheck Locked. Click OK.

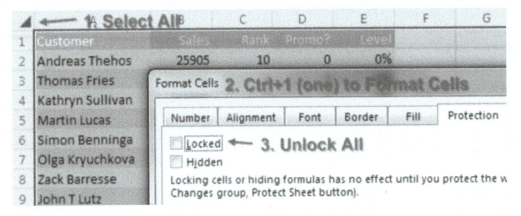

While all cells are still selected, select Home, Find & Select, Formulas.

At this point, only the formula cells are selected. Press Ctrl+1 again to display the Format Cells dialog. On the Protection tab, choose Locked to lock all of the formula cells.

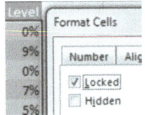

Locking cells does nothing until you protect the worksheet. On the Review tab, choose Protect Sheet. In the Protect Sheet dialog, choose if you want people to be able to select your formula cells or not.

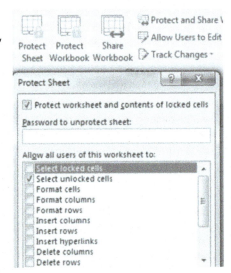

> **Note**: Scroll down a few rows in the Protect Sheet dialog box to reveal popular choices: Use AutoFilter and Use PivotTable & PivotChart. If you want allow people to interact with these features, scroll down and select them.

> **Caution**: Don't bother putting in a password. Passwords are easily broken and easily lost. You will find yourself paying $39 to the Estonians who sell the Office password-cracking software.

#131 Back into an Answer by Using Goal Seek

Do you remember from ""#78 Discover New Functions by Using fx" on page 162, that I showed you how to calculate a loan payment by using the Insert Function dialog? Back in that example, the monthly loan payment was going to be $493.54. I did not mention it at the time, but my monthly budget for car payments is $425.

If you are about the same age as me and spent your summers watching TV, you might remember a crazy game show called *The Price Is Right*. Long before Drew Carey, the venerable Bob Barker would give away prizes using a variety of games. One that I recall is the Hi Lo game. Bob would give you the car if you could state the price of the car. You would guess. Bob would shout "Higher" or "Lower." I think you had 20 seconds to narrow your guesses to the exact price.

A lot of times, I feel like those summers watching Bob Barker trained me to find answers in Excel. Have you ever found yourself plugging in successively higher and lower values into an input cell, hoping to arrive at a certain answer?

	A	B	C	D	E
1	Goal Seek on the Price is Right TV Show				
3	Principal	Term	Rate	Payment	Bob Barker
4	25995	60	5.25%	$493.54	Lower!
5	20000	60	5.25%	$379.72	Higher!
6	23000	60	5.25%	$436.68	Lower!
7	21500	60	5.25%	$408.20	Higher!
8	22300	60	5.25%	$423.39	Higher!
9	22700	60	5.25%	$430.98	Lower!
10	22500	60	5.25%	$427.18	Lower!
11	22400	60	5.25%	$425.29	Lower!
12	22390	60	5.25%	$425.10	Lower!
13	22380	60	5.25%	$424.91	Higher!
14	22385	60	5.25%	$425.00	Winner!

Illustration: Chad Thomas

A tool that is built in to Excel does exactly this set of steps. Select the cell with the Payment formula. On the Data tab, in the Data Tools group, look for the What-If Analysis dropdown and choose Goal Seek….

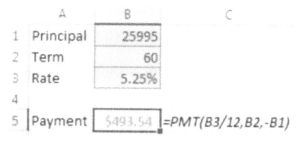

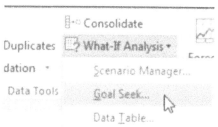

The figure below shows how you can try to set the payment in B5 to $425 by changing cell B1

Goal Seek finds the correct answer within a second.

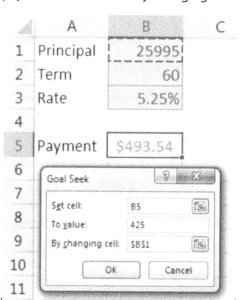

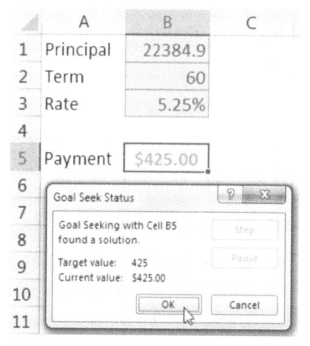

Note that the formula in B5 stays intact. The only thing that changes is the input value typed in B1.

Also, with Goal Seek, you are free to experiment with changing other input cells. You can still get the $425 loan payment and the $25,995 car if your banker will offer you a 71.3379-month loan!

Thanks to Jon Wittwer of Vertex42.com and to @BizNetSoftware for suggesting this Goal Seek trick.

#132 Do 60 What-If Analyses with a Sensitivity Analysis

Goal Seek lets you find the set of inputs that lead to a particular result. Sometimes, you want to see many different results from various combinations of inputs. Provided that you have only two input cells to change, the Data Table feature will do a sensitivity analysis.

Using the loan payment example, say that you want to calculate the price for a variety of principal balances and for a variety of terms.

	A	B	C	D	E	F
1	Principal	25995	Test from $20,995 to $29,995			
2	Term	60	Test from 36 to 72			
3	Rate	5.25%				
4						
5	Payment	$494				

Make sure that the formula you want to model is in the top-left corner of a range. Put various values for one variable down the left column and various values for another variable across the top.

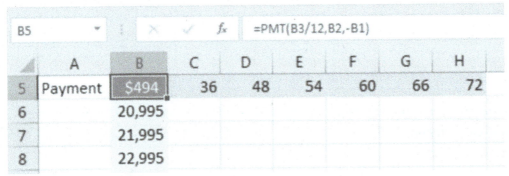

B5			f_x	=PMT(B3/12,B2,-B1)				

	A	B	C	D	E	F	G	H
5	Payment	$494	36	48	54	60	66	72
6		20,995						
7		21,995						
8		22,995						

From the Data tab, select What-If Analysis, Data Table….

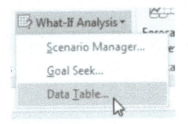

You have values along the top row of the input table. You want Excel to plug those values into a certain input cell. Specify that input cell for Row Input Cell.

You have values along the left column. You want those plugged into another input cell. Specify that cell for the Column Input Cell.

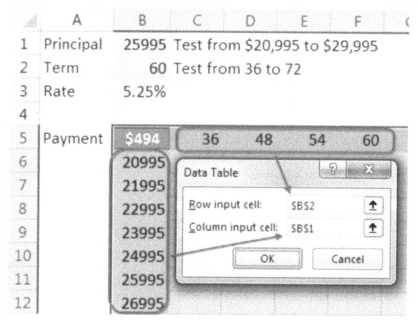

When you click OK, Excel repeats the formula in the top-left column for all combinations of the top row and left column. In the image below, you see 60 different loan payments, based on various inputs.

$494	36	48	54	60	66	72
20,995	632	486	437	399	367	341
21,995	662	509	458	418	384	357
22,995	692	532	479	437	402	373
23,995	722	555	500	456	419	389
24,995	752	578	521	475	437	405
25,995	782	602	542	494	454	422
26,995	812	625	562	513	472	438
27,995	842	648	583	532	489	454
28,995	872	671	604	550	507	470
29,995	902	694	625	569	524	487

Note: I formatted the table results to have no decimals and used Home, Conditional Formatting, Color Scale to add the red/yellow/green shading.

Here is the great part: This table is "live." If you change the input cells along the left column or top row, the values in the table recalculate. Below, the values along the left are focused on the $23K to $24K range.

$494	48	51	54	57	60	63
22,995	532	504	479	457	437	418
23,095	534	506	481	459	438	420
23,195	537	508	483	461	440	422

Tip: You can build far more complex models and still use a data table. In my podcast 2141 "Will Asteroid Bennu Strike the Earth" on YouTube, I had a model with 100K NORM.INV and 100K VLOOKUP. Those 200,000 formulas were sent to a SUM function that summarized them. I used a Data Table to run those 200,001 formulas 100 times. The whole thing recalcs in about 11 seconds.

Thanks to Owen W. Green for suggesting this tables technique.

Bonus Tip: Create a Data Table from a Blank Cell

Note: If you took a class on financial modeling in college, you likely used a textbook written by Professor Simon Benninga. He showed me this cool Excel trick.

Simon Benninga tells a story of a game called Penny Pitching. You and another student would each flip a penny. If you get one head and one tail, you win the penny. If the coins match (heads/heads or tails/tails), the other student gets the penny.

It is simple to model this game in Excel. If RAND()>.5, you win a penny. Otherwise, you lose a penny. Do that for 25 rows and chart the result. Press F9 to play 25 more rounds.

This is known as a Random Walk Down Wall Street. Simon would point out a result like this one, where a hot young stock analyst is on fire with a series of wins, but then a series of losses wipe out the gain. This is why they say that past results are not a guarantee of future returns.

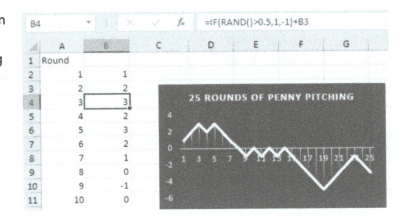

Instead of 25 trials, extend your table in columns A and B to run 250 trials. This would be like playing one round of penny pitching every work day for a year. Build a row of statistics about that year, as shown below.

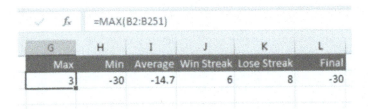

Create an odd data table where the blank cell in column F is the corner cell. Leave Row Input Cell blank. Specify any blank cell for Column Input Cell.

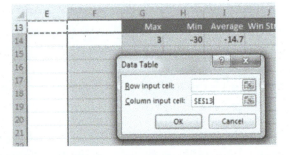

When you create the table, Excel runs the 250 coin flips, once per row. This 30-row table models the entire career of a stock analyst. Every time you press F9, Excel runs the 250-row model for each of 30 years. You can watch an entire 30-year career be modeled with the simple press of F9.

	G	H	I	J	K	L
13	Max	Min	Average	Win Streak	Lose Streak	Final
14	2	-16	-5.412	6	9 ▼	-12
15	3	-26	-14.028	5	6 ▼	-22
16	21	-5	6.772	12	7 ▲	+14
44	19	-3	9.78	12	7 ▭	0

Note: The download file for this chapter shows a few different ways to calculate the Win Streak and Loss Streak.

Thanks to Professor Simon Benninga for showing me this technique.

#133 Find Optimal Solutions with Solver

Excel was not the first spreadsheet program. Lotus 1-2-3 was not the first spreadsheet program. The first spreadsheet program was VisiCalc in 1979. Developed by Dan Bricklin and Bob Frankston, VisiCalc was published by Dan Fylstra. Today, Dan Fylstra runs Frontline Systems. His company wrote the Solver used in Excel. Frontline Systems has also developed a whole suite of analytics software that works with Excel.

If you have Excel, you have Solver. It may not be enabled, but you have it. To enable Solver in Excel, press Alt+T followed by I. Add a checkmark next to Solver Add-in.

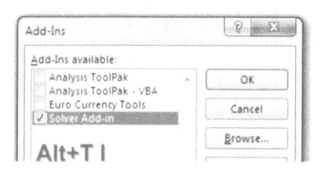

To use Solver, your worksheet needs three elements:

- A single Goal cell to minimize, maximize, or set to a value.
- Multiple input cells—unlike Goal Seek, which allows only one.
- Constraints.

Your task is to build a staffing plan for an amusement park. Each employee works five days with two days off. There are seven possible schedule patterns, listed in A4:A10. The blue cells (B4:B10) are input cells where you enter how many employees follow each pattern.

The Goal cell, B17, is total payroll per week: total staff (B11) × $68/day. Solver will minimize this..

The red box shows required staff per day—30 on weekends, as few as 12 on Monday and Tuesday. The orange cells use SUMPRODUCT to compute scheduled staff by day based on your inputs. Row 15 icons show if you're over, under, or meeting needs.

The red box shows required staff per day—30 on weekends, as few as 12 on Monday and Tuesday. The orange cells use SUMPRODUCT to compute scheduled staff by day based on your inputs. Row 15 icons show if you're over, under, or meeting needs.

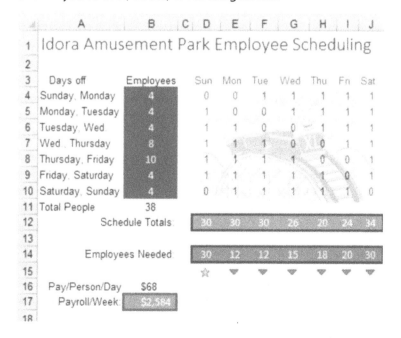

Of course, there is an easier way to solve this problem. Click the Solver icon on the Data tab. Tell Solver that you are trying to set the payroll in B17 to the minimum. The input cells are B4:B10.

Constraints fall into obvious and not-so-obvious categories.

The first obvious constraint is that D12:J12 has to be >= D14:J14.

But, if you tried to run Solver now, you would get bizarre results with fractional numbers of people and possibly a negative number of people working certain schedules.

While it seems obvious to you that you can't hire 0.39 people, you need to add constraints to tell Solver that B4:B10 are >= 0 and that B4:B10 are integers.

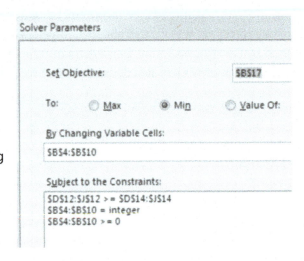

Solver Parameters

Set Objective: $B$17

To: ○ Max   ● Min   ○ Value Of:

By Changing Variable Cells:

$B$4:$B$10

Subject to the Constraints:

$D$12:$J$12 >= $D$14:$J$14
$B$4:$B$10 = integer
$B$4:$B$10 >= 0

Choose Simplex LP as the solving method and click Solve. In a few moments, Solver presents one optimal solution.

Solver finds a way to cover the amusement park staffing by using 30 employees instead of 38. The savings per week is $544—or more than $7000 over the course of the summer.

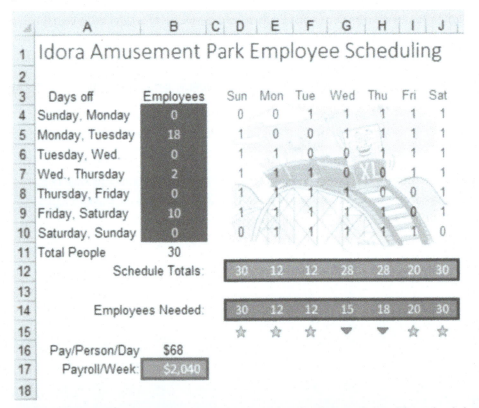

Notice the five stars below Employees Needed in the figure above. The schedule that Solver proposed meets your exact needs for five of the seven days. The by-product is that you will have more employees on Wednesday and Thursday than you really need.

I can understand how Solver came up with this solution. You need a lot of people on Saturday, Sunday, and Friday. One way to get people there on those day is to give them Monday and Tuesday off. That is why Solver gave 18 people Monday and Tuesday off.

But just because Solver came up with an optimal solution does not mean that there are not other equally optimal solutions.

When I was just guessing at the staffing, I didn't really have a good strategy.

Now that Solver has given me one of the optimal solutions, I can put on my logic hat. Having 28 college-age employees on Wednesday and Thursday when you only need 15 or 18 employees is going to lead to trouble. There won't be enough to do. Plus, with exactly the right head count on five days, you will have to call in someone for overtime if someone else calls in sick.

I trust Solver that I need to have 30 people to make this work. But I bet that I can rearrange those people to even out the schedule and provide a small buffer on other days.

For example, giving someone Wednesday and Thursday off also ensures that the person is at work Friday, Saturday, and Sunday. So, I manually move some workers from the Monday, Tuesday row to the Wednesday, Thursday row. I keep manually plugging in different combinations and come up with the solution shown below which has the same payroll expense as Solver but better intangibles. The overstaff situation now exists on four days instead of two. That means you can handle absences on Monday through Thursday without having to call in someone from their weekend.

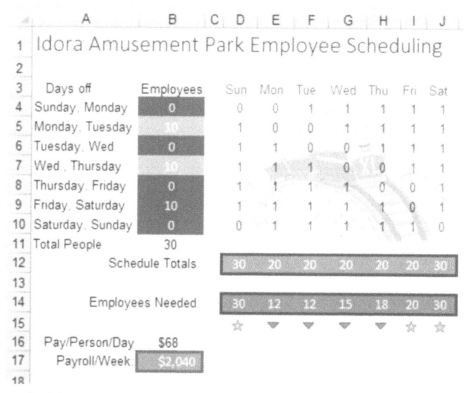

Is it bad that I was able to come up with a better solution than Solver? No. The fact is that I would not have been able to get to this solution without using Solver. Once Solver gave me a model that minimized costs, I was able to use logic about intangibles to keep the same payroll.

If you need to solve problems that are more complex than Solver can handle, check out the premium Excel solvers available from Frontline Systems: mrx.cl/solver77.

Thanks to Dan Fylstra and Frontline Systems for this example. Walter Moore illustrated the XL roller coaster.

#134 Interpolate between a starting and ending number

Say that you need to fill in blank cells between a starting and ending number. Select the range shown.

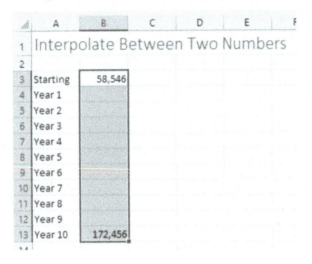

Select the range as shown above. On the Home tab, select Fill, Series.

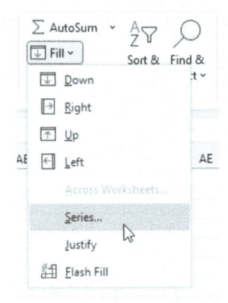

The Fill Series dialog appears, with the correct Step value already filled in.

Click OK to fill interpolate.

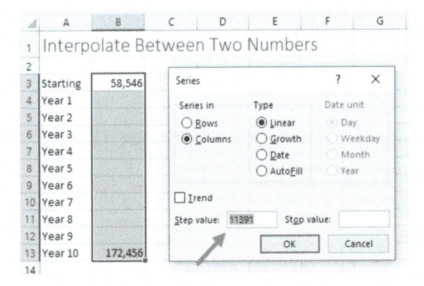

3	Starting	58,546
4	Year 1	69,937
5	Year 2	81,328
6	Year 3	92,719
7	Year 4	104,110
8	Year 5	115,501
9	Year 6	126,892
10	Year 7	138,283
11	Year 8	149,674
12	Year 9	161,065
13	Year 10	172,456

Thanks to Bob Umlas for this technique.

#135 Improve Your Macro Recording

I loved the 1985 version of the Macro Recorder in Lotus 1-2-3. The code was hard to understand, but it worked. There are some defaults in the Excel Macro Recorder that cause misery for anyone trying to record macros. Here are three tips to make the macro experience possibly better.

Tip 1: Turn on Relative Reference for Every Macro

Say that you start in A2 and record a simple macro that moves to A4. I would call that macro MoveDownTwoCells. But if you run this macro while the cell pointer is in J10, the macro will move to cell

A4. This is rarely what you want to have happen. But you can change the behavior of the macro recorder by selecting View, Macros, Use Relative References before you record the macro.

If you record the MoveDownTwoCells macro with this setting turned on, the macro will work from any cell.

Caution: The setting stays turned on only until you close Excel. Tomorrow, you will have to turn it back on again.

Tip: What if you actually need to record a macro that always jumps to cell A4? Even with Relative References enabled, you could press F5 for Go To and use the Go To dialog to go to A4. The macro recorder will record code that will always jump to A4.

Tip 2: Use Ctrl+Shift+Arrow to move to the end of a data set.

Say that you want to add a total at the bottom of yesterday's invoice register. You want the total to appear in row 9 today, but tomorrow, it might need to be in row 17 or row 5, depending on how many rows of data you have.

Find a column that is reliably 100% filled. From the top of that column, record the action of pressing Ctrl+Shift+Down Arrow. Press the Down Arrow key one more time, and you will know you are in the row where the totals should be.

	A	B	C	D	E
1	InvoiceDate	InvoiceNun	SalesReph	Customerh	ProductRe
2	5/8/2021	123829	S21	C8754	21000
3	5/8/2021	123830	S45	C3390	188100
4	5/8/2021	123831	S54	C2523	510600
5	5/8/2021	123832	S21	C5519	86200
6	5/8/2021	123833	S45	C3245	800100
7	5/8/2021	123834	S54	C7796	339000
8	5/8/2021	123835	S21	C1654	161000
9					
10					

Ctrl+Shift+↓

Tip 3: Type =SUM(E$2:E8) instead of pressing the AutoSum button

The macro recorder will not record the intent of AutoSum. When you press AutoSum, you will get a sum function that starts in the cell above and extends up to the first non-numeric cell. It does not matter if you have Relative References on or off; the macro recorder will hard-code that you want to sum the seven cells above the active cell.

Instead of using the AutoSum icon, type a SUM function with a single dollar sign before the first row number: =SUM(E$2:E8). Use that formula while recording the macro, and the macro will reliably sum from the cell above the active cell all the way up to row 2, as shown below.

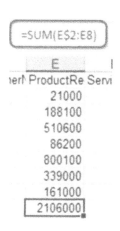

=SUM(E$2:E8)

E	
1erh ProductRe	Serv
21000	
188100	
510600	
86200	
800100	
339000	
161000	
2106000	

Bonus Tip: Use TypeScript to Write Macros for Excel Online

VBA has been the macro language in Excel for decades. This was fine when "Excel" meant Excel running on a PC with Windows or a Mac. But today, there are versions of "Excel" running on an iPhone, on Android, or in an browser. Microsoft is never going to support VBA in those endpoints.

In 2020, they debuted a new macro language called TypeScript. It was designed for those people running Excel in a browser. TypeScript will let you run macros on a PC or Excel Online. As the usage of Excel Online picks up, there will be more scenarios where you want your macros developed in TypeScript.

The new language is hard to find. You need to opt into a preview. This video will get you started: https://www.youtube.com/watch?v=bNbu5ANUeAw

#136 Clean Data with Power Query

Power Query is built in to Windows and Mac versions of Microsoft 365, Excel 2016, Excel 2019, Excel 2021 and is available as a free download in Windows versions of Excel 2010 and Excel 2013. The tool is designed to extract, transform, and load data into Excel from a variety of sources. The best part: Power Query remembers your steps and will play them back when you want to refresh the data. This means you can clean data on Day 1 in 80% of the normal time, and you can clean data on Days 2 through 400 by simply clicking Refresh.

I say this about a lot of new Excel features, but this really is the best feature to hit Excel in 20 years.

I tell a story in my live seminars about how Power Query was invented as a crutch for SQL Server Analysis Services customers who were forced to use Excel in order to access Power Pivot. But Power Query kept getting better, and every person using Excel should be taking the time to learn Power Query.

> **Aha!**: Power Query finally came to the Mac in 2023, but it is missing several important connectors. Suat Ozgur, the database administrator at MrExcel.com created those connectors and provides them free to the world. Get details at Episode 2597.

Get Power Query

You already have Power Query. It is in the Get & Transform group on the Data tab.

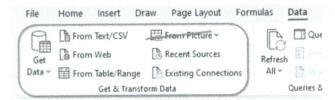

> **Note**: The "From Table/Range" icon refers to three things: (1) Ctrl+T tables. (2) Named ranges. (3) A Dynamic Array formula.

Clean Data the First Time in Power Query

To give you an example of some of the awesomeness of Power Query, say that you get the file shown below every day. Column A is not filled in. Quarters are going across instead of down the page.

To start, save that workbook to your hard drive. Put it in a predictable place with a name that you will use for that file every day.

▲	A	B	C	D	E	F
1	Product	Customer	Q1	Q2	Q3	Q4
2	Apple	SkyWire, Inc.	225	151	126	183
3		Tennessee Moo	156	185	150	273
4		SlinkyRN Excel I	284	111	130	281
5		University of No	185	230	259	123
6		Spain Enterprise	223	281	242	159
7		SkyWire, Inc.	267	174	213	204
8	Banana	Steve Comer	176	252	143	214
9		The Lab with Lec	295	198	134	172
10		Steve Comer	132	234	193	255

In Excel, select Get Data, From File, From Workbook.

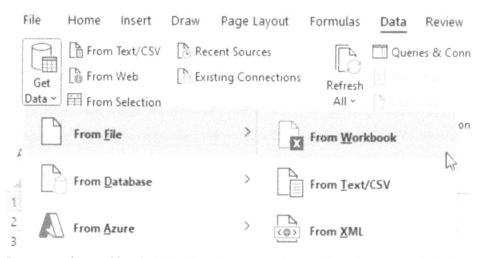

Browse to the workbook. In the Preview pane, click on Sheet1. Instead of clicking Load, click Transform Data. You now see the workbook in a slightly different grid—the Power Query grid.

Now you need to fix all the blank cells in column A. If you were to do this in the Excel user interface, the unwieldy command sequence is Home, Find & Select, Go To Special, Blanks, Equals, Up Arrow, Ctrl+Enter.

In Power Query, select Transform, Fill, Down.

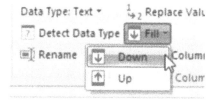

All of the null values are replaced with the value from above. With Power Query, it takes three clicks instead of seven.

Next problem: The quarters are going across instead of down. In Excel, you can fix this with a Multiple Consolidation Range pivot table. This requires 12 steps and 23+ clicks.

In Power Query select the two columns that are not quarters. Open the Unpivot Columns dropdown on the Transform tab and choose Unpivot Other Columns, as shown below.

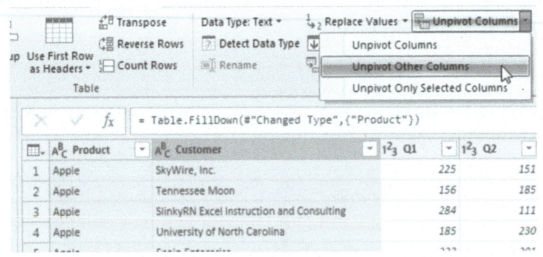

Right-click on the newly created Attribute column and rename it Quarter instead of Attribute. Twenty-plus clicks in Excel becomes five clicks in Power Query.

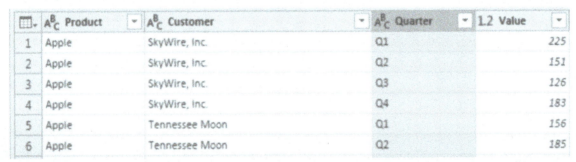

Now, to be fair, not every cleaning step is shorter in Power Query than in Excel. Removing a column still means right-clicking a column and choosing Remove Column. But to be honest, the story here is not about the time savings on Day 1.

When you are done cleaning the data, click Close & Load as shown below.

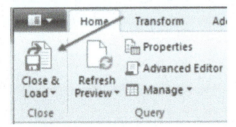

> **Tip**: If your data is more than 1,048,576 rows, you can use the Close & Load dropdown to load the data directly to the Power Pivot Data Model, which can accommodate 995 million rows if you have enough memory installed on the machine.

In a few seconds, your transformed data appears in Excel. Awesome.

	Product	Customer	Quarter	Value
7	Apple	Tennessee Moon	Q2	185
8	Apple	Tennessee Moon	Q3	150
9	Apple	Tennessee Moon	Q4	273
10	Apple	SlinkyRN Excel Instruction and Consulting	Q1	284
11	Apple	SlinkyRN Excel Instruction and Consulting	Q2	111
12	Apple	SlinkyRN Excel Instruction and Consulting	Q3	130
13	Apple	SlinkyRN Excel Instruction and Consulting	Q4	281
14	Apple	University of North Carolina	Q1	185
15	Apple	University of North Carolina	Q2	230

But Wait: Power Query Remembers All of Your Steps

Look on the right side of the Power Query window. There is a list called Applied Steps. It is an instant audit trail of all of your steps. Click any gear icon to change your choices in that step and have the changes cascade through the future steps. Click on any step for a view of how the data looked before that step.

The Payoff: Clean Data Tomorrow With One Click

But again, the Power Query story is not about the time savings on Day 1. When you select the data returned by Power Query, a Queries & Connections panel appears on the right side of Excel, and on it is a Refresh button. (We need an Edit button here, but because there isn't one, you have to right-click the original query to view or make changes to the original query).

It is fun to clean data on Day 1. I love doing something new. But when my manager sees the resulting report and says "Beautiful. Can you do this every day?" I quickly grow to hate the tedium of cleaning the same data set every day.

So, to demonstrate Day 400 of cleaning the data, I have completely changed the original file. New products, new customers, smaller numbers, more rows, as shown here. I save this new version of the file in the same path and with the same filename as the original file.

If I open the query workbook and click Refresh, in a few seconds, Power Query reports 92 rows instead of 68 rows.

Cleaning the data on Day 2, Day 3, Day, 4,...Day 400,...Day Infinity now takes two clicks.

89	Guava	MyOnlineTrainingHub.com	Q4	73
90	Guava	MySpreadsheetLab	Q1	78
91	Guava	MySpreadsheetLab	Q2	49
92	Guava	MySpreadsheetLab	Q3	50
93	Guava	MySpreadsheetLab	Q4	73
94				

This one example only scratches the surface of Power Query. I have several more YouTube videos in a playlist at http://mrx.cl/pqplaylist. You will learn about other features, such as these:

- Combining all Excel or CSV files from a folder into a single Excel grid
- Converting a cell with Apple;Banana;Cherry;Dill;Eggplant to five rows in Excel
- Doing a VLOOKUP to a lookup workbook as you are bringing data into Power Query
- Making a single query into a function that can be applied to every row in Excel

Bonus Tip: Tame the Sequence of Refresh All

Say that you have a Power Query and then build a pivot table on the results. When you go to the Data Tab and click Refresh All, you need the Power Query refresh to complete before the pivot table refreshes. Excel MVP Celia Alves from SolveAndExcel.ca offers this important tip: Right-click the query in the Queries & Connections pane and choose Properties. Make sure to uncheck the Enable Background Refresh setting. This forces the Power Query to finish refreshing before the pivot table is updated. Otherwise, you will have to click Refresh All twice in order to get the pivot table to update.

Bonus Tip: Data Profiling in Power Query

Some excellent data profiling options appeared in late 2019. They are not obvious to find, as they are on the View tab in Power Query. Use the Column Quality, Column Distribution, and Column Profile boxes.

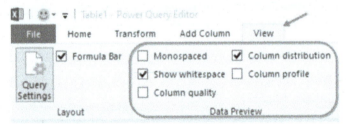

My favorite is the Column Profile. As you would expect, Weekday has 7 distinct values.

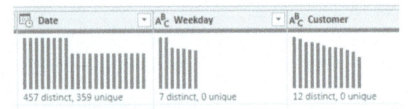

Choose one column and then Column Profile. You will see a window at the bottom with statistics and a frequency distribution.

Column statistics	...	Value distribution	...
Count	563	Wed	
Error	0	Tue	
Empty	0	Mon	
Distinct	7	Thu	
Unique	0	Sat	
Empty string	0	Sun	
Min	Fri	Fri	
Max	Wed		

Column Quality shows if you have any empty or error cells in each column:

A^B_C Product		Date	
● Valid	100%	● Valid	100%
● Error	0%	● Error	0%
● Empty	0%	● Empty	0%

For more Power Query, check out *Master Your Data* by Puls Escobar or books on M by Chhabra or Girvin.

POWER QUERY
BEYOND THE USER INTERFACE

Solving Advanced Data
Cleaning Problems Using

{ **M** }

CHANDEEP CHHABRA

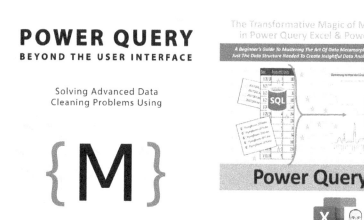

Thanks to Miguel Escobar, Rob Garcia, Mike Girvin, Ray Hauser, and Colin Michael for nominating Power Query.

#137 Use Fuzzy Match in Power Query

There's a research and development team at Microsoft known as Microsoft Labs. Almost 10 years ago, it invented a free Fuzzy Match add-in for Excel. A fuzzy matching algorithm looks for words that share a percentage of characters in common.

The figure shows two data sets: Columns A–B list employees, and D–E list those who returned a required form. You need to find who hasn't responded. VLOOKUP or XLOOKUP won't work because names are formatted differently—"last, first" in column A vs. nickname and last in column D. Use the Fuzzy Match tool in Power Query to match them.

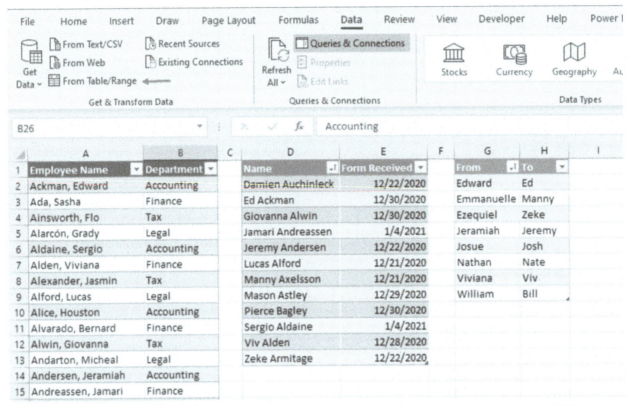

Columns G and H show a translation table that will be used by the fuzzy match to help match full first names with their nicknames. The translation table requires two columns, labeled "From" and "To." The fuzzy match will likely match Kris and Kristy because they share many letters. But it will need an entry in the translation table for Bill and William or Bob and Robert.

Before you can perform the match, all three ranges of data have to be converted to a table by selecting each individual range and pressing Ctrl+T. Then Rrname each table: Select one cell in a table. Go to the Table Tools tab in the Ribbon and type a meaningful name such as "Census," "Forms," and "Nicknames."

You need to convert each of the three tables to a connection in Excel. From cell A1, select, Data, From Table/Range (as shown at the red arrow in Figure 1). Excel will open the Power Query Editor. The first icon on the Home tab says "Close and Load." Click the drop-down menu below it and choose "Close and Load To…" to open the Import Data dialog box.

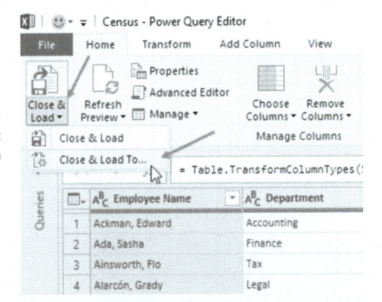

Choose the fourth item, called Only Create Connection.

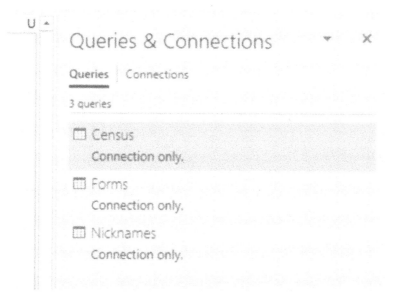

Repeat the process of creating a connection for the other two tables, starting in cell D1 and cell G1, respectively. If you created all three connections correctly, you should see three queries listed as "Connection Only" in the Queries & Connections panel on the right side of the Excel window.

Select a blank cell in your worksheet. From the Data tab, select Get Data, Combine Queries, Merge to open the Merge dialog.

There are many subtle settings in this dialog that aren't intuitive. The figure at right shows the 8 steps:

1. From the top drop-down menu, select the Census table.

2. In the small data preview, click on the heading(s) of the fields to be used for the matching. In this case, it's the Employee Name heading.

3. From the second drop-down menu, choose the name of the lookup table. In this case, Forms.

4. In the data preview, click on the heading(s) of the fields to be used for matching, such as Name.

5. Choose a Join Kind of Left Outer. Choose the box for "Use Fuzzy Matching to Perform the Merge."

6. Several special settings are hidden behind the Fuzzy Matching Options drop-down menu. Click the triangle to reveal this section.

7. Scroll to the bottom of the section and set Nicknames as the Transformation Table.

8. Verify that the number of matches found is the same as the number of records in the Forms table.

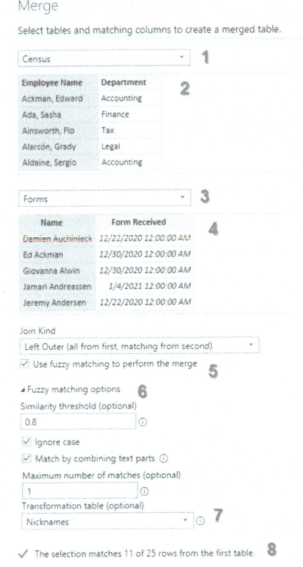

Tip: If you become comfortable with fuzzy matching, you might change the Join Kind from Left Outer to Left Anti in order to return only the list of people in the first table who do not have a match in the second table.

If there are fewer records than you expect, you might experiment with the "similarity threshhold." By default, the similarity threshold requires an 80% match. You could try changing this to 0.7 or 0.6 to see if it improves the number of matches. But be careful. If you set this too low, you risk the chance of false matches happening. For example, at 0.4 similarity, both Mason Astley and Lucy Astley would be seen as a match.

Click OK to perform the Merge. The grid in the Power Query editor will show columns for Employee Name, Department, and then a column called Forms. The value in each row for Forms simply says "Table" in each row. To the right of the "Forms" heading is an Expand icon with two arrows pointing left and right. Click this icon to choose which fields from the Forms table to return.

	A^B_C Employee Name		A^B_C Department		Forms	
1	Ackman, Edward		Accounting		Table	
2	Ada, Sasha		Finance		Table	
3	Ainsworth, Flo		Tax		Table	
4	Alarcón, Grady		Legal		Table	
5	Aldaine, Sergio		Accounting		Table	
6	Alden, Viviana		Finance		Table	
7	Alexander, Jasmin		Tax		Table	
8	Alford, Lucas		Legal		Table	

By default, the new fields will have the table name followed by a period and then the field name (such as "Forms.Form Received"). To prevent this, uncheck the box for "Use Original Column Name As Prefix."

Once you have the preview shown in the Power Query Editor, go to Home, Close & Load to deliver the results to a new table on a new worksheet. You could optionally use Close & Load To… and specify a location on an existing worksheet for the table.

	A	B	C	D	E
1	Employee Name	Department	Name	Form Received	
2	Ackman, Edward	Accounting	Ed Ackman	12/30/2020 0:00	
3	Ada, Sasha	Finance			
4	Ainsworth, Flo	Tax			
5	Alarcón, Grady	Legal			
6	Aldaine, Sergio	Accounting	Sergio Aldaine	1/4/2021 0:00	
7	Alden, Viviana	Finance	Viv Alden	12/28/2020 0:00	
8	Alexander, Jasmin	Tax			
9	Alford, Lucas	Legal	Lucas Alford	12/21/2020 0:00	
10	Alice, Houston	Accounting			
11	Alvarado, Bernard	Finance			
12	Alwin, Giovanna	Tax	Giovanna Alwin	12/30/2020 0:00	
13	Andarton, Micheal	Legal			
14	Andersen, Jeramiah	Accounting	Jeremy Andersen	12/22/2020 0:00	
15	Andreassen, Jamari	Finance	Jamari Andreassen	1/4/2021 0:00	
16	Annan, Aliza	Tax			
17	Annesley, Carissa	Legal			

At this point, review the results to make sure no false matches were found. If everything looks good, you can sort or filter to remove the records that show a match, leaving the people who haven't turned in a form.

There's an easy audit method to look for people in the Forms table who did not show up in the Merge query. Use Data, Get Data, Combine Queries, Merge. Specify Forms as the first table, using Name as the key field. Specify Merge1 as the second table, using Name as the key field. For the Join Kind, specify Left Anti (Rows Only In the First Table}.

Ever since my Accounting 101 class, I was taught that "close" is never acceptable in accounting. This leads to a reluctance to trust the fuzzy matching algorithm. Yet there are cases where the fuzzy match tool is the only solution short of manually matching records.

As more people turn in their forms, choosing Data, Refresh All will automatically perform the fuzzy match again.

#138 Data From Picture is Not Power Query

This is a feature that does deserve to be in this book. I am putting it in the book to warn you about the feature. Data From Picture is not ready for real use. If you want to extract text from an image, you are better reading "#59 Use Copilot to Extract Data From an Image" on page 130.

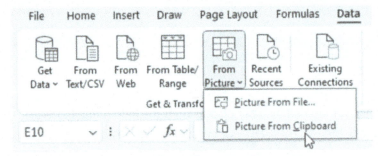

Tip: A tiny start-up company at table2xl.com offers a paid version of this feature that works amazingly well. Microsoft should buy this company and add the functionality to Excel.

#139 Build a Pivot Table on a Map Using 3D Maps

3D Maps (formerly Power Map) has been available in Windows versions of Excel since 2016. Using 3D Maps, you can build a pivot table on a map. You can fly through your data and animate the data over time.

3D Maps lets you see five dimensions: latitude, longitude, color, height, and time. Using it is a fascinating way to visualize large data sets.

3D Maps can work with simple one-sheet data sets or with multiple tables added to the Data Model. Select the data. On the Data tab, open the Data Model drop-down, 3D Map, Open 3D Maps.

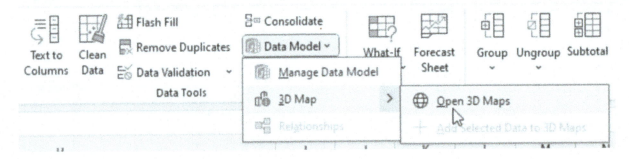

Next, you need to choose which fields are your geography fields. This could be Country, State, County, Zip Code, or even individual street addresses.

GEOGRAPHY
Map by Address (Street)

You are given a list of the fields in your data set and drop zones named Height, Category, and Time.

HEIGHT

Amt (No Aggregation)

CATEGORY

Allotment

TIME

Date (None)

Hover over any point on the map to get details such as last sale date and amount.

In the default state of 3D Maps, each data point occupies about one city block. To be able to plot many houses on a street, select the Gear Wheel, Layer Options and change the thickness of the point to 10%.

To get the satellite imagery, open the Themes dropdown and use the second theme.

3D Maps provides a completely new way to look at your data. It is hard to believe that this is Excel.

Here is a map of Merritt Island, Florida. The various colors are different housing allotments. Each colored dot on the map is a house with a dock, either on a river or one of many canals dredged out in the 1960s and 1970s.

Using the time slider, you can go back in time to any point. Here is the same area at the time when NASA landed the first man on the Moon. The NASA engineers had just started building waterfront homes here, a few miles south of Kennedy Space Center.

March, 2013

December, 1969

Use the wheel mouse to scroll in. You can actually see individual streets, canals, and driveways.

Hold down the Alt key and drag sideways to rotate the map. Hold down the Alt key and drag up to tip the map so your view is closer to the ground.

Thanks to Igor Peev and Scott Ruble at Microsoft for this cool new feature.

Tip: You can create your own regions for 3D Map using custom KML shapes. This process is documented in Episode 2557.

#140 The Forecast Sheet Can Handle Some Seasonality

Before Excel 2016, Excel offered a few forecasting tools that did not fit in every situation. If your sales data included some seasonality, the old forecasting tools would do a bad job. Consider a movie theatre where sales peak on the weekend and plummet on Monday. Using the old linear trendline, Excel shows an R-Squared of 0.02, meaning that the trendline is doing a horrible job of predicting the future.

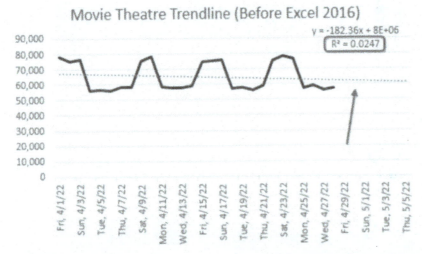

Excel 2016 introduced a new set of forecasting functions and an icon on the Data tab of the Ribbon to create a Forecast Sheet. If you have data with Date in column A and Sales in column B, select the data and choose Data, Forecast Sheet.

In the Create Forecast Worksheet dialog, click Options and review the Seasonality and ask for stats. Click Create and Excel inserts a new worksheet with FORECAST.ETS functions to create a forecast. The 3% error shown means that this forecast is explaining most of the variability.

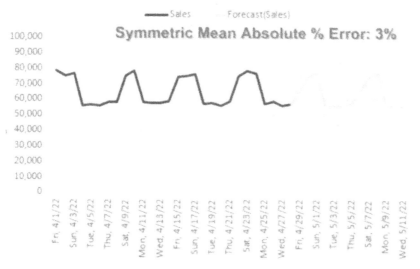

Symmetric Mean Absolute % Error: 3%

Caution: The Forecast Sheet works fine if you have one level of seasonality: More movie-goers on Friday or more gift buyers in November and December. But if your real-life data calls for <u>both</u> a December boom and a Saturday/Sunday peak, the FORECAST.ETS won't handle it.

#141 Fill in a Flash

Excel 2013 added a data-cleansing tool called Flash Fill.

In the figure below, you see full names in column A. You want to get the person's first initial and last name in column B. Rather than try to puzzle out =PROPER(LEFT(A2,1)&" "&MID(A2,FIND(" ",A2)+1,50)), you simply type a sample of what you want in B2.

Type the first initial in B3. Excel sees what you are doing and "grays in" a suggested result.

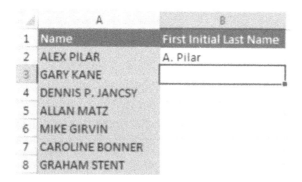

Press Enter to accept the suggestion. Bam! All of the data is filled in.

Look carefully through your data for exceptions to the rule. Two people here have middle initials listed. Do you want the middle initials to appear? If so, correct the suggestion for Dennis P. Jancsy in cell B4. Flash Fill will jump into action and fix Martha K. Wendel in B9 and any others that match the new pattern. The status bar will indicate how many changes were made.

In the above case, Excel gurus could figure out the formula. But Flash Fill is easier.

In the example shown below, it would be harder to write a formula to get the last word from a phrase that has a different number of words and more than one hyphen.

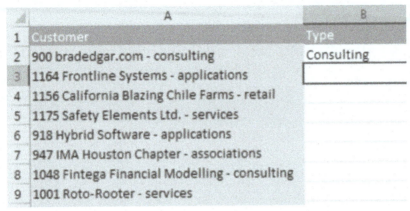

	A	B
1	Customer	Type
2	900 bradedgar.com - consulting	Consulting
3	1164 Frontline Systems - applications	
4	1156 California Blazing Chile Farms - retail	
5	1175 Safety Elements Ltd. - services	
6	918 Hybrid Software - applications	
7	947 IMA Houston Chapter - associations	
8	1048 Fintega Financial Modelling - consulting	
9	1001 Roto-Rooter - services	

Flash Fill makes this easy. Go to cell B3 and press Ctrl+E to invoke Flash Fill.

	A	B
1	Customer	Type
2	900 bradedgar.com - consulting	Consulting
3	1164 Frontline Systems - applications	Applications
4	1156 California Blazing Chile Farms - retail	Retail
5	1175 Safety Elements Ltd. - services	Services
6	918 Hybrid Software - applications	Applications
7	947 IMA Houston Chapter - associations	Associations
8	1048 Fintega Financial Modelling - consulting	Consulting

Note: Flash Fill will not automatically fill in numbers. If you have numbers, you might see Flash Fill temporarily "gray in" a suggestion but then withdraw it. This is your signal to press Ctrl+E to give Flash Fill permission to fill in numbers.

Thanks to Chad Rothschiller at Microsoft for building this feature. Thanks also to Olga Kryuchkova.

#142 Format as a Façade

Excel is amazing at storing one number and presenting another number. Choose any cell and select

	A	B	C	D
1	Rep	Qty	Revenue	Avg Price
2	Andrew Spain	26,850	172,498.50	$6.42
3	Geoffrey G Lilley	24,458	157,921.10	$6.46
4	Kevin J Sullivan	24,754	160,180.30	$6.47
5	Peter Polakovic	24,090	143,880.50	$5.97

Currency format. Excel adds a dollar sign and a comma and presents the number, rounded to two decimal places. In the figure below, cell D2 actually contains 6.42452514. Thankfully, the built-in custom number format presents the results in an easy-to-read format.

The custom number format code in D2 is $#,##0.00. In this code, 0s are required digits. Any #s are optional digits.

However, formatting codes can be far more complex. The code above has one format. That format is ap-

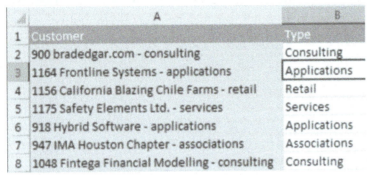

Format
Format >=0;Format<0
Positive;Negative;Zero
Positive;Negative;Zero;Text

plied to every value in the cell. If you provide a code with two formats, the first format is for non-negative numbers, and the second format is for negative numbers. You separate the formats with semicolons. If you provide a code with three formats, the first is for positive, then negative, then zero. If you provide a code with four formats, they are used for positive, negative, zero, and text.

Even if you are using a built-in format, you can go to Format Cells, Number, Custom and see the code used to generate that format. The figure below shows the code for the accounting format.

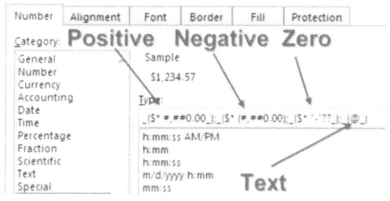

To build your own custom format, go to Format Cells, Number, Custom and enter the code in the Type box. Check out the example in the Sample box to make sure everything looks correct.

In the following example, three zones are used. Text in quotes is added to the number format to customize the message.

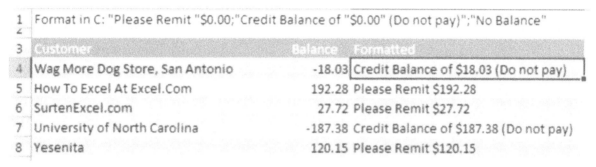

If you create a zone for zero but put nothing there, you will hide all zero values. The following code uses color codes for positive and negative. The code ends in a semicolon, creating a zone for zero values. But since the zone is empty, zero values are not shown.

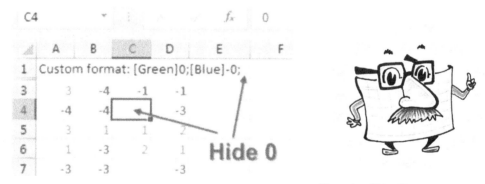

Illustration: Walter Moore

You can extend this by making all zones blank. A custom format code ;;; will hide values in the display and printout. However, you'll still be able to see the values in the formula bar. If you hide values by making the font white, the ;;; will stay hidden even if people change the fill color.

This figure includes some interesting formatting tricks.

	A	B	C
1	Value	Display	Format Code
2	123.45	********** 123.45	**0.00
3	123.45	!!!!!!!!!!!!!!! 123.45	*!0.00
4	123456	123K	0,K
5	4565789	4.6M	0.0,,"M"
6	One	Enter a number!	0;-0;0;"Enter a number!"
7	62	62	[Red][<70]0;[Blue][>90]0;0
8	85	85	[Red][<70]0;[Blue][>90]0;0
9	99	99	[Red][<70]0;[Blue][>90]0;0
10	1234	1 2 3 4	0_W_W0_N0_i0

In B2 and B3, if you put ** before the number code, Excel will fill to the left of the number with asterisks, like the old check writer machines would do. But there is nothing that says you have to use asterisks. Whatever you put after the first asterisk is repeated to fill the space. Row 3 uses *! to repeat exclamation points.

In B4 and B5, each comma that you put after the final zero will divide the number by 1000. The code 0,K shows numbers in thousands, with a K afterward. If you want to show millions, use two commas. The "M" code must include quotation marks, since M already means months.

In B6, add a stern message in the fourth zone to alert anyone entering data that you want a number in the cell. If they accidentally enter text, the message will appear.

In B7 to B9, the normal zones Positives, Negatives, and Zero are overwritten by conditions that you put in square brackets. Numbers under 70 are red. Numbers over 90 are blue. Everything else is black.

In B10, those odd _(symbols in the accounting format are telling Excel to leave as much space as a left parenthesis would take. It turns out that an underscore followed by any character will leave as much white space as that character. In B10, the code contains 4 zeros. But there are different amounts of space between them. The space between the 1 and 2 is the width of 2 W characters. The space between 2 and 3 is the width of an N. The space between 3 and 4 is the width of a lowercase letter i.

The following figure shows various date formatting codes.

	A	B
1	Display	Format Code
2	7/4/22	m/d/yy
3	7/4/2022	m/d/yyyy
4	07/04/2022	mm/dd/yyyy
5	20220704	YYYYMMDD
6	7	m
7	07	mm
8	Jul	mmm
9	July	mmmm
10	J	mmmmm
11	Mon	ddd
12	Monday	dddd
13	Monday the 4 of Jul	dddd" the "d" of "mmm

Note: The mmmmm format in row 10 is useful for producing J F M A M J J A S O N D chart labels.

Thanks to Dave Baylis, Brad Edgar, Mike Girvin, and @best_excel for suggesting this feature.

#143 Show All Open Workbooks in the Windows Taskbar

Here is a great trick from Marlette Toole of the FL Space Coast chapter of the Institute of Internal Auditors. Since you are spending most of your work life in Excel, wouldn't it be nice to see all open workbooks in the Windows taskbar instead of just one tile with the Excel logo?

Right-click in an empty area of the Taskbar and choose Taskbar Settings. In the Combine Taskbar Settings drop-down menu, choose Never.

Combine taskbar buttons

Never	⌄

#144 Paste to Another Computer Using Cloud Clipboard

Do you have two computers on your desk? Go to the Control Panel for the Clipboard and turn on Sync Across Devices and Automatically Sync Text That I Copy for both computers. You can now Ctrl+C some cells on one computer. On the other computer, press Win+V and you can paste the clipboard from the first computer. This eliminates any need to e-mail text from one computer to the other.

Clipboard history

Save multiple items to the clipboard to use later. Press the Windows logo key + V to view your clipboard history and paste from it.

On

Sync across devices ◄────────

Paste text on your other devices. When this is on, Microsoft receives your clipboard data to sync it across your devices.

On

#145 Surveys & Forms in Excel

I often start my live Excel seminars off by asking you to point your cell phone camera at a giant bar code I have projected on the screen. That QR code leads to a three-question survey. Answers automatically flow into my Excel worksheet and those answers get used in the afternoon demo of 3D Maps.

Start right in your Excel workbook. Save your workbook to OneDrive and enable AutoSave. From the Insert tab, open Forms and New Form.

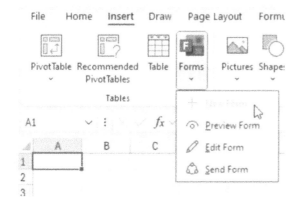

A browser will open and you can build your form. Click New Question. Forms offers support for seven question types. Don't miss the useful Ranking or Likert types hidden behind the three dots.

Type the question and possible answers.

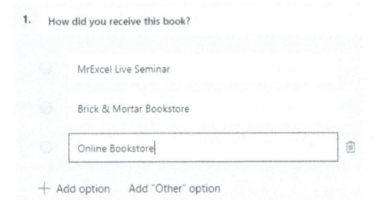

Branching is now supported: Click the 3 Dots icon in the top right corner of Forms.Office.Com.

When you are done with all questions, click Share in the top right corner. You can share via a link, or via e-mail, or using the QR Code. Try it: point your cell phone camera at the bar code on the right.

#146 Use the Windows Magnifier

If you received this book while attending one of my live Power Excel seminars, you likely saw me use the Windows Magnifier. Someone always asks how to use this, so I will write up the key steps.

First, there are three versions of the magnifier. To start the magnifier, press the Windows key and the Plus sign on the Numeric Keypad. To stop the magnifier, press the Windows key and Esc.

The first time that you use the magnifier, it opens in a view called Full Screen. Everything on the screen becomes bigger and you can use the mouse to move around. I don't like this version. Look for the floating Magnifier toolbar. Open Views and choose Lens.

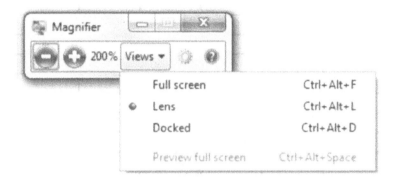

A magnifier lens follows your mouse cursor around the screen. You can use the Settings (gear wheel) icon in the toolbar to change the size of the lens.

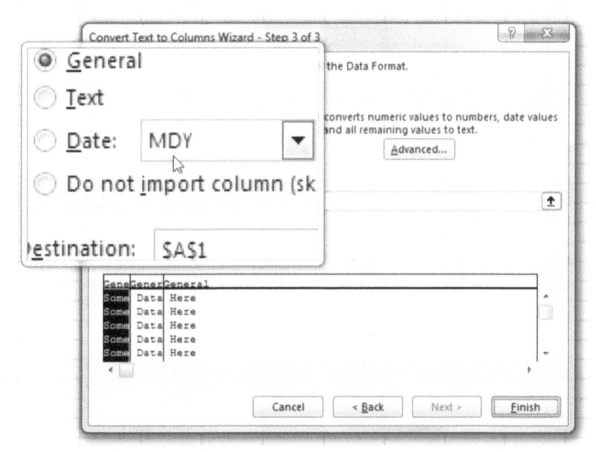

On some computers, the Magnifier toolbar starts out as an icon that looks like a magnifying glass. Click the icon to open the toolbar. More magnifier settings are in Windows, Settings, Ease of Access, Magnifier.

#147 New Scrolling Tricks

Excel now offers horizontal scrolling and smooth scrolling. To scroll with the mouse wheel:

- Spin the mouse wheel to scroll vertically through the grid
- Ctrl+Spin the mouse wheel to change the Zoom level.
- Ctrl+Shift+Spin the mouse wheel to scroll horizontally. This functionality was added to Microsoft 365 during 2021.

Smooth scrolling is a popular improvement, particularly for people who store a lot of text in a cell. Before Smooth scrolling, the following worksheet could be scrolled to show "In B2 and B3" or "In B4 and B5" at the top of the worksheet. There was no way to leave Excel parked with half of row 1 scrolled off the screen.

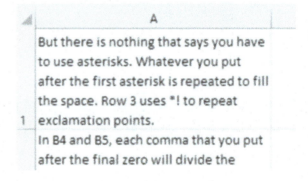

Now, with Smooth Scrolling, you can scroll part way through a cell. In the figure below, you can see that half of cell A1 is scrolled out of view.

You could even scroll sideways and have part of the column visible.

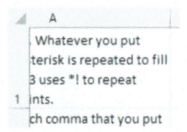

Note: By default, when you scroll with the mouse wheel, it jumps three lines a a time. Visit the Control Panel and search for Scrolling to find these settings.

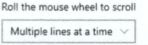

Roll the mouse wheel to scroll

Multiple lines at a time

Choose how many lines to scroll each time

#148 Prevent Default Conversions

Since the beginning, Excel has made some annoying automatic conversions when you (a) import from a CSV or text file, (b) paste from another app, or (c) type data. Here's a summary of the default conversions:

- Remove leading zeroes and convert to a number. For example 00540 becomes 540.

- Keep first 15 digits of long numbers and shows them in scientific notation. First, 12345678901234567 is converted to 12345678901234500 then displays as 1.23456E+16.

- Converts digit-E-digit to Scientific Notation. 123E9 becomes 123000000000 and shows as 1.23E+11

- Converts strings like JAN1 into dates—e.g., January 1 of the current year—and formats them as D-MMM.

Now, under File > Options > Data, you can turn off any or all of these conversions.

Automatic Data Conversion

☐ Enable all default data conversions below when entering, pasting, or loading text into Excel

  ☐ Remove leading zeros and convert to a number ⓘ

  ☐ Keep first 15 digits of long numbers and display in scientific notation ⓘ

  ☐ Convert digits surrounding the letter "E" to a number in scientific notation ⓘ

  ☐ Convert continuous letters and numbers to a date ⓘ

Additional Options

☐ When loading a .csv file or similar file, notify me of any automatic data conversions ⓘ

If you do nothing, these conversions will continue to run—and annoy you.

Many users change data types in step 3 of the Import Text Wizard to preserve leading zeroes. If that's you, go to File > Options > Data and turn off the defaults.

When opening a CSV or text file, Excel will warn you about these conversions. You can decide on a file-by-file basis whether to allow them. If you check "Don't Notify Me About Default Conversions in .CSV or Similar Files," Excel will stop prompting and uncheck the related option automatically.

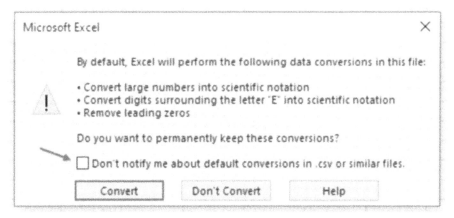

Caution: You can control if the above warning box appears. But this only impacts opening CSV or Text files. It has no impact on pasting from other applications or typing data. Both of those will always automatically follow the first five checkboxes under Automatic Data Conversion.

#149 Check Performance in Excel

A new feature debuted in 2023. Go to the Review tab and choose Check Performance. If you have a workbook that you've been using for years, you should check performance. It looks for excess formatting, unused cell styles, unneeded metadata that can slow your workbook down.

The results appear in a task pane on the right side.

I have a four-year old workbook that I update daily. When I ran Check Performance, Excel found eight ranges where I had previously pasted stray text and then deleted it. The Check Performance offered to clear the text alignment and text properties of these empty cells. That is a great find.

It is tempting to use the Optimize Button in the lower right. But avoid this temptation. Check each worksheet and each range. Check Performance tends to identify "problems" that you included on purpose. Here are some examples of things that I've done on purpose and Check Performance wanted to fix:

- With an image over cells, I had adjusted the height of a row in the middle of the image to allow room for the image before the next text. There is no picture in the tall row, just a picture that extends from above the row to below the row. Check Performance wanted to change the height of this empty row back to the default size.

- I had a cell formatted as an Input cell. I had used Data Validation's Input message to display a tooltip when you selected the cell. Check Performance offered to get rid of the formatting for this blank cell.

- I had never heard of it, but there is something called Pixel Art that is apparently popular in Excel. Check Performance sees this as stray fill color in otherwise empty cells and will remove it.

#150 See Intermediate Calculations

My friend Mike Girvin at the ExcelisFun YouTube channel has a great trick when explaining a long formula. Mike will select part of the formula in the formula bar and press F9 to calculate just that part of the formula. It is a cool trick, but you must remember to press Escape or you will hard-code the intermediate results in the formula.

In 2023, the Excel team provided a better alternative. If you select part of the formula in the formula and pause for a few seconds, a tooltip appears with the intermediate results. Here is an example showing the array stored in the Passcodes named range:

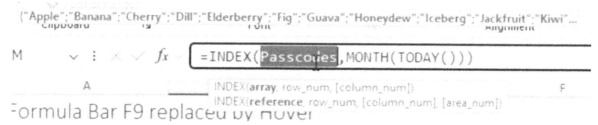

Formula Bar F9 replaced by Hover

This feature also works if you are editing a formula in a cell. Below, a tiny tooltip of "0" shows that the date stored in A10 is not a workday.

Thursday, February 3, 2028
→ 0 ←
Friday, February 4, 2028

=IF(**NETWORKDAYS**(A10,A10,HolidayRange)=1,A10,

IF(**logical_test**, [value_if_true], [value_if_false])

Note that this new feature is related to the Evaluate Formula feature found on the Formulas tab. Below, the same formula is shown in Evaluate Formula. One more press of the Evaluate function will show the result of the intermediate formula. While Evaluate Formula allows you to Step In and drill down, it requires you to evaluate the formula in the same sequence that Excel would use. The new feature to show the intermediate result of any portion of the formula is more flexible.

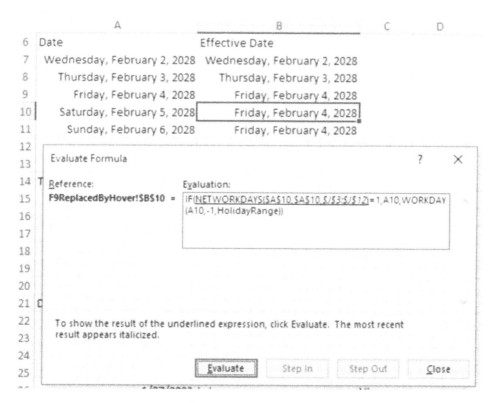

	A	B	C	D
6	Date	Effective Date		
7	Wednesday, February 2, 2028	Wednesday, February 2, 2028		
8	Thursday, February 3, 2028	Thursday, February 3, 2028		
9	Friday, February 4, 2028	Friday, February 4, 2028		
10	Saturday, February 5, 2028	Friday, February 4, 2028		
11	Sunday, February 6, 2028	Friday, February 4, 2028		

Evaluate Formula

Reference:
F9ReplacedByHover!$B$10 = IF(NETWORKDAYS($A$10,$A$10,$J$3:$J$12)=1,A10,WORKDAY(A10,-1,HolidayRange))

To show the result of the underlined expression, click Evaluate. The most recent result appears italicized.

Evaluate   Step In   Step Out   Close

#151 Stale Value Formatting

The Excel team added Stale Value Formatting in late 2023. The idea is that you might be working in a workbook with Manual Calculation enable. The strike-through formatting will remind you that certain cells need to be re-calculated.

To enable the feature, go to Formulas, Calculation Options. Select both Manual and Format Stale Values.

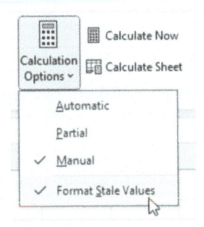

As of January 2024, the stale values will be formatted with a black strikethrough. There is currently no way to change the format. This, of course, annoys people who love to use Ctrl+5 to apply strikethrough formatting.

In the following image, a new value of 300 was just typed in C4. The formulas in row 4, row 9 and column H all need to be re-calculated. To clear the stale value formatting, press F9 or Formulas, Calculate Now.

Manual Calculation Mode & Stale Value Formatting

	Q1	Q2	Q3	Q4	Total	Running
Andy	300	330	360	400	1391	1391
Barb	900	990	1090	1200	4180	5571
Diane	270	300	330	360	1260	6831
Flo	180	200	220	240	840	7671
Ike	250	280	310	340	1180	8851
Total	1901	2100	2310	2540	8851	

Even if you are in Automatic calculation mode, you might see the stale value formatting if the workbook is extremely large and takes multiple seconds to recalculate.

Note that volatile functions will always be crossed out.

These functions will always be stale

Value	Formula
1/17/2024	=TODAY()
1/17/2024 3:39	=NOW()
0.734430291	=RAND()
23	=RANDBETWEEN(1,99)
300	=OFFSET(B3,3,2,1,1)
Diane	=INDEX(B4:B9,3)
0.475294542	=RANDARRAY(5)
0.523905503	

#152 Sort by Font Width?!

This is one of the crazier requests that came in to my YouTube channel. Someone wanted to sort a data set by the width of the text in a column, including differences in font size and font face. This seems like an impossible request.

	Date	Sector	Customer	Quantity	Revenue	COGS	Profit
1	Date	Sector	Customer	Quantity	Revenue	COGS	Profit
2	1/1/2028	Transportation	AAAAAA	100	2257	984	1273
3	1/1/2028	Energy	**AAAAAA**	400	9152	4088	5064
4	1/1/2028	Healthcare	Merck	800	18552	7872	10680
5	1/1/2028	Manufacturing	AAAAAA	1000	22810	10220	12590
6	1/4/2028	Manufacturing	IIIIII	400	8456	3388	5068
7	1/4/2028	Financial	BBBBBB	1000	21730	9840	11890
8	1/7/2028	Retail	BBBBBB	900	21438	9198	12240
9	1/9/2028	Manufacturing	BBBBBB	300	6267	2541	3726
10	1/11/2028	Communications	WWWWWW	100	2401	1022	1379
11	1/13/2028	Financial	OOOOOO	600	11628	5082	6546
12	1/18/2028	Communications	SBC Communications	800	14440	6776	7664
13	2/3/2028	Manufacturing	General Electric	900	21708	8856	12852
14	2/13/2028	Manufacturing	MMMMMM	800	16936	8176	8760
15	2/14/2028	Energy	Exxon	600	11430	5082	6348

Download the workbook for this topic in the book. There are two macros that will sort based on ascending width or descending width. The macro quickly creates a helper column. For each cell in column E, the macro selects the cell, and then does AutoFit Column Width, logging the new column width in the helper column. After repeating this for each value in column E, the data is sorted by the helper column. Finally, the helper column is cleared and column E is set back to the original width. Here is the results sorted from widest to narrow:

	Date	Sector	Customer	Quantity	R
1	Date	Sector	Customer	Quantity	R
2	/18/2028	Communications	SBC Communications	800	
3	2/3/2028	Manufacturing	General Electric	900	
4	/28/2028	Financial	CUNA Insurance	800	
5	/28/2028	Manufacturing	Phillip Morris	800	
6	1/9/2028	Manufacturing	BBBBBB	300	
7	/11/2028	Communications	WWWWWW	100	
8	/13/2028	Manufacturing	MMMMMM	800	
9	4/3/2028	Financial	BankUnited	700	
10	/23/2028	Retail	ABC Stores	900	
11	1/1/2028	Energy	**AAAAAA**	400	
12	1/7/2028	Retail	BBBBBB	900	
13	/13/2028	Financial	OOOOOO	600	
14	/27/2028	Retail	NNNNNN	800	
15	/16/2028	Manufacturing	Motorola	200	
16	1/1/2028	Manufacturing	AAAAAA	1000	
17	/12/2028	Manufacturing	Compaq	1000	
18	1/4/2028	Financial	BBBBBB	1000	
19	1/1/2028	Transportation	AAAAAA	100	
20	/14/2028	Retail	Lowe's	200	
21	/29/2028	Communications	Lucent	300	
22	1/1/2028	Healthcare	Merck	800	
23	/14/2028	Energy	Exxon	600	
24	5/3/2028	Retail	Sears	200	
25	/15/2028	Manufacturing	Ford	800	
26	3/2/2028	Manufacturing	P&G	700	
27	1/4/2028	Manufacturing	IIIIII	400	
28	/16/2028	Manufacturing	HP	200	

#153 Get the Countries from a Column of Phone Numbers

Someone had a long list of international telephone numbers. They asked if there is a formula to figure out the country from the phone number. It turns out that Country Codes are complicated. Some are a single digit. Some are 2 or 3 digits. Sometimes, two countries have the same country code and then you have to look at the country code plus area code to figure out, for example, if it is the USA or Canada.

The formula uses five different XLOOKUPs and five lookup tables that each use a named range.

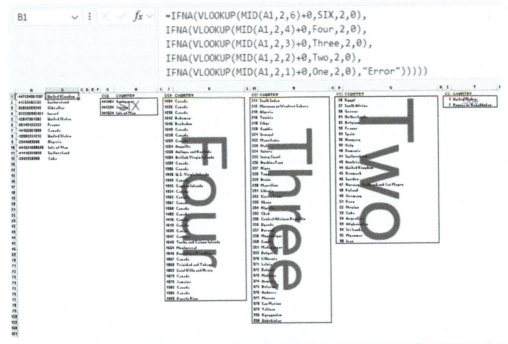

Tip: Set the zoom to 39% or less to see the range names in the grid.

While the system is unwieldy, download the workbook for this chapter and you will have a formula that can identify the country for each phone number.

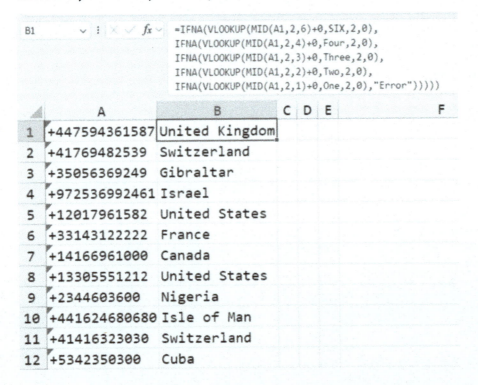

#154 Word for Excellers

Note: Katie Sullivan is a project manager on the Microsoft Word team. For this tip in the book, I turn the podium over to Katie.

While Excel fans sometimes tease that Word and PowerPoint are freeware apps that come with Excel, there are times when Microsoft Word offers a feature that Excel does not. In those cases, it makes sense to copy your data from Excel, paste to Word, do the command, then copy back to Excel. Here are some examples of techniques that are better handled in Word than in Excel.

Technique 1: Convert to Upper, Lower, Proper

If you have to convert from uppercase to lowercase or proper case, Word has a keystroke shortcut. Copy the data to Word and toggle the case using Shift+F3.

Technique 2: Add Bullets

If you want to add bullets to Excel cells, it is far easier in Word than in Excel. Copy the cells to Word and apply a bullet style. Copy from Word and paste back to Excel. You might have to use the Reduce Indent icon a few times.

Tip: Since the first edition of this book, I learned of an easier way to do bullets in Excel. If you have a range of cells that contain text, select the range and press Ctrl+1 to open the Format Cells dialog. Then, on the Number tab, choose Custom from the list on the left. Click in the Type box and clear out whatever is there. Hold down the Alt key while pressing the 7 on the numeric keypad. A bullet should appear. Type a space and then an @.

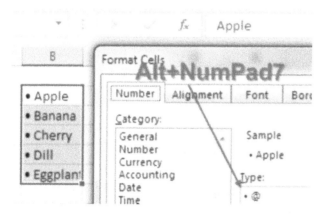

Technique 3: Visualize and Color Formulas

If you have a massively long formula, say one with 10 nested IF statements, you can paste to Word and use colors and Shift+Enter to space the formula to help make sense of it. (One rebuttal from the Excel team: You can expand the formula bar and use Alt+Enter to split a formula into many lines. Or, you can use the great RefTreeAnalyser add-in from Jan Karel Pieterse; see http://mrx.cl/jkpformula.)

Technique 4: Faster SmartArt

Word offers the Convert Text to SmartArt option. While Excel offers SmartArt, too, it is not very handy there because you have to copy the entries one at a time into the SmartArt pane.

Technique 5: Extract Data from a PDF

Say that someone has an Excel workbook and saves that workbook as a PDF. They send it to you. This is annoying, and clearly they don't want you to reuse the data. If you open the PDF in Acrobat Reader, copy the data, and paste to Excel, it will unwind into a single column. But here is the secret: Paste that data to Word first. The rows and columns will paste properly. You can then copy from Word and paste back into Excel. (If you are stuck in a pre-2013 version of Office, I recommend Able2Extract: mrx.cl/pdftoxl.)

The original data is shown on the left below, and you can see on the right and how it looks when you paste directly from PDF to Excel. You can see that the data "unwinds," with B1:C1 going to A2:A3 and so on.

	A	B	C
1	Trait	Dogs	Cats
2	Protective instinct	Yes	No
3	Always happy to see you when return	Yes	No
4	Spit up hairballs	No	Yes
5	Big or small	Yes	Only small
6	Chase tennis balls	Yes	No
7	Herd small children	Yes	No
8	Swim with you	Yes	No
9	Do tricks	Yes	No

	A	B
1	Trait	
2	Dogs	
3	Cats	
4	Protective instinct	
5	Yes	
6	No	
7	Always happy to see you	
8	Yes	
9	No	

Paste that same data to Word (below left), then copy from Word and paste to Excel (below right). The data stays in the original order. You can unapply Word Wrap and adjust the column widths to get back to the original data.

Trait	Dogs	Cats
Protective instinct	Yes	No
Always happy to see you when	Yes	No

Trait	Dogs	Cats
Protectiv e instinct	Yes	No
Always happy to see you	Yes	No

Technique 6: Change Formatting of Words Within Excel

If you have sentences of text in Excel, it is possible to select one word while in Edit mode and change the

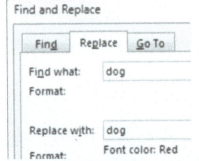

color of that word. But globally changing the color of all occurrences of the word in Excel is tedious. Instead, paste the data to Word and press Ctrl+H. Change dog to dog. Click More>> and then choose Format, Font. Choose Red. Click Replace All. Copy from Word and paste back to Excel. The figure below shows what you end up with.

⊿	A	B	C	D	E	F	G	H
1	Original							
2	A dog is always happy to see you when you return home.							
3	If you have children, a dog will be protective of the children. If it is a herding dog, i							
4	Certain breeds of dog love to swim. You can not keep my dog Bella from diving in t							
5	A dog has no problems chasing a tennis ball all day.							
6								
7	After doing Replace in Word and pasting back to Excel							
8	A dog is always happy to see you when you return home.							
9	If you have children, a dog will be protective of the children. If it is a herding dog, i							
10	Certain breeds of dog love to swim. You can not keep my dog Bella from diving in t							
11	A dog has no problems chasing a tennis ball all day.							
12								

Technique 7: Replace While Keeping Character Formatting

Word also handles a similar problem: replacing text but leaving the text formatting as it is. Below is a survey about the best pet. Someone has highlighted certain words in the text.

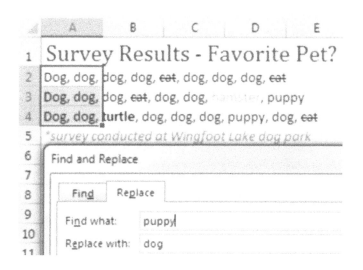

Use Ctrl+H to do a Find and Replace, as shown on the left. When you use Replace All, if a sentence was changed, your in-cell formats will be lost. In the figure below, the strikethrough remains in the first row because that row did not have an occurrence of the word *puppy* and thus was not changed.

Dog, dog, dog, dog, ~~cat~~, dog, dog, dog, ~~cat~~
Dog, dog, dog, cat, dog, dog, hamster, dog
Dog, dog, turtle, dog, dog, dog, dog, dog, cat

To keep the formatting in the original text, copy to Word. Do the replace in Word. Copy from Word and paste back to Excel.

Bonus Tip: Merge Shapes

Here's a brief plug for PowerPoint: If you need to create a shape in Excel that is a combination of other shapes, create the shapes in PowerPoint. Select all the shapes you want to include. On the Drawing Tools Format tab, choose Merge Shapes. You can then select Union, Combine, Fragment, Intersect, or Subtract to combine the shapes. (The Subtract feature lets you cut a hole in a shape.) Then copy that shape and paste to Excel (or Word).

Bonus Tip: Use the Eye Dropper

Another feature unique to PowerPoint is the eye dropper. If you want to use a particular color, you can just click the eye dropper on the color. When you open the Power Point color menu again, choose More Colors, and you can see the RGB colors. To use the eye dropper outside the PowerPoint frame, hold down the left mouse button and pick from any website or picture you have visible on your desktop.

Thanks to Katie Sullivan (a project manager on the Word team!) for contributing this tip. Katie clearly prefers dogs to cats. Thanks to Glenna Shaw and Oz du Soleil for contributing ideas to this tip. Zack Barresse and Echo Swinford pointed out the Merge Shapes option in PowerPoint. Sam Radakovitz added the eye dropper tip and noted the Subtract feature for shapes.

#155 Avoid Whiplash with Speak Cells

I hate having to hand-key data into Excel. Between the Internet and Power Query, there almost always is a way to find the data somewhere. I hate when people send a PDF where they scanned some numbers and are sending the numbers as a picture. A free trial of Able2Extract Pro (mrx.cl/ExtractPDF) will get the actual number into Excel. Even so, sometimes you end up keying data into Excel.

One of the painful parts about keying in data is that you have to proofread the numbers. So, you are looking at the sheet of paper, then the screen, then the paper, then the screen. You will end up with a sore neck. Wouldn't it be nice if you had someone to read you the screen so you can keep your eye on the paper? It's built in to Excel.

Right-click on the Quick Access Toolbar and choose Customize Quick Access Toolbar.

Change the top-left dropdown to Commands Not in the Ribbon. Scroll down to the S entries until you find Speak Cells. Add all five of these commands to the Quick Access Toolbar.

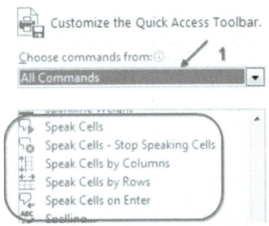

Select your range of numbers and click Speak Cells. Excel reads you the numbers.

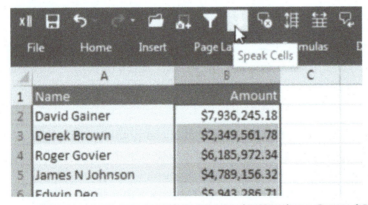

Tip: You can customize the voice in the Windows Control Panel. Search for Text to Speech. There is a setting for Voice Speed. Drag that slider to halfway between Normal and Fast to have the voice read your cells faster.

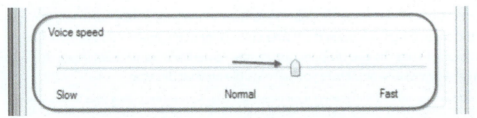

Bonus Tip: Provide Feedback with Sound

New in July 2017: Go to Excel Options. From the left category list, choose Ease of Access. Select the check-box for Provide Feedback with Sound and choose Modern. (The other choice, Classic, should be called Annoying!)

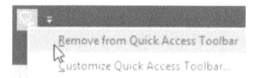

Excel now provides confirmation with gentle sounds when you do any of these tasks: Copy, Paste, Undo, Redo, AutoCorrect, Save, Insert Cells, Delete Cells.

Bonus Tip: A Great April Fool's Day Trick

Do you want a harmless prank to pull on a co-worker? When he leaves his desk to grab a cup of coffee, add the fifth icon to his Quick Access Toolbar: Speak Cells on Enter. Click the icon once, and the computer will say, "Cells will now be spoken on Enter."

Once you've turned on Speak Cells on Enter, right-click the icon in the Quick Access Toolbar and choose Remove from Quick Access Toolbar to hide any sign that you were there.

Your co-worker comes back, sits down, and starts to build a worksheet. The computer repeats back everything the co-worker types.

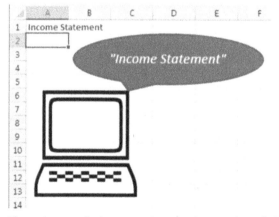

If you have a little more time and want Speak Cells on Enter with attitude, add the following macro to the code pane for the current worksheet..

```
Worksheet                                    ▼    Change

    Private Sub Worksheet_Change(ByVal Target As Range)
        Application.Speech.Speak "Damn Straight!  " & Target.Value
    End Sub
```

#156 Temporarily Make Formula Bar Font Size Larger

Say you have a Zoom or Teams call and you temporarily need to make the font size in the formula bar larger.

Go to File, Options, General. Change the Font Size setting.

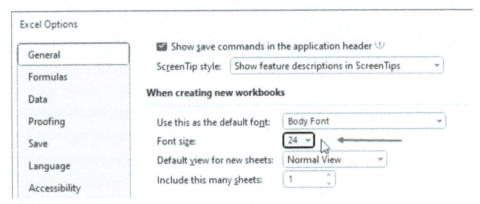

You need to exit and restart Excel for the font changes to take effect. When you re-open Excel, the formula bar font is larger.

	A	B	C	D
			People say you can't change the font size in the formula bar.	
34	Add	Link	xZxKhm9_Xkk Excel Improvements To Picture In Cell - Episode 2608	
36	Add	Link	0NArag0pV7I Excel Place Local Pictures In Cell Using Formula and a VBA Hack - Episode 2607a	
37	Add	Link	mFd8HsHmfpA Excel - Picture Place In Cell - Episode 2606	

M82 fx

After your Zoom or Teams call, remember to change this setting back. Otherwise, Excel will feel wonky with all new workbooks containing a large font.

Note: Every year, I get some strange questions on my YouTube channel. The following topics were answered on YouTube but have not been in this book. They will likely only be in this edition, so enjoy them.

#157 Circle Invalid Data Automatically

You have some numbers in a worksheet. Those cells should be between 60 and 90 inclusive.

Select the range of data. On the Data tab, open Data Validation. Allow a Whole Number. Choose Between and 60 and 90. Click OK.

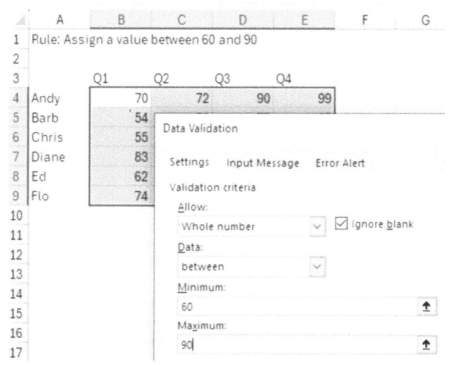

Go back to the Data Validation drop-down and choose Circle Invalid Data.

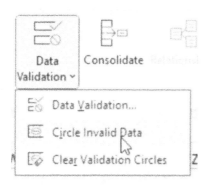

Excel will automatically circle the values that don't meet the validation rule.

	A	B	C	D	E
1	Rule: Assign a value between 60 and 90				
2					
3		Q1	Q2	Q3	Q4
4	Andy	70	72	90	99
5	Barb	54	58	77	69
6	Chris	55	87	50	56
7	Diane	83	92	84	75
8	Ed	62	92	82	99
9	Flo	74	76	98	96
10					

#158 The Advanced Filter Treats Criteria as "Begins With"

Check out this simple use of Advanced Filter. You are asking for all rows with the Product of Apple to be copied to the output range.

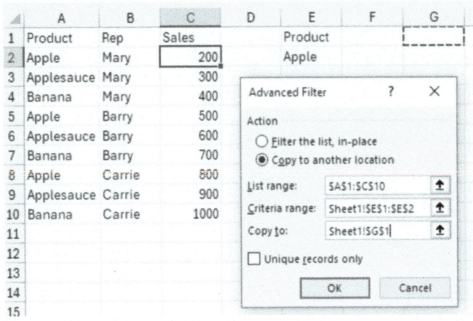

After clicking OK, the output range includes both Apple and Applesauce.

It turns out that this is by design. Microsoft says Excel is supposed to work this way.

If you want to extract just Apple and not Applesauce, you have to set up a formula to make the criteria look like a formula:

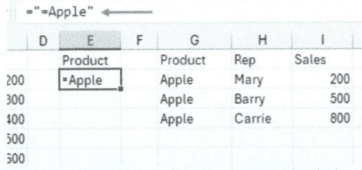

Thanks to Derek Fraley for the heads up about this apparent bug that is not a bug.

#159 Generate All Combinations Using BASE Function

I occassionaly have a model where I need to test all possible combinations of several outcomes. For example, lets say that you have four different manufacturing lines and three scenarios that could happen per line.

You need a fast way to generate rows with 1-1-1-1, 1-1-1-2, 1-1-2-1, 1-1-2-2, and so on all the way down to 3-3-3-3.

Calculate how many rows you will have. The first manufacturing line has 3 possible outcomes. Multiply this 3 by the 3 possible outcomes for Line 2. Continue and you will end up with 3^4 or 81.

Long ago, there were functions in Excel to convert from Decimal to Binary to Octal, or Hexadecimal numbering systems. In Excel 2013, Microsoft improved those with the new BASE function. To see the number 49 in Binary, you could use =BASE(49,2). If you want to make sure that the resulting number has 8 digits, specify 8 as the minimum length.

B6	✓ :	f_x	=BASE(B2,2,8)	
	A	B	C	D
1				
2		49		
3		110001	=DEC2BIN(B2)	
4		110001	=BASE(B2,2)	
5		00110001	=DEC2BIN(B2,8)	
6		00110001	=BASE(B2,2,8)	
7				

The BASE function handles any numbering system from Base-2 to Base-36. For me, I rarely use it since all of my accounting happens in Base-10. However, there is a cool use for the BASE function when you need to generate all possible outcomes.

In the simple model below, you enter the number of columns and choices per column. Cell A5 calculates the number of combinations.

The action starts happening in cell A7. Working from the inside, you generate the numbers 0 to 80 using SEQUENCE(A5,1,0). Send this array into the BASE function for a numbering system of 3 with a minimum sequence of 4. This generates the combinations using the digits 0, 1, and 2. This formula would generate from 0000 to 2222. Since you want 1111 to 3333, you simply add 1111 to the result of the formula.

Note that I've hidden many rows in the middle here so you can see the beginning and end of the results.

▲	A	B	C	D	E	F	G
1	**Arrange Numbers 1 to 3 in Four Columns**						
2							
3	4	Number of Columns					
4	3	Choices Per Column					
5	81	combinations					
6							
7	1111	=BASE(SEQUENCE(A5,1,0),A4,A3)+1111					
8	1112						
9	1113						
10	1121						
11	1122						
12	1123	<--Hiding Rows					
84	3323						
85	3331						
86	3332						
87	3333						
88							

A second formula in B7, copied down to all rows will break the four digits out into columns. This uses the MID function, with a SEQUENCE of 1 row by 4 columns to generate the numbers 1, 2, 3, 4. Copy this formula to the bottom of the array in column A.

B7	⌄ ⋮ ✕ ✓	fx ⌄	=MID(A7,SEQUENCE(1,4),1)				

▲	A	B	C	D	E	F	G
6		Line 1	Line 2	Line 3			
7	1111	1	1	1	1		
8	1112	1	1	1	2		
9	1113	1	1	1	3		
85	3331	3	3	3	1		
86	3332	3	3	3	2		
87	3333	3	3	3	3		
88							

#160 Why a Dark Rectangle Around the Formula Bar?

This brand new feature is annoying half of all Excellers. It all depends on how you edit a formula. I edit by pressing F2 and editing right in the cell. But apparently a lot of people still click up in the Formula Bar. When you do, you get a dark box around the Formula Bar. How do you make it go away? You can't make it go away. What's going on? It's something called the F6 Loop. It's an accessibility feature that jumps around the screen when you press F6.

SUM	⌄ ⋮ ✕ ✓	fx ⌄	=A6^2

#161 High Contrast Color Picker Avoids Accessibility Issues

It used to be all too easy to create ugly, unreadable color combinations in Excel. You'd set a red fill, then choose a dark red font—and end up with something only legible to hawks.

Now, Excel helps us avoid those mistakes with a new High Contrast Only setting built into the color pickers for Font Color and Fill Color.

Let's say you have a red background. If you click Font Color, there's now a High Contrast Only toggle. Turn it On, and Excel filters the list to show only font colors that meet contrast accessibility standards. In this case, you'll probably get two options: black and white.

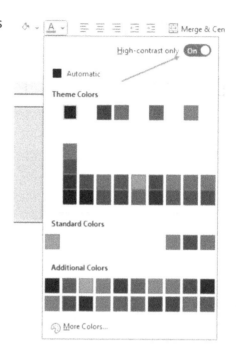

On a yellow background, expect more dark font choices like navy or black. There's even a section for Additional Colors—pre-tested to be readable with your chosen fill color.

It Works in Reverse Too. Got a light font color? When you click Fill Color, High Contrast mode will show only dark backgrounds that provide enough contrast.

If you've ever been dinged by the Accessibility Checker for poor contrast—or if you just want your spreadsheets to look cleaner and more professional—turn on High Contrast Only by default. It'll save your readers' eyes (and maybe your printing budget).

#162 Unhide One Specific Column Without Unhiding Others

You are presenting on a Zoom call. You've hidden columns in your spreadsheet that contain Salary, Manager, and Bonus. You need to unhide the Manager data in E but not unhide the Salary in D or the Bonus in F. Normally, you would select from column D to column G and unhide. But that would reveal the Salary and Bonus information on the call.

Press the F5 key or Ctrl+G to display the Go To dialog box. Specify that you want to Go To cell E2 and click OK. This will select just the hidden E2. You can confirm this by looking in the Name Box to see that you have E2 selected. You can also see the heading of Manager in the Formula Bar.

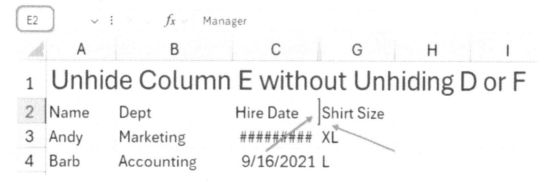

When you unhide the column (perhaps using Alt+OCU or Alt,H,O,U,L or Ctrl+Shift+) if you've followed the steps shown in "41. Hide or Unhide Rows or Columns" on page 310. The result will be that you've left column D and F hidden while unhiding column E.

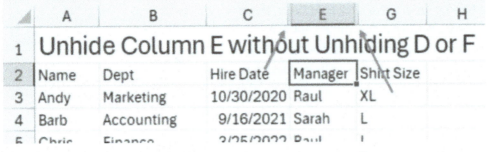

#163 How to Enable ActiveX Controls

Starting in May 2025, Microsoft started disabling ActiveX controls by default. Now, when you open a downloaded Excel file that uses ActiveX controls, you might see this annoying message:

"Blocked content. The ActiveX content in this file is blocked."

Even worse, dismissing the message by clicking the "X" or trying to navigate away with Alt + Tab won't get rid of it. It just keeps coming back!

This is frustrating, but there's a way to fix it. Microsoft changed the default setting to block ActiveX for security reasons—but you can override it if you need those controls to work.

Here's how to enable ActiveX content:

1. Go to File, Options, Trust Center.

2. Click the Trust Center Settings... button.

3. On the left-hand menu, select ActiveX Settings.

4. Choose the third option: "Prompt me before enabling all controls with minimal restrictions."

5. Click OK, and then OK again to exit.

6. To activate the change, you'll need to close and reopen the Excel file that showed the message.

Once you've done this, that pesky warning should disappear. From then on, Excel will prompt you (rather than block you) when opening files with ActiveX—so you can enable content when you trust the source.

#164 Using the Date Picker in Excel Online

Excel does have a built-in Date Picker —but as of June 2025, it is still only in Excel Online. It's been around for over a year and a half, and frankly, it's time this made its way into the desktop versions for Windows and Mac. I am adding it to this book hoping that it makes it to Windows and Mac versions of Excel.

Let's take a look at how the Date Picker works and how to trigger it.

Step 1: Format the Cells as Dates. Select the cells, go to the Number Format dropdown, and choose Short Date or any other date format.

Step 2: Use Excel Online. Open your workbook in Excel Online (the browser version). As soon as you type a date in a cell—say using the shortcut Ctrl + ; to insert today's date—you'll see a calendar appear.

Step 3: Open the Date Picker from a blank cell. This part isn't exactly intuitive: you double-click the cell. That's what opens the date chooser.

From there, you can:

- Pick any day from the calendar.
- Navigate month-by-month using the arrows.
- Click the Month/Year header to open a month selector.
- In the Month Selector, click the Year to open a year selector.
- Click Go to Today (bottom-right) to quickly return to today's date.

#165 Export a PDF from Excel (Even Just One Page!)

Turning your Excel worksheet into a PDF is like printing—whatever shows in Print Preview is exactly what the PDF will show. So, set up everything first: print range, margins, and those handy repeating headers.

To export the PDF, Go to File, Export, Create PDF/XPS Document, Click the Create PDF/XPS button. Choose your file location and enter a file name. Click Publish.

Bonus: Export Only One Page to PDF

The trick is in the Options.

1. Follow the steps above until you're at the Save As window. Click the Options button before publishing.

2. Under Publish what, choose Pages and enter the specific page range—for example, "3 - 4".

3. Click OK, then Publish.

Bonus: Include Gridlines and Headers in the PDF

Angela is printing a spreadsheet for a co-worker who does not use Excel. But, she needs to be able to find cell J42 when colleagues refer to a spot in the spreadsheet. You can save the PDF with gridlines and row/column headings. Here's how to make them appear:

1. Go to the Page Layout tab in the ribbon.

2. In the Page Setup group, click the tiny arrow in the bottom-right corner (called a dialog launcher).

3. In the Page Setup dialog, go to the Sheet tab.

4. Check these two boxes: Gridlines, Row and column headings

5. Click OK, then go back to File, Export, Create PDF/XPS, Publish.

Thanks to Angela B. and Mary Ellen Jelen

#166 Customize the Quick Access Toolbar

There are features you might use frequently that are not on the Home tab. Even though the Excel team does not think many features are Home-tab-worthy, you can add your favorite features to the Quick Access Toolbar (hereafter called QAT).

I always like asking people what they have added to their QAT. In a Twitter poll in January 2019, I had over 70 suggestions of favorite features that could be added to the QAT.

To me, a "good" addition to the QAT is a command that you use frequently that is not already on the Home tab. Any of the features in the Commands Not In The Ribbon category are candidates if you ever have to use them.

Previously in this book, I've suggested the following icons on the QAT:

- The AutoFilter icon was used in "#5 Filter by Selection" on page 7
- Change Shape in "Bonus Tip: Old Style Comments Are Available as Notes" on page 37
- Speak Cells in "#155 Avoid Whiplash with Speak Cells" on page 284
- Speak Cells on Enter in "Bonus Tip: A Great April Fool's Day Trick" on page 285

Below are more icons that you might want to add to your QAT.

The Easy Way to Add to the QAT

The easiest way to add an icon to the QAT is to right-click the icon in the Ribbon and choose Add to Quick Access Toolbar.

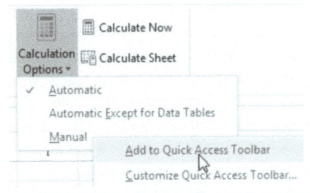

Adding Formulas, Calculation Options, Manual to the QAT gives you a clear indication of when your workbook is in Manual calculation mode:

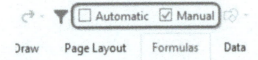

The Hard Way to Add to the QAT

Sometimes, the command you want can not be right-clicked. For example, in "Bonus Tip: Copy the Subtotal Rows" on page 72, I suggested using Alt+; as a shortcut for Visible Cells in the Go To Special dialog box.

Visible Cells Only is available to add to the QAT. But you can't add it by right-clicking in the dialog box. To make matters worse, when you follow these steps, you have to look for a command called "Select Visible Cells" instead of a command called "Visible Cells Only".

1. Right-click anywhere in the Ribbon and choose Customize Quick Access Toolbar. The Excel Options dialog box opens showing a list of Popular Commands. I reject many of these popular commands because they are already a single-click on the Home tab of the Ribbon.

2. Open the drop-down menu to the right of Popular Commands and choose either All Commands or Commands Not In the Ribbon.

3. Scroll through the left list box to find the command.

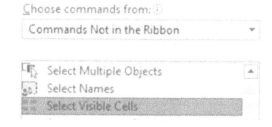

4. Click the Add>> button in the center of the screen.

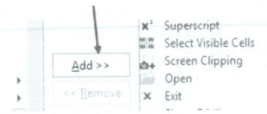

5. Click OK to close Excel Options.

6. Hover over the newly added icon to see the tooltip and possibly learn of a keyboard shortcut.

Favorite QAT Icons From Readers

Presented below are several suggestions from people on Social Media.

Back in "#75 Quickly Convert Formulas to Values" on page 157 I had nine different ways to Paste Values. Here is a tenth way. The most popular suggestion on Twitter was the Paste Values icon.

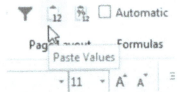

Thanks to ExcelCity, Adam Warrington, Dan Lanning, Christopher Broas. Bonus point to AJ Willikers who suggested both Paste Values and Paste Values and Number Formatting shown to the right of Paste Values above.

Bonus Tip: Sometimes, You Don't Want the Gallery

The next most popular command to add to the QAT is Freeze Panes. Go to the View tab. Open the Freeze Panes drop-down menu. Right-click on Freeze Panes and Excel offers "Add Gallery to the Quick Access Toolbar".

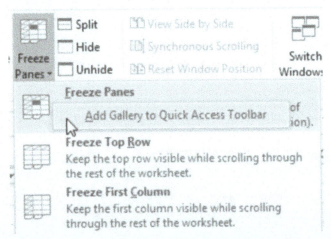

Freeze panes is a tricky command. If you want to freeze row 1 and columns A:B, you have to put the cell pointer in C2 before you invoke Freeze Panes.

Active Cell: First non-frozen cell

	Product	Name	Jan	Feb
1	Product	Name	Jan	Feb
2	Apple	Andy	590	849
3	Banana	Barb	975	128
4	Cherry	Chris	206	920
5	Date	Diane	217	872

Invoke Freeze Panes from here

Some people don't understand this, and in Excel 2007, the Excel team made the Freeze Panes gallery with choices to freeze top row and freeze first column for people who did not know to select C2 before invoking Freeze Panes.

Since you understand how Freeze Panes works, you don't want the gallery on the QAT. You just want the icon that does Freeze Panes.

When you look for commands in the Excel Options, there are two choices for Freeze Panes. The one with the arrow is the gallery. The first one is the one you want.

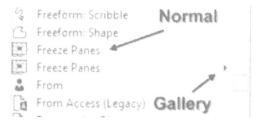

Freeform: Scribble

Freeform: Shape

Freeze Panes   ← Normal

Freeze Panes

From

From Access (Legacy)   Gallery

Thanks to Debra Dalgleish, Colin Foster and @Excel_City for suggesting Freeze Panes

In other cases, the Gallery version is superior to the non-gallery version. Here is an example. Jen (who apparently is a @PFChangsAddict) suggested adding Save As to the QAT. Alex Waterton suggested adding Save As Other Formats. When I initially added the non-gallery version of Save As Other Formats, I realized that both icons open the Save As dialog box.

Instead, use the Gallery version of Save As

Save

Save As   Gallery

Save As Other Format

Save As Other Formats

Here are those four icons in the QAT. The Save As Other Format gallery offers the most choices.

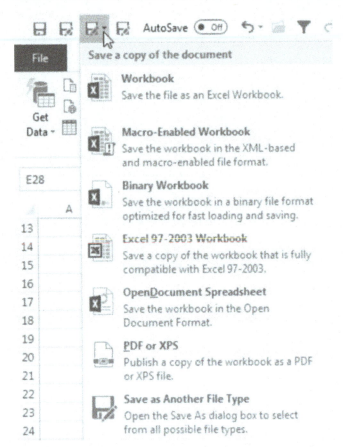

If you are planning on creating a lot of PDF files, Colin Foster suggests adding Publish as PDF or XPS to the QAT.

The First 9 Icons in QAT Have Easy Shortcut Keys

Most people who customize the QAT add new icons after the AutoSave, Save, Undo, Redo commands that are in the default QAT. But those first 9 QAT spots have super-easy keyboard shortcuts. AJ Willikers pointed out that the first 9 icons have easy short cut keys.

Press and release the Alt key. Key tips appear on each ribbon tab. So, Alt, H, S, O would sort descending. If you sort descending a lot, add the icon as one of the first 9 icons on the QAT. Press and release Alt, Then press 1 to invoke the first icon on the QAT. Note that the key tips for items 10 and beyond require you to press Alt, 0, 1 so they aren't quite as easy as the first 9 icons.

Bonus tip: Press and hold Alt+1 to run the first QAT icon repeatedly. This could be useful if it were Increase or Decrease Decimal.

Thanks to AJ Willikers for pointing out the Alt 1-9 keyboard shortcuts.

The Camera Tool versus Paste as Linked Picture

Another popular QAT command on Twitter was the Camera. This awesome hack dates back to Excel 97. It is great because it allows you to paste a live picture of cells from Sheet17 on the Dashboard worksheet. It was hard to use and Microsoft re-worked the tool in Excel 2007, rebranding it as Paste As Linked Picture. But the operation of the tool changed and some people like the old way better.

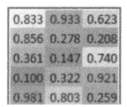

Old way: You could select the cells. Click the Camera icon. The mouse pointer changes to a cross hair. Click anywhere that you want to paste the picture of the cells.

New way: Copy the cells. Click in the new location. Choose Paste As Linked Picture. If you don't want the picture lined up with the top-left corner of the cell, drag to nudge the picture into position.

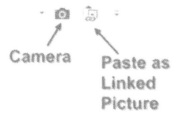

Camera   Paste as Linked Picture

Thanks to Manoel Costa, Brad Edgar, and Duncan Williamson for suggesting the Camera.

Screen Clipping to Capture a Static Image From Another Application

One of my favorite commands for the QAT is Insert Screen Clipping. Say that you want to grab a picture of a website and put it in your Excel worksheet. To effectively use the tool, you need to make sure that the web page is the most-recent window behind the Excel workbook. So - visit the web page. Then switch directly to your Excel Workbook. Choose Insert Screen Clipping and wait a few moments. The Excel screen disappears, revealing the web page. Wait for the web page to grey out, then use the mouse pointer to drag a rectangle around the portion of the web page. When you release the mouse button, a static picture of the web page (or any application) will paste in Excel. The Screen Clipping is also great for putting Excel charts in Power Point. Until you add this command to the QAT, it is hidden at the bottom of Insert, Screenshot. I don't like the Screenshot options because they put the entire full screen in Excel. Screen Clipping lets you choose just a part of the screen.Two Icons Might Lead to the Same Place: Open Recent and Open

One of the popular QAT commands in Excel 2010 and Excel 2013 was the folder with a star - Open Recent File…. This command disappeared from Excel in Excel 2016. But people discovered that if you exported your settings from 2013 and then imported to 2016 or 2019, the icon would appear!

As I considered the prospect of dragging my Excel 2013 .tlb file around for the rest of my life, I inadvertently realized that the Open icon leads to the exact same place as the Open Recent File icon.

Thanks to Colin Foster and Ed Hansberry for suggesting Open Recent File.

Clear Filter and Reapply Filter

You hopefully already have the AutoFilter on your QAT after reading "#5 Filter by Selection" on page 7. Debra Dalgleish, Excel_City, and AJ Willikers suggests Clear Filters. This is a great way to reset your filters without visiting the Data tab.

Bathazar Lawson suggests adding Reapply Filter to the QAT. Here is how this becomes handy. Let's say you have a list of projects. You don't need to see anything where the status code is Complete. You set up a filter for this.

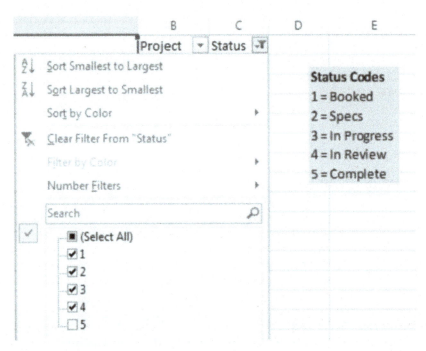

You change the status code on some projects. Some of the projects that used to be In Review are now Complete.

Project	Status
Project 115	3
Project 132	5
Project 38	2
Project 94	5
Project 106	5
Project 22	3
Project 17	5

Instead of re-opening the Filter drop-down, click Reapply Filter.

Sort & Filter

Excel will re-evaluate the data and hide the items which now have a 5.

Project	Status
Project 115	3
Project 38	2
Project 22	3
Project 21	4

CUSTOMIZE THE QUICK ACCESS TOOLBAR

Some Future Features Debut on the QAT and then Become Real Features

I was at a seminar in Topeka when Candace and Robert taught me that you could add an icon called Document Location to the QAT.

If you need to copy the document location to the clipboard, you can select the text from the QAT, right-click and choose Copy.

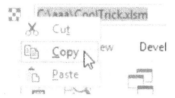

The Document Location has been available since at least Excel 2010. In early 2019, Microsoft 365 subscribers will notice that the File, Info screen now has new equivalents of Copy Path and Open File Location.

Easier Superscript and Subscripts

Add the new Superscript and Subscript icons to the QAT. As you are typing, click either icon to continue typing in subscript or superscript. This might be handy for a single character (such as the 2 in H_2O) or for several characters.

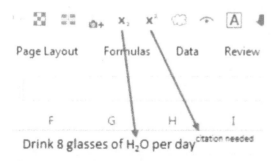

Drink 8 glasses of H_2O per day[citation needed]

Good Features from the Data Tab

The Data tab is like the Boardwalk and Park Place of the Excel ribbon. Every project manager wants to be on the Home tab, but most of the great features end up on the data tab. Excel 2016 introduced Get Data (Power Query), Relationships, and Refresh All. Add those to the QAT.

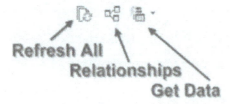

Refresh All
          Relationships
                    Get Data

Build Formulas Without Ever Leaving the Mouse

Ha-ha! This advice flies in the face of what every Excel tipster teaches. Most people want you to build formulas without ever leaving the keyboard. But what if you hate the keyboard and want to use the mouse? You can add these operators to your QAT:

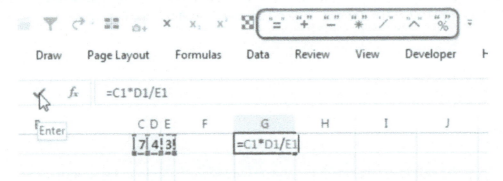

Using the mouse, you can click the Equals sign, then click on C1, then Multiply, then D1, then Divide, then E1. To complete the formula, click the green checkmark next to the formula bar to Enter. Surprisingly, Enter is not available for the QAT. But the formula bar is usually always visible, so this would work.

Those seven icons shown above are not located in one section of the Customize dialog. You have to hunt for them in the E, P, M, M, D, E, and P section of the list.

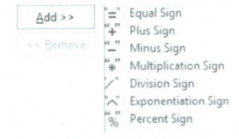

Bonus Tip: Show QAT Below the Ribbon

Right-click the Ribbon and choose Show Quick Access Toolbar Below The Ribbon. There are several advantages. First, it is a shorter mouse move to reach the icons. Second, when the QAT is above the Ribbon, you have less space until the icons run into the file name.

#167 Create Your Own QAT Routines Using VBA Macros

There are several short macros you can add to your Personal Macro Workbook and then add to the QAT. In this tip, you will see how to create the Personal Macro Workbook, type some macros, and then assign them to icons on the QAT.

Create a Personal Macro Workbook

Start from any workbook. Go to View, Macros, Record Macro. In the Record Macro dialog, type a one-word name such as HelloWorld. Choose Personal Macro Workbook. Click OK.

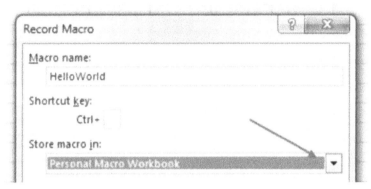

Type Hello in the active cell and press Enter. Then, select View, Macros, Stop Recording. These steps will create a Personal.xlsb on your computer where you can store new macros.

Open the VBA Editor and Find Module1 in Personal.xlsb

From Excel, press Alt+F11. (If you don't have Alt+F11, you can add the Visual Basic command to the QAT and click that.

Your first time in the VBA editor, it might be a vast expanse of grey. From the VBA menu, select View, Project Explorer.

Look for an entry called VBAProject (PERSONAL.XLSB). Click the + icon to expand it.

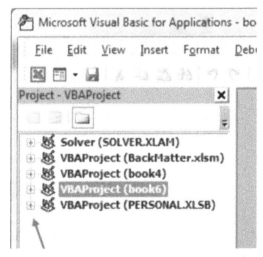

Look for and expand Modules. Right-click Module1 and choose View Code.

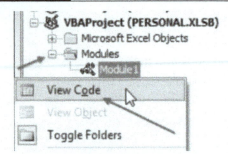

You will see your HelloWorld code. After the End Sub, type any of these procedures.

```
Sub VeryHideActiveSheet()
    ActiveSheet.Visible = xlVeryHidden
End Sub
Sub ShowAllSheets()
    For Each sh In ActiveWorkbook.Worksheets
        sh.Visible = True
    Next sh
End Sub
Sub UpperSelection()
    For Each cell In Selection.SpecialCells(2, 2)
        ' 2, 2 means xlCellTypeConstants, Text
        cell.Value = UCase(cell.Value)
    Next
End Sub
Sub LowerSelection()
    For Each cell In Selection.SpecialCells(2, 2)
        cell.Value = LCase(cell.Value)
    Next
End Sub
Sub ProperSelection()
    For Each cell In Selection.SpecialCells(2, 2)
        cell.Value = Application.WorksheetFunction.Proper(cell.Value)
    Next
End Sub
```

When you customize the QAT, choose Macros from the top left drop-down menu.

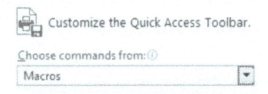

When you choose a macro and click Add>> the icon will default to a flow chart. Click Modify at the bottom right. Choose a new icon. Type a good tooltip.

Here is an explanation of how to use these five macros:

- **Very Hide:** Worksheets can be visible, hidden or very hidden. Few people know about Very Hidden sheets because you have to use VBA to create them. A worksheet that is Very Hidden will not show up in Home, Format, Hide and Unhide, Worksheets. (Thanks to -Sagar Malik)

- **Show All Sheets:** It is easy to select 12 sheets and hide them in a single command. But then unhiding the sheets is a one-at-a-time proposition. This macro will unhide all sheets (including very hidden sheets).

- **Upper Selection:** Converts all text in the selection to upper case.

- **Lower Selection**: Converts all text in the selection to lower case.
- **Proper Selection**: Converts all text in the selection to proper case.

Thanks to MF Wong for suggesting some of these macros.

Bonus Tip: Force Excel to Compile VBA on Each Open of the Workbook

In the 2022-2024 time frame, there is a problem where the VBA project for a workbook becomes corrupted and it appears that your macros are not there. Add this to the registry and try re-opening the workbook. This will force Excel to re-compile the project from the source. It seems to have fixed problems in many case. With RegEdit, locate the key HKEY_CURRENT_USER\Software\Microsoft\Office\16.0\Excel\Options\. Add a new DWORD value called ForceVBALoadFromSource. Assign the value 1 to this DWORD. Then re-open the workbook and see if the macros are back.

Note: Going through a compile on each open can slow Excel down slightly. Feel free to set the DWORD back to 0 if you notice longer load times for complex projects.

Thanks to Ingeborg Hawighorst and Bill Su-Piao for identifying this solution.

Bonus Tip: Settings in the Excel Options Menu

Consider a few of these settings after you choose File, Options:

General, Start Up Options, Unselect Show The Start Screen When This Application Starts to skip the Home screen. Excel will open directly to a blank workbook. (Thanks to Dave Marriott)

Advanced, Editing Options, Unselect After Pressing Enter, Move Selection. When you type a value in a cell, Excel will stay in the same cell. (Thanks to Ed Hansberry)

Advanced, Editing Options, Automatically Insert a Decimal Point. You type 12345. Excel gets 123.45.

#168 Favorite Keyboard Shortcuts

As I started polling readers about their favorite Excel tips, a large number of them were keyboard shortcuts. Some readers, such as Matt Kellett, Olga Kryuchkova, Mike Dolan Fliss, and @model_citizen, suggested that the book has to include a section on favorite keyboard shortcuts.

These are presented in order of popularity. If a lot of readers suggested a tip, it is at the top. After the first eight or so, they are then sorted by my subjective sequence.

1. Ctrl+1 to Format a Selection

Ctrl+1 (the number one) works to format whatever is selected. Whether it is a cell, SmartArt, a picture, a

shape, or the March data point in a column chart, press Ctrl+1.

Thanks to Mitja Bezenšek, Alexa Gardner, Andrej Lapajne, Schmuel Oluwa, Jon Peltier, @ExcelNewss, and @JulianExcelTips.

2. Ctrl[+Shift]+Arrow to Navigate or Select

Your cell pointer is sitting at the top of 50K rows of data, and you need to get to the bottom. If you have a

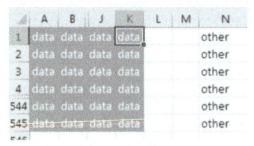 column with no blanks, press Ctrl+Down Arrow to jump to the end of the data set.

In the following figure, Ctrl+Down Arrow will jump to K545. Ctrl+Left Arrow will jump to A1. Ctrl+Right Arrow will jump the gap of empty cells and land on N1.

⊿	A	B	J	K	L	M	N
1	data	data	data	data			other
2	data	data	data	data			other
3	data	data	data	data			other
4	data	data	data	data			other
544	data	data	data	data			other
545	data	data	data	data			other

Add the Shift key in order to select from the active cell to the landing cell. Starting from A1 in the above figure, press Ctrl+Shift+Down Arrow to select A1:A545. While still holding down Ctrl+Shift, press the Right Arrow Key to select A1:K545. If it seems awkward at first, try it for a few days until you get the hang of it.

Thanks to Captain Excel, @Cintellis, José de Diego, Mike Girvin, Elchin Khalilov, Crystal Long, Paul Sasur, and @XLStudioWorks.

3. Ctrl+. to Jump to Next Corner

While you have a large range selected, press Ctrl+Period to move to the next corner of the selection. If the selection is rectangular, you move in a clockwise fashion. From the bottom-right corner, press Ctrl+. twice to move to the top left.

Thanks to Crystal Long, and Steve McCready.

4. Ctrl+5 for Strikethrough

This is great for crossing things off your to-do list. Why 5? If you are making hash marks, the fifth hash mark crosses out the first four.**Ctrl+* to Select Current Region**

This one is easier if you have a number keypad so you don't have to press Shift to get to an asterisk. If I could slow down enough to stop pressing Ctrl+Shift+Down Arrow followed by Ctrl+Shift+Right arrow, I would realize that Ctrl+* is much shorter and does not get tripped up by blank cells. It is really superior in every way to keyboard tip #2. But my muscle memory still prefers tip #2. Thanks to @Excelforo.

5. Ctrl+Enter to Copy Formula into Entire Selection

Ken Puls, who is the king of Power Query, says, "You would think my favorite Excel tip would be Unpivot with Power Query, but my favorite all-time is Ctrl+Enter." Say that you want to enter a formula into 400 cells. Select the 400 cells. Type the formula in the first cell. Press Ctrl+Enter, and Excel enters a similar formula in all cells of the selection.

Gavin White points out another use. You enter a formula in G2. You need to copy the formula down but not the formatting. Select G2:G20. Press the F2 key to put the cell in Edit mode. When you press Ctrl+Enter, the formula is copied, but no formatting is copied. Thanks to Crystal Long, Schmuel Oluwa, Ken Puls, Peter Raiff, Sven Simon, and Gavin Whyte.

6. Ctrl(+Shift)+; to Time or Date Stamp

Press Ctrl+Shift+: to enter the current time. Press Ctrl+; for the current date. Note the shortcut enters the *current* time, not a formula. To put both the Date & time in one cell, type either keystroke, a space, then the other keystroke. Excel will interpret it as the proper Date & time.

Thanks to Olga Kryuchkova, Roger Govier and Tim O'Mara.

7. Ctrl+Backspace to Bring the Active Cell into View

This is a great trick that I never knew. Say that C1 is the active cell. You've used the scrollbars, and now you are looking at ZZ999. To bring the window back to encompass the active cell, press Ctrl+Backspace.

Thanks to Olga Kryuchkova and Schmuel Oluwa.

8. Alt+= for AutoSum

Press Alt+= to invoke the AutoSum function. Thanks to Dawn Bjork Buzbee and Olga Kryuchkova.

9. Ctrl+Page Down and Ctrl+Page Up to Jump to Next Worksheet

If you need to move from Sheet1 to Sheet5, press Ctrl+Page Down four times. If you are at Sheet9 and need to move to Sheet3, press Ctrl+Page Up six times. Thanks to Jeneta Hot.

10. Ctrl+Click to Select Noncontiguous Cells

If you have to select two regions, select the first one, then hold down Ctrl while clicking on other cells or regions. – Thanks toThomas Fries**Tab to AutoComplete**

This one is maddening. You type =VL to start VLOOKUP. The AutoComplete shows that there is only one function that starts with VL. But if you press Enter, you get a #NAME? error.

The correct way to choose VLOOKUP is to press Tab! Thanks to Ashish Agarwal.

11. Shift+F8 to Add to Selection

Select the first range. Press Shift+F8, and you are in Add to Selection mode. Scroll anywhere. Select the next range. Then select another range. And so on, without ever touching Ctrl. To return to normal, press Esc. Thanks to Neil Charles. A bonus tip from Bill Hazlett: if you select A1, press F8, then click in S20, you will select from A1:S20. Press Esc to exit the Extend Selection mode. Watch for the indicator in the status bar:

Ready   Accessibility: Good to go   Extend Selection

12. Ctrl+Spacebar and Shift+Spacebar to Select an Entire Column or Row

Ctrl+Spacebar selects a whole column. Shift+Spacebar selects a whole row. How can you remember which is which? The "C" in Ctrl stands for the "C" in column. Also, the "S" in Shift is adjacent in the alphabet to the "R" in row. Another way to remember which is which: The Shift key is much longer (like a row!) than Ctrl.

Thanks to Michael Byrne, Jeneta Hot, and Bob Umlas.

13. Ctrl+` to See All Formulas

Many folks in the United States think this is Ctrl+~, but it is actually the grave accent to toggle into and out of Show Formulas mode.

14. F3 to Paste a Name into a Formula

I am not a huge fan of this, since you can start typing the name and then choose from AutoComplete. But I know the trick has its fans, including Mike Girvin and Johan van den Brink.

15. Ctrl+Shift+1 to apply Number Formatting

I had never memorized these, but I am going to start using some of them. Ctrl+Shift+1 (also known as Ctrl+!), will apply a number format, 2 decimals, thousands separator, and negatives shown with a minus sign. The other five make some reasonable sense, as described below.

Key	AKA	Formats as	Example
Ctrl+Shift+1	!	Number	-1,234.56
Ctrl+Shift+2	@	Time	2:50 PM
Ctrl+Shift+3	#	Date	29-Jun-15
Ctrl+Shift+4	$	Currency	($1,234.56)
Ctrl+Shift+5	%	Percent	100%
Ctrl+Shift+6	^	Exponential	1.23E+08

Thanks to Matthew Bernath.

16. Ctrl+Shift+2 to Apply Time Formatting

Ctrl+Shift+2 or Ctrl+@ applies a time formatting. Say that you want to meet for dinner @ 5 o'click. Long before it became associated with e-mail addresses, the @ inferred time.**Ctrl+Shift+3 to Apply Date Formatting**

Ctrl+Shift+3 or Ctrl+# applies a date formatting. The # symbol looks a bit like a calendar, if you lived in an alternate universe with three weeks per month and three days per week.

17. Ctrl+Shift+4 to Apply Currency Formatting

Ctrl+Shift+4 or Ctrl+$ applies a currency format with two decimal places.

18. Ctrl+Shift+5 for Percent Format

Ctrl+Shift+5 or Ctrl+% applies a percentage format with 0 decimal places.

19. Ctrl+Shift+6 for Scientific Format

Ctrl+Shift+6 or Ctrl+Shift+^ applies scientific notation. 1.23E+07 infers an exponent. A caret(^) is used to enter exponents in Excel.

20. Ctrl+[to Jump to Linked Cell

You are in a cell that points to Sheet99!Z1000. Press Ctrl+[to jump to that cell. This works if you have links between workbooks, even if the other workbook is closed! Thanks to @Heffa100 and Bob Umlas.

21. Ctrl+F1 to hide or show the Ribbon

To toggle the Ribbon between Pinned and Hidden, use Ctrl+F1.

22. Ctrl+Shift+F1 for Full Screen Mode

New in 2021: Use Ctrl+Shift+F1 to toggle into Full Screen Mode. In this mode, Excel hides the Status Bar, the Ribbon tabs and the Quick Access Toolbar but keeps the Formula Bar. On my large monitor, I can see

55 rows in Excel, 60 rows in Excel after Ctrl+F1, and 64 rows after Ctrl+Shift+F1. None of these beat the QAT icon Full Screen Mode [Toggle Full Screen Mode]. This legacy icon hides the formula bar and shows 66 rows in the grid.

23. Alt+F1 to Chart the Selected Data

Select some data. Press Alt+F1. You get a chart of the data. You might remember F11 doing the same thing. But F11 creates the chart as a chart sheet. Alt+F1 embeds the chart in the current sheet.

24. Shift+F11 to Insert a Worksheet

I never knew this one, but it makes sense as a corollary to F11. If F11 inserts a chart sheet, then Shift+F11 inserts a new worksheet. You can also use Alt+I, W to insert a worksheet, Alt+I, R to insert a row, or Alt+I, C to insert a column. Thanks to Olga Kryuchkova.

25. Alt+E, S, V to Paste Values

I can do Alt+E, S, V, Enter with my eyes closed. Alt+E opened the Excel 2003 Edit menu. S chose Paste Special. V chose Values. Enter selected OK. Thanks to Matthew Bernath and Laura Lewis.

26. Alt+E, S, T to Paste Formats

Alt+E, S, T, Enter pastes formats. Why t instead of f? Because Alt+E, S, F already was in use to paste formulas.

27. Alt+E, S, F to Paste Formulas

Alt+E, S, F, Enter pastes formulas without copying the cell formatting. This is handy to prevent cell borders from copying along with the formula.Alt+E, S, W to Paste Column Widths

Alt+E, S, W pastes column widths. This is great to use with a block of columns. In the following figure. select A1:H1, copy, then select J1 and Alt+E, S, V, Enter to copy all 8 column widths.

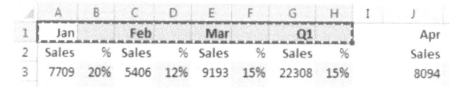

28. Alt+E, S, D, V to Paste Special Add

Alt+E, S, D, V does a Paste Special Add, but does not screw up the formatting.

29. Alt+E, S, E to Turn Data Sideways, I

Alt+E, S, E does a Transpose. To see all the possibilities, press Alt+E, S and then look for the underlined letters.

30. Alt+T, M, S to Change Macro Security.

This shortcut is really useful now that the settings are buried deep in Excel options. Thanks to Ron de Bruin.

31. Alt+T, I to Activate Add-ins

Alt+T, I is faster than File, Options, Add-Ins, Manage Excel Add-ins, Go.

32. Ctrl+Shift+L to Enable the Filter Dropdowns

Toggle the filters on or off with Ctrl+Shift+L. In Excel 2013 and earlier, pressing Ctrl+Shift+L would scroll your screen to the end of the data set. Press Ctrl+Backspace to bring the active cell back in to view. Or, press and release Alt, A, T. Thanks to David Hager and Andrew Walker.

33. Hold Down Alt to Snap to Grid

If you are drawing any shape, Alt will cause that shape to exactly line up with the borders of cells. Thanks to Rickard Wärnelid.

34. Ctrl+W to Close a Workbook but Leave Excel Open

If you have one workbook open and you click the "X" in the top-right corner, you close Excel. Ctrl+W closes that workbook but leaves Excel open. Thanks to Dave Marriott.

35. F5 to Sneak into a Hidden Cell

You've hidden column D, but you need to see what is in D2. Press Ctrl+G or F5 to open the Go To dialog. Type D2 and press Enter. The cell pointer moves to the hidden cell D2, and you can see the value in the formula bar. You can now use the Down Arrow key to move within the hidden column D, and you can always see the value in the formula bar.

36. Alt+D, E, F to Convert Numbers Stored as Text to Numbers

Select a whole column and press Alt+D, E, F. The text numbers are converted to numbers. You are actually doing a default Text to Columns with this shortcut.

37. Alt+O, C, A to AutoFit a Column

Select some cells and press Alt+O, C, A to make the column wide enough for the longest value in the selection.**Ctrl+' to Copy the Exact Formula Down (aka Ditto)**

You have to sum in D10 and average in D11. Create the AutoSum in D10. When you press Enter, you are in D11. Press Ctrl+' to bring the exact formula down without changing the cell reference. If D10 is =SUM(D2:D9), the formula in D11 will also be =SUM(D2:D9).

From there, you can press F2, Home, Right, AVERAGE, Delete, Delete, Delete, Enter. It sounds crazy, but the engineers at General Electric in Cleveland swear by it.

38. Ctrl+Shift+" to Copy the Cell Value from Above

Use Ctrl+Shift+" to bring the value from above into the current cell, eliminating any formula.

39. Hold down Alt while launching Excel to force it into a second instance

You might want each Excel workbook to have separate Undo stacks. This is one way.

40. Press F2 to toggle EDIT or ENTER while editing a formula in any dialog

Say you are typing =VLOCKUP(in the conditional formatting dialog. You press the left arrow key to go back to fix the typo, but Excel inserts a cell reference. Press F2 to change the lower left corner of the status bar from ENTER to EDIT and you can use the arrow keys to move through the formula.

41. Hide or Unhide Rows or Columns

There used to be four great keyboard shortcuts here, but Unhide Columns stopped working.

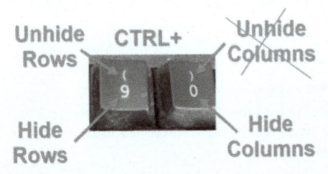

If you want Ctrl+Shift+) to unhide columns again, go to the Control Panel. Search for Typing. At the bottom of Typing, choose Advanced Keyboard Settings. Then choose Input Language Hot Keys to open the Text Services and Input Languages dialog. There are two tabs in this dialog. Choose Advanced Key Settings. You will see that To English is set to Ctrl+Shift+0. Select this item and re-map it to Left Alt + Shift + Grave Accent. When you return to Excel, Ctrl+Shift+) will unhide columns again. Note: If you simply try to unassign To English to nothing, Windows continues to use Ctrl+Shift+0. You must change this setting to something else.

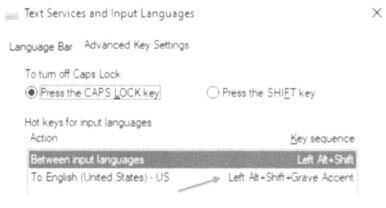

42. Alt+W, F, F to Freeze Panes

There are hundreds more shortcuts like the ones above which you can easily learn. Press and release Alt in Excel to see key tips for each tab in the Ribbon (plus numbered key tips for the Quick Access Toolbar. Press the letter corresponding to a Ribbon tab to see the key tips for all of the commands on that tab. In this particular case, clicking Alt, W, F reveals a third level of key tips, and Alt, W, F, F completes the command. Thanks to Bradford Myers.

43. Ctrl+C to Copy

44. Ctrl+V to Paste

45. Ctrl+X to Cut

46. Ctrl+B for Bold

47. Ctrl+I for Italics

48. Ctrl+U for Underline

49. Ctrl+N for New Workbook

50. Ctrl+P to Print

51. Ctrl+T (or Ctrl+L) to Format as Table

52. Never Forget to Right-click

Many timesavers that are linked to the right mouse button that are often forgotten. Thanks to Colin Foster. Hey! This is not a keyboard shortcut! But wait…it is. You can open that right-click menu by using the Application key on the bottom-right side of your keyboard or Shift+F10. For more on the Application key, see "For Those Who Prefer Using Keyboard Shortcuts" on page 158. Release the Application key and then press any underlined letter to invoke the command.

#169 Ctrl+Click to Unselect Cells

You've always had the ability to select multiple selections in Excel by Ctrl+Dragging to select cells. In the images below, you might click in B2 and drag to C6. Then Ctrl+Click in C8 and drag to C11. Then Ctrl+Click on F2:and drag to B8. Then Ctrl+Click in F11.

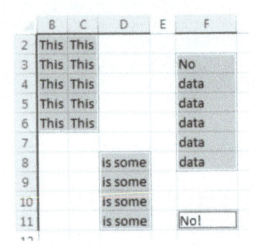

You realize that you did not want to include F3 or F11 in the selection. In the past, there was no way to unselect one cell. You had to start all over with selecting B2:C6 and so on.

If you still have a copy of Excel 2013, try unselecting cells by Ctrl+Clicking them. An odd bug causes the cell to become progressively darker with each Ctrl+Click.

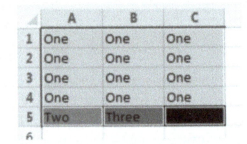

However - that bug was erased and new functionality added to Excel once a posting on Excel.UserVoice.com garnered 327 votes. This is a feature released in 2018 to Microsoft 365 subscribers. You can now Ctrl+Click on a cell that is in the selection and remove the cell from the selection.

> **Note**: In 2021, Excel.UserVoice was replaced by feedbackportal.microsoft.com.

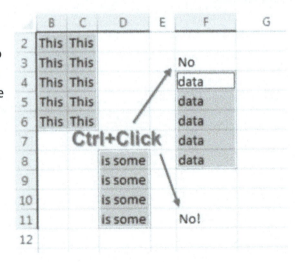

#170 Collapse the Search Box

It takes up way to much space. If you never use it, go to File, Options, General, Collapse the Microsoft Search Box by default. It will collapse to a magnifying glass and move to the top right of the screen.

#171 More Excel Tips

More than 200 ideas were sent in for this book. While the following ideas did not get much press here, they are self-explanatory in a 140-character tweet.

- To make Excel open full-screen, right-click the Excel icon and change the Run setting to Maximized. -David Ringstrom, CPA
- Use a thin light border line to create useful scrollbar maximums when your worksheet contains charts that the scroll bars don't recognize. -Chris Mack
- Highlight duplicate records with Conditional Formatting, Highlight Cells, Duplicate Records. -@Leaf_xl
- A new Partial Calculation mode calcs everything but What-If Tables and Python cells. -@MrExcel
- Color every other row with this conditional formatting formula: =MOD(ROW(),2)=0. -Pedro Millers
- Have a photo appear after a dropdown list in Excel http://t.co/TjbAtSkJ3t -Michael A. Rempel
- Use pictographs for charts (column and pie): Copy picture: select series, paste. -Olga Kryuchkova
- For a pie chart with too many slices: move small slices to second pie using Pie of Pie chart. -Olga Kryuchkova
- Use X/Y charts for drawing artwork. -Joerg Decker
- INDEX can return an entire row/column by using 0 for column/row. -Sumit Bansal
- CHOOSECOLS with negative instance number replaces INDEX but counts from the end. Two get the 2nd to last word from A1, use =CHOOSECOLS(TEXTSPLIT(A1," "),-2). - Diarmuid Early
- Put an apostrophe in front of an Excel formula to stop it from being evaluated. -@DiffEngineX
- DATEDIF(A2,B2,"Y")&" yrs, "&DATEDIF(A2,B2,"YM")&" mos, "&DATEDIF(A2,B2,"MD")&" days." -Paul Wright
- Insert rows without breaking formulas. Cell above is OFFSET(*thisCell*,-1,0) - Jon Wittwer, Vertex42.com
- Subtract 1 from NPV function to get the Net Present Value of the investment. -Olen L. Greer
- Use EDATE to move the date out one month or year. -Justin Fishman
- Find mystery links in the Name Manager. Ta-da! -Lisa Burkett
- Formulas created in Notepad, saved as CSV, & opened in Excel work. Example: mike,=proper(A1) will give Mike. -@mdhExcel
- Double-click a formula. Excel color codes the cells referenced in the formula. -Cat Parkinson
- Turn off Edit Directly in Cell. Then double-click a formula to show cells used in that formula, even if in external workbook. -Sean Blessitt and David Ringstrom
- Go To Special, Constants helps spot constants within a block of formulas where a formula is overwritten with a number. -@HowToExcel
- Select a random 5% of data using =RAND()<.05. -Olga Kryuchkova
- Mark formulas with Conditional Formatting formula =HASFORMULA(A1). -Justin Fishman
- Array formula to count without COUNT: =SUM(IF(ISNUMBER(MyRange),1,0)). -Meni Porat
- In VBA, use Range("A1").CurrentRegion instead of RANGE(). It is like pressing Ctrl+*. -Arnout Brandt
- You can use hyperlinks to launch VBA macros. Smaller than buttons. -Cecelia Rieb
- Use a macro to color the heading cells that have filters applied. -Peter Edwards
- Use Environ("UserName") in VBA code for restricting workbook access. -Angelina Teneva
- Use a UDF in a hyperlink to change cells mrx.cl/udfhyperlink -Jordan Goldmeier
- There are a variety of games written in Excel (2048, MissileCommand, pleuroku, TowerDefense, Pac-Man, Rubic's Cube, Yahtzee, Tetris). -Olga Kryuchkova
- POINT mode in Excel lets you build a formula using arrow keys to point to cells or ranges. If this stops working, see if you inadvertently pressed ScrLk key. You will see SCROLL LOCK near left side of Status Bar. (ScrLk is near PrtScrn and Break keys). -Vijay Krishnan

#172 The MrExcel Message Board

When I launched MrExcel.com in November 1998, I would get up every morning and answers yesterday's e-mailed questions before heading in to work. Initially, it was a question or two each weekday. But, by May 1999, I was getting more questions than I could answer in an hour. I was answering questions from 5 AM to 6 AM and then heading in to work. I either had to start getting up at 4 AM or find another way.

I downloaded WWWBoard from Matt's Script Archive. I asked people to post their question at the message board. And I asked that, after posting, they look at the last few questions to see if they could help someone else out. It was like the take-a-penny, leave-a-penny tray at a cash register. If you need help, post a question. If you can help someone else out, help them out. It worked. People started posting and answering questions.

In the early days, I noticed a few people would stop by almost every day and answer a question or two. Ivan F. Moala. Cecilia. The late Dave Hawley.

One day, at work. I was stumped. I went out to my own message board, and described my problem. An hour later, Ivan F. Moala from New Zealand had posted an amazing answer. I knew I had something.

The board transformed over the years, morphing into bigger platforms. I was on a $10-a-month hosting plan at Pair Networks in Pittsburgh. One day, I get a call from them wondering what I was doing. "You are on a $10-a-month plan, but you are using as much traffic as our $1,000-a-month plan!" Apparently, the MrExcel Message Board had taken on a life of its own.

Today, the amazing people at the MrExcel Message Board have answered 1 million questions about Excel. We've attempted to keep every question live on the site. There are some massive competitors (I won't name them, but their anagram is "is Comfort" or "of Mr Stoic") who have competing forums, but they have no problem wiping out their history. I run into people all the time who say they use my forum. I ask what their UserID is. "Oh – I've never had to post – I just search. Every answer is already there."

The MrExcel community is staffed by volunteers. Over the years, various experts have worked tirelessly as moderators and administrators. My sincere thanks to Andrew Poulsom, barry houdini, Colo, fairwinds, Ivan F Moala, Joe4, Jon von der Heyden, Juan Pablo Gonzalez, NateO, PaddyD, Peter_SSs, Richard Schollar, RoryA, Scott Huish, Smitty, Starl, SydneyGeek, VoG, Von Pookie, zenou, and Zack Barresse. Suat Ozgur and Scott Pierson handled the tech issues with the board.

As far as the people answering questions, 45 people have answered more than 10,000 questions at the board. This is a staggering contribution to the Excel community. Thanks to Aladin Akyurek with 85,000 posts. Norie and Andrew Poulsom have over 70,000 posts each. VoG has over 63,000 posts. Others with over 10K posts: Joe4, Jonmo1, Peter SSs, Rick Rothstein, RoryA, Fluff, Smitty, Richard Schollar, mikerickson, shg, barry houdini, Scott Huish, pgc01, Domenic, erik.van.geit, Michael M, hiker95, jindon, JoeMo, T. Valko, xenou, Marcelo Branco, AlphaFrog, My Aswer Is This, MickG, PaddyD, lenze, Von Pookie, SydneyGeek, Juan Pablo Gonzalez, Mark W., Yogi Anand, MARK858, Tom Urtis, JLGWhiz, GlennUK, tusharm, oldbrewer, Zack Barresse, Jon von der Heyden, just jon, and Greg Truby, and Mole999. Many of the experts at MrExcel.com are awarded the MVP Award in Excel from Microsoft.

If you ask Google any Excel question, the odds are pretty good that one of the top answers will be from MrExcel. If you can't find your answer on Google, it is free to post a new question. Make sure to give the post a title that describes what you are trying to do. Even in the middle of the night, someone will likely have an answer.

In late 2019, the message board was migrated to a modern Xenforo platform, complete with the ability to post screenshots of your Excel problem.

How to Post Your Question to the MrExcel Forum

Here are a few tips to getting an answer quickly at the MrExcel forum.

1. Before posting, do a <u>Search</u>. With a million threads, it is likely someone has had this problem before. You do not have to register to search.

2. In order to post, you have to <u>Register</u>. Give yourself a clever name such as XLGoddess or XLOOKUPKing. We ask for your e-mail address for password resets. I am not doing this to spam you. I won't spam you (because I can't figure out how to spam this many people without getting thrown off the Internet). We used to allow "Anonymous" to post to the board, but when five different "Anonymous" started posting in the same thread, it became impossible to follow the conversation. After registering, click the link in the confirmation e-mail that we send.

3. Start in the <u>Excel Questions</u> forum (there are other forums for Access, Power BI, and so on).

4. Click the Post Thread button in the top right.

5. Include a meaningful title that is specific to your question. Here is an example of a good title: "Excel VBA Type Mismatch Error". Your goal with the title is to get an expert to be interested in your question. Titles such as "Excel Help" or "Help" are not useful.

6. State your question clearly, including your entire need at the start.

7. Add some representative sample data - actual data is much better than an image. There are free tools to help you post your data to the board. See "How to Show Your Worksheet in a Post" below.

8. Tell us what formula/code you have currently, and why your results are not what you want.

9. Include which version of Excel and Operating System you are using.

10. If you are looking for help with an error received, what is the actual error message and where exactly does it occur?

11. Before posting, read your question back to yourself to check it will make sense to somebody unfamiliar with your worksheet.

12. If the answer you receive is inadequate for some reason, post a reply stating why the answer does not work and/or with more information (if needed) in the same thread.

If one or more posts were particularly helpful, click the Like button on that post. Getting Likes increases a person's reputation.

How to Show Your Worksheet in a Post

There are two ways to show your worksheet when posting to the MrExcel Message Board. First, you can use any screen clipping tool, copy a portion of the screen to your clipboard, then paste it into a post at the board. While pasting a picture can allow someone to see what is going on, in many cases, the volunteer who is going to answer your question will want to test some formulas in Excel, and a picture forces them to re-create your worksheet. Instead, our awesome web developer, Suat Ozgur has produced a free Excel add-in called XL2BB which allows you to post your worksheet to the board and allows the volunteer to then copy this data to Excel.

1. Download XL2BB and install following the instructions at https://mrx.cl/XL2BB.

2. You will see a new xl2BB tab in the Ribbon.

3. Select the portion of the worksheet you would like to share and click Mini Sheet.

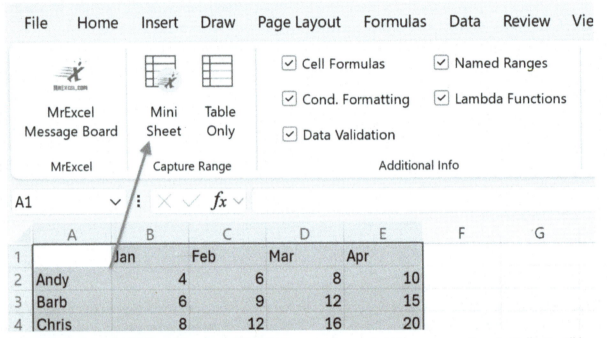

4. Switch back to the MrExcel forum and Ctrl+V to paste the code into your question. Initially, it will be a scary-looking bunch of codes, like this:

5. Click the Preview button

5. And you will see a version of your worksheet:

Can you help with this worksheet?

	Book1			
f(×) Click formula cells to copy formulas.				

📋	**A**	**B**	**C**	**D**	**E**
1		Jan	Feb	Mar	Apr
2	Andy	4	6	8	10
3	Barb	6	9	12	15
4	Chris	8	12	16	20
5	Diane	10	15	20	25
6	Ed	12	18	24	30
7	Flo	14	21	28	35

Sheet1   XL2BB v2.1

Cell Formulas

Range	Formula	
B2:E7	**B2**	=ROW()*COLUMN()

Here is why going to these extra steps will get you a better answer. When you post your worksheet to the board, the volunteer Excel experts love this view of the data for several reasons:

1. They can hover over any value in a cell with a yellow triangle to see the formula in that cell.

2. If they click the value, the formula is displayed in the formula bar and automatically copied to the clipboard so the volunteer expert can paste it into their copy of Excel.

3. If they click the "Select All" icon above and to the left of cell A1, the code for the worksheet is copied to the clipboard. They can then paste this code to a blank workbook and test their formula ideas.

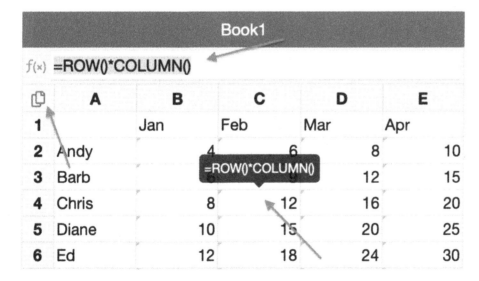

Index

6

6

Take Your Excel Skills to the Next Level

Looking to go deeper? Microsoft Excel Pivot Table Data Crunching is your complete guide to mastering pivot tables, Power Query, and the full analytical power of Excel. Whether you're building dashboards, analyzing millions of rows, or creating reports your manager didn't even know were possible—this book has you covered. Packed with real-world techniques and pro tips from MrExcel himself, it's the deep dive every data wrangler needs.

What's new as of this 2025 edition:

Go further with
MrExcel

Bill Jelen, host of MrExcel.com, is the author of 69 books on Microsoft Excel, including *Excel Gurus Gone Wild* and *Pivot Table Data Crunching*. The first ESPN commentator for the World Excel Championships, he has appeared on over 80 episodes of *Call for Help* with Leo Laporte. Bill writes the Excel column for Strategic Finance magazine and has produced more than 2,500 episodes of the *Learn Excel from MrExcel* video podcast.

Imagine what you can accomplish with MrExcel at your side!
Let's get started!

Visit
MrX.CL/gofurther
to learn more

Hire Bill for a
Webinar for your company

Get up to speed with Power Query
Buy Master Your Data

Learn from 2500+ videos on the
MrExcel YouTube Channel

Explore over 1 million Excel Q&As
Message Board

Search Bill's knowledge
Bill GPT

Get geared up for excelling with
Shirts & Mugs

Discover
How to Contact Bill